Lecture Notes in Computer Science

Commenced Publication in 1973
Founding and Former Series Editors:
Gerhard Goos, Juris Hartmanis, and Jan van Leeuwen

Rogério de Lemos
Cristina Gacek
Alexander Romanovsky (Eds.)

Architecting Dependable Systems II

 Springer

Volume Editors

Rogério de Lemos
University of Kent, Computing Laboratory
Canterbury, Kent CT2 7NF, UK
E-mail: r.delemos@kent.ac.uk

Cristina Gacek
Alexander Romanovsky
University of Newcastle upon Tyne, School of Computing Science
Newcastle upon Tyne, NE1 7RU, UK
E-mail: {Cristina.Gacek, Alexander.Romanovsky}@ncl.ac.uk

Library of Congress Control Number: 2004113649

CR Subject Classification (1998): D.2, D.4

ISSN 0302-9743
ISBN 3-540-23168-4 Springer Berlin Heidelberg New York

Springer is a part of Springer Science+Business Media

springeronline.com

© Springer-Verlag Berlin Heidelberg 2004
Printed in Germany

Typesetting: Camera-ready by author, data conversion by Olgun Computergrafik
Printed on acid-free paper   SPIN: 11314646   06/3142   5 4 3 2 1 0

Foreword

Enforcing the dependability of software systems has been a very active and productive area of research for over 30 years, addressing support for fault prevention, fault tolerance, fault removal and fault forecasting. Such an effort has in particular led to introducing a number of dependability concepts, and related principled methods and tools guiding the structuring of dependable systems, and further allowing reasoning about the systems' dependability. As such, research results in the dependability area impact upon the overall software development process. However, dependability has for long been considered as an aside property in the development of software systems, except for specific classes of systems such as safety-critical systems that cannot tolerate unexpected behavior following the occurrence of failures.

The increasing reliance on software systems that are now surrounding our everyday's life, being embedded in most devices, and providing us with access to a huge amount of content and services via the Internet, makes dependability a prime requirement for today's systems. In particular, dependability requirements should be accounted for in the early phase of the development process, since dependability means significantly impact design choices. In this context, architectural modelling of software systems offers much benefit towards assisting the design of dependable systems and assessing their dependability. By abstracting the low-level details of the system, architectural modelling allows effective exploitation of formal methods for reasoning about the systems' behavior, which constitutes a key dependability means. Architectural modelling further allows developers to comprehensively deal with dependability requirements in the structuring of their systems.

Bringing together researchers from the dependability and software architecture communities, via dedicated workshops and books on improvement to the state of the art on architecting dependable systems, can only be acknowledged as a valuable effort towards eliciting architecture modelling languages, methods and tools that support the thorough development of dependable software systems. This book, the second of an undoubtedly promising series, introduces research results that show how dependability and software architecture research conveniently complement and benefit from each other, addressing specific system architecting for dependability, integration of fault tolerance means with software architecture, and architecture modelling for dependability analysis. Last but not least, reports on industrial experience highlight how such an effort meets industrial practices in dependable software system development. As a result, the breadth and depth of the coverage that is provided by this book on recent research in architecting dependable systems is particularly impressive, and the editors and authors are to be congratulated.

June 2004

Valérie Issarny
INRIA
Research Unit of Rocquencourt

Preface

System dependability is defined as reliance that can be justifiably placed on the service delivered by the system. It has become an essential aspect of computer systems as everyday life increasingly depends on software. It is therefore a matter for concern that dependability issues are usually left until too late in the process of system development. This is why, even though there is a large body of research on dependability, reasoning about dependability at the architectural level is only just emerging as an important theme. It is a theme that needs to be actively pursued since architectural representations have been shown to be effective in helping to understand broader system characteristics by abstracting away from details. Apart from this, there are other factors that make it urgent to consider dependability at the architectural level, such as the complexity of emerging applications and the need for building trustworthy systems from the existing untrustworthy components.

This book comes as a result of an effort to bring together the research communities of software architectures and dependability. It was inspired by the ICSE 2003 Workshop on Software Architectures for Dependable Systems (WADS 2003), where many interesting papers were presented and lively discussions took place. The book addresses issues that are currently relevant to improving the state of the art in architecting dependable systems. It presents a selection of peer-reviewed papers stemming from some original WADS 2003 contributions and several invited ones. The book consists of four parts: architectures for dependability, fault tolerance in software architectures, dependability analysis in software architecture, and industrial experience.

The first part of this book focuses on software architectures for dependability. Its first paper, by Koutsoukos, Loureno, Avillez, Gouveia, Andrade, Fiadeiro, and Wermelinger, is entitled "Enhancing Dependability Through Flexible Adaptation to Changing Requirements". This paper describes an architectural approach that relies on coordination contracts to facilitate the dynamic adaptation of systems to changing domain rules. The approach is illustrated through a case study in the financial systems area, where agreed policies and conditions are negotiated on a case-by-case basis. The paper concludes by reporting on an information system that ATX Software developed for a company specialized in recovering bad credit. The second paper in this part is "A Self-optimizing Run-Time Architecture for Configurable Dependability of Services" by Tichy and Giese. In this paper, Tichy and Giese identify a set of architectural principles that can be used to improve the dependability of service-based architectures. These architectural principles have been instantiated by extending Jini, and have been evaluated qualitatively and quantitatively for a configuration of multiple identical services, showing how the different parameters affect the resulting dependability. The paper by Knight and Strunk on "Achieving Critical System Survivability Through Software Architectures" addresses the idea of making a system survivable rather than highly reliable or highly available by exploring the motivation for survivability, how it might be used, what the concept means in a precise and testable sense, and how it is being implemented in two very different application areas. The subsequent paper is authored by Rodrigues, Roberts and Emmerich. It is on "Reliability Support for the Model Driven Architecture" and elaborates on how the provision of reliability can be suitably realized through Model Driven Architectures (MDA). It is based on a platform-independent reference model that can be mapped to specific platforms. The UML metamodeling language is extended to show how design profile elements reflect on the deployment of the components when transformation rules are applied to the model. The last paper in this part, "Supporting Dependable Distributed Applications Through a Component-Oriented Middleware-Based Group Service" by Saikoski and Coulson, presents a group-based middleware platform that aims at supporting flexibility for controlled redundancy, replication, and recovery of components and services. This flexibility is provided at design time, deployment time and run-time. Their approach is based on concepts of software component technology and computational reflection.

The second part of this book is related to fault tolerance in software architectures. In the first paper, "Architecting Distributed Control Applications Based on (Re-) Configurable Middleware", Deconinck, De Florio and Belmans introduce the DepAuDE architecture developed for industrial distributed automation applications. This architecture provides a fault tolerance middleware, a library for error detection and recovery and fault treatments, and a specialized language called ARIEL for specifying fault tolerance and configuration actions. The paper concludes with a thorough discussion of a case study: a demonstrator of a Primary Substation Automation System controlling a substation for electricity distribution. The second paper of this part is entitled "A Dependable Architecture for COTS-Based Software Systems Using Protective Wrappers". The authors, Guerra, Rubira, Romanovsky and de Lemos, combine the concepts of an idealized architectural component and protective wrappers to develop an architectural solution that provides an effective and systematic way for building dependable software systems from COTS software components. The approach is evaluated using a PID controller case study. The next paper entitled "A Framework for Reconfiguration-Based Fault-Tolerance in Distributed Systems" is co-authored by Porcarelli, Castaldi, Di Giandomenico, Bondavalli and Inverardi. In this framework fault tolerance of components-based applications is provided by detecting failures using system monitoring, and by recovery employing system reconfiguration. The framework is based on Lira, an agent distributed infrastructure employed for component and application level monitoring and reconfiguration, and a decision maker used for selecting new configurations using the feedbacks provided by the evaluation of stochastic Petri net models. In the next paper, "On Designing Dependable Services with Diverse Off-The- Shelf SQL Servers", Gashi, Popov, Stankovic and Strigini argue, based on empirical results from their ongoing research with diverse SQL servers, in favor of diverse redundancy as a way of improving dependability and performance of a SQL server. The paper provides evidence that current data replication solutions are insufficient to protect against the range of faults documented for database servers, outlines possible fault-tolerant architectures using diverse servers, discusses the design problems involved, and offers evidence of performance improvement through diverse redundancy. The last paper of part two, "A New Model and a Design Approach to Building Quality of Service (QoS) Adaptive Systems", is co-authored by Ezhilchelvan and Shrivastava. The focus is on developing Internet-based services provisioning systems. The authors propose a system architecture and identify a model appropriate for developing distributed programs that would implement such systems. The probabilistic asynchronous model proposed abstracts the network performance and dependability guarantees typically offered by the Internet service providers. The system architecture prescribes the role of QoS management algorithms to be: evaluating the feasibility of QoS requests from the end users and adapting system protocols in response to changes in the environment.

Part three of this book deals with dependability analysis in software architectures. In the first paper, which is entitled "Multi-view Software Component Modeling for Dependability", the authors Roshandel and Medvidovic focus on a more comprehensive approach for modelling components. Instead of relying just on the description of the components interfaces, and their respective pre- and post-conditions, the authors propose an approach to modelling components using four primary functional aspects of a software component (known as the Quartet): interface, static behavior, dynamic behavior, and interaction protocol. In addition to describing individually the four aspects, the paper also discusses the relationships between them for ensuring their compatibility. The goal of the work is to obtain support for the architectural-level modelling and analysis of system dependability, in particular, reliability. The second paper, "Quantifiable Software Architecture for Dependable Systems of Systems" by Liang, Puett and Luqi presents an approach for the development and evolution of dependable systems-of-systems. Based on the architectural description of these systems, the approach involves establishing consensus between the different dependability attributes associated with component systems, and translating them into quantifiable constraints. The approach illustrates that with reusable architectural facilities and associated tools support, the quantifiable architecture with multiple perspectives can be effective in supporting the engineering of dependable systems-of-systems. In the last paper of this part, which is entitled "Dependability Modeling of Self-healing Client-Server Applications", the authors Das and Woodside present an analytical model for evaluating the combined performance and dependability attributes of fault-tolerant distributed applications. The authors consider a layered software architecture in which the application and management components can fail and be repaired. It also considers the management of connections, and the application's layered failure dependencies, together with the application performance. In order to show the capability of the approach in evaluating large-scale systems, the authors apply their analytical model to an air traffic control system.

The final part of the book contains two papers that report on existing industrial experiences involving dependability in the context of software architectures. In the first paper, entitled "A Dependable Platform for Industrial Robots", the authors Mustapic, Andersson, Norström and Wall discuss the design of an open software platform for an ABB Robotic System. For them a software platform is the basis for a product-line architecture that aims to increase the number of variations between the different software systems, while maintaining the integrity of the whole robotic system. An initial step in their approach is to model at the architectural level the quality constraints of the platform, which include several dependability attributes. The second paper of this final part, "Model Driven Architecture an Industry Perspective" by Raistrick and Bloomfield, discusses some of the research work that is currently being undertaken within the avionics industry on the usage of Model Driven Architectures (MDA), an initiative of the Object

Management Group (OMG). It has been recognized that the MDA approach might become fundamental in reducing costs in the development and maintenance of software. The authors of this paper identify several fronts in which the usage of the MDA might be effective. These are: the automation of software development with the support of tools, the management of legacy systems, the mapping of avionic applications into standard modular computer systems, and the incremental certification of avionics systems.

We believe that the introduction of the topic of architecting dependable systems is very timely and that work should continue in this area. The first book of the same title, published in the summer of 2003, included expanded papers based on selected contributions to the WADS ICSE 2002 workshop and a number of invited papers. The forthcoming ICSE/DSN 2004 Twin Workshops on Architecting Dependable Systems is another ambitious project, which aims to promote cross-fertilization between the communities of software architectures and dependability.

As editors of this book, we are certain that its contents will prove valuable for researchers in the area and are genuinely grateful to the many people who made it possible. Our thanks go to the authors of the contributions for their excellent work, the WADS 2003 participants for their active support and lively discussions, and Alfred Hofmann from Springer-Verlag for believing in the idea of this book and helping us to get it published. Last but not least, we appreciate the time and effort our reviewers devoted to guaranteeing the high quality of the contributions. They are D. Akehurst, T. Bloomfield, A. Bondavalli, F.V. Brasileiro, M. Castaldi, G. Deconinck, F. Di Giandomenico, M. Correia, G. Coulson, I. Crnkovic, S. Crook-Dawkins, W. Emmerich, J.L. Fiadeiro, G. Fohler, P. Inverardi, V. Issarny, J. Knight, N. Levy, N. Medvidovic, C. Norstrom, A. Pataricza, P. Popov, S. Riddle, G. Roberts, C.M.F. Rubira, S. Shrivastava, F. van der Linden, P. Veríssimo, M. Wermelinger, C.M. Woodside, and several anonymous reviewers.

June 2004

Rogério de Lemos
Cristina Gacek
Alexander Romanovsky

Table of Contents

Part 3. Dependability Analysis in Software Architectures

Part 4. Industrial Experiences

Enhancing Dependability Through Flexible Adaptation to Changing Requirements[*]

Michel Wermelinger[1], Georgios Koutsoukos[2], Hugo Lourenço[2],
Richard Avillez[2], João Gouveia[2], Luís Andrade[2], and José Luiz Fiadeiro[3]

[1] Dep. de Informática, Univ. Nova de Lisboa, 2829-516 Caparica, Portugal
mw@di.fct.unl.pt
[2] ATX Software SA, Alameda António Sérgio, 7, 1C
2795-023 Linda-a-Velha, Portugal
{firstname.lastname}@atxsoftware.com
[3] Dep. of Computer Science, Univ. of Leicester, Leicester LE1 7RH, UK
jose@fiadeiro.org

Abstract. This paper describes an architectural approach that facilitates the dynamic adaptation of systems to changing domain rules. The approach relies on "coordination contracts", a modelling and implementation primitive we have developed for run-time reconfiguration. Our framework includes an engine that, whenever a service is called, checks the domain rules that are applicable and configures the response of the service before proceeding with the call.

This approach enhances dependability in two essential ways: on the one hand, it guarantees that system execution is always consistent with the domain logic because service response is configured automatically (i.e., without any need for programmer intervention); on the other hand, it makes it possible for changes to be incorporated into existing domain rules, and from new rules to be created, with little effort, because coordination contracts can be superposed dynamically without having to change neither the client nor the service code.

Our approach is illustrated through a case study in financial systems, an area in which dependability arises mainly in the guise of business concerns like adherence to agreed policies and conditions negotiated on a case-by-case basis. We report on an information system that ATX Software developed for a company specialised in recovering bad credit. We show in particular how, by using this framework, we have devised a way of generating rule-dependent SQL code for batch-oriented services.

1 Introduction

This paper describes an architectural approach to system development that facilitates adaptation to change so that organisations can effectively depend on a continued service that satisfies evolving business requirements. This approach has been used in a real project in which ATX Software developed an information

---

[*] This paper is a considerably extended version of [1].

R. de Lemos et al. (Eds.): Architecting Dependable Systems II, LNCS 3069, pp. 3–24, 2004.
© Springer-Verlag Berlin Heidelberg 2004

system for a company specialised in recovering bad credit. The approach is based on two key mechanisms:

- the externalisation of the domain rules from the code that implements core system functionalities;
- the encapsulation of the code that enforces those domain rules into so-called coordination contracts that can be created and deleted at run-time, hence adapting computational services to the context in which they are called.

In the concrete case study that we present, the domain rules define the dependency of the recovery process on business concerns of the financial institution and product (e.g., house mortgage) for which the debt is being recovered. At any given time, this business configuration defines the context in which services are called.

These two mechanisms are aimed at two different classes of stakeholders. Domain rules are intended for system users, who have no technical knowledge, so that they can adapt the system in order to cope with requirements of newly or already integrated financial institutions or products. Coordination contracts are intended for system developers to add new behaviour without changing the original service implementation. This is made possible with the ability of coordination contracts to superpose, at run-time, new computations on the services that are being execute locally in system components.

Coordination contracts [2] are a modelling and implementation primitive that allows transparent interception of method calls and as such interfere with the execution of the service in the client. Transparent means that neither the service nor its client are aware of the existence of the coordination contract. Hence, if the system has to be evolved to handle the requirements imposed by new institutions or products, many of the changes can be achieved by parameterising the service (data changes) and by superposing new coordination contracts (behaviour changes), without changing the service's nor the client's code. This was used, for instance, to replace the default calculation of the debt's interest by a different one. The user may then pick one of the available calculation formulae (i.e., coordination contracts) when defining a domain rule.

To be more precise, a coordination contract is applicable to one or more objects (called the contract's participants) and has one or more coordination rules, each one indicating which method of which participant will be intercepted, under which conditions, and what actions to take in that case. In the particular case of the system that we are reporting in this paper, all coordination contracts are unary, the participant being the service affected by the domain rule to which the coordination contract is associated. Moreover, each contract has a single rule. We could have joined all coordination rules that *may be* applicable to the same service into a single contract, but that would be less efficient in run-time and more complex in design time due to more intricate rule definitions. The reason is that once a contract is in place, it will intercept *all* methods given in all the contract's rules, and thus the rule conditions would have to check at run-time if the rule is really applicable, or if the contract was put in place because of another coordination rule.

In this project we used an environment that we have built for developing Java applications using coordination contracts [3]. The environment is freely available from www.atxsoftware.net. The tool allows writing contracts, and to register Java classes (components) for coordination. The code for adapting those components and for implementing the contract semantics is generated based on a micro-architecture that uses the Proxy and Chain of Responsibility design patterns [4]. This microarchitecture handles the superposition of the coordination mechanisms over existing components in a way that is transparent to the component and contract designer. The environment also includes an animation tool, with some reconfiguration capabilities, in which the run-time behavior of contracts and their participants can be observed using sequence diagrams, thus allowing testing of the deployed application.

In the context of this work, we are concerned mainly with the maintainability attribute of dependability, and with faults that are accidental, human-made, and developmental, whereby our approach could be classified as fault prevention [5]. To be more precise, instead of hard-wiring and duplicating domain rules across multiple system services, which makes maintenance of the system error-prone when rules change, we provide support to keep rules separate from the services and to apply them only when needed. Our approach guarantees that whenever a user changes a domain rule, any future invocation of a service (whether it is a web-based interactive service or an SQL-based nightly batch service) that is affected by it will automatically take the rule in consideration. Hence, dependability, i.e., "the ability to deliver service that can justifiably be trusted" [5] is maintained.

The structure of the paper is as follows. The next section provides the wider context of our work, namely our architectural approach to the separation of computation, coordination, and configuration. This explains the design rationale for the framework illustrated, through its application to the debt recovery system, in the following sections. Section 3 starts describing the case study by introducing some example domain rules, taken from the credit recovery domain, and shows how coordination contracts are used to change the default service functionalities according to the applicable domain rules. Section 4 sketches the framework we implemented, describing how the service configuration is done at run-time according to the rules. Section 5 explains how the same framework is used to generate rule-dependent SQL code to be run in batch mode. The last section presents some concluding remarks.

2   The Three Cs of Architectures

The architectural approach that we will be describing is based on the crucial separation between "three Cs": Computation, Coordination, and Configuration. This separation needs to be supported at two different levels. On the one hand, through semantic primitives that address the "business architecture", i.e., the means that need to be provided for modelling business entities (Computation), the business rules that determine how the entities can interact (Coordination),

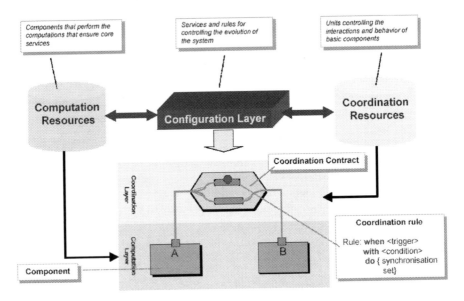

Fig. 1. The configuration framework

and the business contexts through which specific rules can be superposed, at runtime, to specific entities (Configuration). On the other hand, the architectural properties of the deployment infrastructures that can carry this distinction to the design and implementation layers, and support the required levels of agility.

2.1 The CCC System Architecture

As already mentioned, the rationale for the methodology and technologies that we have been building is in the *strict* separation between three aspects of the development and deployment of any software system: the *computations* performed locally in its components, the *coordination* mechanisms through which global properties can emerge from those computations, and the *configuration* operations that ensure that the system will evolve according to given constraints such as organisational policies, legislation, and other. Such layering should be strict in order to allow for changes to be performed at each layer without interfering with the levels below.

The Computation Layer should contain the components that perform the computations that ensure the basic services provided within the system. Each component has two interfaces [6]: a functional interface that includes the operations that allow one to query and change the encapsulated component state; and a configuration interface that provides the component's constructors and destructors, and any other operations that are necessary to the correct management of dynamic reconfiguration. One such operation is querying whether the component is in a "stable" state in which the component may be deleted or its "connections" to other components can be changed; another example is an operation that can temporarily block the component's execution while a reconfiguration that involves it is processed. The reason for separate interfaces is to be able to constrain the access that the various parts of the architecture have to each other and, hence, achieve a cleaner separation of concerns. In the case of the coordination layer, we require that no component should be able to invoke another component's configuration operations: components should not create other components because that is a change to the currently existing configuration and, as such, should be explicitly managed by the configuration layer.

The Coordination Layer defines the way computational components are interconnected for the system to behave, as a whole, according to set requirements. In the terminology of Software Architecture, this layer is populated by the *connectors* that regulate the interactions between the components of the layer below. We call such connectors *coordination contracts* or, for simplicity, *contracts*. We also require each contract to provide a functional and a configuration interface; each constructor in the configuration interface must include as arguments the components that the connector instance to be created will coordinate. We impose two restrictions: a contract may not use the configuration interface of any contract or component; and a contract may not use another contract's functional interface. The rationale for the first condition is again that configuration operations should only be performed by the configuration layer. The reason for the second condition is to make it possible to evolve the system through (un)plugging of individual contracts between components, which is only possible if there are no dependencies among contracts. The coordination effects that contracts put in place are described in terms of trigger-reaction rules as illustrated in Sec. 3.

At each state, the interconnections put in place among the population of basic components via contracts define the current configuration of the system. The Configuration Layer is responsible for managing the current configuration, i.e., for determining, at each state, which components need to be active and what interconnections need to be in place among which components. This layer provides a set of high-level reconfiguration operations that enforce global invariants over the system's configuration. The actual implementation of the configuration layer may follow the technical architecture given in [7]: a configuration database containing updated information about the current configuration, a consistency manager that enforces a "stable" state in which reconfiguration can occur, and a reconfiguration manager that executes the reconfiguration operations, using the services of the database and the consistency manager. The implementation of the reconfiguration operations makes use not only of the configuration interfaces provided by the components and contracts, but also of the functional interfaces because some changes to the configuration may depend on the current state of components and contracts, and may trigger state modifications to restore application-wide consistency.

Systems whose design architecture supports this separation of concerns through a strict layering can be evolved in a compositional way. Changes that do not require different computational properties can be brought about either by reconfiguring the way components interact, or adding new connectors that regulate the way existing components operate, instead of performing changes in the components themselves. This can be achieved by superposing, dynamically, new coordination and configuration mechanisms on the components that capture the basic business entities. If the interactions were coded in the components themselves, such changes, if at all possible thanks to the availability of the source code, besides requiring the corresponding objects to be reprogrammed, with possible implications on the class hierarchy, would probably have side effects on all the other objects that use their services, and so on, triggering a whole cascade of changes that would be difficult to control.

On the other hand, the need for an explicit configuration layer, with its own primitives and methodology, is justified by the need to control the evolution of the configuration of the system according to the business policies of the organisation or, more generally, to reflect constraints on the configurations that are admissible (configuration invariants). This layer is also responsible for the degree of self-adaptation that the system can exhibit. Reconfiguration operations should be able to be programmed at this level that enable the system to react to changes perceived in its environment by putting in place new components or new contracts. In this way, the system should be able to adapt itself to take profit of new operating conditions, or reconfigure itself to take corrective action, and so on.

According to the nature of the platform in which the system is running, this strict layering may be more or less directly enforced. For instance, we have already argued that traditional object-oriented and component-based development infrastructures do not support this layering from first-principles, which motivates the need for new semantic modelling primitives as discussed in the next subsection. However, this does not mean that they cannot accommodate such an architecture: design techniques such as reflection or aspect-oriented programming, or the use of design patterns, can be employed to provide the support that is necessary from the middleware. In fact, we have shown how the separation between computation and coordination can be enforced in Java through the use of well known design patterns, leading to what we called the "Coordination Development Environment" or CDE [4, 3, 8].

The design patterns that we use in the CDE provide what we can call a "micro-architecture" that enforces the externalisation of interactions, thus separating coordination from computation. It does so at the cost of introducing an additional layer of adaptation that intercepts direct communication through feature calling (clientship) and, basically, enforces an event-based approach. In this respect, platforms that rely on event-based or publish-subscribe interaction represent a real advantage over object-based ones: they support directly the modelling primitives that we will mention next.

2.2   The CCC Business Architecture

The separation of coordination from computation has been advocated for a long time in the Coordination Languages community [9], and the separation of all three concerns is central to Software Architecture, which has put forward the distinction between components, connectors and architectures [10]. The Configurable Distributed Systems community [11], in particular the Configuration Programming approach [12], also gives first-class status to configuration. However, these approaches do not provide a satisfying way to model the three concerns in a way that supports evolution. Coordination languages do not make the configuration explicit or have a very low-level coordination mechanism (e.g., tuple spaces); architecture description languages do not handle evolution from first principles or do it in a deficient way; configuration programming is not at the business modelling level.

For instance, the reconfiguration operations that we provide through *coordination contexts* correspond more to what in other works is called a reconfiguration script [13] than the basic commands provided by some ADLs to create and remove components, connectors, and bindings between them [14]. Coordination contexts also make explicit which invariants the configuration has to keep during evolution. It is natural to express these invariants in a declarative language with primitive predicates to query the current configuration (e.g., whether a contract of a given type connects some given components). Such languages have been proposed in Distributed Systems (e.g., Gerel-SL [13]) and Software Architecture approaches (e.g., Armani [15]). However, all these approaches *program* the reconfiguration operations, i.e., they provide an operational specification of the changes. Our position is that, at the modelling level, those operations should also be specified in a declarative way, using the same language as for invariants, by stating properties of the configuration before and after the change. In other words, the semantics of each reconfiguration operation provided in this layer is given by its pre- and post-conditions.

On the other hand, it is true that modelling languages like the UML [16] already provide techniques that come close to our intended level of abstraction. For instance, "use cases" come close to coordination contexts: they describe the possible ways in which the system can be given access and used. However, they do not end up being explicitly represented in the (application) architecture: they are just a means of identifying classes and collaborations. More precisely, they are not captured through formal entities through which run-time configuration management can be explicitly supported. The same applies to the externalisation of interactions. Although the advantage of making relationships first-class citizens in conceptual modelling has been recognised by many authors (e.g., [17]), which led to the ISO General Relationship Model (ISO/IEC 10165-7), things are not as clean when it comes to supporting a strict separation of concerns.

For instance, one could argue that mechanisms like association classes provide a way of making explicit how objects interact, but the typical implementation of associations through attributes is still "identity"-based and does not really externalise the interaction: it remains coded in the objects that participate in the association. The best way of implementing an interaction through an association class would seem to be for a new operation to be declared for the association that can act as a mediator, putting in place a form of implicit invocation [18]. However, on the one hand, the fact that a mediator is used for coordinating the interaction between two given objects does not prevent direct relationships from being established that may side step it and violate the business rule that the association is meant to capture. On the other hand, the solution is still intrusive in the sense that the calls to the mediator must be explicitly programmed in the implementation of the classes involved in the association.

Moreover, the use of mediators is not incremental in the sense that the addition of new business rules cannot be achieved by simply introducing new association classes and mediators. The other classes in the system need to be made aware that new association classes have become available so that the right mediators are used for establishing the required interactions. That is, the burden of deciding which mediator to interact with is put again on the side of clients. Moreover, different rules may interact with each other thus requiring an additional level of coordination among the mediators themselves to be programmed. This leads to models that are not as abstract as they ought to be due to the need to make explicit (even program) the relationships that may exist between the original classes and the mediators, and among the different mediators themselves.

The primitive — *coordination law* - that we have developed for modelling this kind of contractual relationship between components circumvents these problems by abandoning the "identity"-based mechanism on which the object-oriented paradigm relies for interactions, and adopting instead a mechanism of superposition that allows for collaborations to be modelled outside the components as connectors (coordination contracts) that can be applied, at run-time, to coordinate their behaviour. From a methodological point of view, this alternative approach encourages developers to identify dependencies between components in terms of *services* rather than identities. From the implementation point of view, superposition of coordination contracts has the advantage of being non-intrusive on the implementation of the components. That is, it does not require the code that implements the components to be changed or adapted, precisely because there is no information on the interactions that is coded inside the components. As a result, systems can evolve through the addition, deletion or substitution of coordination contracts without requiring any change in the way the core entities have been deployed.

3   Business Rules and Coordination Contracts

ATX Software was given the task to re-implement in Java the information system of Espírito Santo Cobranças, a debt recovery company that works for several credit institutions, like banks and leasing companies. The goal was not only to obtain a Web-based system, but also to make it more adaptable to new credit institutions or to new financial products for which the debts have to be collected. This meant that business rules should be easy to change and implement.

The first step was to make the rules explicit, which was not the case in the old system, where the conditions that govern several aspects of the debt recovery process were hardwired in tables or in the application code itself. We defined a business rule to be given by a condition, an action, and a priority. The condition is a boolean expression over relations (greater, equal, etc.) between parameters and concrete values. The available parameters are defined by the rule type. The action part is a set of assignments of values to other parameters, also defined by the rule type. Some of the action parameters may be "calculation methods" that change the behaviour of the service to which this rule is applicable. The priority is used to allow the user to write fewer and more succint rules: instead of writing one rule for each possible combination of the condition parameter values, making sure that no two rules can be applied simultaneously, the user can write a low priority, general, "catch-all" rule and then (with higher priority) just those rules that define exceptions to the general case. As we will see later, rules are evaluated by priority order. Therefore, within each rule type, each rule has a unique priority.

To illustrate the concept of business rule, consider the agreement simulation service that computes, given a start and ending date for the agreement, and the number of payments desired by the ower, what the amount of each payment must be in order to cover the complete debt. This calculation is highly variable on a large number of factors, which can be divided into three groups. The first one includes those factors that affect how the current debt of the ower is calculated, like the interest and tax rates. This group of factors also affect all those services, besides the agreement simulation, that need to know the current debt of a given person. The second group includes those factors that define what debt should be taken into account for the agreement: the debt on the day before the agreement starts, the debt on the day the agreement ends, or yet another possibility? The last group covers factors concerned with internal policies. Since the recovery of part of the debt is better than nothing, when a debt collector is making an agreement, he might pardon part of the debt. The exact percentage (of the total debt amount) to be pardoned has an upper limit that depends on the category of the debt collector: the company's administration gives higher limits to more experienced employees.

As expected, each group corresponds to a different business rule type, and each factor is an action parameter for the corresponding rule type. The condition parameters are those that influence the values to be given for the action parameters. As a concrete example, consider the last group in the previous paragraph. The business rule type defines a condition parameter corresponding to the category of the debt collector and an action parameter corresponding to the maximum pardon percentage. A rule (i.e., an instance of the rule type) might then be `if category = ''senior'' or category = ''director'' then maxPardon = 80%`. The priorities might be used to impose a default rule that allows no pardon of the debt. The lowest priority rule would then be `if true then maxPardon = 0%`.

However, a more interesting rule type is the one corresponding to the calculation of the debt (the first group of factors for the agreement service). The debt is basically calculated as the sum of the loan instalments that the ower has failed to pay, surcharged with an amount, called "late interest". The rules for calculating this amount are defined by the credit institution, and the most common formula is: instalment amount * late interest rate * days the payment is late / 365. In other words, the institution defines a yearly late interest rate that is applied to the owed amount like any interest rate. This rate may depend only on the kind of loan (if it was for a house, a car, etc.) or it may have been defined in the particular loan contract signed between the institution and the ower. In the first case, the rate may be given as an action parameter value of the rule, in the second case it must be computed at run-time, given the person for whom the agreement is being simulated. But as said before, the formula itself is defined by the institution. For example, there are instutions that don't take the payment delay into account, i.e., the formula is just `instalment amount * late interest rate`. For the moment, these are the only two formulas the system incorporates, but the debt recovery company already told us that in the forseeable future they will have to handle financial institutions and products that have late interest rates over different periods of time, e.g., quarterly rates (which means the formula would have the constant 90 instead of 365).

In these cases, where business rules impose a specific behaviour on the underlying services, we add an action parameter with a fixed list of possible values. Each value (except the default one) corresponds to a coordination rule that contains the behaviour to be superposed on the underlying service (which implements the default behaviour, corresponding to the default value of the parameter). However, from the user's perspective, there is nothing special in this kind of parameter; the association to coordination rules is done "under the hood". For our concrete example, the late interest rule type would have as condition parameters the institution and the product type, and as action parameters the interest rate (a percentage), the rate source (if it is a general rate or if it depends on the loan contract), and the rate kind (if it is a yearly rate or a fixed one). The last two parameters are associated to coordination rules and the first parameter (the rate) is optional, because it has to be provided only if the rate source is general. Two rule examples are

- if institution = 'Big Bank' and productType = 'car loan'
  then rate = 7%, source = 'general', kind = 'fixed';
- if institution = 'Big Bank' and productType = 'house loan'
  then source = 'contract', kind = 'yearly'.

As for the coordination rules, we need one for each computation that differs from the default behaviour, which is implemented directly in the service because it is assumed to be the case occurring most often. For the example, we need a rule to fetch the rate from the database table that holds the loan contract information for all processes handled by the debt recovery company, and another rule to calculate the late interest according to the fixed rate formula.

Continuing with our example, the service has (at least) the following methods:

- `void setRate(double percentage)`, which is used to pass the value of the `rate` action parameter to the service;

- `double getRate()`, which is used by clients of the service, and by the next method, to obtain the rate that is applicable;
- `double getInterest()`, which uses auxiliary methods implemented by the same service to calculate the late interest to be paid. Its implementation is `return getInstalment() * getRate() * getDays() / 365;`.

Given these methods, the coordination rules are as follows:

Fixed Rate This rule intercepts the `getInterest()` method unconditionally, and executes: `return getInstalment() * getRate()`.

Contracted Rate This rule intercepts the `getRate()` method under the condition `!calculated`, and executes: `r =` the rate obtained by consulting the database; `setRate(r); calculated = true`.

The second rule requires the coordination contract to have a local boolean attribute `calculated`, initialized to false. The idea is that, no matter how often the service's clients call the `getRate()` method, the database lookup will be done only for the first call, and the rate is stored into the service object, as if it were given directly by a business rule. This "shortcut" works because we know that the rates stored in the database may only change at the beginning of the nightly batch, not during the interest calculation.

The next section explains how the three parts (business rules, coordinations contracts, and services) work together at run-time in order to ensure that the correct (business and coordination) rules are applied at the right time to the right services.

4 Architectural Framework

The architecture of the configuration framework, and the steps that are taken at run-time, are shown next.

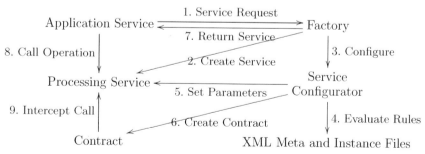

The process starts with the creation of an application service object to handle the user's request, e.g., the request for the simulation of the agreement. This object contains the necessary data, obtained from the data given by the user on the web page, and will call auxiliary processing services. Each service is implemented by a class, whose objects will be created through a factory (step 1 in the figure). After creating the particular instance of the processing service (step 2), the factory may call the service configurator (step 3), if the service is known to be possibly subject to business rules. The configurator consults two XML files containing information about the existing business rules. The one we called meta file defines the rule types (see Fig. 2 for an example), while the instance file contains the actual rules (see Fig. 3).

The configurator first looks into the meta file to check which business rules are applicable for the given processing service. For each such rule, the meta file defines a mapping from each of the rule type's condition (resp. action) parameters into getter (resp. setter) methods of the service, in order to obtain from (resp. pass to) the service the values to be used in the evaluation of the conditions of the rules (resp. the values given by the action part of the rules). There is also the possibility that an action parameter is mapped to a coordination contract. For our example, the mapping could be the one given in Table 1. Notice that the default values general and yearly are not mapped to any coordination contract.

Table 1. Example mapping of parameter (values) to methods and contracts

Parameter	Value	Method	Coordination Contract
institution		getInstitution	
productType		getProductType	
rate		setRate	
source	general		
source	contract		Contracted Rate
kind	yearly		
kind	fixed		Fixed Rate

With this information (which of course is read from the meta file only once, and not every time the configurator is called), the configurator calls the necessary getters of the service in order to obtain the concrete values for all the relevant condition parameters. Now the configurator is able to evaluate the rules in the instance file (step 4), from the highest to the lowest priority one, evaluating the boolean expression in the if part of each rule until one of them is true. If the parameter values obtained from the service satisfy no rules' condition, then the configurator raises an exception. If a suitable rule is found, the configurator reads the values of the action parameters and passes them to the service (step 5) by calling the respective setters. If the action parameter is associated with a coordination contract, the configurator creates an instance of that contract (step 6), passing to the contract constructor the processing service object as the participant. Continuing the example, the configurator would call the getInstitution and getProductType methods. If the values obtained were "Big Bank" and "car loan", respectively, then, according to the example rules in the previous section, the configurator would call setRate(0.07) on the service, and create an instance of the "Fixed Rate" coordination contract.

At this point the configurator returns control to the factory, which in turn returns to the application service a handler to the created (and configured) processing service. The application service may now start calling the methods of the processing service (step 8). If the behaviour of such a method was changed by a business rule, the corresponding contract instance will intercept the call and execute the different behaviour (step 9). To finish the example, if the application service calls `getInterest`, it will be intercepted by the fixed rate contract, returning `getInstalment() * 0.07`.

Of course, the application service is completely unaware that the processing service has been configured and that the default behaviour has changed, because the application just calls directly the methods provided by the processing service to its clients. In fact, we follow the strict separation between computation and configuration described in [6]: each processing service has two interfaces, one listing the operations available to clients, the other listing the operations available to the configurator (like the getters and setters of business rule parameters). The application service only knows the former interface, because that is the one returned by the factory. This prevents the application service from changing the configuration enforced by the business rules.

The user may edit the XML instance file through a tool we built for that purpose to browse (Fig. 4), edit (Fig. 5) and create business rules. The tool completely hides the XML syntax away from the user, allowing the manipulation of rules in a user-friendly manner. Furthermore, it imposes all the necessary constraints to make sure that, on the one hand, all data are consistent with the business rules' metadata (i.e., the rule types defined in the XML meta file), and, on the other hand, that a well-defined XML instance file is produced. In particular, the tool supplies the user with the possible domain values for required user input, it checks whether mandatory action parameters have been assigned a value, facilitates the change of priorities among rules and guarantees the uniqueness of priorities, allows to search all rules for a given institution, etc. You may notice from the presented XML extracts that every rule type, rule, and parameter has a unique identifier and a name. The identifier is used internally by the configurator to establish cross-references between the instance and the meta file, while the name is shown by the rule editing tool to the user (as shown in the screenshots). The `valueType` attribute of a parameter is used by the rule editor to present to the user (in a drop-down list) all the possible values for that parameter. In Fig. 5 the drop-down list would appear by clicking on the button with a down-arrow in the upper right part of the active window.

Notice that the user is (and must be) completely unaware of which services are subject to which rule types, because that is not part of the problem domain. The mapping between the rules and the service classes they affect is part of the solution domain, and as such defined in the XML meta file. As such, each rule type has a conceptual unity that makes sense from the business point of view, without taking the underlying services implementation into account.

```
<service class="ComputeDebt">
  <ruleType name="Late Interest" id="LateInterest">
    <condition>
      <conditionGroup>
        <conditionParameter name="Financial Institution"
                            id="Inst" type="string">
          <valueType name="Institution" />
          <getter name="getInstitutionCd" returnType="String" />
          <SQL>
            <expr>AT_LATE_INTEREST_CALC.INSTITUTION_CD</expr>
            <from>AT_LATE_INTEREST_CALC</from>
          </SQL>
        </conditionParameter>
        <conditionParameter name="Credit Type"
                            id="CredType" type="string">
          <valueType name="CreditType" />
          <getter name="getCreditType" returnType="String" />
          <SQL>
            <expr>ST_PROCESS_CONTRACT.CREDIT_TYPE_CD</expr>
            <from>ST_PROCESS_CONTRACT,AT_LATE_INTEREST_CALC</from>
            <join>ST_PROCESS_CONTRACT.PROCESS_NBR =
                  AT_LATE_INTEREST_CALC.PROCESS_NBR</join>
          </SQL>
        </conditionParameter>
        <!-- the current phase of the recovery process -->
        <conditionParameter name="Phase" id="Phase" type="string">
          <valueType name="ProcPhase" />
          <getter name="getProcessPhase" returnType="String" />
          <SQL>
            <expr>AT_LATE_INTEREST_CALC.ACTUAL_PHASE_CD</expr>
            <from>AT_LATE_INTEREST_CALC</from>
          </SQL>
        </conditionParameter>
        <!-- other condition parameters -->
      </conditionGroup>
    </condition>
    <!-- the action parameters would be given here -->
  </ruleType>
</service>
```

Fig. 2. An extract of the XML meta file

```
<service class = "ComputeDebt" name = "ComputeDebt">
  <ruleType id = "LateInterest">
    <!-- other rules with higher priority -->

    <rule name = "Big Bank, judicial phases" id = "3" priority = "3">
      <conditionset type = "AND">
        <comparison id = "Inst" serviceValue = "0916"
          userValue = "Big Bank" operator = "equal"/>
        <conditionset type = "OR">
          <comparison  id = "Phase" serviceValue = "0005"
            userValue = "External judicial phase" operator = "equal"/>
          <comparison  id = "Phase" serviceValue = "0007"
            userValue = "Internal judicial phase" operator = "equal"/>
        </conditionset>
      </conditionset>
      <!-- the values for the action parameters come here -->
    </rule>

    <!-- remaining rules, with less priority -->
  </ruleType>
</service>
```

Fig. 3. An extract of the XML instance file

5   Batch-Oriented Rule Processing

The approach presented in the previous section is intended for the interactive, web-based application services that are called on request by the user with the necessary data. These data are passed along to a processing service. The configurator queries the processing service for the data in order to evaluate the conditions of the rules.

However, like most information systems, the debt recovery system also has a substantial part working in batch. For example, the calculation of the debt is not only needed on demand to project the future debt for the simulation agreement service, it is also run every night to update the current debt of all the current credit recovery processes registered in the system. In this case, the debt calculation is performed by stored procedures in the database, written in SQL and with the business rules hard-wired.

Hence, when we have a large set of objects (e.g., credit recovery processes) for which we want to invoke the same processing service (e.g., debt calculation), it is not very efficient to apply the service to each of these objects individually. It is better to apply a "batch" strategy, reversing the configuration operation: instead of starting with an object and then choosing the rule that it satisfies, we take a rule and then select all the objects that satisfy it. This is much more efficient because we may use the same configured processing service instance for objects A and B if we are sure that for both A and B the same rule is chosen.

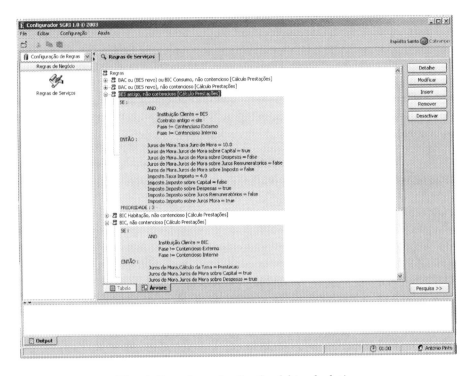

Fig. 4. Browsing rules for the debt calculation

We thus have the need to be able to determine for a given rule the set of objects that satisfy it. Pragmatically speaking, we need a way of transforming the if-part of a rule into an SQL condition that can be used in a SELECT query to obtain those objects. Therefore we extended the rule type information in the XML meta file, adding for each condition parameter the following information:

- an SQL expression that can be used to obtain the parameter value;
- the list of tables that must be queried to obtain the parameter value;
- a join condition between those tables.

Fig. 2 shows a fragment of the meta information for the debt calculation service. There we see, for example, that in order to obtain the value of the product type parameter we have to write the following query:

```
SELECT ST_PROCESS_CONTRACT.CREDIT_TYPE_CD
FROM ST_PROCESS_CONTRACT,AT_LATE_INTEREST_CALC
WHERE ST_PROCESS_CONTRACT.PROCESS_NBR =
      AT_LATE_INTEREST_CALC.PROCESS_NBR
```

Using this information we can now take a rule condition and transform it into a SQL fragment. As an example, consider the rule condition (for the same service) in Fig. 3: it is applicable to all recovery processes of "Big Bank" that

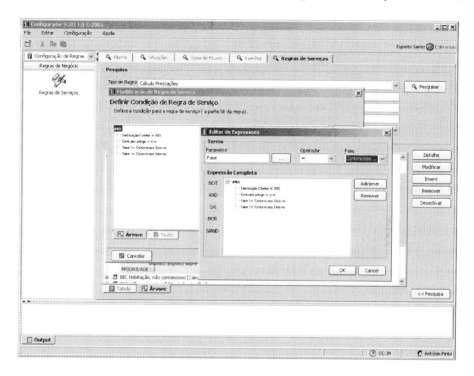

Fig. 5. Editing the condition of a rule

are in the internal judicial phase (i.e., the company's lawyers are dealing with the process) or the external one (i.e., the case has gone to court). We may compose the information for each of the rule parameters in order to obtain a single SQL fragment for the rule condition. This fragment contains the following information:

- the list of tables that must be queried in order to evaluate the rule condition;
- an SQL condition that expresses both the join conditions between the several tables and the rule condition itself.

For our example, the meta file specifies that `Inst` and `Phase`, the two parameters occurring in the condition, only require the table `AT_LATE_INTEREST_CALC` to be queried. As for the rule condition, the meta file specifies that `AT_LATE_INTEREST_CALC.INSTITUTION_CD` corresponds to the usage of the `Inst` parameter, and `AT_LATE_INTEREST_CALC.ACTUAL_PHASE_CD` to the `Phase` condition parameter. By a straightforward replacement of these names in the boolean expression of the rule condition, we get the following SQL expression:

```
((AT_LATE_INTEREST_CALC.INSTITUTION_CD = '0916') AND
((AT_LATE_INTEREST_CALC.ACTUAL_PHASE_CD = '0005') OR
(AT_LATE_INTEREST_CALC.ACTUAL_PHASE_CD = '0007')))
```

The SQL representation of a rule is conveyed by an instance of class `SQLRule`, which is contained in the service configurator, because the XML files are accessed by the latter.

```
public class ServiceConfigurator {
  public class SQLRule  {
      public String getId() { ... }
      public String getName() { ... }
      public String getWhere() { ... }
      public String getFrom() { ... }
  }
}
```

Each processing service class provides a static method for obtaining all of its rules in this "SQL format". This method simply calls a method of the service configurator, passing the service identification, which returns all rules for that service in decreasing order of priority. In the example below we show how we can generate a specialized query for a rule. In this example we first obtain all the service rules in "SQL format" and then generate a query that returns the first object that satisfies the condition of the third rule.

```
ServiceConfigurator.SQLRule[] SQLrules = ComputeDebt.getSQLRules();

ServiceConfigurator.SQLRule rule = SQLrules[2];
System.out.println("Rule : " + rule.getId() + " - " + rule.getName());
String sql = "SELECT TOP 1 AT_LATE_INTEREST_CALC.PROCESS_NBR " +
  " FROM " + rule.getFrom() +
  " WHERE " + rule.getWhere() +
  " AND PROCESSED = false";
System.out.println(sql);
```

The output generated is the following:

```
Rule : 3 - Big Bank, judicial phases

  SELECT TOP 1 AT_LATE_INTEREST_CALC.PROCESS_NBR
  FROM AT_LATE_INTEREST_CALC
  WHERE ((AT_LATE_INTEREST_CALC.INSTITUTION_CD = '0916')
  AND ((AT_LATE_INTEREST_CALC.ACTUAL_PHASE_CD = '0005')
  OR (AT_LATE_INTEREST_CALC.ACTUAL_PHASE_CD = '0007')))
  AND PROCESSED = false
```

Similar queries are generated for each rule and each query is executed. In this way we obtain, for each rule, one object satisfying its condition. This object is basically a representative of the equivalence class of all objects that satisfy the given rule conditions. Now, step 1 of the run-time configuration (section 4) is executed for each object. In other words, we execute the same call as if it were an application service, but passing one of the already created objects as data. The steps then proceed as usual. This means that after step 7, we obtain a service instance that has been configured according to the rule corresponding to the given object.

The generation of the SQL code for the batch version of a service proceeds as follows, for each i from 1 to n (where n is the number of rules for that service). First, generate the SQL query to select all objects satisfying the condition of the i-th rule. This is done as shown above, but without the TOP 1 qualifier. Second, call a special method on the i-th service instance. This method will generate the SQL code that implements the service, based on a template that is customized with the action parameters that have been set by the configurator on the service.

In summary, the SQL code that will be executed in batch is made up of n "modules", one for each rule. Each module first selects all objects to which the rule is applicable, and then executes the parameterized SQL code that corresponds to the Java code for the interactive version of the service. The modules are run sequentially, according to the prioritization of the rules.

This raises a problem. If some object satisfies the conditions of two or more rules, only the one with the highest priority should be applied to that object. To preserve this semantics, each batch service uses an auxiliary table, initialized with all objects to be processed by the service; in the case of the debt calculation service, it is the AT_LATE_INTEREST_CALC table. This table has a boolean column called processed, initialized to false. As each batch module executes, it marks each object it operates on as being processed. Hence, when the next module starts, its query will only select objects that haven't been processed yet. In this way, no two rules will be applied to the same object.

The last, but not least, point to mention are coordination contracts. As said above, one service instance has been created for each rule, and configured accordingly. This means that coordination contracts may have been superposed on some service instances (step 6). Hence, the SQL code generated from those service instances cannot be the same as for those that haven't any coordination contracts. The problem is that services are unaware of the existence of contracts. The result is that when the code generation method of a service object is called (step 8), the service object has no way to know that it should generate slightly different code, to take the contract's behaviour into account. In fact, it *must* not know, because that would defeat the whole purpose of coordination contracts: the different behaviours would be hard-wired into the service, restricting the adaptability and flexibility needed for the evolution of the business rules. Since the Java code (for the web-based part of the system) and the SQL code (for the batch part) should be in the same "location", to facilitate the maintenance of the system, the solution is of course for each contract to also generate the part of the code corresponding to the new behaviour it imposes on the underlying service. For this to be possible, the trick is to make the code generation method of the service also subject to coordination. In other words, when a contract is applied to a service object, it will not only intercept the methods supplied by the service to its clients, it will also intercept the code generation method (step 9) in order to adapt it to the new intended behaviour.

6   Concluding Remarks

This paper reports on the first industrial application of coordination contracts, a mechanism we have developed for non-intrusive dynamic coordination among components, where "dynamic" means that the coordination may change during execution of the system.

Although the examples given are specific to the debt recovery domain, the framework we developed is generic and can be used to help organisations maintain their dependence on business rules and achieve flexibility of adaptation to changing rules. The framework provides a way to separate business rules from services and to apply one or more rules to services depending on the exact service call. Moreover, the approach is applicable to systems with an interactive and a batch part (based on SQL procedures), both subject to the same rules. This avoids the traditional scenario of duplicated business rules scattered among many system services and entangled within their code, thus helping to prevent unintentional faults by developers during software maintenance.

Flexibility of adaptation to change was achieved by two means. The first is the definition of parameterised business rule types. The condition parameters can be combined in arbitrary boolean expressions to provide expressivity, and priorities among rules of the same type allow to distinguish between general vs. exceptional cases. The second means are coordination contracts to encapsulate the behaviour that deviates from the default case. At run-time, from the actual data passed to the invoked service, a configurator component retrieves the applicable rules (at most one of each rule type), parameterises the service according to the rules, and creates the necessary contract instances. The contracts will intercept some of the service's functionalities and replace it by the new behaviour associated to the corresponding business rule.

The architectural framework we designed can be used both for interactive as well as batch application services. The difference lies in the fact that the batch application service has to get one representative data object for each rule, and only then can it create one processing service for each such data. The application service then asks each of the obtained configured services to generate the corresponding SQL code. Coordination contracts will also intercept these calls, in order to generate code that corresponds to the execution of the contract in the interactive case.

This approach has proved to work well for the system at hand. On the one hand it guarantees that the system will automatically (i.e., without programmer intervention) behave consistently with any change to the business rules. On the other hand, it makes possible to incorporate some changes to existing rule types and create new rule types with little effort, because coordination contracts can be added in an incremental way without changing the client nor the service code. Furthermore, the code of the services remains simple in the sense that it does not have to entangle all the possible parameter combinations and behaviour variations.

The main difficulty lies in the analysis and design of the services and the rules. From the requirements, we have to analyse which rules make sense and define what their variability points (the parameters) are. As for the services, their functionality has to be decomposed into many atomic methods because coordination rules "hook" into existing methods of the contract's participants. As such, having just a few, monolithic methods would decrease the flexibility for future evolution of the system, and would require the coordination rule to duplicate most of the method code except for a few changes.

The approach is also practical from the efficiency point of view. The overhead imposed by the configurator's operations (finding the rules, passing action parameter values, and creating coordination contract objects) does not have a major impact into the overall execution time of the application and processing services. This is both true for the interactive and batch parts of the system. In the former case, the user does not notice any delay in the system's reply, in the latter case, the time of generating the SQL procedures is negligible compared to the time they will execute over the hundreds of thousands of records in the database. Moreover, the execution time of the generated SQL code is comparable to the original batch code, that had all rules hard-wired.

To sum up, even though we used coordination contracts in a narrow sense, namely only as dynamic and transparent message filters on services, and not for coordination among different services, we are convinced that they facilitate the evolution of a system that has to be adapted to changing business rules.

7   Acknowledgments

This work was partially supported by project AGILE (IST-2001-32747) and the Marie-Curie TOK-IAP action 3169 (Leg2NET), both funded by the European Commission; by project POSI/32717/00 (Formal Approach to Software Architecture) funded by Fundação para a Ciência e Tecnologia and FEDER; and by the research network RELEASE (Research Links to Explore and Advance Software Evolution) funded by the European Science Foundation.

References

1. Wermelinger, M., Koutsoukos, G., Avillez, R., Gouveia, J., Andrade, L., Fiadeiro, J.L.: Using coordination contracts for flexible adaptation to changing business rules. In: Proc. of the 6th Intl. Workshop on the Principles of Software Evolution, IEEE Computer Society Press (2003) 115–120
2. Andrade, L., Fiadeiro, J.L., Gouveia, J., Koutsoukos, G.: Separating computation, coordination and configuration. Journal of Software Maintenance and Evolution: Research and Practice **14** (2002) 353–369
3. Gouveia, J., Koutsoukos, G., Wermelinger, M., Andrade, L., Fiadeiro, J.L.: The coordination development environment. In: Proc. of the 5th Intl. Conf. on Fundamental Approaches to Software Engineering. Volume 2306 of LNCS., Springer-Verlag (2002) 323–326

4. Gouveia, J., Koutsoukos, G., Andrade, L., Fiadeiro, J.L.: Tool support for coordination-based software evolution. In: Proc. TOOLS 38, IEEE Computer Society Press (2001) 184–196

5. Avizienis, A., Laprie, J.C., Randell, B.: Fundamental concepts of dependability. In: 3rd Information Survivability Workshop, Software Engineering Institute (2000)

6. Wermelinger, M., Koutsoukos, G., Fiadeiro, J., Andrade, L., Gouveia, J.: Evolving and using coordinated systems. In: Proc. of the 5th Intl. Workshop on Principles of Software Evolution, ACM (2002) 43–46

7. Moazami-Goudarzi, K.: Consistency Preserving Dynamic Reconfiguration of Distributed Systems. PhD thesis, Imperial College London (1999)

8. K.Lano, J.L.Fiadeiro, L.Andrade: Software Design Using Java 2. Palgrave Macmillan (2002)

9. Gelernter, D., Carriero, N.: Coordination languages and their significance. Communications of the ACM **35** (1992) 97–107

10. Perry, D.E., Wolf, A.L.: Foundations for the study of software architecture. ACM SIGSOFT Software Engineering Notes **17** (1992) 40–52

11. Magee, J., Kramer, J.: Dynamic structure in software architectures. In: Proceedings of the Fourth ACM SIGSOFT Symposium on the Foundations of Software Engineering, ACM Press (1996) 3–14

12. Kramer, J.: Configuration programming—a framework for the development of distributable systems. In: International Conference on Computer Systems and Software Engineering, Israel, IEEE (1990)

13. Endler, M., Wei, J.: Programming generic dynamic reconfigurations for distributed applications. In: Proceedings of the First International Workshop on Configurable Distributed Systems, IEE (1992) 68–79

14. Medvidovic, N., Taylor, R.N.: A classification and comparison framework for software architecture description languages. IEEE Transactions on Software Engineering **26** (2000) 70–93

15. Monroe, R.T.: Capturing software architecture design expertise with Armani. Technical Report CMU-CS-98-163, School of Computer Science, Carnegie Mellon University (1998)

16. Booch, G., Rumbaugh, J., Jacobson, I.: The Unified Modeling Language User Guide. Addison-Wesley (1998)

17. Kilov, H., Ross, J.: Information Modeling: an Object-oriented Approach. Prentice-Hall (1994)

18. Notkin, D., Garlan, D., Griswold, W., Sullivan, K.: Adding implicit invocation to languages: Three approaches. In: Object Technologies for Advanced Software. Volume 742., Springer-Verlag (1993) 489–510

A Self-optimizing Run-Time Architecture for Configurable Dependability of Services*

Matthias Tichy and Holger Giese

Software Engineering Group, Department of Computer Science
University of Paderborn, Germany
{mtt,hg}@uni-paderborn.de

Abstract. Many human activities today depend critically on systems where substantial functionality has been realized using complex software. Therefore, appropriate means to achieve a sufficient degree for dependability are required, which use the available information about the software components and the system architecture. For the special case of service-based architectures, we identify in this paper a set of architectural principles which can be used to improve dependability. We then describe how the identified architectural principles have been used in a realized service-based architecture which extends Jini. The dependable operation of the infrastructure services of the architecture further enables to systematically control and configure some dependability attributes of application services. We present a qualitative and quantitative evaluation of the dependability for a configuration of multiple identical services which are executed with the architecture and show how the different parameters effect the dependability. Additionally, a scheme for the dynamic control of the required dependability of the application services in the case of changing failure characteristics of the environment is outlined. Finally, we present a first evaluation of the developed architecture and its dynamic control of dependability.

1   Introduction

The dependability of today's complex systems often relies on the employed computers and their software components. Availability, reliability, safety and security (cf. [1]) are the attributes of dependability that are used to describe the required system characteristics. In this paper we only consider the dependability attributes availability and reliability. They can be systematically studied at the level of components and their composition for a given static system architecture by deriving related dependability models which can be quantitatively analyzed (cf. [2, 3]). However, due to the increasingly dynamic character of today's computing environments such as service-based architectures we often do not have a static system architecture.

When further considering dynamic systems where no static *a priori* known system configuration exists, the analysis and prediction of the reliability or availability using a model of the overall configuration is difficult. We therefore propose to build dynamic

* This work was developed in the course of the Special Research Initiative 614 – Self-optimizing Concepts and Structures in Mechanical Engineering – University of Paderborn, and was published on its behalf and funded by the Deutsche Forschungsgemeinschaft.

R. de Lemos et al. (Eds.): Architecting Dependable Systems II, LNCS 3069, pp. 25–50, 2004.

and dependable complex systems not by relying on design-based quantitative analysis of its static overall architecture. Instead, the observed obstacles should be addressed by a component-wise analysis which at run-time monitors and controls the dynamic reconfiguration of the architecture to prevent system reliability and availability to decrease below the required level. Such a software tries to compensate failures (originated from defects of its hardware and software components) by means of repair and it tries to compensate changes of the environment by adaption of its maintenance activities to keep the system's availability and reliability above the required level.

Our architecture consists of an infrastructure, which offers the required generic and configurable maintenance activities, and the application specific services. We further study how the dynamic management of redundant component instances for infrastructure components as well as application services with identical implementation can contribute to improvements for the two considered dependability attributes.

For the infrastructure components we present an in-depth qualitative analysis of relevant hardware failures such as node crashes or network partitioning to show that no single-point-of-failure exists. The application services are in contrast treated as blackboxes with dependability characteristics that may change over time. Following the categorization of [4] we only distinguish whether a service represents an *entity* or only contains an activity (*session*). For session services we further consider stateless and stateful ones where for the latter the history of relevant actions executed throughout this session builds the state.

The failures considered for application services are crash failures, which may either result from defects of the employed hardware or result from the executed software. While the rate of the former may change due to aging or replaced hardware, the later may change over time due to changes in their usage characteristics or software updates. We further make the strong simplification that both kinds of failures simply result in an application service crash failure. As the services will then fail to fulfill their regular behavior expected by the infrastructure the crash can be detected externally by monitoring the services.

A number of established architectural principles are presented in Section 2, which permit to enhance the dependability of service-based architectures. Then, we present in Section 3 our enhancement of the Jini architecture by a number of infrastructure services that systematically employ the identified principles to provide a dependable execution of application services. For a special class of services the possible design alternatives are studied by means of the detailed design of two infrastructure services concerning a dependable operation.

We then discuss the benefits achieved for application specific services concerning availability in Section 4 in a qualitative evaluation. We demonstrate the systematic application of the identified architectural principles within the enhanced architecture. Afterwards, we present a formal model of the architecture. This model provides analytical results of the availability for application services based on the parameters of the architecture and the environment. After that we sketch how to adapt parameters of the control monitors to sustain the availability of application services w.r.t. environmental changes.

Section 5 contains a qualitative and quantitative evaluation of the reliability provided by our architecture for different classes of application services. After that, we describe how our architecture can adapt to environmental changes in order to sustain a required reliability. We show the feasibility of our approach w.r.t. the sustainment of application service dependability based on a simulation experiment in Section 6. Related work is discussed in Section 7 and we close the paper with a final conclusion and some comments on future work.

2 Architectural Principles for Dependability

Established design principles aid in the development of dependable software systems. In this section, a number of these design principles are described which are used in the design of our architecture.

Software systems typically consist of several different parts. Since dependencies between these parts exist, problems occur if one part fails. *Service*-based architectures handle the increasing complexity of today's systems by means of online lookup and binding of services. Services and components [5] share the use of contractually specified interfaces, which makes a black box reuse possible. Thus, a client does not need to know the exact implementation, used fault tolerance techniques, or the service(s) deployment, but only relies on the fulfillment of the interface. The client is working correct as long as the promised functionality of the service is delivered and is, thus, completely decoupled from how the work is processed.

The integral part of a service-based architecture is a *service registry*. The use of such a service registry is a key factor for availability, since service instance connections are not hard-wired and the execution location of services is not fixed. Instead, services can spontaneously connect to recover from failures. One example of a self-healing service-based architecture is the Jini architecture [6, 7]. It has been specially designed to support the development of dependable distributed systems (cf. [8]). One of its features is a *lookup service* that remains operational, even when single nodes in the network have crashed, due to redundancy and replicated data by the usage of multicast messages.

The *leasing* principle extends the allocation of resources with time [9]. The lease represents a period of time during which the resource is offered. Therefore, this lease needs to be extended (renewed) if the resource remains to be offered after the timeout of the lease. If the owner of the resource fails to renew the lease, a client can assume that the resource is no longer available. Leasing is the principle which provides the self-healing behavior of the Jini lookup service. Every service registration on the lookup service is accompanied by a lease. If this lease expires, the lookup service removes the accompanied service registration from its lookup tables. Thus, no service gets this apparently failed service instance in response to a search request. If this service is restarted or the communication system is repaired, the service can re-register on the lookup service.

A *proxy* provides a surrogate or a placeholder for another object [10]. In distributed systems a proxy typically acts as a local placeholder for a remote object encapsulating the forwarding of requests via network communication (e.g. as the stub in Java Remote Method Invocation (RMI) [11]). In the Jini architecture the proxy pattern is an integral part of every service. A service is divided into a proxy and an optional backend. The proxy instance is registered in the lookup service. If a service is to be used by a client, the proxy instance is downloaded as mobile code to the client and executed there. Therefore, the service can execute code on the client's side in addition to code on the backend.

Redundancy of service instances is a key factor to achieve a required degree of reliability. A non redundant service is a single-point-of-failure. Thus, in case of a failure of this service or a communication subsystem failure, which results in a network partition, all dependent clients of that service cease to work. In the Jini architecture more than one lookup service can be used. Thus, a failed lookup service does not compromise the dependability of the complete system.

This leads us to the concept of a *smart proxy* [12, 13]. A smart proxy is not restricted to forwarding but can be used much more flexible. Thus, in the context of reliability the proxy may communicate with multiple backends at once to recover from or mask failures. A client trying to use a service, which has failed although its lease time has not expired, would experience a failure in a proxy-less environment. However, after being downloaded to a client a mobile code proxy, which is stored in the lookup service and thus fails independently from its backend, can revert to another service backend when it detects the failure of its own backend. Hence, a smart proxy can be used to encapsulate and hide the complexity of fault-tolerant code and therefore the use of complex concepts becomes transparent to the user of the service. For example the service registration in the Jini architecture is sent to all available lookup services by the proxy at once using multicast messages. Fault tolerance source code can be integrated in *one* smart proxy, since the proxy is executed in the same process as the using service. Therefore, the smart proxy cannot fail independently from the using service in case of failures. Thus, the using service does not need to include fault tolerance measures in the collaboration with the smart proxy.

Analogue to the redundancy of services a key point for dependability is the availability of data in a distributed system. This can be achieved by the use of *replication*. Replication is the process of maintaining multiple copies of the same entity at different locations. In the Jini architecture the service registrations are replicated in multiple lookup services.

The maintenance of these distributed copies depends on the required consistency for the entity. There exist different *consistency* models (for an overview see [14]). A consistency model provides stronger or weaker consistency in the sense that it affects the values, a read-operation on a data item returns. There is a trade-off between consistency and availability and no optimal solution can be given. The weaker the consistency model the higher availability can be achieved. The possibility to use different consistency models for different data aids in the development of a self-healing architecture as we will show in the next section.

Control theory [15] is a fundamental concept which also permits to improve the dependability of a service-based system. However, in the original domain usually a quasi-continuous rather than a periodic event-based communication between the controller and the controlled subsystem is assumed. For our application, we employ instead an event-based communication. Then, a *monitor* which periodically checks that a service is alive and restarts a new one if not, can be understood as a simple form of controller. If the parameters of the controller are adapted by measuring certain outputs of the system under control we have an *adaptive controller*. If parameter identification for a given dependability model is used to predict the controller parameters, we even have a *self-optimizing controller* [15]. If the required system goals w.r.t. availability are known, this approach can be employed to realize the system which optimally uses its resources to realize these goals.

3   Design of the Architecture

In this section we will show the application of the introduced architectural principles in our architecture. We give a short introduction of the presented architecture and the requirements of the different infrastructure services. The more detailed design and the implementation is available in [16].

The Jini architecture supports ubiquitous computing in ad-hoc networks and provides a dependable infrastructure for service lookup and operation. However, the basic infrastructure only avoids to provide any element that can compromise the dependability of application components. But to achieve the required dependability for any specific service or application remains to be realized by the application developer. Our proposed architecture in contrast permits to configure the required degree of availability for application services at deployment-time.

A key to the improved availability of the infrastructure services is the idea to have redundant instances of every service type running concurrently in the system to prevent a single-point-of-failure as proposed in the last section.

The overall architecture is built on top of Jini. In addition to the Jini lookup service, four different service types are used. In the following we will describe these different services. Ideally on every computation node of the system one instance of each infrastructure service is executed and will be restarted automatically during each reboot (see Figure 1). In addition on each node of the system a Jini lookup service is executed.

On every node of the distributed system an instance of the *node* service is running. Using this node service, new application service instances can be created (and old ones stopped). Additionally, the node service provides information about the node itself. This includes but is not limited to: ip-address, hostname, total memory, free memory, current load, load average.

A *service description storage* contains service descriptions (like name of the service, package-path, required and provided interfaces, deployment constraints, etc.) for all application services which have to be executed. This information has to be read prior to (re)starting them. Each instance of the service description storage contains one replica of the service descriptions. A strong consistency model for these data is required since a weaker consistency model would result in a possible loss of service descriptions in case of failures. This in turn would cause the unavailability of the affected application services, since no repair is possible due to the lost service descriptions. Thus, reading the descriptions is more important than writing. Additionally, read access to these service descriptions occurs more often than write access.

Monitors supervise that the application services contained in the service description storage are indeed executed and available. The availability of the services will be

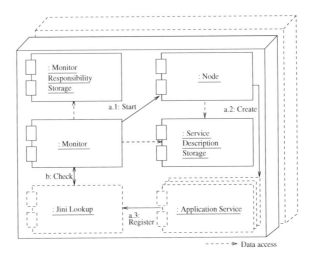

Fig. 1. Architecture design overview

checked periodically. The detection speed of service failures, and thus the mean time to repair (MTTR), can be configured by changing this period. The monitor and the related service instance thus form a closed control loop. To control which monitor is supervising which service, monitors need to acquire a responsibility for a service (i.e. to assure a new instance is started, if a service instance is not available). Thus, another overlaying control loop is used to monitor the monitors themselves. Monitors use the information provided by the node services to choose on which node a certain service will be started.

The monitoring responsibilities are stored in a *monitor responsibility storage*. Responsibilities are accompanied by a configurable lease, which is used to detect failed monitors (i.e. the lease times out). The responsibility lease influences the mean time to repair of the application services, too. Each instance of the monitor responsibility storage contains a copy of these monitor responsibilities. Inconsistencies between these copies only result in changed responsible monitors and potentially additional started service instances. Therefore, we trade overhead for improved reliability and weaken the consistency requirements for these copies. Additionally, after a repaired network partition failure merging the responsibilities in the former partitions must be possible. The monitors whose behavior depends on these responsibilities must be able to cope with a weaker consistency model.

After this overview about the different parts of the architecture, we further describe in more detail the design of two infrastructure services. These services serve as examples how to achieve the required degree of reliability for services, which deal with data, by applying the aforementioned (see Section 2) principles for dependability.

3.1 Service Description Storage

The service description storage contains the descriptions of the services which must be available in the system. These descriptions are replicated in the system on a number of service backends. A strong consistency model is required for this replication. Write operations are only executed by an administrator whereas read operations are regularly executed by the infrastructure services.

Since changes in the service descriptions occur rarely, the number of read operations on these descriptions surpasses the number of write operations. For a certain degree of the system's reliability, it is necessary that the read operations of the infrastructure services succeed with a very high probability in case of failures whereas the write operations are relatively unimportant. To exploit this bias for read operations we have chosen to implement the *weighted voting* approach [17] which provides sequential consistency.

This approach offers the possibility to configure the reliability, based on the assumed distribution of read and write operations. Each node has a number of votes to weight its data specified by the administrator. This number of votes should match the reliability of that node. Quorums are used to determine which nodes participate in a read/write access based on their votes. The weighted voting approach uses a voting where the needed read (n_r) and write quorums (n_w) can be adjusted as long as read-write quorums ($n_w + n_r > n$) and write-write quorums ($2n_w > n$) overlap to prevent inconsistencies (n : total number of votes). For our scenario we chose a high n_w and a low n_r to achieve a high probability for a successful read operation.

Multiple node failures can be masked as long as the required number of votes is available to reach the required quorum. In case of a network partition, read operations are possible in every partition containing more than n_r votes. Write operations are only possible in the rare case that during a network partition one partition contains more than n_w votes. Since we chose a low n_r value, the probability is high that read access is possible in all partitions. We state the reasonable requirement that the network partition must be repaired, before a write access by the administrator is possible.

The weighted voting approach is implemented in the service's smart proxy. Thus, a using service does not need to know about the specific implementation; it just calls read and write operations on the proxy and all replication and consistency management is done internally. JavaSpaces [18] are used as backends. JavaSpaces are a tuple-based storage [19] implemented as Jini services. Therefore, they exhibit the aforementioned principles like leases. Additionally, JavaSpaces can be used as participants in the Jini implementation of the Two-Phase-Commit-Protocol [20]. The backends store the data and an associated version number.

The smart proxy does a lookup on the lookup service gathering the required number of available JavaSpaces for a read respective write access. Executing a write access, the proxy simply writes the data in all gathered JavaSpaces using the Two-Phase-Commit-Protocol and increments the version number. Executing a read access is slightly more complex. After gathering the correct number of JavaSpaces, the smart proxy reads the data of every JavaSpace and then internally selects the data, which has been written by the last write access. This selection is based on the highest version number.

3.2 Monitor Responsibility Storage

Storing the monitor responsibilities is a problem similar to storing the service descriptions. In contrast to that, here write and read operations are equally important. In case of failures it is necessary that another monitor can take over the responsibility of a broken monitor and needs to store this information in the responsibility storage.

Therefore, we can weaken the consistency requirements for the responsibility storage to be able to read and write to it anytime especially in the failure case. An appropriate weaker consistency model is *eventual consistency* [14]. Eventual consistency demands that in absence of write operations the storages eventually stabilize in a globally consistent state after a certain amount of time.

Our approach to achieve eventual consistency is based on multicast messages and a decentral majority voting on every responsibility storage in the network. Because of the multicast messages, every message is received by every storage. Thus, in case of a read operation, all available storages receive the read request and respond by returning their local data as a multicast message. Therefore every storage and the requester get the responsibilities stored in every storage. Since the number of storages is unknown in case of failures, a timeout is used to finish waiting for responses. After that, all storages and the requester do a decentral majority voting on the received data. In case of parity each participant chooses the data with the highest hashcode to achieve a consistent result. A write operation simply sends a write multicast message which is processed by all storages, which receive the message.

Before a globally consistent state is reached there may exist local inconsistencies. For example, during a network partition failure the local data in the storages in the different partitions diverge because updates are only visible within one partition. After the failure is repaired the conflicts between all partitions are resolved by the next read operation. After the decentral majority voting the data of only one partition holds, the others are discarded. Therefore only one monitor is responsible for a specific service description. All other, former responsible monitors notice their responsibility loss on their next responsibility check.

From a user point of view this complex dealing with multicast messages and the voting is completely encapsulated within a smart proxy.

4   Ensuring Availability of Application Services

After presenting the design of the architecture and the individual services, we show how the architecture achieves availability for application services in case of node failures and network partition failures. According to [21] availability is the probability that an item will perform its required function under given conditions at a stated instant of time. Since systems without repair have in the long run an availability of zero, we have to repair the services if they have experienced a failure.

4.1   Qualitative Evaluation

In case of a node failure different scenarios, w.r.t. failures of a responsible monitor and monitored application services, are possible. The case that neither a responsible monitor nor a monitored service is affected by the node failure is trivial. If a node is affected by the failure, which does host only application services, the monitors responsible for these application services will detect the services' failures because the application services do not renew their leases with the lookup service. The monitors will choose new nodes for the application services and start new instances there. Figure 2 shows this scenario. Note, the displayed monitor and lease periods, which influence the achievable degree of availability.

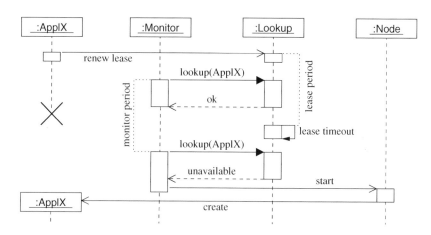

Fig. 2. Scenario of a node failure

In the case of failures in the responsible monitor as well as in the monitored service, the responsibility lease of the monitor expires and another monitor takes over the supervising responsibility. This monitor replaces the failed monitor, and starts supervising the currently unmonitored service which includes starting new instances when needed. Figure 3 shows the events in a sequence diagram, in the case that a service and its supervising monitor are executed on the same node, which experiences a failure.

During a network partition failure, communication is only possible inside the different partitions and no communication can cross the borders between the different partitions. A monitor, which has been responsible for services in the complete network, is in one part of the system during the partition. In this part the monitor recognizes the absence of some monitored services and restarts them. In the other parts the monitor's responsibility times out, other monitors step in, and restart all needed service instances. Thus, in each partition a responsible monitor and all service instances are available after a certain amount of time (cf. Figure 3). If the partitions become too small during a network partition to execute all services, a solution might be to execute only important services due to some specified service levels.

After reuniting the different partitions, the responsibility storages are merged by the above described decentral majority voting to determine a new unified responsible monitor. This new monitor takes over the responsibility for the service instances started by the other responsible monitors in the other partitions. Additionally, it can consolidate the number of service instances in the reunited network by asking some service instances to shut themselves down in a graceful manner. The monitors formerly responsible in the other partitions stop monitoring their started service instances after noticing their responsibility loss.

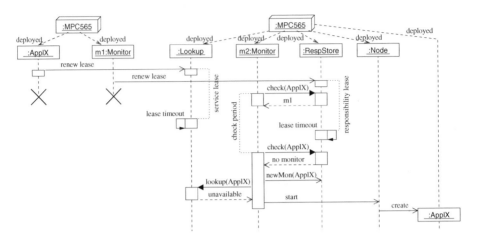

Fig. 3. Timing of a monitor failure

4.2   Quantitative Evaluation

In the previous section, we presented how the architecture is designed to improve the availability of application services in case of failures of application services or architecture services. In the following, we show how the availability of application services can be analytically determined using a formal model. The behavior of the architecture and application services depends on a number of parameters. Obviously, the values of most of the relevant parameters change over time and therefore can only be approximated by their expected mean values.

A first category of parameters are *configurable parameters*, which allow to adjust the system behavior to the required bounds:

Monitoring period p_{mean}**:** As described in Section 3 the monitor checks periodically, whether all of its monitored service instances are executed. Decreasing this monitor period leads to faster recognition of service failures but higher resource consumption.

Monitor responsibility lease m_{mean}**:** A lease is attached to each monitor responsibility. Decreasing this lease leads to faster recognition of monitor failures but higher resource consumption.

Service registration lease l_{mean}**:** A lease is attached to the registration of each service in the registration service (e.g. Jini lookup service). Decreasing this lease leads to faster recognition of service failures but higher resource consumption.

Number of monitors mp**:** The number of monitors is crucial to the dependability of the solution. Increasing the number of monitors decreases the probability, that all monitors have failed, but increases the resource consumption.

Number of service description storages d**:** The number of service description storages affects the availability of the service descriptions. Increasing the number of service description storages leads to a higher probability, that the service descriptions are available, but increases the resource consumption.

Number of application service instances i**:** The number of concurrent application service instances directly affects the availability of the application service. Increasing the number of concurrent instances leads to a higher availability, but increases the resource consumption.

Since availability is determined by $MTTF/(MTTF + MTTR)$ (cf. [21]), we can reach higher availability by reducing the mean time to repair. We can configure the MTTR by changing the lease given by the Jini lookup service, the monitoring period and the responsibility lease. Therefore, the proposed architecture can be customized for the required degree of availability subject to the condition that the number of working monitors, service description storages is sufficient.

Two other parameters affect the availability of application services. These parameters are *system parameters*, which are imposed by the environment, and therefore cannot be changed by the architecture. They have to be estimated up front and may later be identified at run-time using our model (e.g. in a self-optimizing controller):

Mean operating Time Between Failures (MTBF) b_{mean}**:** It is affected by the underlying hardware and software platform.

Hardware Mean Time To Repair (MTTR) r_{mean}**:** The time needed to repair a broken hardware platform on which monitors and service description storages are executed.

As it is apparent from the above parameter descriptions, unreflecting changes to the parameters lead to either low availability results for the application services or extraordinary resource consumption. A quantitative analysis is required to determine appropriate values for the configuration parameters for a required availability of application services and to permit system parameter identification. For this purpose we use generalized stochastic Petri nets.

Generalized stochastic Petri nets (GSPN) [22] can be utilized for quantitative analyses of the dependability of models (cf. [23]). A steady-state analysis of the modeled behavior gives quantitative results for the availability of a single service group managed by the architecture. We give a short introduction to GSPNs in Appendix A.

We model the architecture and some application services in a certain example scenario w.r.t. crash failures. In our example scenario, we have three instances of a certain application service group which are executed by the architecture. Further we will use the term service groups for one group of identical application services. We use the model to compute the probability, that at least one application service instance of the service group is working ($p0$), i.e. one service instance is sufficient for performing the required function (1-out-of-3 redundancy). The timed behavior of the model is determined by the above described dependability parameters.

$$p0 = p\{\#working\_instances > 0\}. \tag{1}$$

In Figure 4 the model of our example scenario is shown in form of a generalized stochastic Petri net. All architecture parameters (times and quantities), which have been described in the previous section, are used in this architectural model of a group of identical application services.

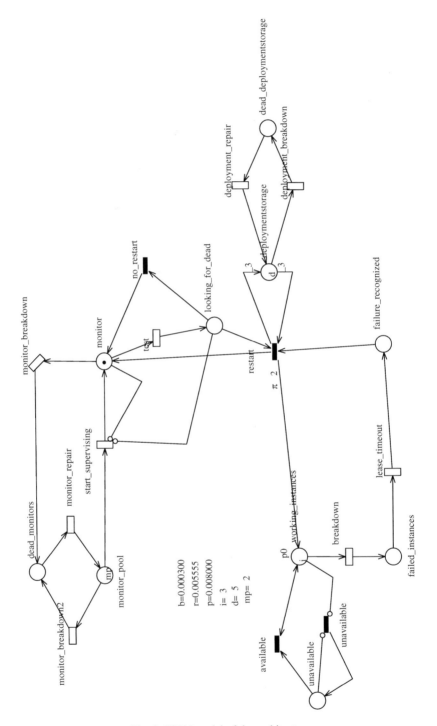

Fig. 4. GSPN model of the architecture

The net consists of mainly three parts. The lower left part of the system models the different states of the application service instances. An instance can be in three different states: (1) it is working (the token is in state working_instances), (2) it has failed (parameter b_{mean}) but the lease has not expired yet (token in state failed_instances), and (3) the lease has timed out (parameter l_{mean}) and the token is in state failure_recognized. We abstract from the small amount of time (compared to the other parameter values) which is required to restart a service on another node. We added two immediate transitions unavailable and available. The first fires, when no service instance is available, and thus the system of three application service instances has failed. The second fires, when there is at least one service available again, and thus the system has been repaired. These two transitions are used to analyze the mean time to failure of the complete system of the three application services.

In the lower right part of the figure the service description storages are modeled. For our example we used five service description storages (5 tokens in state deploymentstorage). Three votes are required for a read quorum. If a service description storage experiences a failure (parameter b_{mean}), a stochastic transition fires and a token moves to the state dead_deploymentstorage. After a certain amount of time (parameter r_{mean}) the deployment storage is repaired and the token moves back to state deploymentstorage.

In the upper part of the model the behavior of the monitors is specified. Initially, one monitor is supervising the application service instances (the token in state monitor). Two other monitors are running but are not supervising any application service instance (two tokens in state monitor_pool). When a monitor fails (either a supervising monitor or a monitor in the pool) determined by the parameter b_{mean}, the token moves to the state dead_monitors. If the supervising monitor fails (no token in monitor or looking_for_dead), another available monitor starts supervising the application services. The transition start_supervising models this behavior. The time value of this transition m_{mean} models the monitor responsibility lease of our architecture.

In the middle of the figure, the restarting of failed application service instances is modeled. The supervising monitor periodically checks whether a service application instance has failed (token moves from state monitor to looking_for_dead). If there is a token in state failure_recognized and enough votes can be gathered from the service description storages, the immediate transition restart fires based on the transition priority 2. If not, the transition no_restart fires to end the supervising period.

In GSPNs stochastic transitions are specified with a rate value. This rate value is the inverse of the mean duration (cf. Appendix A). In Figure 4 the rate values are shown, which are the inverse of the parameters which we described at the beginning of this section. All transitions concerning the failure of services (application and architecture) have the rate $b = 1/b_{mean}$. Typical embedded pc platforms have a MTBF of over 200,000 hours [24]. Since influences from the operating system and other infrastructure is unknown, we pessimistically assume a MTBF of 3,333 minutes, which equals 2.3 days. Thus, we get a failure rate $b = 0.0003$ (in failures/minute). All transitions concerning hardware repair have the rate $r = 1/r_{mean}$. We assume, that repairing hardware or replacing it is done in a mean time of 180 minutes which leads to $r = 0.005555$ (repairs per minute). The time needed for a repair of an application service instance is based on the values for the lease time (l_{mean}), the monitoring period (p_{mean}), and the monitor responsibility lease (m_{mean}). All these three parameters can be configured to reach a certain availability. Since their cost in terms of network bandwidth and processing power is equal and they equally influence the availability, we use the same value for all parameters: $p_{mean} = l_{mean} = m_{mean} = 125$ minutes. This simplifies the analysis and in the next section the adaption of the controller. Hence, we get the rate $p = 0.008$ (per minute).

We analyzed the GSPN model and got the result, that in the steady-state the probability of at least one working service instance is $p0 = 0.999281$, i.e. the availability of the service group is 99.9281%.

To be able to reach a required availability of the application services for different environmental parameters b_{mean}, we did a steady-state analysis of the model ($p0$) with different values for the parameter (p_{mean}) and the probability of service failures (b_{mean}) computing the probability of at least one working service. Figure 5 shows the results of the steady-state analysis. Note, that the parameter values shown in the figure are the reciprocal values of the means. Considering any curve b, we can improve the availability by reducing the parameter p_{mean} (reducing p_{mean} leads to higher p because of $p = 1/p_{mean}$). We used the GreatSPN tool [22] for modeling the net and the steady-state analysis.

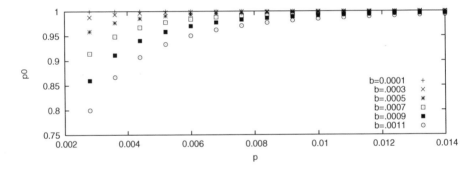

Fig. 5. Parameterized steady-state analysis of the availability

4.3   Controlling the Availability

The steady-state analysis computes the availability achievable by the architecture w.r.t. different estimated values for the architecture parameter p_{mean} and the hardware mean time to failure b_{mean}. For the initial deployment we use a reasonable b_{mean} and the according p_{mean} to achieve the required $p0$, which we computed during the steady-state analysis. Our estimated value for b_{mean} may be wrong. Therefore, if the estimated value for the service failure b_{mean} proves incorrect after deploying the system and executing it, we may adjust the monitoring period p_{mean}, based on the values of the steady-state analysis to reach the same required availability $p0$ despite the incorrect estimated b_{mean}. Additionally, the rate of the service failure may change over the course of time. The architecture parameter will be changed accordingly to sustain the required availability.

However, we can only perform a steady-state analysis for a distinct number of parameter values. The parameter values, gathered during the execution of the system, will not be equal to the values computed by the steady-state analysis. Thus, we need to be able to compute a monitoring period for a service failure rate which we did not consider during the steady-state analysis. We assume that the steady-state results are continuous w.r.t. the parameter values (p and b). Therefore, we may approximate a graph $p0 = f(p, b)$ by using a cubic bi-spline function.

The approximation by the cubic bi-spline function results in a set of polynomial functions. For each patch based on the initial discrete values, one polynomial function is used to compute the p0 value. Figure 6 shows a scaled plot of the set of functions. The figure shows which availability (shown on the z-axis) is the result of the failure rate b and the architecture parameter p. Increasing the architecture parameter p, which increases the repair rate of the architecture, increases the availability $p0$ for a given failure rate b. Vice versa, in case of a higher failure rate b, we can increase the repair rate p to reach a required availability $p0$.

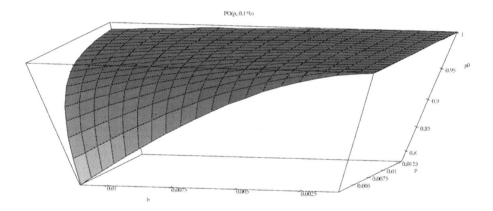

Fig. 6. Interpolated function of the distinct values provided by the steady-state analysis

Based on this function, we can change the architecture parameter to achieve a required degree of availability in response to the measured changes of the service failure rate. Thus, we are controlling the availability of the system by reading inputs (service availability) and changing outputs (architecture parameter) to reach a certain goal, i.e. we are applying control theory to software systems as proposed in [25]. Our approach for adjusting the parameter p is a special feedback adaptive controller named *model identification adaptive controller* (MIAC). Following [15], it is also named a *self-optimizing controller*.

As depicted in Figure 7, the basic control loop in the system is built by the service group and the monitor. The service group represents the controlled process. It can be influenced by the monitor by restarting crashed services. The feedback from the process to the monitor is only implicitly present in the architecture. The monitor periodically checks via the lookup service if a specific service has not crashed.

The availability of the application service group is influenced by the service failure rate b. The measured availability of the application services $p0$ is fed into the parameter identification unit. Using the pre-computed approximation of $p0(p, b)$ the related service failure rate b can be determined and propagated to the parameter adaptation unit. There, the approximation of $p0(p, b)$ is again used to determine the parameter p to reach the assigned availability goal $p0$.

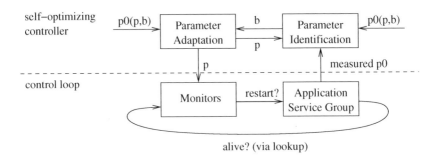

Fig. 7. Self-optimizing availability controller

5   Ensuring Reliability of Application Services

As outlined in the preceding section, the presented infrastructure of the architecture can ensure a required degree of availability for a group of application services by restarting failed ones. Due to failures, application services are failing over time and are restarted on other nodes in the network by the architecture.

Reliability is known as the probability that an item will perform its required function under given conditions for a stated time interval [21]. Thus, we can also aim at raising the reliability of the application system by employing redundancy. As long as the failure rate of the services does not exceed a certain level, which would make it impossible to synchronize the redundant service instances, we can use the available redundant services to fulfill the incoming service requests.

5.1   Qualitative Evaluation

For each class of application services we have to reflect the specific condition when the service will fail.

For stateless session services it is irrelevant which service instance is used for a given action, since the actions are independent of each other. If a service instance fails, simply another instance can be used. It is not needed to keep the service instance consistent with each other, since there is no state which needs to be shared between the individual service instances.

If a stateful session service instance fails in the middle of a session, just using another service instance from thereon does not work. Essentially, the last state of the failed service instance must be recreated on the newly used service instance. Thus, the history (relevant actions) until the point of failure needs to be replayed. As a smart proxy will only crash together with the client employing it, we can rely on this principle to ensure that the client is able to replay the history on its own as long as at least one application service instance is available.

For obtaining reliable entity services, it is necessary to replicate the entity and to distribute the replicas among a number of service instances to be able to tolerate failures. Additionally, the consistency of the entity according to a suitable consistency model must be assured. The required consistency model is application-specific and for every degraded service level a different number of active application service instances might be required. For standard consistency models like sequential consistency, application independent replication algorithms may be used, which provide the required consistency model. For example, in our architecture we have data with two very different requirements (service descriptions and monitor responsibilities) which can be provided by appropriate consistency models (see Section 3.1). For the service descriptions we have two different service levels. Either we have the full service including read and write access or the degraded service read access only.

The implementation of the above mentioned concepts leads to a system where reliability can be configured to some extend. But the maintainability[1] of the resulting system deteriorates due to the increased application of fault tolerance techniques throughout the system's source code. To overcome the situation that each client of a service must include the appropriate fault tolerance code, we apply in our architecture the smart proxy pattern (see Figure 8).

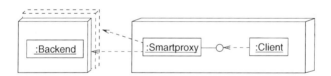

Fig. 8. A smart proxy hides the employed fault tolerance scheme

5.2   Quantitative Evaluation

For an appropriate model of the reliability of a specific group of application services the same general dependability characteristics as employed in the GSPN model of Figure 4 have to be considered.

For a specific group of redundant service components we can model the expected reliability using a GSPN model such as in Figure 4 where additionally the failure rate λ of the service failure condition for the whole group is analyzed. Note, that this condition is not the failure rate of the single service instances but a condition on the whole set of service instances which is specific for the class of service and the employed redundancy scheme.

Using a steady-state analysis of the model we can then derive the failure rate. Due to the steady-state result we can assume that the measured mean transition throughput of

---

[1] "the ease with which a software system or component can be modified to correct faults, improve performance, or other attributes, or adapt to a changed environment" [26].

a set of transitions detecting the failing of the service actually corresponds to a constant failure rate λ which describes the rate at which the whole group of services is failing to provide the required service.

At first we can ensure a required minimal mean time to failure. Using the formula $\mathrm{MTTF} = 1/\lambda$ for a system with constant failure rates ($\mathrm{MTTF} = \int_0^\infty R(t)$) we can derive the required upper bound $\lambda \leq 1/\mathrm{MTTF}$ on the failure rate. The value of λ is dependent on the configurable architecture parameter p. Thus, by changing p we can indirectly influence the mean time to failure.

Secondly, to ensure the required minimal reliability r for a given time interval of length l such that $R(l) \geq r$ holds, we can use the formula $R(t) = e^{-\lambda t}$ for the case of a constant failure rate to derive an upper bound for the failure rate with $\lambda_r \leq -\ln(r)/l$.

In the same manner as the availability value $p0$ can be computed using the GSPN model, we can thus use the steady-state analysis results of an appropriately extended GSPN model to derive the required results for the service failure rate of the group of services.

For stateless session services any service instance is sufficient. To derive the failure rate for this simple case we have thus added to the GSPN model in Figure 4 an additional place unavailable and transitions available and unavailable which model the event that none of the service instances is available. For the example configuration presented in Figure 4 the throughput of the transition unavailable determined by the steady-state analysis is 0.000005, i.e. the $MTTF_S$ for the complete system is $1/0.000005 = 200,000$ minutes, which is 138.8 days. The resulting reliability over a month is thus $e^{-0.000005*43,200} = 0.805735$.

For a stateful session service with a smart proxy which records the relevant history, the same extension of the GSPN model as used for the stateless case can be employed for analysis. The reliability for an entity service group, where a simple majority voting of the service instances is employed such that at least two of all three service instances have to be up, can be analyzed by extending the GSPN model of Figure 4 as follows: Two transitions unavailable1 and unavailable0 for the case of only one or zero available services and their combined transition rate has to be used to model the failure of service provisioning. Transition available has to be replaced by two transition available2 and available3 which fire when two or three of the service instances are available. It is to be noted that a different employed redundancy scheme would also result in a different required extension of the GSPN model.

5.3   Controlling the Reliability

Like in Figure 7, we can exploit an approximation of the parameterized GSPN model to realize a self-optimizing controller on top of the basic control loop build by the service group and the monitor. The required changes to the infrastructure parameters are derived from the parameterized model for multiple identical services at run-time by measuring the failure rate $r0$ of the service group.

The reliability of the application service group is influenced by the crash failure rate b. Equivalent to the controller loop used for ensuring the availability $p0$, the measured failure rate of the whole application service group $r0$ is used in an additional parameter identification unit where the pre-computed approximation of $r0(p,b)$ is used to estimate the single service failure rate b. In the parameter adaptation unit this estimation and the $r0(p, b)$ is then used to compute the parameter p to reach the assigned reliability goal $r0$.

In Section 4.3 we presented a controller for the availability of the application service group, which controls the availability for not falling below a certain required level. If we employ both controllers, we may get different values for the architecture parameter p. In this situation we simply choose the higher value. Consider a situation where the controllers compute two values p_r and p_a to ensure a required level of reliability respective availability. If $p_r > p_a$ holds, $p = p_r$ is used for controlling availability *and* reliability. Since a higher value for p than p_a is used for controlling the availability, the availability of the application service group will be higher than required.

6   Evaluation

We presented in the last sections an approach to control the availability and reliability of application services executed by the architecture in the case of changes to the crash failure rate due to external influences. In this section, we present results of a number of simulation experiments, which show that (1) our GSPN model is a correct abstraction of the simulation and (2) the controlling approach presented can indeed ensure the requested availability and reliability in case of changes to the crash failure rate.

For the simulation experiments, the scenario of the GSPN model of Section 4.2 is used: a service group of 3 application service instances is executed by the architecture, 1 running application service instance is sufficient for working (1-out-of-3 redundancy), 3 monitors are used to supervise the service group, 5 deployment storages contain the service group deployment information of which 3 must be working (3-out-of-5 redundancy).

The simulation is event driven, i.e. for each event a distinct trigger time is computed when this event will happen. This trigger time computation is either based on a negative exponential distribution or based on deterministic periods. Events are (1) crash failures, (2) repair of infrastructure services, (3) lease expirations of application service instances, (4) monitor checks, and (5) monitor responsibility checks. The simulation sequentially processes the events in the order of the trigger time. During processing an event, new events are created, e.g. processing a lease expiration event creates a monitor check event. The simulation skips all time steps between events, since no change to the system is expected to occur between events.

In the course of the evaluation, 75 simulation runs have been conducted each running for 100,000 events. Due to the stochastic distributed event trigger times, the simulated total time of each simulation run varies. The mean simulation time for a simulation run is 12,551,511 minutes, which roughly equals 24 years.

The availability values gathered during the simulation experiments and computed in the GSPN analysis are very similar. In addition the results of the simulation run are slightly better than the analysis results of the more abstract GSPN model in the majority of the simulation runs. Table 1 shows the results for an architecture parameter $p = 0.0092$ and the different values for the crash failure rate b for different simulation runs.

Table 1. Availability results of simulation and GSPN analysis for $p = 0.0092$ and different b

	0.0001	0.0003	0.0005	0.0007	0.0009	0.0011
GSPN	0.999980	0.999516	0.997921	0.994637	0.989166	0.98102
Simulation	0.999985	0.999710	0.997589	0.994958	0.989306	0.97026

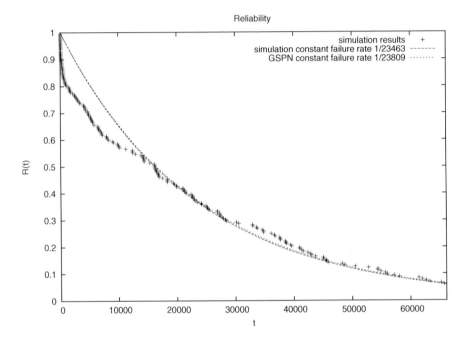

Fig. 9. Reliability results of simulation and GSPN analysis for $p = 0.0092$ and $b = 0.0007$

Concerning reliability, Figure 9 shows the reliability curve for different time intervals t gathered during the simulation experiment. During a simulation run, the time intervals x_i in which the application group performs its required function are stored in the set M. The set $N_t = \{x_i | x_i > t\}$ contains all time intervals x_i which are longer than the time interval t. The points depicted in the figure are computed as $R(t) = |N_t|/|M|$, i.e. the fraction between the number of time intervals bigger than t and the total number of time intervals. Hence, these individual points $R(t)$ depict the experimental results for the probability that the application group performs its required function for at least the time interval t. In addition the mean time to failure of the simulation experiment and the MTTF computed by the GSPN analysis are included to show, that concerning reliability our GSPN model is a good abstraction of the simulation.

In Sections 4.3 and 5.3, we presented the idea to use the values computed by the GSPN analysis to control availability and reliability in case of changes to the crash failure rate b. To support this claim, we conducted simulation runs, where we externally change the crash failure rate b during the simulation run. Figure 10 shows the plot of one simulation run. The average availability of the system over a time frame of 1,000 minutes is displayed as a line. The reconfigurations done by the controller are displayed

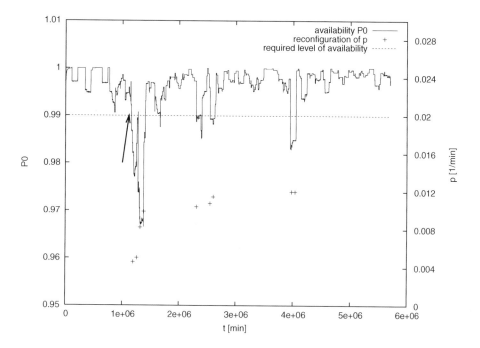

Fig. 10. Availability results showing the reaction to induced changes of the crash failure rate

as small crosses. In this run, we started with the crash failure rate $b = 0.0003$. Note, that we externally induced an increase of the crash failure rate b at time 1,114,365 (visualized by the arrow) to $b = 0.0009$. The controller is set to reconfigure the architecture parameter p, when the availability falls below a required level of 0.99. It is apparent from the figure, that after the externally induced increase of the crash failure rate, the availability falls below the required level of 0.99. Thereafter the controller reacts by increasing p, and the availability rises again above 0.99. Due to the random distributed crash failures in the simulation, there have been three additional points in time, where the availability falls below 0.99 and the controller reacts again by increasing the architecture parameter p.

In this section, we have shown by the extensively conducted simulation runs, that (1) our GSPN model is a good abstraction w.r.t. the simulation and based on that (2) our controller can indeed ensure the availability of the application service group in spite of external increases of the crash failure rate.

7   Related Work

In the Jini-context the problem of availability is somewhat addressed by the RMI-Daemon [11]. This daemon supports the on demand creation of remote objects. Additionally if the node fails, after a reboot and a restart of the daemon all remote objects are recreated. Nevertheless this daemon only restarts the remote objects on the same node. Therefore, this is not a solution if a node fails permanently or if the remote objects should be available during the repair of the node.

The RIO-Project [27] uses a somewhat similar approach compared to ours. One single monitor is loaded with the service descriptions and ensures the availability of the contained services in the system. The fact that the service descriptions are only available inside of the monitor makes the monitor a single-point-of-failure in the system. If the monitor process fails, the service descriptions are lost since they are not replicated. No other monitor can use those service descriptions and replace the existing monitor without manual intervention. Thus the reliability of the RIO approach depends heavily on the reliability of one monitor instance. Additionally during a network partition failure the approach does not work since the monitor instance cannot be in more than one partition of the network. Hence this approach is not applicable for dependable systems.

The Master-Slave pattern [28] can be applied when services are replicated and a result must be selected which is returned to the client. This is similar to our smart proxy approach. In our approach the slaves are the different service instances and the smart proxy is the master. The Master-Slave pattern is aimed at stateless session services whereas our approach can also be used for the consistent management of entity services.

The Willow-Architecture by Knight et al. [29] provides survivability for critical distributed systems. As a response to faults reconfiguration is used to ensure the survivability of the system. The response to failures is based on a monitor/analyze/respond-control loop which is similar to our behavior of the monitor.

The SAFEGUARD project [30] aims at a scalable multi-agent environment for maintaining an acceptable level of system's operability. Anomaly Detection Agents initiate countermeasures in response to bad events in order to maintain the acceptable operability level. Those agents employ *learning* algorithms (case based reasoning, neural networks, etc.) to detect previously unknown bad events. Voting schemes are used to decrease the probability that false positives are detected or anomalies are not detected. In the SAFEGUARD project the quite ambitious effort is proposed to employ artificial intelligence approaches for fault detection. In contrast we use self-optimizing behavior to recover from known faults.

Kon et al. present in [31] the distributed middleware 2K which is built on top of standard operating systems and CORBA [32]. The 2K middleware provides means for dynamic instantiation of components including management of dependencies. To react to changes in the environment, 2K uses mobile reconfiguration agents which contain reconfiguration commands and/or new implementations for system and application commands. The resource management component of 2K uses also lease times as means for the detection of resource unavailability [33]. While fault tolerance is addressed for the 2k middleware components, for application components fault tolerance and reliability is left to the developer.

Gustavsson and Andler describe in [34] a distributed real-time database which uses eventual consistency. Similar to our approach they use this consistency model to improve the availability and efficiency and to avoid blocking for unpredictable periods of time.

The general approach to analyze the reliability in the presence of maintenance activities such as the restart of services by the monitors with models is restricted to fixed structure and derives one large GSPN (cf. [23]). In the presented approach in contrast dynamic structures are supported and GSPNs are only build off-line for each service group to determine the general characteristics. This model is then used at run-time to adapt the parameters of the monitors to sustain the required availability. The required availability is itself adapted taking the service dependencies into account.

8   Conclusions and Future Work

For the presented architecture implemented on top of Jini, we have shown that the infrastructure services itself build a dependable system. This includes that in contrast to related proposals no single-point-of-failure for node crashes or network partition failures is possible. For different kinds of application services we presented appropriate concepts to also realize a higher reliability. The required additional efforts for availability and reliability are systematically hidden to the service clients using the smart proxy concept of Jini.

As the number of parallel running service instances and lease times for registry and monitoring can be freely configured, the architecture permits to adjust the deployment and maintenance scenario for a given application service such that the required availability and reliability can be achieved by determining the parameters using the presented quantitative dependability models.

Additionally, we used the results of the formal analysis to react to run-time measurements of dependability characteristics. Thus, we adjust the system parameters such as monitor supervision periods accordingly to control the required degree of availability or reliability. We supported our approach by extensive simulation experiments.

In accordance with [35], which defines *self-adaptive software* as software that modifies its own behavior in response to changes in its operating environment, we thus classify our architecture as *self-healing software*. Our scheme to employ a model of the system under control to predict the controller parameters is in the control theory community named a *self-optimizing controller* [15]. Therefore, our architecture is a *self-optimizing* system for service-based software that at run-time does not only ensure self-healing behavior, but also optimizes the system w.r.t. the known required dependability and operation costs.

In addition to the implementation of the presented dependable architecture and its run-time system, tool support by means of UML component and deployment diagrams has been realized [36, 16]. This includes code generation for the services, generation of XML deployment descriptions, and the visualization of the current configuration by means of UML deployment diagrams.

As future work, we want to employ classical approaches for learning to improve our results. E.g., instead of the approximation $p0(p, b)$ or $r0(p, b)$ derived from the GSPN model, the measured relation between the parameters can be accumulated during operation. These selected field data may permit to find more cost effective solutions which still provide the required degree of dependability. When the predictive accuracy of this approach is detected to be not sufficient any more, the system may switch back to the model-based approach outlined in this paper to ensure the required availability in the long run. We plan to conduct real-life tests, to show whether the results of the simulation runs are repeatable under real-life conditions.

Acknowledgments

The authors thank Katrin Baptist, Sven Burmester, Matthias Gehrke, Ekkart Kindler, Matthias Meyer, and Daniela Schilling for discussions and comments on earlier versions of the paper.

References

1. Laprie, J.C., ed.: Dependability : basic concepts and terminology in English, French, German, Italian and Japanese [IFIP WG 10.4, Dependable Computing and Fault Tolerance]. Volume 5 of Dependable computing and fault tolerant systems. Springer Verlag, Wien (1992)
2. Majzik, I., Pataricza, A., Bondavalli, A.: Stochastic Dependability Analysis of System Architecture Based on UML Models. In Lemos, R.D., Gacek, C., Romanovsky, A., eds.: Architecting Dependable Systems. Volume 2677 of Lecture Notes in Computer Science. Springer-Verlag, New York (2003) 219–244
3. Gokhale, S.S., Horgan, J.R., Trivedi, K.S.: Specification-Level Integration of Simulation and Dependability Analysis. In Lemos, R.D., Gacek, C., Romanovsky, A., eds.: Architecting Dependable Systems. Volume 2677 of Lecture Notes in Computer Science. Springer-Verlag, New York (2003) 245–266
4. DeMichiel, L.G., Yalcinalp, L.Ü., Krishnan, S.: Enterprise JavaBeans^{TM} Specification. Sun Microsystems. (2001) Version 2.0.
5. Szyperski, C.: Component Software, Beyond Object-Oriented Programming. Addison-Wesley (1998)
6. Arnold, K., Osullivan, B., Scheifler, R.W., Waldo, J., Wollrath, A., O'Sullivan, B.: The Jini(TM) Specification. The Jini(TM) Technology Series. Addison-Wesley (1999)
7. Sun Microsystems: Jini Specification. (2000) Revision 1.1.
8. Waldo, J., Wyant, G., Wollrath, A., Kendal, S.: A Note on Distributed Computing. techreport, Sun Microsystems Laboratories (1994) TR-94-29.
9. Waldo, J.: The Jini architecture for network-centric computing. Communications of the ACM **42** (1999) 76–82
10. Gamma, E., Helm, R., Johnson, R., Vlissides, J.: Design Patterns, Elements of Reusable Object-Oriented Software. Addison-Wesley (1994)
11. Sun Microsystems: Java^{TM} Remote Method Invocation Specification. (2002) Revision 1.8, JDK 1.4.
12. Koster, R., Kramp, T.: Structuring QoS-Supporting Services with Smart Proxies. In: Proceedings of Middleware'00 (IFIP/ACM International Conference on Distributed Systems Platforms and Open Distributed Processing), Springer Verlag (2000)
13. Ledru, P.: Smart proxies for jini services. ACM SIGPLAN Notices **37** (2002) 57–61
14. Tanenbaum, A., van Steen, M.: Distributed Systems, Principles and Paradigms. Prentice Hall (2002)
15. Isermann, R., Lachmann, K.H., Matko, D.: Adaptive control systems. Prentice Hall International series in systems and control engineering. Prentice Hall, New York (1992)
16. Tichy, M.: Durchgängige Unterstützung für Entwurf, Implementierung und Betrieb von Komponenten in offenen Softwarearchitekturen mittels UML. Master's thesis, University of Paderborn, Department of Mathematics and Computer Science, Paderborn, Germany (2002)
17. Gifford, D.K.: Weighted Voting for Replicated Data. In: Proceedings of the seventh symposium on Operating systems principles. Volume 7 of ACM Symposium on Operating Systems Principles., ACM press (1979) 150–162

18. Freeman, E., Hupfer, S., Arnold, K.: JavaSpaces Principles, Patterns, and Practice. Addison-Wesley (1999)
19. Carriero, N., Gelernter, D.: How to Write Parallel Programs. MIT Press (1990)
20. Gray, J.N.: Notes on Database Operating Systems. In: Operating Systems an Advanced Course. Lecture Notes in Computer Science, Springer Verlag (1978)
21. Birolini, A.: Reliability engineering : theory and practice. Springer Verlag, Berlin (1999) 3rd Edition.
22. Marsan, M.A., Balbo, G., Conte, G., Donatelli, S., Franceschinis, G.: Modelling with Generalized Stochastic Petri Nets. John Wiley and Sons, Inc. (1995)
23. Malhotra, M., Trivedi, K.S.: Dependability modeling using Petri-nets. IEEE Transactions on Reliability **44** (1995) 428–440
24. Advanced Digital Logic Inc.: MSMP3SEN/SEV Datasheet `http://www.adlogic-pc104.com/products/cpu/pc104/datasheets/msmp3sen-sev.pdf`. (2001)
25. Kokar, M.M., Baclawski, K., Eracar, Y.A.: Control Theory-Based Foundations of Self-Controlling Software. IEEE INTELLIGENT SYSTEMS **14** (1999) 37–45
26. Standards Coordinating Committee of the IEEE Computer Society, The Institute of Electrical and Electronics Engineers, Inc. 345 East 47th Street, New York, NY 10017-2394, USA: IEEE standard glossary of software engineering terminology, IEEE Std 610.12-1990. (1990)
27. Sun Microsystems: RIO - Architecture Overview. (2001) 2001/03/15.
28. Buschmann, F., Meunier, R., Rohnert, H., Sommerlad, P., Stal, M.: Pattern Oriented Software Architecture. John Wiley and Sons, Inc. (1996)
29. Knight, J.C., Heimbigner, D., Wolf, A., Carzaniga, A., Hill, J., Devanbu, P., Gertz, M.: The Willow Architecture: Comprehensive Survivability for Large-Scale Distributed Applications. In: The International Conference on Dependable Systems and Networks (DSN-2002), Washington DC (2002)
30. Bologna, S., Balducelli, C., Dipoppa, G., Vicoli, G.: Dependability and Survivability of Large Complex Critical Infrastructures. In: Proceedings of the 22nd International Conference on Computer Safety, Reliability and Security (SAFECOMP 2003). Volume 2788 of Lecture Notes in Computer Science., Springer Verlag (2003) 342 – 353
31. Kon, F., Campbell, R.H., Mickunas, M.D., Nahrstedt, K., Ballesteros, F.J.: 2K: A Distributed Operating System for Dynamic Heterogeneous Environments. In: Proc. of the Ninth IEEE International Symposium on High Performance Distributed Computing (HPDC'00), Pittsburgh, USA. (2000)
32. Object Management Group: The Common Object Request Broker: Architecture and Specification, Version 3.0 formal/02-06-33. (2002)
33. Kon, F., Yamane, T., Hess, C., Campbell, R., Mickunas, M.D.: Dynamic Resource Management and Automatic Configuration of Distributed Component Systems. In: Proceed. of the 6th USENIX Conference on Object-Oriented Technologies and Systems (COOTS'2001), San Antonio, USA. (2001)
34. Gustavsson, S., Andler, S.F.: Self-stabilization and eventual consistency in replicated real-time databases. In: Proceedings of the first workshop on Self-healing systems, ACM Press (2002) 105–107
35. Oreizy, P., Gorlick, M.M., Taylor, R.N., Heimbigner, D., Johnson, G., Medvidovic, N., Quilici, A., Rosenblum, D.S., Wolf, A.L.: An Architecture-Based Approach to Self-Adaptive Software. IEEE Intelligent Systems **14** (2002) 54–62
36. Tichy, M., Giese, H.: Seamless UML Support for Service-based Software Architectures. In: Proc. of the International Workshop on scientiFic engIneering of Distributed Java applIcations (FIDJI) 2003, Luxembourg. Lecture Notes in Computer Science (2003)
37. Reisig, W.: Petri nets - An introduction. EATCS Monographs on Theoretical Computer Science. Springer Verlag (1985)

A   An Introduction to Generalized Stochastic Petri Nets

In this section, we give a small, simplified, and informal introduction to generalized stochastic Petri nets (GSPN). We assume that the reader is familiar with s/t-nets (cf. [37]). For further information and a formal introduction for GSPNs see [22].

A GSPN consists of states and transitions. Two ideas merely have been added compared with s/t-nets: (1) the introduction of timed transitions, (2) the association of a random, exponentially distributed firing delay with timed transitions.

(a) Immediate   (b) Stochastic

Fig. 11. Different transition types

The first idea leads to the distinction between immediate transitions which immediately fire, if they are enabled, and timed transitions. If a timed transition becomes enabled, it gets a timer which decreases constantly until it reaches zero. Then, the transition fires. The second idea leads to the association of a random, exponentially distributed firing delay with timed transitions. For mathematical reasons negative exponential probability density functions (pdf) are adopted. Figure 11 shows the different types of transitions in a GSPN, which are used throughout this paper.

A stochastic transition is specified using a rate. This rate is the inverse of the mean of the negative exponential pdf. For example, if you want to model an activity with an average duration of $t = 10$ time units, the respective timed transition has a rate $\lambda = \frac{1}{t} = 0.1$.

Priorities and weights are used to specify how conflicts between two immediate transitions are resolved. Using priorities the transition fires, which has the higher priority. Weights are used to specify the probability of the conflicting transitions. For example, if two immediate transitions with the weights $w_1 = 1$ and $w_2 = 4$ are in conflict to each other, the probability that transition one fires is $p_1 = \frac{w_1}{w_1+w_2} = 0.2$ and the probability that transition two fires is $p_1 = \frac{w_2}{w_1+w_2} = 0.8$.

If an immediate and a timed transition are in conflict with each other, always the immediate transition fires. The resolution of two conflicting timed transitions is based on the facts that (1) the two timers of the transitions are sampled from the negative exponential pdf and (2) the probability of two timers expiring at the same instant is zero.

Generalized stochastic Petri nets can be mapped to continuous-time Markov chains for steady-state analysis. The GreatSPN tool [22] has been used in the paper for this analysis. It is available from www.di.unito.it/~greatspn/index.html on request.

Achieving Critical System Survivability
Through Software Architectures

John C. Knight and Elisabeth A. Strunk

Department of Computer Science
University of Virginia
151, Engineer's Way, P.O. Box 400740
Charlottesville, VA 22904-4740, USA
{strunk,knight}@cs.virginia.edu

Abstract. Software-intensive systems often exhibit dimensions in size and complexity that exceed the scope of comprehension of system designers and analysts. With this complexity comes the potential for undetected errors in the system. While software often causes or exacerbates this problem, its form can be exploited to ameliorate the difficulty in what is referred to as a *survivability architecture*. In a system with a survivability architecture, under adverse conditions such as system damage or software failures, some desirable function will be eliminated but critical services will be retained. Making a system survivable rather than highly reliable or highly available has many advantages, including overall system simplification and reduced demands on assurance technology. In this paper, we explore the motivation for survivability, how it might be used, what the concept means in a precise and testable sense, and how it is being implemented in two very different application areas.

1 Introduction

Sophisticated hardware systems have been providing dependable service in many important application domains for some time. Systems such as electro-mechanical railway signals and aircraft hydro-mechanical controls are safety critical, and many strategies for achieving and analyzing dependability properties in these systems have been developed. Introducing software-intensive components into engineered systems, however, adds extra dimensions in size and complexity. Combining powerful computation facilities with high-speed digital communications can lead to systems that are thousands of times more complex than would normally be considered in a hardware system, such as the electronic funds transfer system within the financial network or the supervisory and control mechanisms within the electric power grid. Such systems are referred to as *critical infrastructure systems* because of the very high dependence that society now has on them.

Software also enables function to be implemented that would be impractical to implement in hardware. In *safety-critical embedded systems*, important facilities—including many that enhance safety—depend on complex software systems for correct operation. An example of this is stability augmentation in aircraft flight-control, where the digital system calculates a stream of small adjustments that must be made to control surfaces in addition to the pilot's commands.

R. de Lemos et al. (Eds.): Architecting Dependable Systems II, LNCS 3069, pp. 51–78, 2004.
© Springer-Verlag Berlin Heidelberg 2004

Both critical infrastructure systems and safety-critical embedded systems can quickly exceed not only the scope of current approaches to analysis but also the comprehension capability of even talented, experienced system designers and analysts. When this happens, the potential for introducing undetected errors into the system is greatly increased. While software function causes or exacerbates some of the difficulties in system design, its form can be exploited to ameliorate them in what is referred to as a *survivability architecture*. In a system with a survivability architecture (referred to as a *survivable system*), the full set of system functions, though highly desirable, will not always be provided and need not be provided in order to prevent a catastrophic failure. Under certain adverse conditions that preclude the provision of total functionality, the system can offer an alternative service. This alternative service provides critical system functions, sacrificing some of the preferred service to ensure a level of continued operation that is considered acceptable even though it is not optimal.

Requiring that a system be survivable rather than reliable provides two major advantages. First, the amount of hardware replication required to meet hardware dependability goals can be reduced by architecting the system to allow and account for some unmasked failures; this confers considerable cost savings, particularly in large systems. Second, assurance of correct software function can be limited to the function whose correctness is crucial. Certain software faults can be tolerated by transitioning to providing only the crucial functionality, and the more limited size of the crucial functionality gives designers and analysts a much better chance of being able to cope with the complexity of the system.

In this paper, we examine the characteristics and dependability requirements of critical infrastructure and embedded systems. With these requirements in mind, we present the detailed definition of survivability and show how the definition can be applied. We then give examples of survivable systems and discuss the implementation of survivability using survivability architectures for both types of system.

2   Types of System

2.1   Critical Information Systems

Powerful information systems have been introduced into critical infrastructure applications as the cost of computing hardware has dropped and the availability of sophisticated software has increased [18]. Massive computerization has enabled efficiencies through tightened coupling of production and distribution processes. Just-in-time delivery of automotive parts by rail, for example, has enabled dramatic inventory reductions. Some forms of damage to these systems have no external effect because of appropriate redundancy; mirrored disks, for example, mask the effect of disk failure. But in other cases, the effects of damage will be so extensive that it will be visible to the system's users in the form of a lack of service or reduction in the quality of service. Events that disrupt critical infrastructure applications are inevitable; in practice, the continued provision of some form of service is necessary when damage precludes the provision of full service.

For the developer of a critical information system, knowing what service is required in the event that full service cannot be provided is very important. The current notion of dependability for critical information systems does not provide the necessary concepts of degraded service and the associated spectrum of factors that affect the choice of degraded service as an explicit requirement. Survivability is the term that has come into use for this composite form. To provide a basis for a discussion and to motivate the definition, we enumerate the characteristics of infrastructure applications that affect the notion of survivability. The most important characteristics are:

- *System Size.* Critical information systems are *very* large. They are geographically diverse, topologically complex, and include large numbers of heterogeneous computing, storage and network elements.

- *Damage and Repair Sequences.* Events that damage a system are not necessarily independent nor mutually exclusive. A sequence of events might occur over time in which each event causes more damage. In effect, a bad situation gets progressively worse meaning that a critical infrastructure application might experience damage while it is in an already damaged state, and that a sequence of partial repairs might be conducted. A user might experience progressively less service over time as damage increases and progressively more as repairs are conducted.

- *Time-Dependent Damage Effects.* The impact of damage tends to increase with time. The loss associated with brief (seconds or less) interruptions of electric power, for example, can be mitigated in many cases. A protracted loss (days) is much more serious, with impact tending to increase monotonically with time.

- *Heterogeneous Criticality.* The requirements for dependability in infrastructure systems are considerable but some functions are more important than others and the importance of some functions often varies with time.

- *Complex Operational Environments.* The operating environments of critical infrastructures are of unprecedented complexity. They carry risks of natural, accidental, and malicious disruptions from a wide variety of sources.

2.2   Safety-Critical Embedded Systems

As with critical infrastructure systems, immense amounts of software have been introduced into safety-critical embedded systems for similar reasons and with similar results. There has been a shift towards digital implementation of many functions that used to be electro- or hydro-mechanical (fly by wire, for example), and many new service and software-intense safety functions have been introduced (enhanced ground proximity warning, for example).

All forms of damage to safety-critical systems must be anticipated and considered in system design and analysis. The emphasis in these systems has always been to mask the effects of faults, yet that is becoming increasingly difficult as the complexity of the systems increases. In addition, the overall complexity of the software upon which the systems rely has long surpassed the point at which comprehensive analysis is possible. Exploiting the notion of survivability for these systems can reduce system complexity and limit the amount of software that is crucial to dependable operation.

Mandated dependability requirements are set by regulating agencies such as the U.S. Federal Aviation Administration (FAA), Food and Drug Administration (FDA), and Nuclear Regulatory Commission (NRC). The FAA, for example, categorizes aircraft functionality into three levels of criticality according to the potential severity of its failure conditions [14]. The most extreme criticality level is "**Catastrophic**: Failure conditions which would prevent continued safe flight and landing" [14]. Catastrophic failure conditions must be "extremely improbable" [14] or "so unlikely that [the failure condition is] not anticipated to occur during the entire operational life of all airplanes of one type" [14]. "Extremely improbable" corresponds to a quantitative failure rate of 10^{-9} failures per hour of operation.

Using survivability in systems of this type enables the extent of the system that is required to meet this extreme level of dependability to be reduced significantly. As in the critical infrastructure case, we enumerate the characteristics of safety-critical embedded systems that affect the notion of survivability. These characteristics are:

- *System Timing and Resource Constraints.* Embedded systems are often severely limited in power, cost, space, and weight, and so they are tuned to take the best possible advantage of their underlying resources.

- *System Coupling.* System components frequently have a very strong dependence on one another, and so the state of various system components must be seen individually and also as a whole when determining appropriate system behavior.

- *Damage and Repair Sequences.* Failures can occur in sequence, and while sometimes the system size allows reinitialization, at other times system criticality precludes any service interruption.

- *Heterogeneous Criticality.* Criticality of embedded system services also varies with function and with time. A medical application, for instance, is less dangerous during surgical planning than during the surgery itself.

- *Complex Operational Environments.* While the operational environments of embedded systems are fairly localized, they can still be affected by a variety of factors. Avionics systems are affected by factors such as weather, altitude, and geographic location.

3   What Is Survivability?

3.1   Existing Definitions of Survivability

Like many terms used in technologies that have not yet matured, several notions of survivability have appeared, and a rigorous definition has been presented only recently. Survivability has roots in other disciplines; for instance, a definition used by the telecommunications industry is:

Survivability: A property of a system, subsystem, equipment, process, or procedure that provides a defined degree of assurance that the named entity will continue to function during and after a natural or man-made disturbance; e.g., nuclear burst. Note: For a given application, survivability must be qualified by specifying the range of conditions over which the entity will survive, the minimum acceptable level or [sic] post-disturbance functionality, and the maximum acceptable outage duration [46].

The sundry definitions of survivability (see also, for example, [12, 13]) vary considerably in their details, but they share certain essential characteristics. One of these is the concept of service that is essential to the system. Another is the idea of damage that can occur; and a third, responding to damage by reducing or changing delivered function. Further, the definitions used outside of computing introduce the idea of probability of service provision as separate from the probabilities included in dependability.

While these definitions offer a firm starting point for a definition, they offer only an *informal* view of what survivability means. This view is analogous to the colloquial view of reliability—that the system rarely or never fails. The *formal* view of reliability, on the other hand, states that a system is reliable if it meets or exceeds a particular probabilistic goal. It is the formal definition that provides criteria for reliability that can be tested. Likewise, a formal definition for survivability that provides testable criteria is needed. If a system's survivability characteristics cannot be tested, then system developers cannot tell whether they have met users' requirements. The informal definitions above, for example, do not specify: which functions are essential; under what fault conditions the essential functions will be provided; or the timing requirements on transitioning to provide only essential functions.

Knight et al. give a definition based on specification: "A system is survivable if it complies with its survivability specification" [20]. They draw on the properties mentioned above and present a specification structure that tells developers what survivability means in an exact and testable way. It is this definition that we characterize and build on here.

3.2   A More Precise Intuitive Notion

What has been implied so far, but has not been made explicit, is the idea of *value* provided by a system to its users. In the critical infrastructure case, this value is essentially an aggregate over time; provision of electric service, for instance, is not critical at a single point in time or even for a short length of time, but the service is crucial over the long term. In contrast, in many embedded systems provision of service at a particular point in time is paramount; a nuclear shutdown system, for example, is of no use if it is operational continuously only until it is called upon.

The core of the survivability concept is that value is not a Boolean variable. A system is not constrained to provide service or not; it can provide service whose value to the user is less than that of the system's standard service, but still enough to meet critical user requirements. For an aircraft, such service might be basic control surface actuation without enhanced fly-by-wire comfort and efficiency algorithms.

The general idea of survivability is that a system will "survive" (i.e., continue some operation), even in the event of damage. The operation it maintains may not be its complete functionality, or it might have different dependability properties, but it will be some useful functionality that provides value to the users of the system, possibly including the prevention of catastrophic results due to the system's failure. Such a strategy is used extensively in industrial practice, but it does not rest on a rigorous mathematical foundation and so the properties of such a system are not guaranteed.

One might want to pursue survivability of a system for two reasons. First, while many services that critical systems provide are helpful or convenient, not all of them are necessary. Dependability guarantees on the noncrucial services can be extremely expensive to implement, particularly in the case of infrastructure systems where thousands of nodes would have to be replicated were the system engineered to provide all services with high dependability. In this case, survivability increases value delivered to the user because it decreases the cost of the services that are rendered.

Second, it might be the case that a system is so complex that there is no way to determine with sufficient confidence that the system meets its dependability goals. Cost can influence a decision to use survivability in this sense as well—sufficient assurance, if possible, could be extremely costly—but even more difficult is the question of validation. Validation is an informal activity [42], and must ultimately be performed by humans. The larger and more complex the system, the more difficulty humans have in determining whether it will meet their informal notion of what it should accomplish. If the system is survivable, human oversight need only ensure to ultradependable levels the crucial function and the transition mechanism, a simpler task than ensuring ultradependability of the entire system.

We now describe the different facets of the survivability concept that lead into a more rigorous definition:

- *Acceptable services.* A simple strategy for specifying a survivable subsystem is to define what constitutes the system's desired functionality and what constitutes its crucial functionality. The crucial functionality can then be ultradependable and the desired functionality *fail-stop* in the sense of Schlichting and Schneider [37]. This strategy is oversimplistic, however, for three reasons. First, the user is likely to expect some minimum probability that the full function is provided. Operating exclusively in backup mode is almost certain to be unacceptable. Second, there can be more than two major classes of function. If the system must degrade its services, some services are likely to be more valuable than others even if they are not essential, and the subsystem should continue to provide those services if possible. Third, the functionality that is determined to be crucial by domain experts will usually depend upon operating circumstances. As an example, consider an automatic landing system. It could halt and simply alert pilots of its failure if it were not in use (i.e., in standby mode), but if it were controlling an aircraft it would have to ensure that pilots had time to gain control of the situation before halting. The *set of acceptable services* contains those services which provide the best possible value to the user under adverse circumstances, and which take account of the three factors above.

- *Service value.* If we are to base design decisions on delivered value, it is important to have a precise characterization of that value. The metrics by which delivered value can be measured vary among applications, and can become incredibly complex. Absolute value is not important, however, because the purpose of a value metric is to decide what will provide the most benefit under specific circumstances: a quality that can be specified with relative values among the set of acceptable services. The relative value provided by a service can change under varying operational conditions, but for a system with a small number of separate services and a small number of salient environmental characteristics, the specification of relative service values can be done simply in a tabular form without having to conduct a detailed utility analysis.

- *Service transitions.* The system will provide only one member of the set of acceptable services at a time. Under normal circumstances, that member will be the *pre-*

ferred service which includes all desired functionality. If the preferred service can no longer be maintained, the system must transition to a different acceptable service. Which service it transitions to will depend on which services can still be provided and the operational conditions at the time of the transition. The set of valid transitions defines the specifications to which the system can transition from a particular specification. When a reconfiguration occurs, the service with the highest relative service value in that set for the prevailing operational conditions will be chosen. Transitions also might be triggered by a change in operational conditions as well as some form of damage if the system is not delivering its preferred service.

• *Operating environment.* Since different services provide different relative values under different operating conditions, the characteristics of the operating environment that affect relative service values must be enumerated, so that the environmental state can be determined and used in calculating the most appropriate transition to take. As an example, note that time of day has a serious impact on usage patterns of infrastructure services and can affect the risks associated with critical embedded systems such as aircraft and automobiles.

• *Service probabilities.* Users will demand that they have more than strictly crucial operational capability the vast majority of the time. Simply listing a set of acceptable services, then, is insufficient because that would imply that implementing only the basic service fulfills the specification. Rather, a set of minimal probabilities on value of delivered service are required. These probabilities are requirements on a system's meeting the dependability requirements of the operational specification. In other words, if the system were operating under the specification S_1, then the probability would be that S_1's dependability requirements were met.

This is not the same as strict composition of dependability and survivability probabilities, because if the survivability probability is not met, then the system will transition to another specification with a new set of dependability probabilities.

It might be the case that specification probabilities should be grouped. For example, if a system can transition from S_1 to either S_2 or S_3 depending on operating conditions, and (S_2 OR S_3) provides some coherent level of service, then the desired probability would be on (S_2 OR S_3) rather than the specifications individually. Generally, the same probability might be assigned to both S_2 and S_3 so that that probability would then hold over (S_2 OR S_3). Specifying that the probability hold over the disjunction, however, leaves more slack in the implementation of the system as well as being more intuitive.

3.3 Defining Survivability

Now that we have presented an informal explanation of the meaning and characteristics of survivability, we summarize the definition [20]. The definition is phrased as a specification structure; a system specification that has each of these elements is defined to be a survivability specification, and a system built to that specification has a survivability architecture. Such a specification contains six elements:

S: *the set of functional specifications of the system.* This set includes the *preferred* specification defining full functionality. It also includes alternative specifications representing forms of service that are acceptable under certain adverse conditions (such as failure of one or more system components). Each member of **S** is a full specification, including dependability requirements such as availability and reliability for that specification.

E: *the set of characteristics of the operating environment* that are not direct inputs to the system, but affect which form of service (member of **S**) will provide the most value to the user. Each characteristic in **E** will have a range or set of possible values; these also must be listed.

D: *the states of E that the system might encounter.* This is essentially the set of all modes (i.e., collection of states) the environment can be in at any particular time. Each element of **D** is some predicate on the environment. **D** will not necessarily be equal to the set of combinations of all values of elements in **E** since some combinations might be contradictory. Including **D** as a specific member allows completeness checks across environmental modes.

V: *the matrix of relative values each specification provides.* Each value will be affected both by the functionality of the specification and the environmental conditions for which that specification is appropriate. Quantifying these values is impossible, but using relative values gives the ordering needed to select a service based on prevailing conditions.

T: *the valid transitions from one functional specification to another.* Each member of **T** includes the specification from which the transition originates (source specification), the specification in which the transition ends (target specification), and a member of **D** defining the environmental conditions under which that transition may occur (the transition guard). The guard enables a specifier to define which transitions are valid under certain circumstances, and the developer can then use **V** to decide which target specification is most valuable under those conditions.

   In information systems this is sufficient because while there will be some approximate time constraint on the transition's occurrence, it is unlikely to be a very tight time bound. In embedded systems, on the other hand, the time required to transition often will be an integral part of the transition specification, and some global state invariant might need to hold during the course of the transition. Thus **T** has two optional members: the transition time, the maximum allowable time for a particular transition during which the system may be noncompliant with all members of **S**; and the transition invariant, which may not be violated at any point in which the system is noncompliant with all members of **S**.

P: *the set of probabilities on combinations of specifications.* Each member of **P** will be a set of specifications containing one or more elements that is mapped to a probability. The specifications in each set provide approximately the same level of functionality, under different environmental conditions. The probability is the probability of a failure in the system when the system is in compliance with one of the specifications (or the single specification, if there is only one in the set for that probability). Each probability is a minimum; for example, a failure of the primary specification might in reality be extremely improbable, so that the system never transitions to another specification. The probabilities are set by the systems owners to document the required service guarantees and they serve to provide a lower-bound guarantee of system operation.

4 System Examples

4.1 An Example of Survivability in Critical Information Systems

To illustrate the definition, we present an example based on a hypothetical financial payment system. We assume a hierarchical network topology in which there are a large number of nodes associated with *branch* banks (small retail institutions), a smaller number of *money-center* banks that are the primary operations centers for major retail banking companies, and a small set of nodes that represent the *Federal Reserve Bank*. Examples of identified hazards to the system include major hardware disruption in which communications or server machines become non-operational; coordinated security attacks in which multiple commercial bank regional processing centers are penetrated; and regional power failure in which either many branch banks are disabled or several money-center banks are disabled.

For this example, we assume several forms of tolerable service for the payment system (shown in Fig. 1): (S_0) *Preferred*, including electronic funds transfers, check processing, support for financial markets such as stocks and bonds, and international funds transfers; (S_1) *Industry/Government*, which limits service to transfer of large sums among major industrial and government clients only; (S_2) *Financial Markets*, which defines service for all the major financial markets but no other client organizations; (S_3) *Government Bonds*, which defines service for processing of sales and redemptions of government bonds only and only by major corporate clients; and (S_4) *Foreign Transfers*, in which transfers of foreign currency into or out of the country are the only available service.

To decide upon the relative value seen by users of the payment system associated with the services in this example (V in Fig. 1), we note: (1) that settlement by the clearing houses and the Federal Reserve Bank occurs during the late afternoon; (2) domestic markets are closed at night; and (3) stock, bond, and commodity markets must be accommodated when trading volumes are exceptionally and unexpectedly high. There is little value to providing processing service to domestic financial markets overnight, for example, and thus international transfers of funds have higher value. Similarly, extreme volume in domestic financial markets leads to a high demand on the financial payment system and this demand must be met if possible. Finally, during times of political crisis, sentiment turns away from most traditional financial instruments and government bonds become heavily sought after. Thus, during such times, the ability to maintain a market in government bonds is crucial. The relevant members of E, then, are time of day, trading volume, and political climate. D is the powerset of members of E, except that: (1) all states where the political climate is unstable are grouped together, since their values are the same; and (2) high trading volume cannot occur during late afternoon or at night. P for this specification is the set of individual specifi-

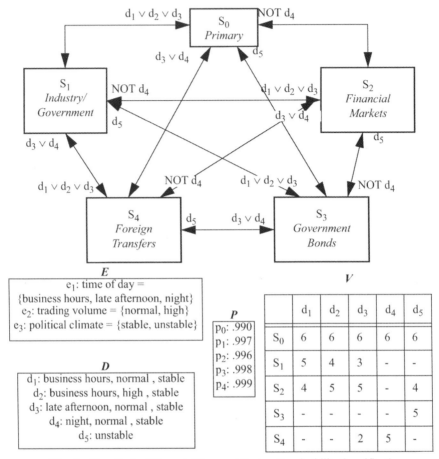

Fig. 1. Hypothetical Financial Payment System Survivability Specification

cation probabilities; composing specification probabilities does not make sense in this situation.

In our example, consider first the occurrence of a fault with a major file server that occurs during the middle of a normal market day (i.e., system state d_1) and which cannot be masked. To meet its survivability specification, the options that the system has are to transition to providing either service S_1, S_4, or S_2, (see Fig. 1) and the maximum relative value to the user (from the V table indexed by the current conditions d_1) would be in service S_1 in this case. Were this to occur during the night, the transition would be to service S_4 because the current conditions would be d_4. Now suppose that while the server is down, a coordinated security attack is launched against the system (a bad situation getting worse). In that case, the response to the attack might be to shut down as much of the system as possible. The system would transition to service S_3 since that would permit the best support in the event that the situation developed into a governmental crisis.

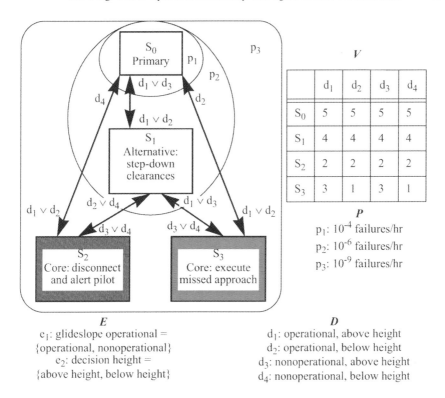

Fig. 2. Hypothetical ALS Survivability Specification

V

	d_1	d_2	d_3	d_4
S_0	5	5	5	5
S_1	4	4	4	4
S_2	2	2	2	2
S_3	3	1	3	1

P

p_1: 10^{-4} failures/hr
p_2: 10^{-6} failures/hr
p_3: 10^{-9} failures/hr

E
e_1: glideslope operational =
{operational, nonoperational}
e_2: decision height =
{above height, below height}

D
d_1: operational, above height
d_2: operational, below height
d_3: nonoperational, above height
d_4: nonoperational, below height

4.2   An Example of Survivability in Embedded Systems

As an illustration of how survivability might be applied to a safety-critical system, consider a hypothetical automatic landing system for a commercial aircraft. Assume four functional specifications, as shown in Fig. 2. The primary specification (S_0) will have all of the functionality the pilot desires for the system. The consequences of any failures will be minor because, if they have the potential to be more severe, the system can transition to one of the other three specifications. Therefore, using the FAA's criticality levels (see section 2.2), any failure in the primary specification may be "probable" provided that failure of a transition to another specification is "extremely improbable".

The first alternative specification (S_1) will have much of the functionality desired by the user, but some desirable yet unnecessary functionality removed. For example, the system might have to follow the step-down altitude clearances for the runway to descend at the proper rate rather than using the glideslope. All failures in this specification must be "improbable"; its functionality is important enough that frequent interruptions could have adverse consequences. However, provided that failure of a transition to another specification is "extremely improbable", none of it need be "extremely improbable" because any failures with potentially catastrophic consequences will cause a transition to a different alternative specification (S_2 or S_3).

S_2 and S_3 are the specifications that have very high dependability requirements. We will let S_2 be the specification requiring that the system disconnect and alert the pilot while remaining on course if the system fails and S_3 be the specification requiring the aircraft to execute a missed approach and alert the pilot on system failure. They contain the minimum functionality necessary to maintain safe operation of the system. Any non-masked failure of either of these specifications—such as failure to alert the pilot that the system has malfunctioned and the pilot is now in control—must be "extremely improbable", as the specifications are designed to include only the system functionality whose failure could have catastrophic consequences.

Whether the system transitions to S_2 or S_3 on a failure of S_1 depends on whether the aircraft is above or below decision height at the time of the transition, based on the assumption that presenting the possibility of a go-around is more valuable under those circumstances. The new probability requirement, then, would be that a failure of S_2 *above* decision height is "extremely improbable", and a failure of S_3 *below* decision height is "extremely improbable". In some cases the environmental conditions might change, and a transition between specifications appropriate to different conditions must occur in order to keep the system operating with its optimal functionality.

5   Implementation of Survivable Systems

5.1   The Role of Fault Tolerance

Survivability is a system property that can be required in exactly the same way that the other facets of dependability can be required. There is no presumption about how survivability will be achieved in the notion of survivability itself—that is a system design and assessment issue. However, the probabilities associated with each of the tolerable forms of service are important design constraints since they will determine which design choices are adequate and which are not.

A practical survivability specification will have achievable probabilities and carefully selected functionality specifications. Thus, in such a system, the effects of damage will not be masked necessarily; and, provided the probabilities are met in practice, degraded or alternative service will occur. In effect, this implies that the survivability requirement will be achieved by the fault-tolerance mechanism, i.e., the system will have a fault-tolerant design. Note, however, that the N different functions in the survivability specification do not correspond to functions that can be achieved with the resources that remain after N different faults. The N functions in the survivability specification are defined by application engineers to meet application needs and bear no prescribed relationship to the effects of faults. Many different faults might result in the same degraded or alternative application service. The role of a survivability architecture is to provide the necessary system-level framework to implement the fault tolerance necessary to meet the system's survivability goal. In the next two sections, we discuss two examples.

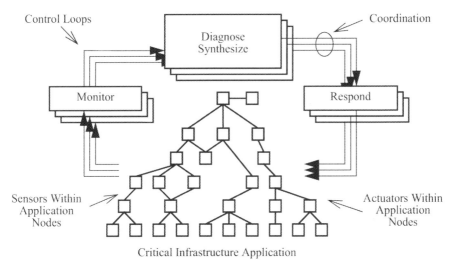

Control Loops

Coordination

Diagnose
Synthesize

Monitor

Respond

Sensors Within
Application
Nodes

Actuators Within
Application
Nodes

Critical Infrastructure Application

Fig. 3. The Willow Reactive System.

5.2   The Willow Reactive Mechanism

The fundamental structure of the Willow architecture [19] is a set of *control loops* each of which has monitoring, diagnosis, synthesis, coordination, and response components [45]. These components provide application-level fault tolerance. Monitoring and diagnosis provide error detection and synthesis; coordination and response provide error recovery. The overall structure is depicted in Fig. 3. The control loops begin with a shared *sensing* capability shown within the application nodes. Sensors can include reports from application software, application heartbeat monitors, intrusion detection alarms, or any other means of measuring actual application properties.

From sensing events, independent *diagnosis and synthesis* components build models of application state and determine required application state changes. Synthesis components issue their intended application changes as *workflow* requests. These are coordinated by the workflow and resource managers to ensure that changes occur correctly and smoothly within the application. When workflows are allowed to activate, workflow events are received by the application nodes and result in local system state changes. *Actuation* completes the control loop cycle.

As an example of the way in which the Willow reactive mechanism might be used, consider the hypothetical financial system introduced in section 4.1. The system might consist of several hundred servers of different types and tens of thousands of clients all communicating via a private network. Such a system provides services that are critical to several communities, and both security and availability are important properties. The Willow reactive mechanism could be used to deal with a variety of faults, both malicious and non-malicious, that might affect the system. A control loop could be deployed to deal with node failures that might occur because of hardware or software failures. A second control loop could be deployed to deal with coordinated security attacks. We discuss how these loops might work in the remainder of this section.

Dealing with Complex Faults

The reactive controller is a fully automatic structure that is organized as a set of finite state machines. The detection of the erroneous state associated with a fault (i.e., error detection) is carried out by a state machine because an erroneous state is just an application system state of interest. As the effects of a fault manifest themselves, the state changes. The changes become input to the state machine in the form of events, and the state machine signals an error if it enters a state designated as erroneous. The various states of interest are described using predicates on sets that define part of the overall state. The general form for the specification of an erroneous state, therefore, is a collection of sets and predicates. The sets contain the application objects of concern, and the predicates range over those sets to define states either for which action needs to be taken or which could lead to states for which action needs to be taken.

In the financial system example, events occurring at the level of individual servers or clients would be sent to the diagnosis and synthesis element of the Willow system where they would be input to a finite-state machine at what amounts to the lowest level of the system. This is adequate, for example, for a fault such as one causing commercial power to be lost. Dealing with such a fault might require no action if a single server or some small number of clients is affected because local equipment can probably cope with the situation. If a serious power failure affects a complete critical data center along with its backups, then the system might need to take some action. The action taken would be determined by the system's survivability specification as discussed in section 4.1. Recognizing the problem might proceed as follows. As node power failures are reported so a predefined set maintained by the diagnosis element, say *nodes_without_power*, is modified. When its cardinality passes a prescribed threshold, the recognizer moves to an error state. Once the recognizer is in the error state, the response mechanism would generate the appropriate workflows and individual nodes throughout the system would undertake whatever actions were defined by the workflows.

Sometimes, damage to a system is more complex. For example, a set of financial system nodes losing power in the West is the result of one fault, a set losing power in the East is the result of a second, but both occurring in close temporal proximity might have to be defined as a separate, third fault of much more significance. Such a fault might indicate a coordinated terrorist attack or some form of common-mode hardware or software failure. No matter what the cause, such a situation almost certainly requires a far more extensive response. We refer to such a circumstance as a *fault hierarchy*. A fault hierarchy is dealt with by a corresponding hierarchy of finite-state machines. Compound events can be passed up (and down) this hierarchy, so that a collection of local events can be recognized at the regional level as a regional event, regional events can be passed up further to recognize national events, and so on.

A coordinated security attack launched against the example financial system might include a combination of intrusions through various access points by several adversaries working at different locations, targeted denial-of-service attacks, and exploitation of previously unknown software vulnerabilities. Detection of such a situation requires that individual nodes recognize the circumstances of an attack, groups of nodes collect events from multiple low-level nodes to recognize a wide-area problem,

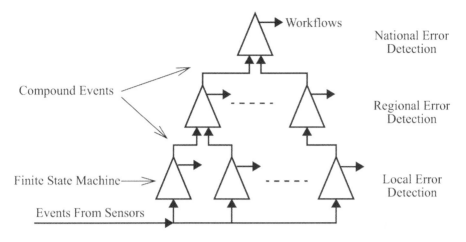

Fig. 4. Recognizing a Fault Hierarchy

and the high-level error-detection mechanism recognize the variety of simultaneous wide-area problems as a coordinated attack.

Provided sensor data was available from elements such as host intrusion-detection systems, network traffic monitors, and liveness monitors, a scenario such as this could generate an appropriate set of events as the different elements of the attack took place. A finite-state-machine hierarchy that might be used in such circumstances is shown in Fig. 4. As sensor events arrive from intrusion detection systems, an initial indication of the severity of the situation would be created. Local error detection might show that multiple clients were reporting intrusions. Each one might not be serious in its own right, but the temporal proximity of several would be a concern. The finite state machines receiving these intrusion events might not act on them other than to shut down the nodes reporting intrusions. Instead, they would generate compound events that would be sent to finite machines detecting regional security problems.

Regional error detection might determine that action needed to be taken after several local error detectors signalled a problem by forwarding a compound event. The action taken at the regional level might be to immediately switch all nodes in the region to a higher security level and limit service. If network traffic monitors then detected traffic patterns that were indicative of a denial of service attack, the error detection mechanism could trigger a national response.

Communication
The communication challenges presented by the Willow reactive system are considerable because of the scale of the networked applications that it seeks to address. The greatest challenge comes from the need to send reconfiguration commands to sets of nodes (those that have to act in the face of damage or an attack) where the relevant set is determined by analysis of the state.

The obvious way to approach such a requirement is for the Willow reactive system to maintain a central database with details of all the nodes in the system—how they are configured, what software they are running, their network addresses, and so on. This is completely infeasible for systems of the type we address. With hundreds of thousands of nodes, the size of the database would be prohibitive and it would constantly be in danger of being out of date—network changes would not be reflected in the database until some time after they occurred.

To send reconfiguration commands, the Willow system uses a novel communications approach called *selective notification*, an event communication mechanism combining content-based addressing, intentional addressing, and sender qualification in a unified structure for the delivery of events [33]. It has three primary components: (1) *symmetric decoupled communication* that combines content, sender, and receiver addressing in a single property-based addressing language; (2) *descriptive communication policies* in which communication relationships are defined at the level of policies constraining properties of objects relevant to communication; and (3) *simultaneous addressing* in which content-based, intentional, and sender-qualified addresses are applied simultaneously in determining the delivery of each event.

Returning to the example security attack on the hypothetical financial system, the actions needed for defense as the attack develops would be communicated to the nodes that need to take action by selective notification. The regional response of shutting down all nodes signalling intrusions and switching all other nodes in the affected region to a higher security level would be effected by two uses of selective notification. In the first, a command to shut down would be transmitted to "All Nodes In Region X With Triggered Intrusion Detection Alarms" where "X" is identity of the affected region. In the second, a command to change security parameters would be sent to "All Operating Nodes In Region X". The phrases in quotations are the addresses used by selective notification. By selecting nodes based on properties, only essential network state information needs to be maintained by the Willow system.

The Willow reactive system has been evaluated as a means of defending against fast-moving worms. Using a single control loop implementation, worm propagation has been studied by simulation and the effect of a Willow-based defense system assessed. The details of that study can be found in the work of Scandariato and Knight [36].

Dealing with Conflicting Goals

The Willow reactive system consists of multiple asynchronous control loops, and each could initiate reconfiguration at any time. Clearly, this means that either all but one has to be suspended or there has to be a determination that they do not interfere. In the financial system example, we hypothesized that there might be two control loops and it is clear that they could easily conflict. If one were reconfiguring the information system to deal with a common-mode software failure when a security attack was initiated, it would be essential to take whatever actions were deemed necessary to counter the effects of the security attack. Reconfigurations underway might have to be suspended or even reversed. In such a situation, unless some sort of comprehensive control is exercised, the system can quickly degenerate into an inconsistent state.

One approach would be to have each source make its own determination of what it should do. The complexity of this approach makes it infeasible. An implementation would have to cope with on-the-fly determination of state and, since initiation is asynchronous, that determination would require resource locking and synchronization across the network.

The approach taken in Willow is to route all requests for reconfiguration through a resource manager/priority enforcer. The prototype implementation uses predefined prioritization of reconfiguration requests and dynamic resource management to determine an appropriate execution order for reconfiguration requests. It does this using a distributed workflow model that represents formally the intentions of a reconfiguration request, the temporal ordering required in its operation, and its resource usage. Combined with a specified resource model, this information is the input to a distributed scheduling algorithm that produces and then executes a partial order for all reconfiguration tasks in the network.

Scheduling is preemptive, allowing incoming tasks to usurp resources from others if necessary so that more important activities can override less important ones. Transactional semantics allow preempted or failed activities to support rollback or failure, depending on the capabilities of the actuators that effect the reconfiguration.

5.3   Embedded System Reconfiguration

Turning now to embedded systems, the notion of reconfiguration to deal with faults has been used extensively in safety-critical and mission-critical systems. For example, the Boeing 777 uses a strategy similar to that advocated by Sha's Simplex architecture in which the primary flight computer contains two sets of control laws: the primary control laws of the 777 and the extensively tested control laws of the 747 as a backup [38]. The Airbus A330 and A340 employ a similar strategy [41] as have embedded systems in other transportation, medical, and similar domains. Existing approaches to reconfigurable architectures are, however, ad hoc; although the system goals are achieved, the result is inflexible and not reusable. Another important issue is the difficulty of achieving the necessary level of assurance in a system that has the capability of reconfiguring.

A prototype experimental survivability architecture for embedded systems designed to deal with these issues is illustrated in Fig. 5. In this architecture, these subsystems interface with the Subsystem Control Reconfiguration Analysis and Management (SCRAM) middleware. The SCRAM layer interfaces with the host operating system and various error-detection mechanisms deployed throughout the system.

The goal of this architecture is to permit the entire system to be survivable and consequently to provide the service required for safety (but not necessarily any other services) with a very high level of assurance. System survivability is achieved: (a) by ensuring that subsystems possess certain crucial properties; (b) by precise composition of the properties of the individual subsystems; (c) by controlled reconfiguration of subsystems if they experience local damage; and (d) by controlled reconfiguration at the system level if necessary.

Each subsystem is constructed individually to be a survivable entity and to provide a set of acceptable services in the sense of the survivability framework described

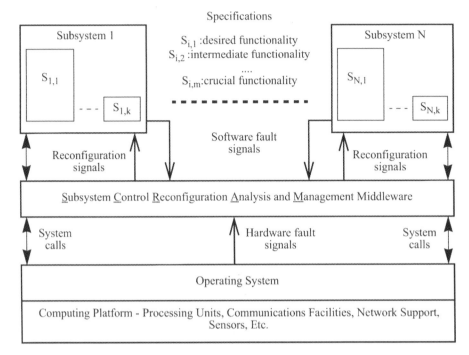

Fig. 5. Survivable Embedded System Architecture Overview

above. During operation, the SCRAM layer is responsible for reconfiguring the system so as to ensure the continued provision of essential aspects of the system's functionality. Reconfiguration is initiated by any sequence of events that either preclude the system from providing full functionality or indicate that providing full functionality would be unwise. An example of the former would be the defective operation or loss of any major system component, and an example of the latter would be an anticipated loss of power or communications in the near future. These events are detected by various means, including checking mechanisms within the different software subsystems themselves.

Protection Shells and Fail-Stop Software
The argument for the efficacy of survivability in embedded systems is based on the notion that in practice, many functions in safety-critical systems do not need to be ultradependable, they need to be fail-stop [37]. In other words, it is sufficient for the function to either work correctly or to stop and signal that it has failed. As an example, consider the hypothetical automatic landing system (ALS) from Section 4.2. Although part of the overall avionics system, the ALS could be defective during cruise without posing a serious threat to the aircraft. Provided the ALS either works correctly or stops and alerts the pilot, the aircraft is unlikely to come to harm.

The software analog of fail-stop machines is the concept of *safe programming* introduced by Anderson and Witty [2]. The concept of safe programming is (in part) to modify the postcondition for a program by adding an additional clause stating that stopping without modifying the state and signalling failure is an acceptable result of execution. A *safe* program in this sense is one that satisfies its (modified) postcondition. The problem of assurance has thus been reduced to one of assuring comprehensive checking of the program's actions rather than assuring proper overall functionality.

Related to safe programming, and providing a mechanism for implementing it, is the idea of a *safety kernel*. The idea has been studied in various contexts. Knight has introduced the term *protection shell* to more accurately describe what a small, simple policy enforcement mechanism for safety should be. The term "shell" implies that, rather than basing safety policies on what information can pass to and from the processor, the policies should be based on what outputs can be returned to the hardware controlled by the application.

Protection shells can be used to implement fail-stop function in survivable subsystems. Less critical components can have shells that guarantee the entire piece of function is fail-stop, while crucial components' shells can guarantee fail-operational capability or provide assurance that failures are acceptably improbable. Whichever capability is needed, the analysis associated with the shell will be much simpler than that associated with the full system because the shell for each component is much simpler than the component itself and is explicitly designed to facilitate that analysis.

The software subsystems that interact with the SCRAM layer can leverage the simpler analysis that protection shells afford to achieve the goal of obtaining a high level of assurance that the subsystem will, in fact, be survivable. Each major software component in a subsystem will be encapsulated in a shell that is geared to provide some set of guarantees for each possible operational level (individual specification). They can then be combined into a survivable subsystem structure using a standard architecture that provides subsystem reconfiguration and an interface allowing the SCRAM middleware to control subsystem internal reconfiguration.

Assurance Characteristics of a Reconfigurable System
The mechanism through which embedded system reconfiguration is achieved is complex, and going about its development in an ad hoc way could lead to lower overall system dependability than would have been exhibited by a system that could not reconfigure. Furthermore, dependability is a characteristic that typically must be met with very high assurance, and it cannot be assured without a rigorous characterization of this assurance.

We have described single-process reconfiguration informally as "*the process through which a system halts operation under its current source specification S_i and begins operation under a different target specification S_j.*" [43]. From the definition of survivability, we know that a survivable embedded system has:

- A set S: $\{S_1, S_2, ..., S_n\}$ of service specifications of the system
- A set E of possible environmental factors and their values
- The maximum time T_{ij} allowable for reconfiguration
- An invariant Inv_{ij} that must hold during reconfiguration

Using these concepts, reconfiguration can be defined as the process R for which [43]:

1. R begins at the same time the system is no longer operating under S_i
2. R ends at the same time the system becomes compliant with S_j
3. S_j is the proper choice for the target specification at some point during R
4. R takes less than or equal to T_{ij} time units
5. The transition invariant holds during R
6. The precondition for S_j is true at the time R ends
7. The lifetime of R is bounded by any two occurrences of the same specification

This is still an informal characterization of reconfiguration; a more thorough character-ization upon which a rigorous argument can be built is available elsewhere [43].

Using the Software Architecture to Facilitate Proof
For large, complex systems, showing that an implementation has the characteristics outlined above can be a daunting task. Building in the potential for arguments of reconfiguration assurance in a more detailed software architecture can facilitate the creation of assurance arguments, just as the survivability architecture is designed to facilitate arguments of overall system dependability.

Software architectures have an advantage over software design in that they are general enough to be reusable across a number of systems. We argue that if we can show overall assurance properties of an architecture, we no longer have to show those assurance properties for each individual system that employs the architecture. Thus, assurance of such a system is defined as assurance of compliance with the architecture rather than assurance of overall reconfiguration.

Protection shells are a useful basic component of such an architecture in that they can export an interface whose properties can be assured by comprehensive checking of outputs if necessary. In addition to providing such functional properties, shells can be used to ensure invariants are held by restricting access to the interface. They can include definitions of preconditions and postconditions of module data, and call mod-ule functions that ensure preconditions and postconditions are met at appropriate times. Finally, each interface function of a shell can carry strict timing guarantees of its operation.

In our architecture, each function in a module interface presents a set of functional service levels. Reconfiguration to a similar but degraded service is accomplished by calling degraded versions of the same functions. The modules (and their shells) are linked through a *monitoring layer*, the architectural component that knows which member of S must operate, and passes this information along to the modules hierarchi-cally to effect reconfiguration of function. Any detected and unmasked fault during computation of a module function causes control to be returned to the monitoring layer. The layer then activates the *reconfiguration mechanism*, which will choose the target specification, cause the data elements of the individual modules to conform to the precondition of the target specification, and instruct the monitoring layer to restart operation under the new specification.

Our architecture is designed to facilitate reconfiguration of a single application. A more extensive characterization of its structure and applicability is available elsewhere [43]. We have outlined above how multiple applications can be combined using the SCRAM layer into an overall reconfigurable system. A similar assurance structure for the set of interacting systems is currently in development.

6   Related Work

Many concepts in the field of dependability are similar or related to the notion of survivability. In addition, many techniques for improving dependability are related to survivability architectures. We review this related work in this section.

6.1   Related Concepts

- *Dependability*

    Avizienis et al. argue that survivability and dependability are equivalent—"names for an essential property" [4] although that statement was based on an earlier, informal definition of survivability [13]. Given the extremely broad definition of dependability, it is possible to argue that survivability is subsumed by dependability. However, survivability meets a need not adequately addressed by the standard definition of dependability since the latter's breadth includes no structure and suggests a single-service view. Survivability emphasizes the need to specify systems that can provide different forms of service, each with its own complete set of dependability requirements, under different conditions. The problem with the single-service view is that it might not be cost effective to provide assurance of full service across the entire spectrum of potential damage; in a survivable system, a narrower subset of damage is selected to be addressed by the dependability requirements. Whether survivability is seen as a facet of dependability, or a composite of functional and dependability requirements, is a matter of definition. We use it as a composite of dependability requirements, i.e., a set of specifications each of which has its own dependability requirements in the traditional sense. This allows the standard technical notion of dependability to remain unchanged while adding another means of addressing informal dependability requirements on system function.

- *Graceful degradation*

    The general notion of graceful degradation is clearly related to survivability. One definition, from the telecommunications industry, is: "Degradation of a system in such a manner that it continues to operate, but provides a reduced level of service rather than failing completely" [46]. According to this definition, survivability is a specific form of graceful degradation where reduced levels of service are specified and analyzed rigorously. Other perspectives on graceful degradation (e.g., Shelton et al. [40] and Nace and Koopman [28]) choose not to assume a specific set of alternative services, but rather determine the best possible value provided on-the-fly based on stated utility values of available functional components. Graceful degradation and survivability address a similar problems, but in subtly different ways. Graceful degradation attempts to provide the maximum value possible given a certain set of working functional components, which means it provides fine-grained control of functionality each form of which is determined dynamically. Survivability, on the other hand, supplies only prescribed functionality sacrifices some of graceful degradation's postulated utility in order to provide tight control over the analysis and certification process of software. A gracefully degrading system is likely to degrade in steps as resources are lost, but those steps are not necessarily determined at design time. A survivable system degrades in explicit, tightly-controlled steps that provide predictability and the opportunity for stronger formal analysis at the expense of some potential utility.

- *Quality of service*
  The telecommunications industry also has a definition for quality of service: "Performance specification of a communications channel or system" [46]. Quality of service (QoS) focuses on providing the most value with available resources and, like survivability, does this by incorporating some number of discrete functional levels. However, the term is generally used to refer to specific aspects of a system, for instance video quality or response time. QoS could be used by a survivable system, but survivability typically has a much broader impact on system function, changing the function more dramatically or replacing it altogether.

- *Performability*
  The concept of performability is related in a limited way to survivability [26]. A performability measure quantifies how well a system maintains parameters such as throughput and response time in the presence of faults over a specified period of time [27]. Thus performability is concerned with analytic models of throughput, response time, latency, etc. that incorporate both normal operation and operation in the presence of faults but does not include the possibility of alternative services. Survivability is concerned primarily with system functionality, and precise statements of what that functionality should be in the presence of faults.

6.2   Related Embedded Architectures

Some architectural aspects of survivable embedded systems have been discussed by other researchers. In this section, we review two particular approaches: the simplex architecture and safety kernels.

- *Simplex architecture*
  The Simplex architecture of Sha et al. [39] uses a simple backup system to compensate for uncertainties of a more complex primary system. The architecture assumes analytic redundancy: that two major functional capabilities with some significant design difference between them are used. The examples given primarily involve control systems. A survivability architecture is similar, but: (1) takes a more general view of possible user requirements, allowing more than two distinct functions; (2) uses tighter component control, disallowing software replacement (as opposed to reconfiguration) online in order to facilitate stronger analysis; and (3) addresses the problems associated with non-independence of software failures without requiring knowledge of completely separate methods to accomplish a goal (which might be an unreasonable assumption in many digital systems).

- *Safety Kernels*

  The idea of a safety kernel derives from the related concept of a security kernel. Both are related to survivability since they have a goal of assuring that certain important properties (safety or security) hold even if functionality has to be abandoned. Leveson et al. use the term *safety kernel* to describe a system structure where mechanisms aimed to achieve safety are gathered together into a centralized location [22]. A set of fault detection and recovery policies specified for the system is then enforced by the kernel. Subsequently, Rushby defined the role of a safety kernel more precisely based on the maintenance of crucial properties when certain conditions hold [34]. In a discussion about the implementation issues of safety kernels, Wika and Knight introduced the idea of *weakened properties*, properties that are not checked in the kernel, but which the kernel ensures are checked by the application [53]. Weakened properties compromise between the need for assurance and the need for kernel simplicity. Burns and Wellings define a safety kernel as a *safe nucleus* and a collection of *safety services* [8]. The safe nucleus manages safety properties computing resources; the safety services check safety and timing invariants of individual applications. The safety services evade the problem of enforceability of only negative properties; including them means that all computation requests of an application can be monitored to check that safety assertions hold. Peters and Parnas [29] use the idea of a *monitor* that checks the physical behavior of a system by comparing it with a specification of valid behaviors. They explore the imprecision in a system's ability to detect its precise physical state and how this relates to the properties that must be checked by the monitor. These ideas apply to the safety kernel concept as well, as there may be some slack in safety policies or known imprecision in the physical system.

6.3   Fault-Tolerant Distributed Systems

A very wide range of faults can occur in distributed systems and fault tolerance in such systems has been an active area of research for many years. In this section, we mention briefly some of this research. For a more comprehensive overview, see Gartner [16] and Jalote [17].

Cristian surveyed the issues involved in providing fault-tolerant distributed systems [10]. He presented two requirements for a fault-tolerant system: (1) mask failures when possible; and (2) ensure clearly specified failure semantics when masking is not possible. The majority of his work, however, dealt with the masking of failures. Birman introduced the "process-group-based computing model" [7] and three different systems—ISIS, Horus [48] and Ensemble [49]—that built on the concept. In a recent system design, Astrolabe [50], Birman introduced a highly distributed hierarchical database system that also has capabilities supporting intentionally addressed messaging. By using a gossip-based communications protocol, Astrolabe organizes a hierarchical database of aggregated information about large-scale distributed computer systems. A virtual collection of high-level information contains highly aggregated information about the system as a whole, while lower level 'nodes' contain more localized information about distributed sub-systems.

In the WAFT project, Marzullo and Alvisi are concerned with the construction of fault-tolerant applications in wide-area networks [1]. The Eternal system, developed by Melliar-Smith and Moser, is middleware that operates in a CORBA environment, below a CORBA ORB but on top of their Totem group communication system. The primary goal is to provide transparent fault tolerance to users [25]. Babaoglu and Schiper are addressing problems with scaling of conventional group technology. Their approach for providing fault tolerance in large-scale distributed systems consists of distinguishing between different roles or levels for group membership and providing different service guarantees to each level [5]. Finally, the CONIC system developed by Kramer and Magee addresses dynamic configuration for distributed systems, incrementally integrating and upgrading components for system evolution. The successor to CONIC, Darwin, is a configuration language that separates program structure from algorithmic behavior [23, 24].

Kaiser introduced KX, Kinesthetics eXtreme, an architecture supporting the distribution and coordination of mobile agents to perform reconfiguration of legacy software systems [47]. The architecture allows mobile code (or SOAP message enabled code) to travel around a network and coordinate activities with one another through the Workflakes distributed workflow engine, which is in turn built atop the COUGAAR distributed blackboard system.

6.4 Intrusion-Tolerant Systems

The notion of Intrusion Tolerance emerged in the 1990's as an approach to security in which reliance would not be placed totally on preventing intrusion. Rather systems would be engineered to detect intrusions and limit their effect. Intrusion tolerance is closely related to fault tolerance for a specific type of deliberate fault, and provides a form of survivability.

Two major projects of note in the area are OASIS and MAFTIA. For detailed discussions of intrusion tolerance, see the text by Lala [21] and the report by Powell and Stroud [30]. For a discussion of the architectural issues, see the report by Verissimo et al [51]. We summarize some of the major research concepts here.

Some of the research in the field of intrusion tolerance has addressed important basic issues that can be viewed as building blocks for intrusion-tolerant systems. Examples include communications protocols that provide important quality guarantees [6, 31], approaches to the secure use of mobile code [3], file systems that resist or tolerate attacks [44], software wrappers that permit legacy code to have certain important quality attributes retrofitted [15], security protocols that help ensure certain security properties [11], mechanisms for dealing with buffer overflow attacks, and approaches to the creation of a secure certification authority [54].

As well as building blocks, experimental systems have been designed and built to demonstrate system-level concepts and techniques. Examples include HACQIT—a system that provides Internet services to known users through secure connections [32], ITDOS—an intrusion-tolerant middleware system based on CORBA [35], and SITAR—an intrusion tolerant system based on COTS servers [52].

7   Summary

The notion of survivability is emerging as an important concept in a number of areas of computer system design. In this paper, we have explored the motivation for survivability, how it might be used, what the concept means in a precise and testable sense, and how it is being implemented in two very different application areas.

Making a system survivable rather than highly reliable or highly available has many advantages including overall system simplification and reduced demands on assurance technology. Both of these advantages contribute to the potential for building systems and with assured operation that would otherwise be infeasible. Although service to the user will be limited during some periods of operation for a system that is survivable, the potential for overall cost-effective system development will often outweigh this limitation.

Acknowledgements

We thank Jonathan Rowanhill and Philip Varner for their significant contributions to the design and implementation of the Willow reactive system. This work was supported in part by NASA Langley Research Center under grants numbered NAG-1-2290 and NAG-1-02103. This work was supported in part by the Defense Advanced Research Projects Agency under grant N66001-00-8945 (SPAWAR) and the Air Force Research Laboratory under grant F30602-01-1-0503. The views and conclusions contained in this document are those of the authors and should not be interpreted as necessarily representing the official policies or endorsements, either expressed or implied, of DARPA, the Air Force, or the U.S. Government.

References

[1]   Alvisi, L. and K. Marzullo. "WAFT: Support for Fault-Tolerance in Wide-Area Object Oriented Systems." *Proc. 2nd Information Survivability Workshop*, IEEE Computer Society Press, Los Alamitos, CA, October 1998.

[2]   Anderson, T., and R. W. Witty. "Safe programming." *BIT* 18:1-8, 1978.

[3]   Appel, A. "Foundational Proof-Carrying Code." IEEE Symposium on Logic in Computer Science, Boston MA, 2001

[4]   Avizienis, A., J. Laprie, and B. Randell. "Fundamental Concepts of Computer System Dependability." *IARP/IEEE-RAS Workshop on Robot Dependability: Technological Challenge of Dependable Robots in Human Environments*, Seoul, Korea, May 2001.

[5]   Babaoglu, O. and A. Schiper. "On Group Communication in Large-Scale Distributed Systems." *ACM Operating Systems Review* 29(1):62-67, January 1995.

[6]   Backes, M. and C. Cachin. "Reliable Broadcast In A Computational Hybrid Model With Byzantine Faults, Crashes, And Recoveries" International Conference on Dependable Systems and Networks, San Francisco CA, June 2003

[7]   Birman, K. "The Process Group Approach to Reliable Distributed Computing." *Communications of the ACM*, 36(12):37-53 and 103, December 1993.

[8] Burns, A., and A. J. Wellings. "Safety Kernels: Specification and Implementation." *High Integrity Systems* 1(3):287-300, 1995.

[9] Carzaniga, A., D. Rosenblum, and A. Wolf. "Achieving Scalability and Expressiveness in an Internet-scale Event Notification Service." Symposium on Principles of Distributed Computing, 2000.

[10] Cristian, F. "Understanding Fault-Tolerant Distributed Systems." *Communications of the ACM* 34(2):56-78, February 1991.

[11] Deswarte, Y., N. Abghour, V. Nicomette, D. Powell. "An Intrusion-Tolerant Authorization Scheme for Internet Applications." Sup. to Proc. 2002 International Conference on Dependable Systems and Networks, Washington, D.C. June 2002.

[12] Deutsch, M. S., and R. R. Willis. *Software Quality Engineering: A Total Technical and Management Approach.* Englewood Cliffs, NJ: Prentice-Hall, 1988.

[13] Ellison, B., D. Fisher, R. Linger, H. Lipson, T. Longstaff, and N. Mead. "Survivable Network Systems: An Emerging Discipline." Technical Report CMU/SEI-97-TR-013, Software Engineering Institute, Carnegie Mellon University, November 1997.

[14] Federal Aviation Administration Advisory Circular 25.1309-1A, "System Design and Analysis."

[15] Fraser, T., L. Badger, and M. Feldman. "Hardening COTS Software with Generic Software Wrappers." in OASIS: Foundations of Intrusion Tolerant Systems (J. Lala Ed.), IEEE Computer Society Press, 2003.

[16] Gartner, Felix C. "Fundamentals of Fault-Tolerant Distributed Computing in Asynchronous Environments." *ACM Computing Surveys* 31(1):1-26, March 1999.

[17] Jalote, P. *Fault Tolerance in Distributed Systems.* Prentice Hall:Englewood Cliffs, NJ, 1994.

[18] Knight, J., M. Elder, J. Flinn, and P. Marx. "Summaries of Four Critical Infrastructure Systems." Technical Report CS-97-27, Department of Computer Science, University of Virginia, November 1997.

[19] Knight, J. C., D. Heimbigner, A. Wolf, A. Carzaniga, J. Hill, P. Devanbu, and M. Gertz. "The Willow Architecture: Comprehensive Survivability for Large-Scale Distributed Applications." Intrusion Tolerance Workshop, The International Conference on Dependable Systems and Networks, Washington, DC, June 2002.

[20] Knight, J. C., E. A. Strunk and K. J. Sullivan. "Towards a Rigorous Definition of Information System Survivability." DISCEX 2003, Washington, DC, April 2003.

[21] Lala, J. "Foundations of Intrusion Tolerant Systems." IEEE Computer Society Press, Catalog # PR02057, 2003.

[22] Leveson, N., T. Shimeall, J. Stolzy and J. Thomas. "Design for Safe Software." AIAA Space Sciences Meeting, Reno, Nevada, 1983.

[23] Magee, J., N. Dulay and J. Kramer. "Structuring Parallel and Distributed Programs." *Software Engineering Journal*, 8(2):73-82, March 1993.

[24] Magee, J., and J. Kramer. "Darwin: An Architectural Description Language." http://www-dse.doc.ic.ac.uk/research/darwin/darwin.html, 1998.

[25] Melliar-Smith, P., and L. Moser. "Surviving Network Partitioning." *IEEE Computer* 31(3):62-68, March 1998.

[26] Myers, J.F. "On Evaluating The Performability Of Degradable Computing Systems." *IEEE Transactions on Computers* 29(8):720-731, August 1980.

[27] Myers, J.F., and W.H. Sanders. "Specification And Construction Of Performability Models." *Proc. Second International Workshop on Performability Modeling of Computer and Communication Systems*, Mont Saint-Michel, France, June 1993.

[28] Nace, W., and P. Koopman. "A Product Family Based Approach to Graceful Degradation." DIPES 2000, Paderborn, Germany, October 2000.

[29] Peters, D. K., and D. L. Parnas. "Requirements-based Monitors for Real-time Systems." *IEEE Trans. on Software Engineering* 28(2):146-158, Feb. 2002.

[30] Powell, D. and R. Stroud (Eds). "Conceptual Model and Architecture of MAFTIA." http://www.newcastle.research.ec.org/maftia/deliverables/D21.pdf

[31] Ramasamy, H., P. Pandey, J. Lyons, M. Cukier, and W. Sanders. "Quantifying the Cost of Providing Intrusion Tolerance in Group Communications." in OASIS: Foundations of Intrusion Tolerant Systems (J. Lala Ed.), IEEE Computer Society Press, 2003.

[32] Reynolds, J., J. Just, E. Lawson, L. Clough, R. Maglich, and K. Levitt. "The Design and Implementation of an Intrusion Tolerant System." in OASIS: Foundations of Intrusion Tolerant Systems (J. Lala Ed.), IEEE Computer Society Press, 2003.

[33] Rowanhill, Jonathan C., Philip E. Varner and John C. Knight. "Efficient Hierarchic Management For Reconfiguration of Networked Information Systems." The International Conference on Dependable Systems and Networks (DSN-2004), Florence, Italy, June 2004.

[34] Rushby, J. "Kernels for Safety?" *Safe and Secure Computing Systems*, T. Anderson Ed., Blackwell Scientific Publications, 1989.

[35] Sames, D., B. Matt, B. Niebuhr, G. Tally, B. Whitmore, and D. Bakken. "Developing a Heterogeneous Intrusion Tolerant CORBA Systems." in OASIS: Foundations of Intrusion Tolerant Systems (J. Lala Ed.), IEEE Computer Society Press, 2003.

[36] Scandariato, Riccardo and John C. Knight. "An Automated Defense System to Counter Internet Worms." Technical Report CS-2004-12, Department of Computer Science, University of Virginia, March 2004.

[37] Schlichting, R. D., and F. B. Schneider. "Fail-stop processors: An approach to designing fault-tolerant computing systems." *ACM Transactions on Computing Systems* 1(3):222-238.

[38] Sha, L. "Using Simplicity to Control Complexity." *IEEE Software* 18(4):20-28, 2001.

[39] Sha, L., R. Rajkumar and M. Gagliardi. "A Software Architecture for Dependable and Evolvable Industrial Computing Systems." Technical Report CMU/SEI-95-TR-005, Software Engineering Institute, Carnegie Mellon University, 1995.

[40] Shelton, C., P. Koopman, and W. Nace. "A framework for scalable analysis and design of system-wide graceful degradation in distributed embedded systems." Eighth IEEE International Workshop on Object-oriented Real-time Dependable Systems, Guadelajara, Mexico, January 2003.

[41] Storey, N. *Safety-Critical Computer Systems*. Prentice Hall: Harlow, U.K., 1996.

[42] Strunk, E. *The Role of Natural Language in a Software Product*. M.S. Thesis, University of Virginia Dept. of Computer Science, May 2002.

[43] Strunk, E. A., and J. C. Knight. "Assured Reconfiguration of Embedded Real-Time Software." The International Conference on Dependable Systems and Networks (DSN-2004), Florence, Italy, June 2004.

[44] Strunk, J., G. Goodson, M. Scheinholz, C. Soules and G Ganger. "Self Securing Storage: Protecting Data in Compromised Systems." in OASIS: Foundations of Intrusion Tolerant Systems (J. Lala Ed.), IEEE Computer Society Press, 2003.

[45] Sullivan, K., J. Knight, X. Du, and S. Geist. "Information Survivability Control Systems." *Proc. 21st International Conference on Software Engineering*, IEEE Computer Society Press, Los Alamitos, CA, May 1999.

[46] U.S. Department of Commerce, National Telecommunications and Information Administration, Institute for Telecommunications Services, Federal Std. 1037C.

[47] Valetto, G. and G. Kaiser. "Using Process Technology to Control and Coordinate Software Adaptation." 25th International Conference on Software Engineering. Portland, Or. May, 2003.

[48] van Renesse, R., K. Birman, and S. Maffeis. "Horus: A Flexible Group Communications System." *Comm. of the ACM* 39(4):76-83, April 1996.

[49] van Renesse, R., K. Birman, M. Hayden, A. Vaysburd, and D. Karr. "Building Adaptive Systems Using Ensemble." Technical Report TR97-1638, Department of Computer Science, Cornell University, July 1997.

[50] Van Renesse, R., K. Birman and W. Vogels. "Astrolabe: A Robust and Scalable Technology for Distributed System Monitoring, Management, and Data Mining." *ACM Transactions on Computer Systems*, Vol. 21, No. 2, pp. 164–206, May 2003.

[51] Veríssimo, P., Neves, N.F., and Correia,M. "Intrusion-Tolerant Architectures: Concepts and Design (extended)." Technical Report DI/FCUL TR03-5, Department of Computer Science, University of Lisboa, 2003

[52] Wang, F., F. Jou, F. Gong, C. Sargor, K. Goseva-Popstojanova, and K. Trivedi. "SITAR: A Scalable Intrusion-Tolerant Architecture for Distributed Services." in OASIS: Foundations of Intrusion Tolerant Systems (J. Lala Ed.), IEEE Computer Society Press, 2003.

[53] Wika, K.J., and J.C. Knight. "On The Enforcement of Software Safety Policies." *Proceedings of the Tenth Annual Conference on Computer Assurance* (COMPASS), Gaithersburg, MD, 1995.

[54] Zhou, L., F. Schneider and R. Renesse. "COCA: A Secure Distributed Online Certification Authority." in OASIS: Foundations of Intrusion Tolerant Systems (J. Lala Ed.), IEEE Computer Society Press, 2003.

Reliability Support for the Model Driven Architecture

Genaína Nunes Rodrigues*, Graham Roberts, and Wolfgang Emmerich

Dept. of Computer Science
University College London
Gower Street, London WC1E 6BT, UK
{G.Rodrigues,G.Roberts,W.Emmerich}@cs.ucl.ac.uk

Abstract. Reliability is an important concern for software dependability. Quantifying dependability in terms of reliability can be carried out by measuring the continuous delivery of a correct service or, equivalently, the mean time to failure. The novel contribution of this paper is to provide a means to support reliability design following the principles of the Model Driven Architecture(MDA). By doing this, we hope to contribute to the task of consistently addressing dependability concerns from the early to late stages of software engineering. Additionally, we believe MDA can be a suitable framework to realize the assessment of those concerns and therefore, semantically integrate analysis and design models into one environment.

1 Introduction

Component-based development architectures (CBDA) are increasingly being adopted by software engineers. These architectures support distributed execution across machines running on different platforms (e.g. Unix, Windows). Examples of component models include Sun's Enterprise Java Beans (EJB), OMG's CORBA Component Model (CCM) and Microsoft's .NET. Additionally, CBDAs rely on the construction and deployment of software systems that have been assembled from components [6].

One of the advantages of applying a component-based approach is reusability. It is easier to integrate classes into coarse-grained units that provide one or more clearly defined interfaces. However, the lack of interoperability among diverse CBDAs may be one of the major problems that hinders the adoption of distributed component technologies. Once a platform has been chosen and the system has been developed, porting to a different platform becomes troublesome.

To fill this gap, the OMG(Object Management Group) has focused on paving the way to provide CBDAs interoperability standards through the Model Driven Architecture (MDA). To accomplish this approach, MDA structures the system into key models: the Platform Independent Models (PIMs) and the Platform Specific Models (PSMs). A PIM specifies the structure and functions of the system abstracting away technical details. A PSM expresses that specification in terms of the model of the target platform.

The Unified Modeling Language(UML) is the core language to represent those models. Through UML complex formalization can be carried out in a abstract way by

---

* Funded by CAPES, Brazil.

R. de Lemos et al. (Eds.): Architecting Dependable Systems II, LNCS 3069, pp. 79–98, 2004.

modeling states of an object as well as its functions and parameters. Furthermore, UML models facilitate the assessment of a design in the early stages of software development, when it is easier and cheaper to make changes.

The defined and standard structure of MDA would seem suitable to address software dependability, in that the MDA designates the system function as required by the stakeholders. Issues such as reliability, safety, security and availability comprise software dependability [13, 21]. However, there is no standard representation for dependability in MDA models. During the software execution this can lead to situations not foreseen in the platform models.

Reliability assurance is an important concern in software dependability. Quantifying dependability in terms of reliability can be carried out by measuring the continuous delivery of correct services or equivalently, of the mean time to failure [12]. A system can be considered reliable if it performs at a constant level, as the stresses on that system change. For example, if a request takes 10 ms to complete with one user, then it takes the same time to process the same request with 1000 concurrent users.

The novel contribution we propose is to provide a means to support reliability design following the principles of MDA. By doing this, we hope to contribute to the task of consistently carrying out dependability concerns from the early to the late stages of software engineering. Besides, MDA appears to be a suitable framework to realize the assessment of those concerns and therefore, semantically integrate analysis and design models into one environment. Although UML profiles that thoroughly address dependability cannot be found currently, MDA seems to be a feasible environment to consistently assess and express dependability by means of properly constructed profiles.

In this paper, we elaborate our approach on how the provision of reliability can be suitably realized through a standard model-driven architecture approach. In section 2, we show how we plan to provide reliability modeling in MDA and the steps to be followed to accomplish this goal. The reference model, in section 3, is the first step towards a platform-independent reliability model and the EJB Profile, in section 4, represents the appropriate platform specific mapping of that reference model. In section 5, we highlight the design profile elements extending the UML metamodeling language and show how it reflects on the deployment of the components when transformation rules are applied to the model. In section 6, we provide a sample scenario of how our approach of reliability support in MDA applies to a given modeled system. In section 7, we present the related work targeting reliability support and analysis in the CBDA scenario. Finally, section 8 summarizes our contribution and discusses future work towards achieving standard reliability support from designing models to programatic interfaces.

2   MDA and Reliability

Nowadays, the demand for distributed systems is increasing as they promote the integration of legacy components and the design of non-functional properties. However, the construction of distributed systems would be far more complex than building a client-server system if it were not for the use of middleware. In order to simplify the construction of distributed systems, middleware has had an important influence on the software engineering research agenda.

The choice of which middleware a software system is based on is mostly influenced by non-functional requirements. However, the support for non-functional requirements usually differ from one platform to another. For example, components developed for Enterprise Java Beans are quite different from components for CORBA or .NET. Once a software system is built based on a particular middleware, the cost of future change to a different underlying platform can be extremely high [5]. Therefore, the construction of distributed systems using middleware requires principles, notations, methods and tools compatible with capabilities provided by current middleware products. And more importantly, as the underlying infrastructure shifts over time and middleware continues to evolve, the designed business logic of a system should be kept stable.

To address these problems, the OMG has developed a set of specifications that are referred to as the Model Driven Architecture [6]. Essentially, "the MDA defines an approach to IT system specification that separates the specification of system functionality from the specification of the implementation of that functionality on a specific technology platform" [17]. The Platform Independent Models (PIMs) and the Platform Specific Models (PSMs) are the basic structure where the MDA approach relies on. While a PIM provides a formal specification of the structure and function of the system that abstracts away technical details, a PSM expresses that specification in terms of the model of the target platform. PIMs are mapped to PSMs when the desired level of refinement of PIMs is achieved. The ability to transform a higher level PIM into a PSM raises the level of abstraction at which a developer can work. This ability allows a developer to cope with more complex systems with less effort.

Fig. 1. Major Steps in the MDA Development Process [11]

Although the MDA software development life-cycle may seem to resemble the same of the traditional one, there is a crucial difference. Traditionally, tools generate some code from a model, but such generation is not complete enough to prevent handmade work. MDA transformation, on the other hand, are always executed by tools as shown in Figure 1. In fact, the transformation step from the PSM to the code generation is not new. The innovation and benefits of MDA relies on the automatic transformation from PIM to PSM. This is where time and effort can be saved when, for example, software analysts and software engineers have to decide on which underlying platform the designed system will be applied to and how the database model will look like based on the design model.

However, there is no standard approach to carry out transformations in MDA. The OMG Query, View, Transformations (QVT) Request for Proposals [16] is on the way of specifying transformations of MDA models. Unfortunately, the final QVT specification, though essential, may not come soon. In this regard, [8] has proposed ways to carry this out. That work defines a mapping from model-to-model transformation, from PIM to

PSM, instead of a model-to-text transformation. In our work, we define our own mechanisms and rules of making transformation between models. We agree with [8] that the success of the MDA vision towards QVT requires the development of an effective means of defining model transformations.

The Unified Modeling Language (UML) is the core element to represent those models. According to the OMG, UML supports the formalization of abstract, though precise, models of the state of an object, with functions and parameters provided through a predefined interface [17]. In fact, UML provides a wide set of modeling concepts and notations to meet current software modeling techniques. The various aspects of software systems can be represented through UML, what makes it suitable for architecture modeling. As a consequence, UML has been widely used as a basis for software analysis and development.

To model complex domains in UML, new semantics can be added through extension mechanisms packages that specify how specific model elements are customized and extended with those semantics. In particular, UML profiles make extensive use of UML stereotypes and tagged values. For example, the stereotype <<EJBSessionHome>> indicates that a UML class represents an EJB Session Home [9]. Additionally, profiles list a number of constraints that stem from the consistency constraints defined in the UML semantics guide. The language to express these constraints is called the Object Constraint Language (OCL)[1] and is used to specify well-formedness(correct syntax) rules of the metaclasses comprising the UML metamodel. OCL can also be used to specify application-specific constraints in the UML models.

2.1 Bringing Reliability to MDA

As there is a lack of dependability specification in the current MDA, we propose to tackle this problem in the levels of abstraction suggested by OMG's MDA, depicted in Figure 1. It is feasible to accomplish this task using the standard meta-modeling approach of MDA and specifications. Such a task has been demonstrated in the context of performance specification [19].

Our current focus is on reliability for software systems, one of the properties of dependability. To guarantee and assess reliability properties of software systems using the MDA approach, we plan to achieve reliability in such a way that it is specified in the early stages of software architecture design. In this way, we aim to provide reliability in a platform-independent way. In the context of MDA and current distributed component-based architectures, early reliability assessment is important as the software architecture design is specified in the context of software development.

The main contribution of this research is, therefore, to provide a means to support reliability design following the principles of a model driven approach. By doing this, we hope to contribute to the task of systematically addressing dependability concerns from the early to the late stages of software engineering. Besides, MDA appears to be a suitable framework to realize the assessment of those concerns and thus to semantically integrate analysis and design models into one environment.

---

[1] For more references of this language, see chapter 6 in [9].

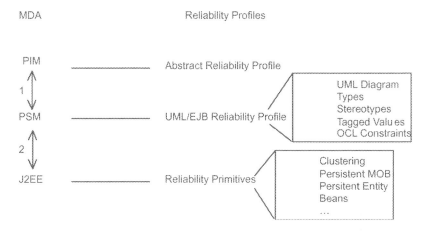

Fig. 2. Reliability Profiles in MDA

To provide a reliability profile for MDA, we follow the MDA approach: from PIM to PSM and from PSM to code (see Figure 2). Current component-based development architectures (CBDA), such as Enterprise Java Beans, address a considerable range of features to support system reliability. These CBDAs guarantee some mechanisms that provide reliable services [4]:

- Replication by means of clustering;
- Transaction management (which comprises both concurrency and replication transparency) ;
- Message driven communication supporting various kinds of reliability request (unicast or group);
- Persistency through stateful and persistent component objects;

In the J2EE platform, for instance, these mechanisms are provided in the respective order:

- Instance pooling and the fail-over mechanism;
- The two-phase commit protocol and the Java Transaction API (JTA);
- Asynchronous communication with persistent Java Message Service(JMS) and Message Driven Beans;
- Stateful Session Beans and Entity Beans.

Our first target platform to apply our reliability profile is the J2EE. In this regard, we plan to extend the UML Profile for EJB [9], henceforth EJB Profile, to express the above listed J2EE reliability mechanisms in a standardized way. That is, we aim to specify a subset of UML meta-model that describes the semantics of mechanisms in J2EE to achieve reliability. This subset contains stereotypes, tagged values and OCL constraints.

In order to realize this task, UML meta-models must be designed to reflect each of those reliability mechanisms, relying on the UML Specification 1.4 [20]. A meta-model is a model of a language expressed using modeling techniques. This feature

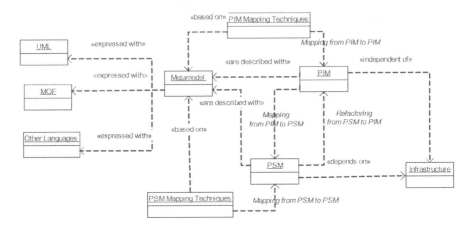

Fig. 3. MDA Metamodel Description [17]

in UML allows us to express the design and analysis domains seamlessly using the concepts inherent to these domains. Moreover, this facility permits to map the behavior of distributed component architectures into a domain knowledge keeping the semantics of the modeling requirements of UML.

Following this principle, our approach to meta-modeling using the UML lightweight extension mechanisms, i.e. profiles, is consistent with the official MDA white paper [17], which defines basic mechanisms to consistently structure the models and formally express the semantics of the model in a standardized way. Moreover, the profiles define standard UML extensions to describe platform-based artifacts in a design and implemented model. For example, the EJB Profile supports the capture of semantics expressible with EJB through the EJB Design Model and the EJB Implementation Model.

Addressing reliability mechanisms following MDA's approach will be possible to express semantics and notations that adequately address those mechanisms in a standard way. In MDA, a mapping is a set of rules and techniques used to modify one model in order to get another model. So as to design and formalize those reliability mechanisms, we will first map them into a profile, according to the mapping mechanism in Figure 3.

3   A Profile for Replication

This section shows how we plan to achieve the previously stated goals through UML profiles. We build a profile for replication and map the core elements of the profile to the EJB architecture. At the end of this process of mappings and refinements, the elements required to design, implement and deploy reliability according to the OMG model driven architecture are identified.

In this section, we exploit the first reliability mechanism described in section 2, the replication transparency through clustering. The initial step towards achieving reliability in MDA principles is to define the architecture of the application that expresses how reliable the method invocations should be, as well as the deployment relationships between the application components. Therefore, a reliability profile is needed. Figure 4 shows what the overall scenario looks like. Basically, there are three main profiles: the design (where the reliability mechanism is modeled), the deployment (to determine how the components are distributed in the network according to the required reliability support) and the mapping (to map the desired reliability to the designed classes). In particular, the mapping profile is represented by the hexagon described by *PIMxPSM* and the pentagon *DSxDP*. They represent respectively the transformation from one design profile (Reliability PIM) to another (Reliability PSM) and the transformation required to map the design profile elements to the deployment profile

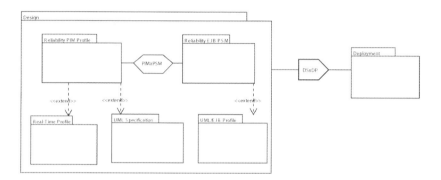

Fig. 4. Profiles to model reliability in EJB applications

In the design profile, meta-modeling techniques are used to map the reliability mechanisms we define. In the PSM level, we chose to apply the design profile to the J2EE platform at first. Therefore, we extend the EJB Profile to define the architecture of the application, in EJB terms, concerning resource demands and deployment relationships required to accommodate the reliability profile. All together, this profile extends four main specifications:

1. UML Profile for Schedulability, Performance and Real-Time Specification (briefly, Real-Time Profile) [19] - to specify how applications requiring a quantitative measure of time can be modeled in a MDA-standard way.
2. UML Specification [20] - to complement the reliability profile with feature lacking in the specifications above following standard UML notations, definitions and semantics.
3. UML Profile for Modeling Quality of Service and Fault Tolerance Characteristics and Mechanisms [18] - an ongoing specification that addresses definition of individual QoS characteristics and a generic fault-tolerant framework.
4. EJB Profile - to express the reliability profile in the semantics of EJB using UML notation.

The first step towards identifying the stereotypes, tagged values and constraints of a profile is to design a reference model. The Reliability Reference Model in Figure 5 is an adaptation of the Generic Fault-Tolerant Framework in [18] and consists of the following elements:

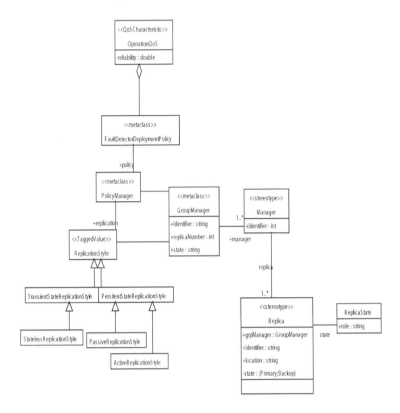

Fig. 5. Core Reliability Reference Model for Replication

- `FaultDetectorPolicy`: This policy describes the mechanisms safety engineering uses to describe how to monitor software faults. It can be of three different types:
  - `StaticallyDeployedFaultDetectors`: In an operating environment with a relatively static configuration, location-specific Fault Detectors will typically be created when the FT infrastructure is installed.
  - `InfrastructureCreatedFaultDetectors`: The FT infrastructure may create instances of the Fault Detectors to meet the needs of the applications. Therefore, the infrastructure is configured to match those needs.
  - `ApplicationCreatedFaultDetectors`: For some particular reason (e.g lack of support from the infrastructure), it may be necessary for applications to create their own Fault Detectors.
- `PolicyManager`: Establishes the type of replication and the type of fault detector to be used. The policies include approaches to detect the errors and styles of replication management. Examples of policies are of type `ReplicationStyle` (i.e. Transient or Persistent State), initial number of replicas and minimum number of replicas. The `PolicyManager` defines default policies that apply to all object groups associated to this model element.

– GroupManager: Manages the object group of a fault-tolerant object by managing the several Manager instances. A reference to the entire group makes transparent to the clients the concept of replication. Finally, the state is used for the synchronization between primary and backups.

– Manager: Used by the GroupManager to detect faults and to create a new instance of a replica as a Factory object, where each replica has its own identity. Each group's GroupManager has one or many Manager instances: one instance for each host where a replica is deployed. The set of Manager instances is controlled by a GroupManager. In the case of a fault detected by the Manager, the GroupManager automatically reconfigures the system by reassigning task among non-failed components. Then the GroupManager will try to reconstruct that failed component by using the factoring mechanism to recover the components to a saved state prior to error detection.

– Replica: A redundant entity. Its number or location are the basic parameters to support the fail management.

– ReplicaState: Defines the dynamic state information of a Replica, which depends on the role of the replica in the group. This role determines whether the replica is primary, backup or transient and it will vary according to the policy used.

– TransientStateReplicationStyle: This replication style defines styles for objects having no persistent state. For StatelessReplicationStyle, the one kind of TransientStateReplicationStyle, the history of invocation does not affect the dynamic behavior of the object group.

– PersistentStateReplicationStyle: This replication style defines styles for objects that have a persistent state. Two distinctive persistent replication styles can be identified:

   1. PassiveReplicationStyle: Requires that only one member of the object group, the primary member, executes the methods invoked on the group. Periodically, the state of the primary member is recorded in a log, together with a sequence of method invocations. In the presence of a fault, a backup member becomes a primary member. The new primary member reloads its state from the log, followed by reapplying request messages recorded in the log. When it is cheaper transferring a state other than executing a method invocation in the presence of a failure and the time for recovery after a fault is not constrained, passive replication is worth considering. The style of the PassiveReplicationStyle can be Warm or Cold. In the Warm style, the state of the primary member is transferred to the backups periodically. While in the Cold style, the state of the primary member is loaded into the backup only when needed for recovery.

   2. ActiveRepicationStyle: A second type of persistent replication which requires that all the members of an object group execute each invocation independently but synchronously. The handleMessages operation detects and suppresses duplicate requests and replies, and delivers a single request or reply to the destination object. When it is cheaper to execute a method invocation rather than transferring a state or when the time available for recovery after a fault is tightly constrained, active replication is worth considering. If the voting attribute is active, the requests from the members of the client object group are

Table 1. Reliability Profile Stereotypes for Replication

Profile Elements	Base Class	Tags	Element Type
GroupManager	ClassifierRole, Object, Node	ReplicationStyle, TransientState, PersistentState	Metaclass
PolicyManager	ClassifierRole, Object, Node	RPFaultDetectorPolicy	Metaclass
Replica	ClassifierRole, Object, Node	ReplicaState, TransientState, Per-sistentState	Stereotype
Manager	ClassifierRole, Object, Role	ReplicationStyle, TransientState, PersistentState	Stereotype

Table 2. Tag Values of the Reliability Profile

Tag Name	Applies To	Tag Type
FaultDetectorPolicy	Subsystem	Enumeration{ 'StaticallyDeployed', 'InfrastructureCre-ated', 'ApplicationCreated'}
ReplicationStyle	Subsystem	Enumeration{ 'TransientState', 'PersistentState'}
ReplicaState	Class	Enumeration{ 'Primary', 'Backup', 'Transient'}
TransientState	Class	StatelessReplication Value
PersistentState	Class	Enumeration{ 'PassiveReplication', 'ActiveReplication'}
ReliabilityValue	Class	Real

voted, and are delivered to the members of the server object group only if the majority of the requests are identical. The situation is analogous to replies from the members of the server object group.

Based on this reference model, we are able to identify the stereotypes and the tagged values in the design profile, as described in Tables 1 and 2.

4   Mapping from the Reliability Profile to the EJB PSM

The reliability sub-profile for replication we show in this section is intended to show how the profile we designed can be applied to the J2EE platform. In Figure 6 we depict the elements that constitute the profile we built from extending the EJB Profile.

On the left-hand side of the picture, we depict the five core stereotypes that constitute our design domain profile for EJB. They are presented in Table 3. The core elements that constitute this EJB PSM are the following:

1. ReplicaHome - The client never makes request directly to the EJB beans, but through the EJB objects. Clients get a reference of EJB objects through an EJB object factory, which is responsible for instantiating, finding existing and destroying EJB objects. The ReplicaHome carries out the functionality of this factory.

2. ReplicaSession and ReplicaEntity - The classes stereotyped as such implement the Replica class from the Reference Model (figure 5) and the functionalities of the EJB Session and EJB Entity Beans, respectively. As a type of Replica, the classes having these stereotypes will be monitored by the object group that implements the Manager functionalities.

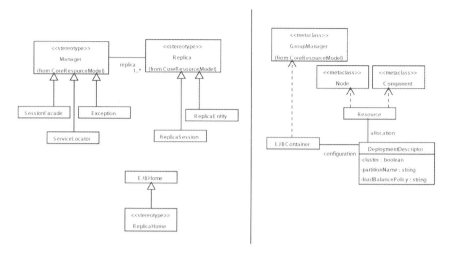

Fig. 6. Reliability Model Mapping to EJB

3. SessionFacade and ServiceLocator - These stereotypes will indicate the classes that implement the Session Facade and Service Locator J2EE Patterns [1] and primarily the functionalities of the Manager required to monitor the behavior of the replica objects.

4. ReplicaException - Each replica is associated to a ReplicaException stereotyped object, so that each business method of a replica reports this exception. Each ReplicaException will be caught by the class implementing the SessionFacade.

On the right-hand side of Figure 6, we show how we relate the GroupManager from the Reference Model to the EJB architecture. Essentially, the deployment descriptor file declares the service requirements for the EJB components, such as transaction control and partition management. This information is used by the EJB Container where the EJB components will be deployed. Therefore the EJB Container is the element in the EJB architecture that fits the functionalities of our GroupManager. In particular, every resource to be deployed in the EJB Container needs an association with the deployment descriptor file.

4.1   The Transformation Rules

After identifying the elements that constitute the replication transparency profile for EJB, we define transformation rules to generate a coarse-grained EJB model. Based on the target model we aim to reach (see Figure 6), we define rules to map from the source model (PIM) to the EJB model (PSM) based on our profile:

1. For each PIM class, an EJB key class is generated.
2. Each PIM class is transformed into an EJB component.
3. Each PIM association is transformed into an EJB association.

Table 3. Reliability Stereotypes for the J2EE

Stereotypes	Base Class	Parents	Tags
ReplicaHome	Class	EJBHome	No tag associated
ReplicaSession	Object	Replica, Session-Bean	ReplicationStyle, ReplicaState, ReliabilityValue
ReplicaEntity	Object	Replica, Entity-Bean	ReplicationStyle, ReplicaState, ReliabilityValue
SessionFacade	ClassifierRole, Object	Manager	ReplicaState, Reliability Value
ServiceLocator	ClassifierRole, Object	Manager	No tag associated
ReplicaException	Object	Manager, Exception	No tag associated

4. Each PIM attribute of a class is transformed into an EJB attribute of the mapped EJB class.
5. Each PIM operation is transformed into an EJB operation of the generated EJB component from the PIM class.
6. Each <<Replica>> (Entity and/or Session Bean) component is associated to a Session Facade EJB pattern [1] (i.e. a Session Facade remote interface and a Session Facade Bean).
7. Each <<Replica>> has to be associated to a <<ReplicaException>>.

In the lack of a standard specification for model transformation, we formalize the above rules in OCL in order to (1) keep the consistency between PIMs and PSMs and (2) avoid ambiguities between the models. For example, rule 7 above is expressed in OCL as follows:

```
package Foundation::Core

context Class  inv:

  self.stereotype -> exists(c:ModelElement|
                          c.oclIsTypeOf(Replica)
  implies

  self.allOppositeAssociationEnds.participants ->
    exists(m:ModelElement|
        m.stereotype -> exists("ReplicaException"))
```

5   Mapping from Design to Deployment

In the mapping profile, where the elements in the design profile are mapped to the deployment profile, constraints rule how the desired reliability mechanisms should be mapped to provide the kind of refinement that the cannot be fulfilled by UML diagrams. Those constraints are specified in accordance with the `PolicyManager` from our Reference Model. Finally, the deployment profile provides the configuration of how the components communicate and are distributed throughout the network.

In order to map replication in the deployment diagram, we should know what is the desired reliability assurance of the system, according to the `PolicyManager` policy. By this means, it is possible to know how many replicated components there should be in each cluster to guarantee the desired reliability level. We use the approach where components are grouped in parallel to improve reliability through replication [15]. In this mapping, we do not include the probability of failure of the Replica Manager. Taking this assumption into consideration, the reliability of the parallel system, R_p, is the probability that it is in operation when needed. This probability is equal to one minus the probability that the system is not in operation (P_r). For this to happen, all n components must be down, which is

$$P_r = \prod_{i=1}^{n}(1 - r_i) \tag{1}$$

where r_i is the reliability of each component. So, assuming independence of failures between components, we get:

$$R_p = 1 - P_r[\text{all components are down}]$$
$$R(p) = 1 - [(1 - r_1) \times (1 - r_2) \times \ldots (1 - r_n))] \tag{2}$$

When all the components have the same reliability, the functional formula for this assurance is:

$$1 - (1 - r)^n > a \tag{3}$$

where r is the reliability of each component, a is the required reliability of the system and n is the number of components that should be comprised in each cluster. To reflect this scenario, the classes of the design profile to be replicated should be mapped to the deployment profile through the mapping profile. A fragment of the mapping profile to assure the reliability property above is described in OCL as follows:

```
package Foundation::Core

context Abstraction def:
```

– *Calculating n*

```
  let exp(x : Real, y : Real) : Real =
     if(y = 1) then x
  else x * self.exp(x, y - 1)
     endif

context Abstraction  inv:
```

– Identifying the Mapping Profile

```
self.stereotype->forAll(name = "mapping") implies
```

– Reading from every EJB component stereotyped as "Replica" the tagged value "ownedReliability", which is the actual reliability property of the EJB component, and the tagged value "reliabilityValue", which is the reliability to be achieved

```
self.supplier.oclAsType(Classifier).ownedElement->forAll(
    m : ModelElement | m.oclIsTypeOf(Class) implies
      (1 - self.exp((1 - m.taggedValue->any(type =
          "ownedReliability").dataValue),
        self.client.oclAsType(Classifier).ownedElement->select(
            n : ModelElement | n.oclIsTypeOf(Component) and
    m.stereotype->exists(name = "Replica") and
            n.name = m.name)->size())) >
        m.taggedValue->any(type =
          "reliabilityValue").dataValue)
```

where `self.supplier` refers to the classes in the designed profile and `self.client` refers to the components in the deployment profile.

There is, however, one important step that is not described here but must be accomplished, which is the support in MDA for formal analysis. In this regard, a formal analysis profile is required to separately express dependability in an analysis model. This might follow the approach in [23], which aims at providing a MDA performance analysis to enterprise applications and has shown that worthwhile benefits arise, such as:

– Flexible application of analysis techniques to design domains by defining new mappings;
– Use of model checking tools to check the semantic validity of the analytic model against the design model.

6   Example

In this section we show an example of how to apply the profile to an EJB application. This example is based on the IBM ITSO Bank model shown in the Examples section of the EJB Profile.

In Figure 7 we show how the overall architecture of the ITSO Bank example looks like when we apply our Reliability Profile based on replication. On the whole, for each set of objects in the EJB container we want to replicate there is a Replica Manager, which corresponds to the `Manager` type in our profile. The Group Manager object stands for the one with equivalent name in our profile.

The analysis model of the ITSO Bank system has four main objects: Bank, BankAccount, Customer and TransactionRecord, as depicted in Figure 8. A BankAccount of Bank can be of three types: CheckingAccount, SavingsAccount and CorportateAccount. Each transaction executed on a BankAccount is recorded as a TransactionRecord.

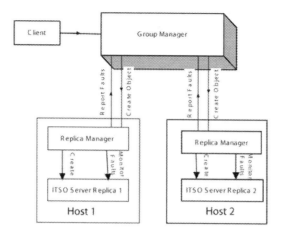

Fig. 7. Architecture of the Replication Profile applied to the ITSO Bank Example

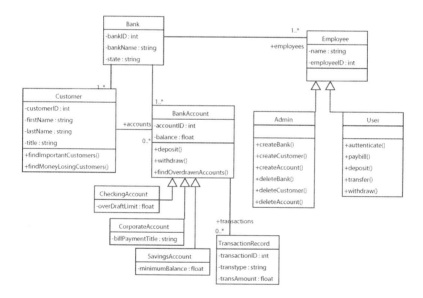

Fig. 8. ITSO Bank Example-Analysis Model

Each BankAccount is owned by a Customer, that has an authentication information. From this analysis model, we want to build a PSM for the J2EE platform and apply our profile.

We create from the analysis model an external view of the system describing an EJB-based implementation of the model, applying our profile. As we constrain to the external view, we show how the `Customer` class is mapped into EJB components according to our profile. Figure 9 shows part of those EJB components. For the sake of brevity, we concentrate our example only on the `Customer` class, which business objects are implemented in `CustomerSession` as an EJB Session Bean.

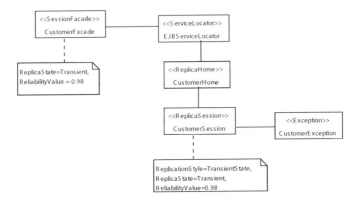

Fig. 9. ITSO External View for Customer

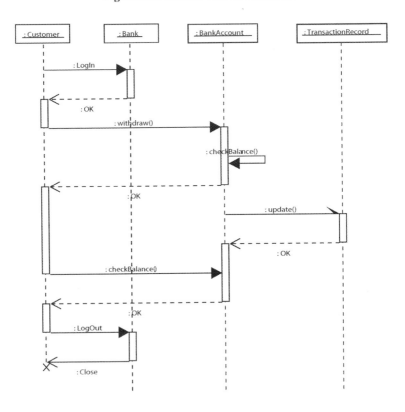

Fig. 10. Sequence Diagram for the Customer Object

In order to deploy the Customer component consistently, we need to identify which other components make invocation to and receive invocation from it. In this regard, the UML Sequence Diagrams play an important role. We show in Figure 10 the dynamic relationship between Customer and the other ITSO classes. We notice that the reliability of `Customer` is also related to the reliability of other classes, such as: `Bank`, `BankAccount` and `TransactionRecord`. Therefore, we should apply the same reliability value to those classes. Given that $JBoss^{TM}$ is the chosen J2EE server to run this example, a fragment of the deployment descriptor for this scenario has the following configuration:

– *The CustomerSession Bean configuration*

```
<session>
   <ejb-name>CustomerSession</ejb-name>
   <jndi-name>CustomerSession/Home</jndi-name>
   <local-jndi-name>CustomerSession/LocalHome</local-jndi-name>
     <clustered>true</clustered>
     <cluster-config>
       <partition-name>DefaultPartition</partition-name>
     </cluster-config>
</session>
```

– *The BankEntity Bean configuration*

```
<entity>
   <ejb-name>BankEntity</ejb-name>
   <jndi-name>BankEntity/Home</jndi-name>
   <local-jndi-name>BankEntity/LocalHome</local-jndi-name>
     <clustered>true</clustered>
     <cluster-config>
       <partition-name>DefaultPartition</partition-name>
     </cluster-config>
</entity>
```

– *The BankAccountEntity Bean configuration*

```
<entity>
   <ejb-name>AccountEntity</ejb-name>
   <jndi-name>AccountEntity/Home</jndi-name>
   <local-jndi-name>AccountEntity/LocalHome</local-jndi-name>
     <clustered>true</clustered>
     <cluster-config>
       <partition-name>DefaultPartition</partition-name>
     </cluster-config>
</entity>
   . . .
```

Suppose the target reliability for `Customer` is 95% and the reliability of each component deployed in JBoss, version 3.0 on top of a Linux server is 75%. Then, according to our mapping profile (see section 5), the `Customer` component classes (as well as `Bank`, `BankAccount` and `TransactionRecord`) should be replicated across at least 3 nodes of a cluster.

7   Related Work

There are plenty of work dealing with reliability in the design level [3, 10, 22]. Those work look at some of the issues we identify in our work, in terms of addressing dependability concerns in the early stages of software development. We can primarily find in those work analysis techniques to validate design tools based on UML.

However, they differ from our approach in some aspects. MDA uses the straight-forward approach through the concepts of mapping models among different platforms. Adopting the MDA approach we believe that we can construct an environment where one can consistently integrate the analysis and design of dependability issues, as well as the integration of design and implementation. [2] provides a useful transformation technique to automate dependability analysis of systems designed through UML. Nev-ertheless, to properly contemplate dependability in all stages of the software engineer-ing process, we believe that one of the main concern is to provide a unified semantic between the analysis and the design models. Recently, [14] has presented a more elabo-rated work of how UML 1.4 can be applied to stochastic analysis of system architecture dependability. Additionally, they extend the OMG General Resource Model in the UML Profile for Real–Time, Schedulability and Performance [19], shortly the Performance profile, to adequate to their analysis model, which may be considered in a future step of our work.

Another approach to address software dependability is to provide mechanisms to improve reliability of software after it has been implemented through testing techniques. Works such as [7] use those techniques to identify faults in the software that are likely to cause failures. Testing for reliability carries out an important research agenda, and is an important tool to measure the reliability of software systems. In our work, we first assume that the reliability property of the system components will be already provided most likely through testing. Secondly, our purpose is to concentrate on the reliability assurance of the system from design to deployment level through transformation tech-niques. Therefore, concentrating on these levels, we believe that the desired reliability of software systems will be reported in the testing phase according to the required reli-ability property defined in the architecture level.

The OMG has also requested proposals in order to standardize profiles for particu-lar application areas, particularly the UML Profile for Modeling Quality of Service and Fault Tolerance Characteristics and Mechanisms [18], briefly QoS profile. The major concern of the QoS profile are the QoS aspects, but it also addresses some dependabil-ity concerns. However, it can be viewed only as a starting point towards the specification of an MDA profile for dependability. The revised submission does not provide enough details in terms of the relationship between Dependability profile and the Performance profile. The proposal points out fault-tolerance solutions to mitigate reliability prob-lems. However, the semantics to model fault-tolerant systems in the MDA approach are quite informal, which may result in ambiguities. A more refined level is required for the QoS profile in order to make use of it as a reference model and in terms of solutions to mitigate reliability problems it seems to be so far restricted.

8   Concluding Remarks and Future Work

This work is expected to support a practical approach for the provision of reliability for software systems. There are current techniques to provide reliability for software systems. However, techniques such as process algebras are generally considered time consuming, in regard to the software development. The model driven approach is suitable for filling in this gap. We expect to provide a solution where reliability can be assured along the life cycle of software development.

We have currently defined the abstraction level where reliability can be addressed in MDA through replication. Our future work includes:

– Identify those qualities that require formal analysis to determine. Choose an appropriate analysis technique for reliability analysis and define a profile to represent the entities within the analysis domain.
– Define a mapping between the design domain and the analysis domain from the previous step that correctly represents the semantics of each.
– Extend a platform-specific profile such as [9] to represent the reliability mechanisms of interest.
– Define a mapping between the design domain and the deployment diagram.
– Automate the mapping from the design domain to the deployment diagram.

There are other aspects we do not deal with in this stage of our work, although we must consider them in the forthcoming steps. These aspects include:

– Identifying a general procedure to build a Reference Model. What are the main aspects that a Reference Model should include? In building our Reliability Reference Model we noticed that some of these aspects include identifying resource types, timed events, and so on. We therefore noticed the lack of consistent information in what would be the most important design issues a Reference Model should embrace. We are aware that it depends on the sort of subject to be modeled, but we noticed in our first constructed model there are main points that should be considered to make easier identifying the model elements.
– Finding ways to guarantee that the Reference Model and the Profile are consistent with each other and how to reason about the various elements that come out in the profile based on the reference model. Identifying the elements in the profile that is complete and consistent with the elements in the reference model seems to rest mostly on the informal judgement of expert individuals.

Acknowledgment

We would like to thank Rami Bahsoon and Licia Capra for assisting in the review of this document. We would like to give special thanks to James Skene for discussions during the accomplishment of this work.

References

1. D. Alur, J. Crupi, and D. Malks. *Core J2EE Patterns*. Sun Microsystems Inc., 2001.
2. A. Bondavalli, I. Majzik, and I. Mura. Automatic Dependability Analysis for Supporting Design Decisions in UML. In R. Paul and C. Meadows, editors, *Proc. of the 4th IEEE International Symposium on High Assurance Systems Engineering*. IEEE, 1999.

3. V. Cortellessa, H. Singh, and B. Cukic. Early reliability assessment of uml based software models. In *Proceedings of the Third International Workshop on Software and Performance*, pages 302–309. ACM Press, 2002.
4. W. Emmerich. *Engineering Distributed Objects*. John Wiley & Sons, Inc, 2000.
5. W. Emmerich. Software Engineering and Middleware: A Roadmap. In A. Finkelstein, editor, *The Future of Software Engineering*, pages 119–129. ACM Press, Apr. 2000.
6. W. Emmerich. Distributed Component Technologies and Their Software Engineering Implications. In *Proc. of the 24th Int. Conference on Software Engineering, Orlando, Florida*, pages 537–546. ACM Press, May 2002.
7. P. Frankl, R. Hamlet, B. Littlewood, and L. Strigini. Choosing a Testing Method to Deliver Reliability. In *International Conference on Software Engineering*, pages 68–78, 1997.
8. A. Gerber, M. Lawley, K. Raymond, J. Steel, and A. Wood. Transformation: The missing link of MDA. In *Proc. 1st International Conference on Graph Transformation, ICGT'02*, volume 2505 of *Lecture Notes in Computer Science*, pages 90–105. Springer Verlag, 2002.
9. J. Greenfield. UML Profile for EJB. Technical report, http://www.jcp.org/jsr/detail/26.jsp, May 2001.
10. G. Huszerl and I. Majzik. Modeling and analysis of redundancy management in distributed object–oriented systems by using UML statecharts. In *Proc. of the 27th EuroMicro Conference, Workshop on Software Process and Product Improvement, Poland*, pages 200–207, 2001.
11. A. Kleppe, J. Warmer, and W. Bast. *MDA Explained*. Addison–Wesley Series Editors, 2003.
12. J.-C. Laprie. *Dependability: Basic Concepts and Terminology*. Springer–Verlag, 1992.
13. B. Littlewood and L. Strigini. Software Reliability and Dependability: A Roadmap. In A. Finkelstein, editor, *The Future of Software Engineering*, pages 177–188. ACM Press, Apr. 2000.
14. I. Majzik, A. Pataricza, and A. Bondavalli. Stochastic Dependability Analysis of System Architecture Based on UML Models. In R. de Lemos, C. Gacek, and A. Romanovsky, editors, *Architecting Dependable Systems, LNCS–2667*, pages 219–244. Springer Verlag, 2003.
15. D. A. Menascé and V. A. F. Almeida. *Capacity Planning for the Web Services*. Prentice Hall PTR, 2001.
16. Object Management Group. OMG MOF 2.0 Query, Views, Transformations - RFP. Technical report, http://www.omg.org/techprocess/meetings/schedule/ MOF_2.0_Query_View_Transf._RFP.html.
17. Object Management Group. Model Driven Architecture. Technical report, http://cgi.omg.org/docs/ormsc/01-07-01.pdf, July 2001.
18. Object Management Group. UML Profile for Modeling Quality of Service and Fault Tolerance Characteristics and Mechanisms. Technical report, http://www.omg.org/docs/ad/02-01-07.pdf, December 2002.
19. Object Management Group. UML Profile for Schedulability, Performance and Real-Time Specification. Technical report, http://www.omg.org/cgi-bin/doc?ptc/02-03-02.pdf, March 2002.
20. Object Management Group. Unified Modeling Language (UML), version 1.4. Technical report, http://www.omg.org/cgi-bin/doc?formal/01-09-67.pdf, January 2002.
21. B. Randell. Software Dependability: A Personal View (Invited Paper). In *Proc. 25th Int. Symp. Fault-Tolerant Computing (FTCS-25, Pasadena)*, pages 35–41. IEEE Computer Society Press, 1995.
22. H. Singh, V. Cortellessa, B. Cukic, E. Gunel, and V. Bharadwaj. A bayesian approach to reliability prediction and assessment of component based systems. In *Proc. of the 12th IEEE International Symposium on Software Reliability Engineering*, pages 12–21. IEEE, 2001.
23. J. Skene and W. Emmerich. Model Driven Performance Analysis of Enterprise Information Systems. *Electronical Notes in Theoretical Computer Science*, March 2003.

Supporting Dependable Distributed Applications Through a Component-Oriented Middleware-Based Group Service

Katia Saikoski and Geoff Coulson

Computing Dept., Lancaster University
Lancaster LA1 4YR, UK
Phone: +44 1524 593054
ksaikoski@terra.com.br, geoff@comp.lancs.ac.uk
http://www.comp.lancs.ac.uk

Abstract. Dependable distributed applications require flexible infrastructure support for controlled redundancy, replication, and recovery of components and services. However, most group-based middleware platforms, which are increasingly being used as implementation environments for such systems, fail to provide adequate flexibility to meet diverse application requirements. This paper presents a group-based middleware platform that aims at maximal flexibility. In particular, flexibility is provided at design time, deployment time and run-time. At design and deployment time, the developer can configure a system by assembling software components shaped to a specific use. Then, at run-time, s/he can dynamically reconfigure the resulting system to adjust it to new circumstances, or can add arbitrary machinery to enable the system to perform self-adaptation. As examples, levels of fault tolerance can be dynamically increased and decreased as desired by adding, removing or replacing replicas; or the underlying communications topology can be adapted by switching from point-to-point TCP to multicast as numbers of replicants increase. Importantly, it is not necessary that the shape that run-time reconfiguration takes has been foreseen at design or deployment time. Our proposed solution employs software component technology and computational reflection as the basic means by which to perform and manage configuration and reconfiguration.

1 Introduction

The past few years have seen a significant increase in the importance of group-based distributed applications. Although they have in common the use of multiple end-points, the class of group applications is characterised by great diversity: while the support of *dependability* (e.g. fault-tolerance or high availability based on replication of servers) is perhaps the largest subset, dissemination of audio and video, distribution of events, and computer supported cooperative work are also important constituents of this class. Ideally, both dependability scenarios and these other group-related areas would be supported by a common underlying distributed platform.

R. de Lemos et al. (Eds.): Architecting Dependable Systems II, LNCS 3069, pp. 99–119, 2004.

Unfortunately, present day distributed object based middleware platforms (e.g. the Common Object Oriented Architecture (CORBA) [1] or the The Distributed Component Object Model (DCOM) [2]), which are increasingly being used as implementation environments for such applications, fail to provide suitable support for group applications in their full generality. And where they do provide support it is typically targeted at a limited subset of group applications, or is piece-meal and non-integrated. Examples from the CORBA world are the fault tolerance service [3], and the (completely separate) CORBA event service [4]. This lack of integration is problematic in a number of ways. In particular, it leads to missed opportunities for common solutions (e.g. in multicast channels, group addressing, access control and management) and makes it harder than it should be to combine related services (e.g. to provide a fault tolerant event service).

The broad aim of the research described in this paper is to provide a fully general and integrated platform for the support of group applications. Because of the diversity involved, this is a challenging undertaking. The different types of group applications vary dramatically in their requirements in terms of topology, dynamicity of membership, authentication of membership, logging of messages, reliability of communications, ordering guarantees on message delivery, use of network multicast etc.

Our approach is to attempt to satisfy all such requirements in a middleware environment known as OpenORB [5–7] which, in addition to supporting (group) applications, also supports the development of generic group services. This is primarily achieved through the use of component technology [8] which allows programmers to build applications and generic group services in terms of an extensible library of basic building blocks (components). Components are used not only at the application/ services level; the middleware itself is built from components. This allows groups to be used recursively to support communication among the various middleware components themselves. As a simple example, basic middleware components such as the name service can be made fault tolerant by means of groups.

A further aspect of our work is the support of *run-time reconfiguration* of running group applications or services. Runtime reconfiguration is essential for those applications that need to cope with changing requirements; in particular, for systems that cannot be switched off easily (e.g., control systems), or systems that cannot be switched off for long periods (e.g., telecom systems). As an example, consider a highly available service built from a group of server replicas. In such a scenario, it may be desirable to change the inter-replica reliability protocol (e.g. from an active replica to a passive replica scheme) as the number of replicas, the number of clients, or the performance/ reliability needs change over time. Another (non-dependability-related) example could involve adding or removing media filters such as video compressors to support media dissemination in multimedia conferences involving nodes with heterogeneous network connectivity and processing capability [9]. To support such requirements, we apply the notion of *reflection* [10]. For example, we maintain run-time component graphs, which allow component configurations to be adapted in a "direct manipulation" style (see Sect. 2).

This paper is structured as follows. First, Sect. 2 describes our basic middleware architecture and its reflective, component based, computational model. Next we discuss, in Sects. 3 and 4, our support for the construction and runtime reconfiguration of component-based groups (with a focus on dependability-related services). Section 5 then presents an example of the use of our group support services. Finally, Sect. 6 deals with related work and Sect. 7 offers concluding remarks.

2 Background on OpenORB

OpenORB [5-7] is a flexible middleware platform built according to a component-based architecture. It is loosely inspired by the ISO Reference Model for Open Distributed Processing (RM-ODP) [11]. At deployment-time, components are selected and appropriately composed to create a specific instance of the middleware. For example, components encapsulating threads, buffer management, the (Internet Inter-ORB Protocol) IIOP protocol and the Portable Object Adapter may be selected, among others, for placement within a CORBA address space. In addition, components can be loaded into address spaces (using RM-ODP terminology, we will refer to address spaces as *capsules*) at run-time, and there are no restrictions on the language in which they are written. Components can be either *primitive* or *composite*. The former have no internal structure (at least not at the level of the component model) whereas the latter are formed as a composition of nested components (either primitive or composite). As we explain below, reflection is used to facilitate the reconfiguration of the set of components configured into a composite component or a capsule, and thus dynamically adapt the middleware functionality at run-time.

In OpenORB, component interfaces are specified in (an extended version of) the CORBA Interface Definition Language (IDL), and components may export any number of interface types. Furthermore, new interface instances can be created on demand at run-time. Multiple interface types provides separation of concerns; for example, operations to control the transfer of state between replicas in a fault tolerant service can be separated from operations to provide the service itself. Multiple interface instances are then useful in giving multiple clients their own private "view" of the component.

As well as standard operational interactions (i.e. method calls), our extended IDL supports the *signal* and *stream* interaction types defined in RM-ODP. Signal interactions, which are one-way messages, are typically used for primitive events; and stream interactions, which additionally involve isochronous timing properties, are used for audio or video etc. Along with the authors of RM-ODP, we claim that this set of interaction types is canonical and functionally complete, or at least can serve to underpin any other conceivable interaction type. Apart from interaction types, each interface takes one of two possible roles: either *provided* or *required*. Provided interfaces represent the services offered to the component's environment, while required interfaces represent the services the component needs from its environment (in terms of the provided interfaces of other components). This explicit statement of dependency eases the task of composing components in the first place and also makes it feasible to replace components in running configurations (see below).

Communication between the interfaces of different components can only take place if the interfaces have been *bound*. In terms of role, required interfaces can only be bound to provided interfaces and vice versa. To-be-bound interfaces must also match in terms of their interaction types (i.e. method signatures etc.). There are two categories of bindings: local bindings and distributed bindings (see Fig. 1). The former, which are simple and primitive in nature, can be used only where the to-be-bound interfaces reside in the same capsule; they effectively terminate the recursion implicit in the fact that distributed bindings have interfaces which need to be bound to the interface they are binding! Distributed bindings are composite and distributed components which may span capsule or machine boundaries. Internally, these bindings are composed of sub-components (themselves bound by means of local bindings) that wrap primitive facilities of the underlying system software. Examples are primitive network-level connections (e.g., a "multicast IP binding"), media filters, stubs, skeletons etc. Distributed bindings are often constructed in a hierarchical (nested) manner; for example a "reliable multicast binding" may be created by encapsulating a "primitive" multicast IP binding and components that offer SRM-like functionality [12].

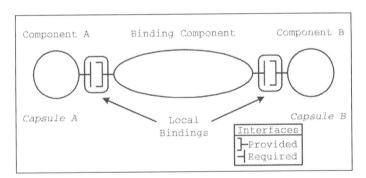

Fig. 1. Bindings supporting local and distributed interaction between components

It should be noted that distributed bindings are not unique in being composite and distributed components; any OpenORB component is allowed to have these properties. In other words, distributed binding components do not enjoy any particular status as compared to other components.

Components are created by *factory* components (or simply "factories"). Factories for composite components are implemented as compositions of factories, each of which deals with the composite component's various constituents. Often, factories are parameterised with *templates* which define the required configuration and characteristics of to-be-created components. Templates are specified in the Extensible Markup Language (XML) [13]; specifically group-oriented templates are discussed in detail below.

In terms of *reflection*, every OpenORB component has an associated "meta-space" that is accessible from any of the component's interfaces, and which provides reflective access to, and control of, the component in various ways. To help separate concerns, meta-space is partitioned into various orthogonal "meta-models". For example, the *interface meta-model* allows access to a component's interface signatures and bindings, and the *resources meta-model* gives access to the resources (e.g. threads or memory) used by the component. The meta-model of most relevance to this paper is the *compositional meta-model*. This takes the form of a graph data structure which serves as a causally-connected self-representation of a capsule's internal topological structure (in terms of component composition). This means that manipulations of the graph's topology result in corresponding changes in the capsule's internal topology (and vice versa). Support is provided to make such changes atomic (e.g. by freezing any threads executing in the changed component). The other meta-models, which are beyond the scope of this paper, are described in [6]. More generally, OpenORB itself is discussed in more detail in [7].

3   An Overview of GOORB

GOORB (*Group support for OpenORB*) is a flexible OpenORB-based infrastructure for the creation and maintenance of both *group types* and *group instances*. At design and start up time, group types are defined based on templates, and on the re-use and assembly of software components from an extensible library. Then, at run-time, group instances are created on the basis of group type specifications and can subsequently be flexibly reconfigured to adjust them to dynamically varying environments. The design of GOORB follows the basic concepts and the infrastructure employed in the OpenORB reflective architecture discussed above. In particular, each group type is represented as a template and each group instance is represented as a composite component. The constituents (see Fig. 2) of these composite components are as follows:

— *Group members* are composite components whose internal constituents are *application components* (e.g. databases access, audio and video playout etc.) combined with zero or more *system components* (e.g. stubs, skeletons, distributors, collators). Application components implement the basic functionality of the application whereas system components implement functionality associated with the GOORB group semantics.

— *Group bindings* are explicit representations of the topology and communication semantics of a given group type. It is not a default requirement that members of a group should use a specific communication pattern such as multicast. Although multicast is widely used as a support for groups, an application designer might equally well decide that members should communicate using several point-to-point communications, or any other composition of communication patterns. Thus, GOORB remains agnostic as to how members communicate among themselves while providing generic support for specifying and controlling this communication.

– *Management components* are system components that manage the group; e.g., components to control the membership of the group, or components to detect faults, or monitor the status of quality of service (QoS) of the group.

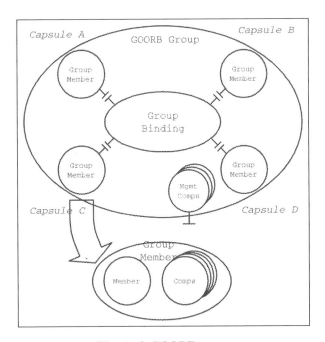

Fig. 2. A GOORB group

4   GOORB in Detail

4.1   Overview

The overall GOORB architecture, see Fig. 3, constitutes the following generic services: *i*) a *group binding service* which is responsible for providing functionality with which to configure and instantiate group bindings, *ii*) a *configurable group service* which is responsible for the configuration, creation, destruction and control of group instances, and *iii*) a *group reconfiguration service* which supports the reconfiguration of group instances. All these services are accessed through a set of well-defined interfaces and rely on an extensible library of default components.

In the following subsections we discuss in detail the design and operation of the above three services.

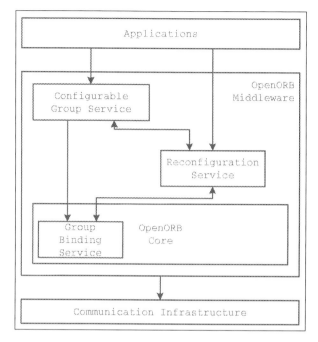

Fig. 3. The GOORB architecture

4.2   The Group Binding Service

The group binding service is responsible for the creation and maintenance of group bindings. As mentioned, group bindings provide the core communications services in a GOORB group. However, it is important to notice that group bindings could also be used to realise interaction among components that are not part of a GOORB group. The difference between a GOORB group and a set of components connected via a group binding is the level of service provided. A GOORB group provides control over members of the group as default functionality while the group binding just enables the communication between several end-points. The group binding service can be considered a low-level enabler for groups while the GOORB group provides more comprehensive facilities.

Group bindings can be either primitive or composite. Primitive bindings implement or wrap basic communication functionality (e.g., IP multicast). These are directly supported by the infrastructure and their implementation is inaccessible to the programmer. Composite bindings then take the form of value-added encapsulations of one or more simpler bindings (e.g., IP multicast improved with components to guarantee reliability such as SRM [12] or RMT [14]). The basic building blocks of the group binding service architecture are the various factories. Factories for primitive group bindings are provided by the infrastructure and are parameterised with the references of the interfaces that will be connected by the binding. As well as setting up the protocol infrastructure necessary to support the group binding, they instantiate (in remote address spaces as required) necessary auxiliary system components such as stubs, controllers, etc. We have so far implemented the following primitive group binding factories:

- Multicast Stream Binding Factory. This creates primitive multicast stream bindings that can be used to connect several application interfaces, typically for the transmission of audio and video (e.g. to support an audio/video conferencing application). The application interfaces connected to these bindings can be either producers or consumers of audio/ video. An application component can be made both a producer and a consumer by implementing both interface types. The precise semantics of the binding can be flexibly configured. In particular, it is possible to create any of the following topologies: $1 - n$ (1 sender and n receivers), $n - m$ (n senders and m receivers), $n - 1$ (n senders and 1 receiver). Also, when several application interfaces are sending video, a receiving application can select which signals it wants to see.
- Multicast Operational Binding Factory. Primitive multicast operational bindings are used to bind multiple application interfaces in a request/ reply style of interaction. There are two roles defined: clients and servers. Clients make invocations on *stub* components, which forward the invocations to all currently bound server interfaces. By default, stubs block until the first reply arrives (cf. CORBA's deferred synchronous operation semantic [15]). However, this can be changed using a stub control interface so that the stub can instead be made to wait for any number of replies. All replies are then passed to a *collator* component. Different collators can implement alternative collation policies-i.e. alternative ways of combining replies so that a single consolidated reply can be presented to the client interface.
- Multicast Signal Binding Factory. Multicast signal bindings offers means for firing events in several capsules. Their structure is similar to that of multicast stream bindings; i.e., source components send events that are captured by sink components.

Each primitive group binding instance has a control interface that provides methods for dynamically adding and removing interfaces to the binding. As explained below, GOORB groups take advantage of this to realise changes in their membership.

Composite group bindings embody more complex communication semantics. For example, an operational primitive binding can be associated with encryption components to produce a secure binding. In addition, such a secure binding can be further improved with compression components to form yet another type of binding. Following the approach taken for general OpenORB composite components, configurations are described in terms of a set of components and bindings between them as explained in Sect. 2. These can be local bindings, which connect components in the same capsule, or distributed bindings, which connect components in different capsules. In the particular case of distributed groups, the configuration will typically include at least one distributed binding.

Unlike primitive group bindings, composite bindings are designed by application developers and are created by a single generic factory. A template, which embodies a description of the to-be-created composite binding, is sent to this factory which evaluates the internal details of the template and sends requests to other factories (component and binding factories) according to the configuration and location of the components to be instantiated to create the binding. The binding template is realised as an XML document. In more detail, configurations are specified by a graph that is formed by a list of components and a list of local bindings to be established between specified interfaces of these components. Because only local bindings are specifiable, nested distributed binding components must be used to bind any interfaces not located in a common capsule.

Finally, it is worth mentioning that the configurable group service framework includes an extensible selection of pre-defined generic protocol components that can be used in the specification of arbitrary composite bindings. For example, the stubs and collators mentioned above are included in this selection. Collators are, in fact, an instance of a more general class of components called *filters*. These support standard interfaces which allow them to be composable into stacks. Other examples of filters are *encryptors/ decryptors* and *compressors/ decompressors*. A further example is an *orderer* component which orders incoming messages according to some policy (e.g. for use in a totally ordered multicast binding).

4.3   The Configurable Group Service

In GOORB, group types are defined using XML-specified *group type templates* which specify the configuration and characteristics of to-be-created groups. These are similar in concept to the above-described Group Binding Service templates, but with additional complexity and functionality. Group type templates, which are passed to a generic group factory, include information about the types of potential members that can be part of the group, how these members communicate among themselves, the externally-visible services the group provides, any QoS parameters associated with the group etc. The template is an explicit representation of the group at creation time. In addition, though, a version of the template is retained during the lifetime of the group instance to facilitate reconfiguration (see Sect. 4.4). Essentially, the initial template describes the possible compositions that can be realised for the associated group type, while the run-time version represents the actual configuration of a running group at any instant of time.

The XML Schema for group type templates is shown in Appendix A; an example of its use is given in Sect. 5. Essentially, the template embodies both *structure* and *constraints*: the group structure is represented by a graph defining components and the bindings between them; the constraints then define design-time and run-time limitations associated with the composition of the graph (e.g., the maximum or minimum number of elements of a certain type in the graph).

In more detail, the group template defines a group as consisting of a *group binding* configuration (as described above in Sect. 4.2), one or more *member types* (e.g., it may be useful to distinguish producer and consumer members in a media dissemination group), and zero or more *service types*. A member type is a template for the creation of future members of the group. Each consists of a *member interface type* and a *per-member configuration*. The member interface type is the type of interface that a prospective member of the associated member type will present to the group, while the per-member configuration is a graph of application and system components that is dynamically instantiated each time such a member joins the group. It is used to specify things like per-member stubs, skeletons, protocol stacks, collators, etc. In addition to the member interface type and per-member configuration, a member type can also include *attributes* that specify, e.g., the minimum and maximum number of instances of this type that may be in existence.

Service types are useful only in connection with "open groups" [16]. These are groups that provide a service that can be invoked by parties external to the group-e.g. in the case of a replicated service. As with member types it is possible to define multiple service types, and each service type similarly consists of an interface type, a per-service instance configuration, and attributes. "Closed groups", i.e. those with no service types, are also quite common: a typical example is a video conference.

The most important of the Configurable Group Service's run-time elements are the *generic group factory* and the *local factory*. The generic group factory interprets group type templates and calls on local factory instances, one of which runs on every participating node, to actually create the required components in the required location.

Each running group supports a default *group management* component that interacts with local factories to request the creation of new member and service instances. The generic group factory implicitly creates an instance of this default group management component type when the group is first created, and binds it into the group composite-unless another membership component (presumably with non-standard semantics) is defined in the group type template (it is also possible to change this later using the Reconfiguration Service). All group management components must implement at least the minimal *IGroup* interface that provides methods for components to join or leave a group. IGroup offers two methods for inserting members in a group and another two methods for removing them: *join()* inserts an already-instantiated actual member (i.e. application components only; no system components) into the group while *createMember()* instantiates a set of application components in a specified capsule and then inserts them into the group. (This is similar to the *MembershipStyle* property defined in the CORBA-FT Specification [3] where the membership can be either "infrastructure-controlled" or "application-controlled".) *IGroup* also supports *leave()* and *destroyMember()* methods. In the case of *leave()* only the infrastructure is destroyed while in the case of *destroyMember()*, the member component is also destroyed. *IGroup* additionally provides a *getView()* method which returns the list of current members in the group.

4.4   The Reconfiguration Service

The final element of GOORB is its support for run-time reconfiguration of group instances for purposes of adaptation and evolution. This is based on a *composi-*

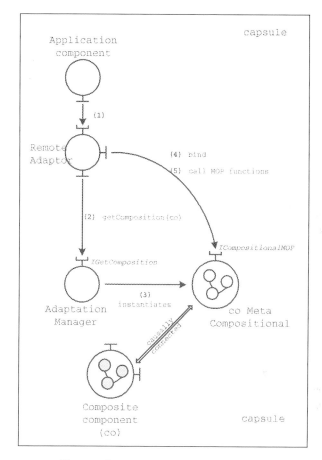

Fig. 4. The reconfiguration architecture

tional meta model which is an extension of the basic OpenORB compositional meta-model mentioned in Sect. 2. In outline, an application wishing to perform a reconfiguration operation on a group obtains an interface to the group's compositional meta-model. It then manipulates this (causally-connected) meta-model-which takes the form of a topological graph plus operations to manipulate this graph-to effect corresponding changes in the actual underlying group. For example, nodes in the graph can be added, removed, and replaced to effect the corresponding addition, removal and replacement of actual underlying components (e.g. group members), as can arcs to effect the addition etc. of local bindings.

The implementation of the compositional meta-model mirrors the fact groups are inherently-distributed composite components-i.e. the compositional meta-model graph is itself decomposed and distributed. This helps with both scalability and fault tolerance. To further contribute to scalability, individual decomposed parts of the graph are dynamically instantiated on demand in an incremental way. The way in which remote access to meta-models is achieved is illustrated in Fig. 4. Basically, if the target component (or subcomponent) is non-local, requests to instantiate its compositional meta-model are transparently forwarded, by a local, per-capsule, *remote adaptor*, to the appropriate per-capsule *adaptation manager* in the capsule in which the target resides. Then, this adaptation manager requests a local factory (not shown in the figure) to create the local part of the target component's compositional meta-model and returns a reference to this. Finally, the remote adaptor can dynamically bind to the remote meta-model and invoke method calls to inspect and adapt the sub-graph (and hence the underlying component topology) just as if it were local.

Adaptation managers are responsible for ensuring that only permitted requests are processed and that only secure adaptations occur. To confirm the security of requested adaptations, adaptation managers call on per-group *adaptation data* components. These hold a set of adaptation constraints, expressed in XML and derived from the group template, for a particular group instance. For example, it is possible to forbid the deletion of parts of a per-member configuration such as a sub-composite that implements security checks. Because adaptation is a distributed operation, the constraints associated with a composite component are correspondingly distributed in per-capsule adaptation data components so that the failure of one host does not compromise the whole system. Additionally, local adaptations do not have to rely on information residing in another host.

Figure 4 actually presents an abstraction of the reconfiguration architecture. At a finer level of detail, two specific types of adaptation managers are employed: *group adaptation managers* (GAMs) and *member adaptation managers* (MAMs). These are respectively created when a group and members of a group are created. The GAM is responsible for receiving and delegating all adaptation requests to be performed on a group, while MAMs are responsible for performing adaptation on a specific member of a GOORB group[1]. Essentially, GAMs and MAMs deal with two issues: transactional updates and replicated updates. Transactional updates are important to ensure that distributed group reconfiguration operations are performed either completely or not at all. Replicated updates, on the other hand, are useful to enable updates to be performed on all members or services in one action. For example, in one request one can add a compression component to all the receiving video members in a media dissemination group.

Finally, the reconfiguration architecture incorporates an *adaptation monitor*, which is a per-capsule composite component that embodies the OpenORB QoS management architecture [17]. This is capable of being configured to monitor some particular QoS metric (e.g. "the frequency of invocations on a replicated group service"), and then to select an appropriate adaptation strategy (e.g. "move from active to passive replication") when a particular trigger is detected (e.g. "more than n invocations per second are occurring"). Following the proto-

---

[1] In the context of reconfiguration, service instances (as defined in Sect. 4.3) are considered members of the group. Therefore, each service instance has its own MAM as well as every member.

type presented in [17], monitors and strategy selectors are defined in terms of FC2 timed automata, while strategy activation consists of a script containing a sequence of calls on the group's compositional meta-model. Crucially, adaptation monitors can be dynamically instantiated in capsules so that it is not necessary that modes of adaptation in a group have been foreseen at design or deploy time (although these must not violate the adaptation constraints referred to above).

5   An Example of the Use of GOORB

In this section, we illustrate the use of GOORB by means of a simple dependability-related application scenario. The scenario involves a group of actively replicated servers (these are "calculators") in an open group with a single service type. The cardinality of the service type is restricted to a single instance, and there is a single member type with unconstrained cardinality to represent the replicants. The group template is as follows:

```
<?xml version="1.0" encoding="UTF-8"?>
<group xmlns="http://site/GOORB/ggr"
       xmlns:gbs="http://site/GOORB/gbs"
       xmlns:ggb="http://site/GOORB/ggb"
       xmlns:ggm="http://site/GOORB/ggm"
       xmlns:xsi="http://www.w3.org/2001/XMLSchema-instance"
       xsi:schemaLocation="http://site/GOORB/ggr
       E:\Schema\GOORBGroup.xsd" groupName="ActiveReplication">
  <groupBinding groupBindingType="ReliableMulticastBinding.xml"/>
  <managementComponents/>
  <memberTypes>
    <member memberType="CalcReplica.xml" minCardinality="1" maxCardinality="unbounded"/>
  </memberTypes>
  <serviceTypes>
    <member memberType="CalcService.xml" minCardinality="1" maxCardinality="1"/>
  </serviceTypes>
</group>
```

A reliable distributed binding (separately described in *ReliableMulticastBinding.xml*) is employed as the basis of communication within the group. *CalcReplica.xml* and *CalcService.xml* are templates that describe the configuration of the member and service types of the group respectively. *CalcService.xml*, which is shown below, contains a proxy component that receives the replies from the requests on the replicas and sends the first reply back to the client.

```
<?xml version="1.0" encoding="UTF-8"?>
<member xmlns="http://site /GOORB/ggm"
        xmlns:gbs="http://site/GOORB/gbs"
        xmlns:xsi="http://www.w3.org/2001/XMLSchema-instance"
        xsi:schemaLocation="http://site/GOORB/ggm E:\Schema\GroupMember.xsd">
  <gbs:configuration name="calcService">
    <gbs:graph>
      <gbs:component template="GetFirstCalcProxy.xml">proxy</gbs:component>
    </gbs:graph>
    <gbs:externalInterface>
      <gbs:bindable>
        <gbs:componentName>proxy</gbs:componentName>
        <gbs:interfaceName>ICalc___</gbs:interfaceName>
      </gbs:bindable>
      <gbs:bindable>
        <gbs:componentName>proxy</gbs:componentName>
```

```
            <gbs:interfaceName role="service">ICalc</gbs:interfaceName>
        </gbs:bindable>
    </gbs:externalInterface>
  </gbs:configuration>
  <externalBinding>
    <gbs:localBinding>
        <gbs:bindable>
            <gbs:componentName>proxy</gbs:componentName>
            <gbs:interfaceName role="server">ICalc___</gbs:interfaceName>
        </gbs:bindable>
        <gbs:bindable>
            <gbs:componentName>mob</gbs:componentName>
            <gbs:interfaceName>iface</gbs:interfaceName>
        </gbs:bindable>
    </gbs:localBinding>
  </externalBinding>
</member>
```

As explained in Sect. 4, the group template is passed as a parameter to the generic group factory's *create()* method. After the group has been created, it can be populated with member and service instances, as explained in Sect. 4.3, by calling operations the *join()* or *createMember()* operations on the (default) group management component's *IGroup* interface.

Having established and populated the group, it is possible to adapt it by employing the Reconfiguration Service. As a somewhat contrived example (chosen for simplicity of exposition), it may be desired to replace the initial proxy component mentioned above with one that returns the result of a voting process between the replicas. To achieve this, the client application (or a strategy activator if reconfiguration is being initiated automatically by an embedded QoS manager) needs to access the group's GAM's *IGAdapt* interface in order to invoke its *adaptType()* method (this enables an adaptation to be atomically performed on every member of the specified type). *AdaptType()* takes as a parameter the name of an adaptation script which, in our case, contains the following single call:

```
comp_meta_model.replaceComponent("proxy", {"name":"vproxy",
                                    "template":"VotingProxy.xml",
                                    "module":"Comps.VotingProxy"});
```

As a result of executing this script, every member of the group has its original proxy component replaced by a new "vproxy" component. The compositional meta-model's *replaceComponent()* method substitutes a component in the group composite for another component of the same type, i.e., one with the same set of provided and required interfaces. The first parameter is the component to be removed and the second is either the new component (if this has already been instantiated), or a template for a component that needs to be created (as shown in the example). Both the *IGAdapt* interface and the more general facilities of the compositional meta-model are discussed in more detail in [18].

6   Related Work

Adaptive fault tolerance has been described by Kalbarczyk [19] as the ability for a system to adapt dynamically to changes in the fault tolerance requirements of an application. Some issues of adaptive fault tolerance have been addressed by projects such as *Chameleon* [19], *AFTM* [20] and *Proteus* [21] (part of the AQuA system). Chameleon is an infrastructure that supports multiple fault tolerance strategies. These are realised by objects called ARMORs which can be used (and reused) to build different fault tolerance strategies. Furthermore, ARMORs can be added/removed or changed at run-time, thus providing dynamic reconfiguration. Such reconfiguration, however, is aimed at modifying the fault tolerance level only-it is less general than the capabilities offered by GOORB. In the AFTM (Adaptive Fault Tolerant Middleware) [20], several fault-tolerant execution modes are available, from which the most suitable mode can be selected according to application's requirements. However, only a small selection of execution modes is available in the AFTM environment and there are no guidelines on how to develop new modes-in other words, unlike GOORB, the system in not easily extensible. The Adaptive Quality of Service for Availability (AQuA) [21] architecture provides a flexible infrastructure for developing dependable systems. It relies on a group of technologies to provide applications with their required availability. First, it uses the Quality Objects (QuO) framework for specifying dynamic quality of service (QoS) requirements. Second, it uses the Proteus framework to handle fault tolerance through replication. Finally, at the lowest level of the platform, AQuA uses the Maestro/Ensemble [22] group communication system to provide reliable multicast to a process group. Although AQuA is highly flexible in terms of the configuration, it lacks support for run-time reconfiguration.

A number of researchers have attempted to build group services in terms of components (in a loose interpretation of the term). Notable examples are the Ensemble toolkit from Cornell University [22], work at Michigan [23] and the "building block" based reliable multicast protocol proposed by the IETF [14]. However, these efforts are primarily targeted at low levels aspects of group provision (i.e. communications services) and their component models are far less general than ours. A more general approach is proposed by projects such as Coyote [24], Cactus [25] and Apia [26], however, they also address low-level protocol stack issues.

At a higher system level, the Object Management Group (OMG) has defined a multi-party event service [4] for CORBA and has recently added fault tolerance by replication of objects to its specification [3]. However, as mentioned in the introduction, these efforts are limited in scope and fail to address the needs of the full diversity of group applications. This can also be said of a number of other group-oriented efforts in the CORBA world. For example Electra [27], Eternal [28], OGS [29], OFS [30] and NewTop Object Group Service [31] are all targeted solely at fault tolerant application scenarios and cannot easily be employed in the construction of other types of group application. Furthermore, they tend to provide flexibility though the setting of per-defined properties, which, naturally enough, represent only those degrees of freedom envisaged by the designer of the system. There is no support for the definition of entirely new group services that meet as yet unforeseen needs.

Groups have been developed for middleware platforms other than CORBA such as JGroup [32] for the Java RMI (Remote Method Invocation), the work described in [33] in the context of the Regis platform, and ARMADA [34] which is another middleware system designed specifically for fault tolerance. Similar comments to the above can be applied to all these systems. ARMADA explicitly address the need for adaptivity, but not though a component/ reflection-based approach.

Work at Cornell on the Quintet system [35] uses COM components to build reliable enterprise services. This work recognises an increased need for flexibility (e.g. rather than prescribe transparency, they allow groups to be explicitly configured), but it is not as radical as our reflection-based approach. In addition, the work is not targeted at the full range of group applications.

Our component model is influenced by models such as COM+ [2], Enterprise JavaBeans [36] and CORBA Components [15], all of which support similar container-based models for the construction of distributed applications. We add a number of novel aspects to such models including the support of multiple interaction types, and the notion of local/ distributed bindings. We also add sophisticated reflection capabilities in the form of our multiple meta-model approach.

7   Conclusions

This paper has described a flexible architecture for building groups with a wide diversity of requirements. In particular, the architecture aims to address three main areas: i) providing group support in a generic middleware environment; ii) the need for flexibility in creating groups, and iii) the further need for flexibility during the group operation. Our experience to date with the architecture has been very favourable: we have been able to build, with minimal effort, a wide range of group services using only a relatively limited set of base components. In this paper, the focus has been on dependability scenarios; however, it is important to emphasise that GOORB has been successfully applied in other group-related areas. For example, its application in a multimedia group-based scenarios is discussed in [37].

As mentioned, XML templates serve as the basis for both group creation and for restricting reconfiguration at run-time (where required) by means of constraints inserted in the template. However, this heavy reliance on XML templates raises a possible drawback of our design: the potential complexity of templates; particularly for large and complex groups. To alleviate this we are currently investigating the provision of 'front-end factories' that are specially designed for different application areas (e.g. replicated services, or multimedia groups). Building on the current generic factory/ template architecture, these will provide a custom interface and map to the standard XML templates accepted by the generic group factory. Another important extension that we are investigating is the use of a graphical front-end as a means of composing groups from components in repositories. We also envisage that this can be used at run-time to initiate reconfiguration operations.

In a future implementation phase we will migrate our implementation to the OpenORB v2 environment [7]. This performs significantly better than the Python based prototype that is discussed in this paper (it is based on a binary level inter-component communication scheme, called OpenCOM [38], which is superset of a subset of Microsoft's COM). The use of OpenORB v2 will permit more realistic experimentation with media dissemination groups and will also allow us to address questions regarding the performance implications of our approach.

A final area of future work is to investigate in more detail the full power of the reflective capability of groups. apart from its use in reconfiguration as discussed in this paper, the use of reflection opens up many further possibilities; e.g., passivating and activating groups, inserting quality of service monitors into group configurations, or add interceptors to perform logging of messages. There are many unsolved problems in this area, not the least of which is the difficulty of maintaining the integrity of configurations when they are adapted at run-time [39]. However, it seems a highly desirable goal to offer such facilities.

References

1. Object Management Group: CORBA Object Request Broker Architecture and Specification - Revision 2.3 (1999)
2. Microsoft Corporation: COM Home Page. Available at <http://www.microsoft.com/com/> (1999)
3. Object Management Group: Fault Tolerant CORBA Specification, V1.0. Available at <http://www.omg.org> (2000) OMG document: ptc/2000-04-04.
4. Object Management Group: Event service, v1.0. Formal/97-12-11 (1997)
5. Blair, G., Coulson, G., Robin, P., Papathomas, M.: An Architecture for Next Generation Middleware. In: Proceedings of IFIP International Conference on Distributed Systems Platforms and Open Distributed Processing (Middleware'98), Springer-Verlag (1998) 191–206
6. Costa, F.M., Duran, H.A., Parlavantzas, N., Saikoski, K.B., Blair, G., Coulson, G.: The Role of Reflective Middleware in Supporting the Engineering of Dynamic Applications. In Cazzola, W., Stroud, R.J., Tisato, F., eds.: Reflection and Software Engineering. Lecture Notes in Computer Science 1826. Springer-Verlag, Heidelberg, Germany (2000) 79–99
7. Coulson, G., Blair, G., Clark, M., Parlavantzas, N.: The Design of a Highly Configurable and Reconfigurable Middleware Platform. ACM Distributed Computing Journal 15 (2002) 109–126
8. Szyperski, C.: Component Software - Beyond Object-Oriented Programming. Addison-Wesley (1998)
9. Coulson, G., Blair, G., Davies, N., Robin, P., Fitzpatrick, T.: Supporting Mobile Multimedia Applications through Adaptive Middleware. IEEE Journal on Selected Areas in Communications 17 (1999) 1651–1659
10. Maes, P.: Concepts and Experiments in Computational Reflection. In: Proceedings of OOPSLA'87. Volume 22 of ACM SIGPLAN Notices., ACM Press (1987) 147–155
11. ISO/IEC: Open Distributed Processing Reference Model, Part 1: Overview. ITU-T Rec. X.901 — ISO/IEC 10746-1, ISO/IEC (1995)

12. Floyd, S., Jacobson, V., Liu, C., McCanne, S., Zhang, L.: A Reliable Multicast Framework for Light-weight Sessions and Application Level Framing. IEEE/ACM Transactions on Networking **5** (1997) 784–803
13. World Wide Web Consortium: Extensible Markup Language (XML) 1.0. W3C Recommendation (1998)
14. Whetten, B., Vicisano, L., Kermode, R., Handley, M., Floyd, S., Luby, M.: Reliable Multicast Transport Building Blocks for One-to-Many Bulk-Data Transfer. INTERNET-DRAFT - RMT Working Group, Internet Engineering Task Force (2000) draft-ietf-rmt-buildingblocks-02.txt.
15. Object Management Group: CORBA Components Final Submission. OMG Document orbos/99-02-05 (1999)
16. Olsen, M., Oskiewicz, E., Warne, J.: A Model for Interface Groups. In: Proceedings of IEEE 10th Symp. on Reliable Distributed Systems. (1991)
17. Blair, G.S., Andersen, A., Blair, L., Coulson, G.: The role of reflection in supporting dynamic QoS management functions. In: Seventh International Workshop on Quality of Service (IWQoS '99). Number MPG-99-03 in Distributed Multimedia Research Group Report, London, UK, IEEE/IFIP, Lancaster University (1999)
18. Saikoski, K., Coulson, G.: Experiences with OpenORB's Compositional Meta-Model and Groups of Components . In: The Workshop on Experience with Reflective Systems, Kyoto, Japan (2001)
19. Kalbarczyk, Z.T., Bagchi, S., Whisnant, K., Iyer, R.K.: Chameleon: A Software Infrastructure for Adaptive Fault Tolerance. IEEE Trans. on Parallel and Distributed Systems **10** (1999) Special Issue on Dependable Real Time Systems.
20. Shokri, E., Hecht, H., Crane, P., Dussalt, J., Kim, K.: An Approach for Adaptive Fault Tolerance in Object-Oriented Open Distributed Systems. In: Proceedings of the Third International Workshop on Object-oriented Real-Time Dependable Systems (WORDS'97), Newport Beach, California (1997)
21. Sabnis, C., Cukier, M., Ren, J., Rubel, P., Sanders, W.H., Bakken, D.E., Karr, D.A.: Proteus: A Flexible Infrastructure to Implement Adaptive Fault Tolerance in AQuA. In: Proceedings of the 7th IFIP Working Conference on Dependable Computing for Critical Applications (DCCA-7), San Jose, CA, USA (1999) 137–156
22. van Renesse, R., Birman, K., Hayden, M., Vaysburd, A., Karr, D.: Building Adaptive Systems Using Ensemble. Technical Report TR97-1619, Cornell University (1997)
23. Litiu, R., Prakash, A.: Adaptive Group Communication Services for Groupware Systems. In: Proceedings of the Second International Enterprise Distributed Object Computing Workshop (EDOC'98), San Diego, CA (1997)
24. Bhatti, N., Hiltunen, M., Schlichting, R., Chiu, W.: Coyote: A system for constructing fine-grain configurable communication services. ACM Transactions on Computer Systems **16** (1998) 321–366
25. Hiltunen, M., Schlichting, R.: The Cactus Approach to Building Configurable Middleware Services. In: Proceedings of the SRDS Dependable System Middleware and Group Communication Workshop (DSMGC), Nürnberg, Germany (2000)
26. Miranda, H., Pinto, A., Rodrigues, L.: Appia: A Flexible Protocol Kernel Supporting Multiple Coordinated Channels. In: Proceedings of the 21st International Conference on Distributed Computing Systems, Phoenix, Arizona, IEEE (2001) 707–710
27. Maffeis, S.: Adding Group Communication Fault-Tolerance to CORBA. In: Proceedings of USENIX Conference on Object-Oriented Technologies, Monterey, CA (1995)

28. Narasimhan, P., Moser, E., Melliar-Smith, P.M.: Replica consistency of CORBA objects in partitionable distributed systems. Distributed Systems Engineering Journal 4 (1997) 139–150
29. Felber, P.: The CORBA Object Group Service: A Service Approach to Object Groups in CORBA. PhD thesis, Départment D'Informatique – École Polytechnique Fédérale de Lausanne (1997)
30. Sheu, G.W., Chang, Y.S., Liang, D., Yuan, S.M., Lo, W.: A Fault-Tolerant Object Service on CORBA. In: Proceedings of the 17th International Conference on Distributed Computing Systems (ICDCS '97), Baltimore, MD (1997)
31. Morgan, G., Shrivastava, S., Ezhilchelvan, P., Little, M.: Design and Implementation of a CORBA Fault-tolerant Object Group Service. In: Proceedings of the Second IFIP WG 6.1 International Working Conference on Distributed Applications and Interoperable Systems (DAIS'99), Helsinki, Finland (1999)
32. Montresor, A.: The Jgroup Reliable Distributed Object Model. In: Proceedings of the Second IFIP WG 6.1 International Working Conference on Distributed Applications and Interoperable Systems (DAIS'99), Helsinki, Finland (1999)
33. Karamanolis, C., Magee, J.: A Replication Protocol to Support Dynamically Configurable Groups of Servers. In Press, I.C.S., ed.: Proceedings of the Third International Conference on Configurable Distributed Systems (ICCDS'96), Annapolis MD (1996)
34. Abdelzaher, T.F., Dawson, S., Feng, W.C., Jahanian, F., Johnson, S., Mehra, A., Mitton, T., Shaikh, A., Shin, K.G., Wang, Z., Zou, H.: ARMADA Middleware and Communication Services. Real-Time Systems 16 (1999) 127–153
35. Vogels, W., Dumitriu, D., Pantiz, M., Chipawolski, K., Pettis, J.: Quintet, Tools for Reliable Enterprise Computing. In: Proceedings of the 2nd International Enterprise Distributed Object Computing Workshop (EDOC '98), San Diego, CA (1998)
36. Sun Microsystems: Enterprise JavaBeans Specification Version 1.1. Available at <http://java.sun.com/products/ejb/index.html> (2000)
37. Saikoski, K.B., Coulson, G., Blair, G.: Configurable and Reconfigurable Group Services in a Component Based Middleware Environment. In: Proceedings of the SRDS Dependable System Middleware and Group Communication Workshop (DSMGC), Nürnberg, Germany (2000)
38. Clark, M., Blair, G., Coulson, G., Parlavantzas, N.: An Efficient Component Model for the Construction of Adaptive Middleware. In: Proceedings of the IFIP Middleware Conference 2001. Volume 2218., Heidelberg, Germany. Lecture Notes in Computer Science (2001)
39. Blair, G., Coulson, G., Andersen, A., Blair, L., Clark, M., Costa, F., Limon, H.D., Parlavantzas, N., Saikoski, K.B.: A Principled Approach to Supporting Adaptation in Distributed Mobile Environment. In: 5th International Symposium on Software Engineering for Parallel and Distributed Systems (PDSE-2000), Limerick, Ireland (2000)

Appendix A: XML Schema for GOORB Groups

Below is the standard XML Schema for describing GOORB groups. As can be seen, a group is a composition of group members and services, a group binding and management components. Some of these elements are described in other XML schemas as follows: OpenORB's basic elements such as composite components, interfaces and local bindings are described in *GOORBBasics.xsd* (*gbs* namespace); group bindings are described in *GroupBinding.xsd* (*ggb* namespace); and group members and services are described in *GroupMember.xsd* (*ggm* namespace). Note that, for ease of reuse, separate templates can be used to describe some of the elements. For example, a group member can be included either as a separate template or directly described in the group template itself. The same option can be used for service types and group bindings.

Another important issue is related to the constraints associated to groups. For example, it is possible to restrict the cardinality of the group or the cardinality of a specific member type. Another set of constraints, which are not shown in the schema below, is related to adaptation. For example, it is possible to define if adaptation can be realised in a particular group or what level of adaptation can be realised. Each set of rules (constraints) is associated to a number of management components. New set of rules requires new versions of these components.

```xml
<?xml version="1.0" encoding="UTF-8"?>
<xs:schema targetNamespace="http://site/GOORB/ggr"
xmlns:ggm="http://site/GOORB/ggm" xmlns:ggr="http://site/GOORB/ggr"
xmlns:xs="http://www.w3.org/2001/XMLSchema"
xmlns:gbs="http://site/GOORB/gbs"
xmlns:ggb="http://site/GOORB/ggb"
elementFormDefault="qualified" attributeFormDefault="unqualified">
   <xs:import namespace="http://site/GOORB/gbs" schemaLocation="GOORBBasics.xsd"/>
   <xs:import namespace="http://site/GOORB/ggb" schemaLocation="GroupBinding.xsd"/>
   <xs:import namespace="http://site/GOORB/ggm" schemaLocation="GroupMember.xsd"/>
   <xs:element name="group">
      <xs:annotation>
         <xs:documentation>A group is a composition of group members and services, a
                           group binding and management components
         </xs:documentation>
      </xs:annotation>
      <xs:complexType>
         <xs:sequence>
            <xs:choice>
               <xs:element ref="ggb:groupBinding"/>
               <xs:element ref="ggr:groupBinding"/>
            </xs:choice>
            <xs:element ref="ggr:managementComponents"/>
            <xs:element ref="ggr:memberTypes"/>
            <xs:element ref="ggr:serviceTypes"/>
         </xs:sequence>
      </xs:complexType>
   </xs:element>
   <xs:element name="memberTypes">
      <xs:annotation>
         <xs:documentation>A member of the group</xs:documentation>
      </xs:annotation>
      <xs:complexType>
         <xs:sequence>
            <xs:element ref="ggr:participantType" maxOccurs="unbounded"/>
         </xs:sequence>
      </xs:complexType>
   </xs:element>
   <xs:element name="serviceTypes">
      <xs:annotation>
         <xs:documentation>A service offered by the group</xs:documentation>
      </xs:annotation>
      <xs:complexType>
         <xs:sequence>
            <xs:element ref="ggr:participantType" minOccurs="0" maxOccurs="unbounded"/>
         </xs:sequence>
      </xs:complexType>
   </xs:element>
```

```
    <xs:element name="participantType">
      <xs:annotation>
        <xs:documentation>A participant in the group (service or member)
        </xs:documentation>
      </xs:annotation>
      <xs:complexType>
        <xs:choice>
          <xs:element ref="ggr:member"/>
          <xs:element ref="ggm:member"/>
        </xs:choice>
        <xs:attribute name="name" type="xs:string" use="required"/>
        <xs:attribute name="type" type="xs:anyURI" use="required"/>
        <xs:attribute name="minCardinality" type="xs:integer" use="required"/>
        <xs:attribute name="maxCardinality" type="xs:integer" use="required"/>
      </xs:complexType>
    </xs:element>
    <xs:element name="groupBinding">
      <xs:annotation>
        <xs:documentation>A reference to an external groupBinding xml file
        </xs:documentation>
      </xs:annotation>
      <xs:complexType>
        <xs:attribute name="groupBindingType" type="xs:anyURI" use="required"/>
      </xs:complexType>
    </xs:element>
    <xs:element name="managementComponents">
      <xs:annotation>
        <xs:documentation>A list of management components</xs:documentation>
      </xs:annotation>
      <xs:complexType>
        <xs:sequence>
          <xs:element ref="gbs:component" minOccurs="0" maxOccurs="unbounded"/>
        </xs:sequence>
      </xs:complexType>
    </xs:element>
    <xs:element name="member">
      <xs:annotation>
        <xs:documentation>A reference to an external member</xs:documentation>
      </xs:annotation>
      <xs:complexType>
        <xs:attribute name="memberType" type="xs:anyURI" use="required"/>
      </xs:complexType>
    </xs:element>
</xs:schema>
```

Architecting Distributed Control Applications Based on (Re-)Configurable Middleware

Geert Deconinck, Vincenzo De Florio, and Ronnie Belmans

K.U.Leuven-ESAT, Kasteelpark Arenberg 10, B-3001 Leuven, Belgium
{Geert.Deconinck,Vincenzo.DeFlorio,
Ronnie.Belmans}@esat.kuleuven.ac.be

Abstract. Industrial distributed automation applications call for reusable software components, without endangering dependability. The DepAuDE architecture provides middleware to integrate fault tolerance support into such applications based on a *library* of detection, reconfiguration and recovery functions, and a *language* for expressing non-functional services, such as configuration and fault tolerance. At run time, a middleware layer orchestrates the execution of recovery actions. The paper further provides a hierarchical model, consisting of a dedicated *intra-site* local area network and an open *inter-site* wide area network, to deal with the different characteristics and requirements for dependability and quality-of-service, when such applications rely on off-the-shelf communication technology to exchange management or control information. The middleware can be dynamically reconfigured when the environment changes. This methodology has been integrated in the distributed automation system of an electrical substation.

1 Introduction

In many industrial automation applications, dependability requirements have been traditionally fulfilled by *dedicated* hardware-based fault tolerance solutions. This was also the case in the distributed embedded automation system in an electrical substation which drove this research. Today however, the evolution towards a new generation of automated substations demands for a reduction of development and maintenance costs and requires the use of lower cost hardware, software and communication components from the market. This trend is motivated by the growing need for more functionality: development of new, dedicated (hardware-based) solutions is considered too expensive and not flexible enough to keep up with the evolving requirements of the liberalized electricity market. It has a direct impact on the selection of the target platforms for automation, where industrial computers with commercial real-time operating systems are pushed as alternatives to previously adopted dedicated boards or customized Programmable Logic Controllers (PLC's). The migration away from dedicated hardware-based fault tolerance solutions imposes the adoption of software-based fault tolerance strategies to cope with dependability requirements, especially if the target platform does not offer fault tolerance capabilities off-the-shelf. The use of a distributed architecture is then the key issue for this migration, since this provides redundancy based on standardised hardware and networking modules. As such, industrial distributed embedded systems – like those used in the control and automation of electrical energy infrastructures – rely on *off-the-shelf* components and protocols to ensure cost-efficient exploitation [1, 2, 3].

R. de Lemos et al. (Eds.): Architecting Dependable Systems II, LNCS 3069, pp. 123–143, 2004.
© Springer-Verlag Berlin Heidelberg 2004

Furthermore, as a particular application can be deployed on a variety of hardware platforms (with different sets of sensors and actuators attached) and within different environments (e.g. with different levels of electromagnetic interference), flexibility is needed both to instantiate the application functions appropriately and to react adequately to disturbances to the information and communication infrastructure on which the application is executing. For instance, system reconfiguration and recovery may be different, depending on which I/O devices are connected to the different parts of the distributed controllers. Hence, software and component reusability is necessary; more generally, adaptability is required to reconfigure fault tolerance strategies depending on the environment.

The DepAuDE architecture (called after a European IST-project with the same name) deploys a set of middleware modules to provide fault tolerance by exploiting the embedded systems' distributed hardware and by separating functional behaviour from the recovery strategy, i.e., the set of actions to be executed when an error is detected [4, 5, 6]. This is described in section 2.

Furthermore, such industrial applications often rely also on off-the-shelf communication and networking technology (e.g. Ethernet and IP protocols) to exchange management or even control information over wide area networks. The paper provides a hierarchical model, consisting of a dedicated *intra-site* network and an open *inter-site* network, to deal with the different characteristics and requirements for dependability and quality-of-service (Section 3). In Section 4, a methodological approach is presented that captures the dependability requirements of the application and allows to instantiate the appropriate configuration of the middleware components, and to validate the requirements in the implementation. This DepAuDE approach has been applied to a primary substation automation system (PSAS) as a case study (Section 5).

The added value of the DepAuDE approach comes from the flexibility to deploy automation applications on heterogeneous standardised hardware platforms by exploiting the redundancy and from the ability to modify recovery strategies without requiring major modifications to the application (based on the separation of functional behaviour from the recovery strategy), while tolerating the same physical faults as in the dedicated hardware solutions.

2   DepAuDE Approach

As indicated in Figure 1, a *middleware layer* and the *ARIEL language* are the two major components of the DepAuDE approach [4, 5, 6, 7]. The latter is used at design-time to describe non-functional aspects of the application, while the former acts at run-time.

The first part of this **middleware layer** consists of a *library of fault tolerance mechanisms* (FTM): this library provides basic elements for error detection, localization, containment, recovery and fault masking. The tools are software-based implementations of well-known fault tolerance mechanisms, grouped in a library of adaptable, parametric functions. Examples include watchdogs, voters, support for acceptance tests, replicated memory, etc. [8]. These FTM's can be used on their own, or as co-operating entities attached to a *backbone,* which is the second part of the middleware layer. Both the backbone and the FTM's are implemented on top of the *Basic Services Layer* (BSL), which is the third part of the middleware. The BSL provides a homogeneous interface for task handling and inter process communication on top of heterogeneous platforms with different hardware modules and different real-time operating systems (RTOS).

At run-time, this backbone behaves as a distributed application that maintains information on application progress, on system status and on network topology. At start-up, the backbone creates such information from events received notifications from the BSL, which contains the libraries for communication and task management that were instrumented in such a way as to forward their return value to the backbone or from application tasks, when a predefined breakpoint is reached in the application code. At run-time, this information is updated by the FTM's (for instance, when an error is detected), by the BSL or by the application (e.g. when an application error is detected). All this information is retained in a replicated database. When such event notification is received, the recovery scripts that orchestrate fault tolerance actions are triggered (see below). When a node is restarted, the middleware supports the reintegration of backbone, BSL and FTM modules into the rest of the continuing system; it can also reload application tasks. The application in itself is responsible for reintegrating these restarted tasks into the ongoing execution, as no checkpoint/restore mechanisms are designed (yet). The backbone is hierarchically structured to maintain a consistent system view and contains self-testing and self-healing mechanisms [6].

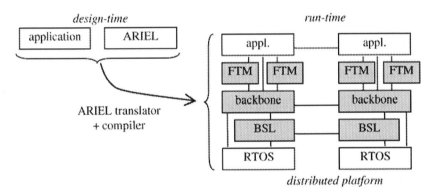

Fig. 1. The ARIEL language and the DepAuDE middleware (grey boxes) are the major components.

The second major component of the DepAuDE approach is the **configuration-and-recovery language** (ARIEL): this high-level language is used to configure the middleware and to express recovery strategies [4, 5, 6, 7, 9]. For configuration purposes, ARIEL is able to set parameters and properties of FTM's. For expressing recovery strategies, ARIEL allows can check conditions on the contents of the database of the backbone and act according to the results by e.g. terminating or starting a node or a task. As such, these scripts indicate fault tolerance actions by detailing localization, containment and recovery steps to be executed when an error is detected. Both aspects are detailed below.

2.1 ARIEL as Configuration Support Tool

Within ARIEL the developer describes the configuration of the parametric FTM's, their integration in the application, and the allocation of tasks to nodes. A *translator* processes these ARIEL descriptions and issues header files defining configured objects and symbolic constants [7]. These header files are to be compiled with the application.

(Example 1) The initial allocation of tasks to nodes is described in ARIEL.

```
NNODES 3
...
DEFINE NODE1 '192.166.61.132', port 5001
...
NODE1 HAS task10, task201, task30
NODE2 HAS task14, task18, task202, task40
NODE3 HAS task203, BB_master
...
GROUP {task20} IS task201, task202, task203
```

(Example 2) A software-implemented watchdog task (task10) can be configured in ARIEL by indicating the heartbeat period (100 ms), the task to be guarded (task14) and the task to be informed when an exception occurs (task18):

```
WATCHDOG task10 WATCHES task14
  HEARTBEAT 100 ms
  ON_ERROR WARN task18
END WATCHDOG
```

At run-time this will result in a separate task10, spawned by the middleware that will be waiting for heartbeat messages send by application task14 (which needs one additional periodic call from the application process). When such messages are not received, a separate message is send by this middleware task10 to application task18, and the backbone is notified as well.

(Example 3) ARIEL can be used to implement transparent task replication, and to indicate how voting is to be handled. The voting algorithm and the metric for comparison of the objects can be selected. Within ARIEL, one can include a timeout for a slow or missing voting party, and either choose to continue as soon as two of the three inputs are received or to wait until all three inputs are received or the timeout has elapsed (which is the default option).

```
REPLICATED task20 IS task201, task202, task203
  METHOD MODULAR_REDUNDANCY
   VOTING_ALGORITHM MAJORITY
   METRIC "int_cmp"
   TIMEOUT 400 ms
  END METHOD
  ON_SUCCESS task30
  ON_ERROR task40
END REPLICATED
```

Other ARIEL-templates have been designed to handle recovery blocks, backup tasks, voting support, exception handling, and other well-known fault tolerance techniques [7].

2.2 ARIEL as Recovery Language

The second usage of ARIEL is as an ancillary application layer, to describe –at design time– the recovery strategies to be executed when an error is detected. Basically, the ARIEL language allows querying the database of the backbone for the state of entities of the application, and attaching run-time actions to be executed on these entities if the condition is fulfilled – for instance:

```
IF FAULTY task1 THEN RESTART node1
```

Such an entity can be a single task, a node, a group of tasks, a connection, etc. As such, one can query the database in the backbone to check whether an entity has been found in error, is running, has been restarted/rebooted, etc. and then perform recovery actions on it. The actions allow starting, terminating, isolating or sending information to an entity. It is also possible to start an alternative (backup) task, to reset a node or link, to generate synchronization signals (to initiate restart after reconfiguration), etc. Not only the status of application tasks can be tested in the condition of the ARIEL clause, but also the status of the network, or of the RTOS. The entire, context-free grammar of ARIEL is presented in [7].

Following this DepAuDE approach, increasing the dependability of an application implies the configuration and integration of the middleware with the application and writing the recovery strategies in ARIEL.

At compile-time, a translator processes these ARIEL scripts and produces binary recovery code to be compiled with the application. At run-time, the backbone will execute these strategies devoted to error processing. These strategies are switched in either asynchronously - when an error is detected within the system by one of the basic error detection tools -, or synchronously - when the user signals particular dynamic conditions like, for instance, a failed assertion, or when the control flow runs into user-defined breakpoints.

The innovative aspects of this approach do not come from the implementation of the library of (well-known) FTM's, but rather from the combination with the middleware that executes *user-defined* recovery actions written in ARIEL, when an error is detected. The power of ARIEL is the ability to describe *local, distributed or system-wide* recovery strategies. The backbone takes care of passing the necessary information to other nodes in the system and of initiating the recovery actions on the different nodes via the BSL. Such recovery strategies separate the (*non-functional*) aspects of application recovery from those concerning the (*functional*) behaviour that the application should have in the absence of faults. Furthermore, separating these aspects allows modifying recovery strategies with only a limited number of changes in the application code, and vice-versa (i.e. the application functionality can be changed without adjusting the recovery strategy). This results in more flexibility and a better maintainability of the application (assuming a reliable interface and an orthogonal division of application functionality from fault tolerance strategies) [5].

As an example consider the following ARIEL snippet:

```
IF FAULTY task1 THEN
  STOP task1
  START task4
  WARN task2, task3
FI
```

This script is a part of a three-and-a-spare system (i.e., a triple-modular redundant task with a standby component that can take over in case one of the three replicas fails). Three such scripts describe the entire three-and-a-spare system.

Several meta-characters allow the writing of more powerful ARIEL scripts:

- Meta-character '*' refers to any entity in the system.
- Meta-character '$' can be used to refer in a section to an entity mentioned in the condition. For instance, 'IF [FAULTY task1 AND RUNNING node1] THEN REBOOT $2 RESTART $1 FI' means that the entity, which fulfils the second condition, needs to be rebooted, and the entity that fulfils the first condition needs to be restarted.
- Meta-character '@' refers to the entity fulfilling the condition, while meta-character '~' refers to those entities that do not fulfil the condition.

Figure 2 uses these meta-characters to describe the three-and-a-spare recovery strategy as a single IF THEN section, in which group1 is defined as the set of tasks {task1, task2, task3}.

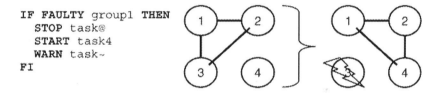

```
IF FAULTY group1 THEN
    STOP task@
    START task4
    WARN task~
FI
```

Fig. 2. Recovery script for a three-and-a-spare configuration.

Furthermore, the recovery strategies can be replaced whenever needed (e.g. when deployed on a different hardware platform. For instance, the example from Figure 3 shows that a different ARIEL script allows the application to behave as a three-and-a-spare system or as a gracefully degrading set of tasks. In the latter case, the voting function in the middleware is transparently modified from 2-out-of-3 majority voting to 2-out-of-2 duplication with comparison.

2.3 Assumptions

This DepAuDE approach has been implemented as middleware on top of the real-time operating systems such as *Windows CE and VxWorks,* and on top of the general purpose operating systems *Linux* and *Windows.* It relies on the following assumptions.

- Fault model: a single physical fault affects execution or communication entities (tasks, nodes, links). Experiments from the case study from section 5 below confirm that electromagnetic interference affects only the entity to which the responsible I/O element is connected [10]. Depending on the underlying hardware and RTOS (i.e. if a memory management unit is available), a fault containment region is a task or node. Crash failure semantics (fail-silent behaviour) is assumed for the fault containment region.

- A synchronous system model is assumed (i.e. known & bounded processing delays, communication delays, clock differences and clock drifts [11]). This is realistic for the set of targeted real-time automation applications, because of their implementation on dedicated hardware with a dedicated communication network.
- Communication, provided by the middleware at level 5 of the OSI protocol stack, is assumed to be perfect (no lost messages, no duplicates, keeping message order). In order to increase the coverage for this assumption, a set of mechanisms can either be deployed or developed at the lower OSI levels; DepAuDE relies on the Ethernet CRC error detection mechanism and level 2 retransmission mechanisms. For the pilot application from section 5, UDP/IP over a switched Ethernet network was adequate; for other situations TCP/IP might prove better if the real-time constraints are fulfilled.
- As the communication mechanism addresses groups of tasks, there is an OSI level 5 multicast service, whose behaviour is assumed to be *atomic*. If this assumption coverage is too low, dedicated atomic multicast support and group membership functions can be added to the middleware.

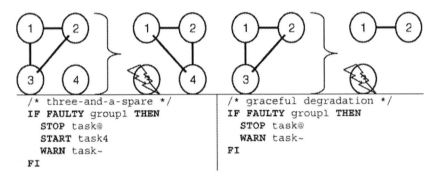

```
/* three-and-a-spare */
IF FAULTY group1 THEN
   STOP task@
   START task4
   WARN task~
FI
```

```
/* graceful degradation */
IF FAULTY group1 THEN
   STOP task@
   WARN task~
FI
```

Fig. 3. Changing recovery strategies from three-and-a-spare to graceful degradation.

It is important to note that the ARIEL recovery scripts have to be triggered by the error detection mechanisms from the FTM library, from the application or from the platform, in order to trigger the recovery. This implies that the coverage of the fault tolerance strategy driven by the ARIEL scripts cannot be higher than the coverage of the error detection tools which trigger their execution. Furthermore, it is the task of the developer to provide the ARIEL configuration parameters and recovery scripts that are appropriate for a given application on a given platform. The developer also needs to assess if the application-specific timing constraints are met under the worst execution times of the recovery strategies.

3   Inter-site Aspects

Up to now, the considered automation application onto which the DepAuDE approach was deployed, was running on several nodes of a particular site, interconnected via a local area network. However, distributed embedded automation systems become more and more interconnected with each other via non-dedicated, wide area networks, making use of off-the-shelf communication technology (IP networks). For instance, all control systems for electricity distribution (considered as case study in section 5 below) that are spread over a country or region, are interconnected to allow load balancing and orchestrated reactions in case of partial breakdown of the electricity distribution or in case of local overloads. In this context, one can take advantage of modelling these systems at two levels (see Figure 4).

- Intra-site level: this corresponds to the distributed embedded application for which its nodes are connected via a local area network, or via dedicated point-to-point connections. This **intra-site** network is only used by this application, and the application has complete control over it. This network also provides *real-time* support to the application.
- Inter-site level: this interconnects the local systems via a non-dedicated wide area network (for instance, the intranet of a global company, or the Internet) that is not under control of the application, and that is shared with other applications. This **inter-site** network is mainly used for *non-real-time* communication; however, nowadays and future industrial demands impose quality-of-service or (soft) real-time requirements on this inter-site communication.

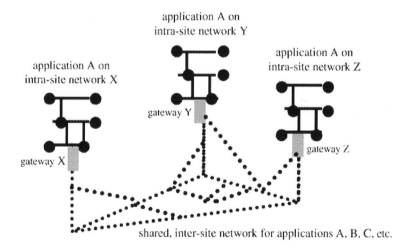

Fig. 4. Architecture of the target (distributed)[2] system. The application A runs on 3 sites (X, Y, Z) as a distributed real-time application. The interconnection among the different parts of the application A happens via an open inter-site network that is also used by other applications B, C.

If a certain quality-of-service can be guaranteed by the inter-site communication system, this inter-site network allows introducing cost-saving features into the applications, such as remote diagnosis, maintenance or control of embedded systems over non-dedicated inter-site connections.

These interconnected distributed embedded automation applications are not only subject to hardware (physical) faults affecting parts of the intra-site system or the inter-site connections, leading to unavailability of computing nodes, or of parts of the network. They can also suffer from malicious faults (intrusions) affecting inter-site connections, which may cause the unavailability of these networks (for instance, denial-of-service attacks) or which endanger the integrity of the data. Furthermore the presence of other applications that make use of the same inter-site network results in a *dynamic environment*, leading to bandwidth reduction or non-deterministic reception of messages.

Many emerging quality-of-service schemes (e.g. *diffserv*, *intserv*) are not widespread or simple enough to be applied over open communication infrastructures [12]. The DepAuDE architecture provides *gateway* functionality in the middleware to handle such inter-site networks without a need to modify intermediate routers. The gateway connects the intra-site network with the inter-site network (see Figure 4). It is responsible for sending several replicas of a message through different paths that are as disjoint as possible; such a system has been called redundant source routing (RSR), because the entire path from source to destination is described in the header of a message [13]. The criticality of a message or of that particular part of the application determines the required number of redundant paths. Redundant paths are obtained by enabling source routing in IP packets (completely supported in IP protocol v6, and partially in IPv4). As Internet has no known or regular structure, the gateways contain a *map discovery* module able to identify the possible inter-site paths with an accuracy that decreases with the distance from the probing points (gateways) [12]. Each gateway exchanges the collected local maps to build a global map with high details. These maps are updated periodically to deal with topology changes and congested areas.

Simulations and measurements have shown that the RSR increases the delivery probability when the number of disjoint paths increases. Additionally, several redundant paths provide the possibility that one path will be faster than others, leading to a lower latency. These results also show that the additional increase in traffic does not slow down the communication (as only a fraction of the communication is considered critical enough to be replicated) [13].

The inter-site network can be considered as a dynamic environment: when monitoring characteristics such as throughput and latency, the application behaviour can be adapted to it. As an example, if the inter-site connection bandwidth is too low, only the most critical application messages are transmitted, while less important information (e.g. logging information) is retained until later. Alternatively, a backup connection can be established (e.g. a dial-up line); this is more expensive but has also a more predictable bandwidth. As such, the gateway software has been extended by monitoring modules [14, 15]; based on ARIEL scripts and middleware support, the automation application can be adapted accordingly. Analogously, when a site is under intrusion or eavesdropping attack, the gateway node can encrypt the inter-site communication with a different encryption algorithm, at the cost of a higher performance overhead.

The data measured by network and node monitoring mechanisms can also be used to make recovery scripts less statically defined: e.g. they allow a task to be restarted on a node with the lowest CPU usage.

Furthermore, one set of ARIEL recovery scripts can be replaced by a different set, based on monitored parameters in the environment. For example, if all internet-based inter-site networks are highly congested, the recovery scripts based on retransmission via a different internet service provider can be replaced by a script that retransmits over a dial-up line. Such scripts are not executed until an error (a communication blackout) actually takes place.

This allows a three-tiered separation between functional complexity, fault tolerance complexity and environment complexity (Figure 5).

Fig. 5. Three-tiered complexity. If environmental parameters change, a different set of recovery strategies can be pushed onto the middleware, to be executed when an error is detected.

4 Methodological Guidance

The deployment of the DepAuDE architecture for a particular distributed automation application is not a trivial task. Therefore a methodology was developed, making use of formal and semi-formal techniques available on the market, to collect and analyse dependability requirements of the application, to support configuration and instantiation of the middleware with its FTM's, and to derive modelling scenarios.

The methodology has been conceived according to the principles of IEC standard 60300 on dependability management [16]. The DepAuDE methodology supports the application designer in carrying out the initial definition/specification/analysis activities through the use of three complementary modelling formalisms: UML Class Diagrams (CD's), a static paradigm, TRIO [17], a logic paradigm, and Stochastic Petri Nets (SPN), an operational paradigm. Since these three formalisms are general-purpose and they originated independently from the system dependability analysis domain, a methodology on the synergic use of the three formalisms was defined. It provides a generic CD scheme, predefined TRIO/SPN model libraries and guidelines on how to customize them for a specific application [18, 19, 20]. For a detailed description, see [21].

Class Diagrams are the "entry level" in the methodology: a set of predefined CD's is provided for the automation system domain, together with guidelines on how to tailor the generic scheme to the target application. CD's are meant as a support for collecting and structuring the functional and dependability requirements. Examples include how physical components contribute to automation functions, which deadlines need to be met, which availability requirements apply to certain components, etc.

TRIO is used for the specification and analysis of dependability requirements and fault tolerance strategy in a formal temporal logic framework [22]. A TRIO domain dependent structure is derived from the CD scheme by exploiting the class structure of the CD scheme and by applying construction rules that map a subset of classes, attributes and associations of the CD scheme onto TRIO classes, axioms, properties and Abstract Test Cases. Such TRIO structure is then customized and refined by the modeller according to its knowledge of the application; this allows generating temporal logic models and property proofs. The dependability analysis then allows verifying qualitative properties of the system (such as application progress and absence of deadlocks).

The role of SPN in the methodology is to support the system designer constructing and analyzing dependability models. The construction of analyzable SPN models follows a compositional approach based on a layered view of the system. Compositionality and layered structuring allow to master the complexity of the system and to get more flexibility and re-usability of models, which are key issues when comparing different FTM's. A library of predefined (parametric and labelled) SPN component models is at the disposal of the modeller, together with a layered interaction structure for the component models. The SPN component models are created from standard models and they represent the behaviour of classes of the generic CD scheme, while the layered structure is obtained by applying construction rules derived from the generic CD scheme. The methodology gives customization and refinement guidelines to support the modeller in the construction of an analyzable SPN model based on application-specific CD schemes. However, CD's being static in nature, the set up of an analyzable SPN requires that the information derived from CD's is integrated with information of the behaviour of some system entities. As such, different ARIEL scripts can be modelled. Models can be produced by hand, or they can be obtained through the automatic translation of UML StateCharts and Sequence Diagrams to Generalized Stochastic Petri Nets [18]. Once an analyzable SPN model of the system has been built it can be used for the computation of dependability metrics (such as availability).

5   Case Study

The DepAuDE architecture has been integrated in a demonstrator of a Primary Substation Automation System (PSAS), i.e. the embedded hardware and software in a substation for electricity distribution, connecting high voltage lines (HV) to medium voltage (MV) lines over transformers. The PSAS requires protection, control, monitoring and supervision capabilities. It is representative of many applications with dependability requirements in the energy field [10, 23, 24]. The major source of faults in the system is electromagnetic interference caused by the process itself (opening and closing of HV/MV switchgear) in spite of the attention paid to designing for electromagnetic compatibility. Software and hardware faults in the automation system have to be considered as well. These cause errors in communication, execution and memory subsystems. In an ongoing renovation of these substations, the dedicated hardware platforms are being replaced by standardised components. The lack of built-in fault tolerance capabilities at each node can be compensated by software-implemented fault tolerance (e.g. based on DepAuDE middleware) that exploits the redundancy. The need for adaptability to new situations and maintainability of the software can be accomplished using the configuration-and-recovery language ARIEL. Although software-based fault tolerance may have less coverage than hardware-based solutions, this is not considered inhibitive, because the physical (electrical, non-programmable) protection in the plant continues to act, as a last resort, as a safeguard for non-covered faults [24]. Besides, high-quality software engineering and extensive on-site testing remain important to avoid introduction of design faults that could hamper mission-critical services.

As indicated on Figure 6, a primary substation (grey lines) consists of switches, insulators, bus bars, transformers, capacitors and other electrical components. The dedicated PSAS architecture (black lines) consisted of a controller (LCL - Local Control Level) and a number of Peripheral Units (PU) distributed on the plant. (The inherent electrical redundancy of the substation is not shown.) Each PU is associated with sensors and actuators on the plant. The LCL provides for the entire substation functionality for control, monitoring and PU supervision. It also provides an interface to the operator and -over the inter-site network- to remote control systems and remote operators [10].

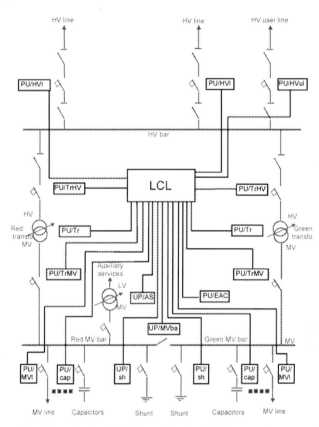

Fig. 6. Primary Substation electric circuit (grey lines) and PS automation system (black lines).

More specifically, the LCL in the pilot application controls the switches to two HV/MV transformers, the switch connecting the Red MV bar (on the left) to the Green MV bar (on the right), as well as switches local to the MV lines (Figure 6). The pilot application implements two automation functions from the LCL module: *automatic power resumption* (function1) and *parallel transformers* (function2) [23].

Function1 allows automatic power resumption when a HV/MV transformer shuts down, e.g. triggered by internal protection (temperature too high, oil alarm, ...). It disconnects the MV lines connected to the bus bar of the transformer, computes the load carried by the transformer just before the event happened, and if possible, causes the remaining transformer to take the entire load, as e.g. in the following scenario:

- (Initial situation) Red transformer carries 32 MVA (8 lines of 4 MVA) and Green transformer 24 MVA (8 x 3 MVA); the switches connecting the Red and Green bars to the transformers are closed; the switch connecting the Green MV bar to the Red MV bar is open.

- (Anomaly) An internal protection mechanism shuts down the Green transformer, and its power drops from 24 MVA to zero. The switch connecting the Green bar to the Green transformer opens. (The switch connecting the Red bar to the Red transformer remains closed and the switch connecting the two bars remains open.)
- (Reaction) The switch connecting the Green bar to the Red bar receives the command to close. It closes 1 execution cycle (100 ms) later and the load carried by the Red transformer rises to 56 MVA.

`Function2` (parallel transformers) consists of a series of automatic actions, assisting operators. E.g., an operator can request to turn on a transformer and `function2` translates this request into a specific sequence of commands of opening and closing breakers and insulators. Such a re-insertion scenario can be applied some time after transformer exclusion.

5.1 System Setup

The PSAS application has been developed using a proprietary, automata-based, design environment based on the specification technique *ASFA* [25, 26]. Application development consists of several steps:

- `Function1` and `function2` are extracted from the PSAS application and specified through the *ASFA Graphical Editor* [27], obtaining a tabular description of the pilot application.
- These ASFA tables are processed by the *ASFA-C Translator* [26], producing a target-independent C-code version of the application, and by the *ASFA Partitioner*, allowing an application to be mapped to a single task or decomposed into a set of tasks [25]. A four-task version was selected for testing on the distributed system below.
- At run time, the *Execution Support Module* (ESM) enforces cyclic execution, typical for PLC-based automation systems. Robust execution is ensured by cyclically refreshing the I/O image and the non-protected memory areas, while the application's state is safeguarded by hardware or software mechanisms [24]. The ESM takes care of synchronization, exception handling and a set of ASFA-specific library functions.

A peculiarity of the ASFA environment is that the application code is automatically obtained by translating the automata-based specification [25]. Besides reducing the probability of introducing coding errors, this approach provides portability to all platforms supported by the Execution Support Module. This eased the porting of the application from the dedicated to the standardised platform.

This pilot application was deployed on a distributed, standardised system consisting of three dedicated, heterogeneous industrial processors for the automation functions and two standard PCs for support functions, interconnected by an Ethernet switch:

- N1 and N2: two industrial PCs (*VMIC* and *INOVA*), with *VxWorks* as RTOS;
- N3: *Siemens SIMATIC M7*: an extended PLC with I/O modules, with *RMOS32* as RTOS;
- N4: Linux-based standard PC, which hosts the coordinating tasks of the backbone (i.e. the task which orchestrates the execution of recovery actions);
- N5: Windows-NT PC with Operator Console functions. For inter-site connections (*not considered in this case study*), this node also hosts the gateway software.

Table 1. Allocation of middleware tasks to nodes.

	N1 VxWorks *VMIC* *IPC*	N2 VxWorks *INOVA* *IPC*	N3 RMOS32 *Siemens* *PLC*	N4 Linux *PC*	N5 WinNT *PC*
BSL tasks	*	*	*	*	*
Backbone	slave	slave	slave	master	slave
FTM	*	*	*	*	*
Operator Console					*
ESM	*	*	*		

The pilot automation application (function1 and function2) runs on nodes N1, N2 and N3 of this heterogeneous hardware equipment on which an RTOS is installed. All three *RTOS* nodes (N1, N2 and N3 in Table 1) are attached to I/O components on the field (PU = Peripheral Units on Figure 6). In initial tests, input and output from/to the field is simulated.

Synchronization signals, for the cyclic application execution, are generated by the internal clock of one of the nodes (in a real set-up, they are obtained from an independent, external device). In this setup, node N3 handles the synchronization signal; in order to provide a backup solution in case of a fault on N3, synchronization signals are also available at N1 and N3.

5.2   Instantiating DepAuDE on PSAS

The run-time components of the DepAuDE approach are integrated into the PSAS pilot application (see Table 1). The fault containment region is an entire node, and not a single task, as the involved RTOS does not provide any memory protection functionality.

- A VxWorks resp. RMOS32 implementation of the BSL tasks run on the RTOS nodes N1, N2, resp. N3; a Linux resp. WinNT version runs on the nodes N4 resp. N5.
- An FTM used for detecting crashed or isolated nodes – is present on all nodes.
- The master backbone task, responsible for orchestrating the recovery strategies, is allocated to N4.
- Each of the three RTOS nodes N1, N2, N3 hosts an instance of the ASFA Execution Support Module. Each instance of the ESM is able to act as master (ESM_M, on the master node) or slave (ESM_S, on the slave nodes). The role is chosen depending on the specific system configuration. All ESM_S make up the ESM_SLAVE_GROUP. The configuration with highest performance (see below) requires ESM_M to be allocated to N3 and the ESM_S processes to run on N1 and N2.

The application tasks of the two automation functions (function1 and function2), among which there is no communication, can be allocated in different ways to the RTOS nodes. Function2 consists of a single task, PARALLEL_TRS, while function1 (automatic power resumption) consists of three tasks: two tasks (BUSBAR1 and BUSBAR2) handle low-level, I/O dependent, computations relative to the MV lines attached to each bus bar; one task, STRAT, coordinates the whole function and performs no field I/O. There is no communication between the two BUSBAR tasks, while both communicate with STRAT. The basic constraint for allocating tasks to nodes is that a task that controls a specific sensor or actuator should be allocated to a processor that is attached to these I/O ports. As both functions of the pilot application control the same set of field components (same transformers and switches), all RTOS nodes are assumed to be connected to that portion of the field. In our setup, node N2 provides better computing performance than N1, while N3 has the lowest performance.

The start-up configuration is the optimal distribution of application tasks onto the heterogeneous hardware. The best performing configuration, Config_0 in Table 2, does not require off-node communication among the application tasks:

- no application task is allocated to N3, whose ESM acts as master and handles communication with the operator console on N5;
- PARALLEL_TRS runs on N1;
- BUSBAR1, BUSBAR2, and STRAT are allocated to N2.
- Each application task has at least one standby replica task_Ri on a different target node Ni (i=1..3).

Table 2. Different configurations to allocate active PSAS application tasks to target nodes.

	N1	N2	N3
Config_0	PARALLEL_TRS	STRAT, BUSBAR1, BUSBAR2	–
Config_1	*CRASHED*	PARALLEL_TRS STRAT, BUSBAR1, BUSBAR2	–
Config_2	PARALLEL_TRS	*CRASHED*	STRAT BUSBAR1, BUSBAR2
Config_3	STRAT, BUSBAR1, BUSBAR2	–	*CRASHED*

5.3 PSAS Recovery Strategy

In order to cope with temporary and permanent physical faults affecting the information and communication infrastructure of the PSAS, an appropriate recovery strategy has been designed and coded as a set of Ariel recovery scripts. It combines different kinds of error detection mechanisms, error recovery and system reconfiguration: if a node crashes, the system is reconfigured. If two nodes crash simultaneously, no reconfiguration is possible. The following scripts are examples of recovery actions.

(Example 1) If one of the slave target nodes (e.g., N1) crashes, the FTM detects this event and notifies the backbone executing the following ARIEL code:

```
IF
  [FAULTY NODE{N1} AND RUNNING NODE{N2} AND \
  RUNNING NODE{N3} AND \
  PHASE(TASK{ESM_M}) == {NEW_CYCLE_PH}]
THEN
  ISOLATE NODE{N1}
```

```
SEND {Config_1} TASK{ESM_MSG_M}
SEND {Config_1} GROUP{ESM_SLAVE_GROUP}
RESTART TASK{PARALLEL_TRS_R2}
FI
```

If the condition of the above script is fulfilled, application tasks are reconfigured as
Config_1 from Table 2. Config_1 maintains the full PSAS functionality by transferring Parallel_TRS to N2, actually by activating its backup replica. To avoid
interference among recovery mechanisms, a condition on the current execution phase
of the ESM_M task (**PHASE**(TASK{ESM_M}) == {NEW_CYCLE_PH}) must be satisfied
in conjunction with the crash test. The **ISOLATE** NODE action corresponds to inform-
ing other nodes that they may not accept any message from the isolated peer -even if
it comes alive again- until the isolation is undone.

(Example 2) If a target node (e.g. N2) crashes during a different execution phase of
the master ESM, then this error is notified by the ESM_M to the backbone (through
RaiseEvent(RE_ESM_error)), causing the execution of the following ARIEL
code:

```
IF [EVENT {RE_ESM_error}]
THEN
 IF [FAULTY NODE{N2} AND RUNNING NODE{N3}]
 THEN
  ISOLATE NODE{N2}
  SEND {Config_2} TASK{ESM_MSG_M}
  SEND {Config_2} TASK{ESM_MSG_S1}
  RESTART TASK{BUSBAR1_R3}, TASK{BUSBAR2_R3}, \
TASK{STRAT_R3}
  RESTART TASK{PARALLEL_TRS_R1}
 FI
FI
```

Hence, the system is reconfigured as Config_2: the spare replicas of BUSBAR1,
BUSBAR2 and STRAT are activated on N3.

(Example 3) In case of a fault on target node N3 (where ESM_M is running), the following ARIEL code is executed, triggered by one of the FTM's that detected an error
and subsequently notified the backbone:

```
IF
 [FAULTY NODE{N3} AND RUNNING NODE{N1} AND \
 RUNNING NODE{N2}]
THEN
 ISOLATE NODE{N3}
 SEND {Config_3} GROUP{ESM_SLAVE_GROUP}
 SEND {BACKUP_MASTER} TASK{ESM_MSG_S2}
 STOP TASK{PARALLEL_TRS}
 RESTART TASK{STRAT_R1}, TASK{BUSBAR1_R1}, \
TASK{BUSBAR2_R1}
FI
```

Hence, the function of master ESM node is transferred to N2 and the application
tasks of N2 are moved to N1. As N1 cannot support both application functions simul-

taneously, PARALLEL_TRS is disabled, thus proceeding to a graceful degradation of the automation system (Config_3).

Other recovery strategies, such as restarting all tasks on a node after a transient fault, or shutting down the system when reconfiguration is not possible, have also been coded in ARIEL and implemented. We did not provide recovery strategies associated with a crash of N4 or N5, because they are not RTOS nodes and they are not concerned with the automation control function itself; so even if they crash, the application is not endangered. In a real deployment they could be replicated or could backup each other. Figure 7 shows the user interface of the pilot application demonstrator.

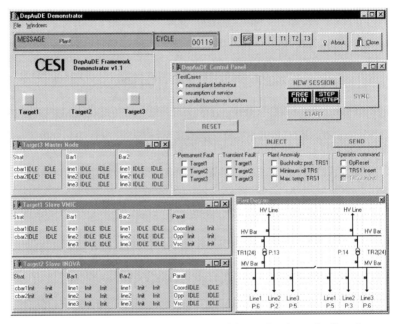

Fig. 7. User interface for application supervision and active task allocation.

The implementation effort required to integrate the DepAuDE BSL into the ASFA design environment was limited (about 2400 lines of code for the RMOS and VxWorks targets). The communication mechanism supplied by the DepAuDE BSL provided transparent inter-process communication among ASFA application tasks. The grouping of tasks revealed useful when implementing the standby replicas. Inter-processor communication among application tasks strongly influences application performance and reconfiguration time in case of faults. Therefore inter-processor data flow should be avoided if possible, or at least minimised.

5.4 Stabilizing Memory

As a different example of a DepAuDE-FTM, a software module has been designed, implementing so-called *stabilizing memory* [27], as a mechanism combining physical with temporal redundancy (and with several protocols) to recover from transient faults affecting memory or computation, and preventing incorrect output to the field. With respect to a pre-existing solution relying exclusively on dedicated hardware boards, this software implementation of the stable memory module supports better maintainability. For instance, it is possible to set parameters for the size of the stabilizing memory, for the number of physically redundant copies, for the number of temporally redundant copies, etc. The developer can also modify the allocation of the physically distributed copies to the available resources. The configuration-and-recovery language ARIEL sets all these configuration parameters as well as the recovery actions to be taken in case an error is detected. The additional flexibility offered by these recovery strategies allows for instance for reconfiguration by re-allocating the distributed copies to non-failed components in case that a fault occurred. The recovery strategies are not hard-coded in the application code, but are described in ARIEL and executed by the backbone that interacts with the modules. As the application interface to the pre-existing dedicated board is identical to the one for software-based stabilizing memory module, the complexity for the designer is equivalent in both implementations.

The DepAuDE-based implementation of the stabilizing memory module meets the real-time requirements of the application, which are in the range from 50 milliseconds to 500 milliseconds. When deployed in an operational PSAS for testing, subject to the electromagnetic interference from the opening and closing of breakers and switches, no incorrect output was identified during the test-period, while the log-files indicated that the stabilizing memory module functioned correctly and masked the introduced errors.

6 Related Work and Conclusion

The configuration-and-recovery language ARIEL and the DepAuDE approach borrow several ideas from existing research and implementations. For instance, the suitability of libraries of software-implemented fault tolerance solutions to improve the dependability of distributed applications has been shown in [8, 29, 30]. Besides, the *middleware* approach towards fault tolerance gained much support recently [31, 32, 33]. The concept of de-coupling the functional application aspects from the non-functional ones concerning fault tolerance, is also present in the meta-object approach, where a call to a method in an object-oriented application is trapped in order to transparently implement some fault tolerance functionality [34, 35].

The presented approach combines the advantages of software-implemented fault tolerance, via a library of functions, with the decoupling of the meta-object approach (but without requiring object orientation) by specifying recovery actions as a sort of ancillary application layer. In addition, the ARIEL language allows for a concise description of distributed actions, especially for expressing recovery strategies.

An alternative strand of work has been performed in the framework of the Common Object Request Broker Architecture (CORBA), where specifications for fault-tolerant CORBA [36] and real-time CORBA [37] have been issued, and several academic and commercial implementations of one of both specifications exist; other implementations try to combine both specifications [38]. However, object-oriented computing (and hence CORBA) was not compatible with our target applications that were written in plain C-code, or in the ASFA design environment that produces C-code as well. Also the TRIO approach was applied to CORBA applications [39].

The DepAuDE approach is two-tiered, comprising middleware with a library of fault tolerance mechanisms and a control backbone, and a configuration-and-recovery language ARIEL. It integrates software-implemented FTM's into distributed automation systems, exploiting the available hardware redundancy. Software-implemented fault tolerance may need to be complemented or replaced by other approaches or techniques on lower levels (hardware or operating system), for instance, to be able to meet hard real-time requirements [40, 41], and/or by application-specific mechanisms.

The DepAuDE approach is especially useful when the lack of flexibility that is inherent to dedicated hardware-based fault tolerance solutions (as often used for automation applications) makes their adoption not cost-effective in cases where similar functionality has to be deployed in several sites, each characterized by a different platform, configuration, environment, etc. The deployment of this DepAuDE architecture on off-the-shelf, heterogeneous platforms allows different recovery scripts to be integrated with the application. Given the generality of the methods and techniques used, the designed solution is applicable to a wide class of process automation systems. Furthermore, the middleware can be reconfigured when the application requirements change, or when environment parameters (such as inter-site bandwidth) change; industrial experience on the Primary Substation Automation System confirms that this adds to the flexibility and the maintainability of the automation application.

Further research is concentrating on collecting dependability data from the deployed configurations and on the challenges posed by the inter-site connections, as well as on a detailed quantitative and qualitative comparison with existing approaches.

Acknowledgements

This project has been partially supported by the K.U.Leuven Research Council (GOA/2001/04), European project IST-2000-25434 (www.depaude.org), and the Fund for Scientific Research - Flanders through "Krediet aan Navorsers" 1.5.148.02. The authors like to thank the DepAuDE project partners for their contributions.

References

1. M. Amin, "Towards self-healing energy infrastructure systems," *IEEE Computer Applications in Power*, vol.14, no.1, pp. 20-28, Jan. 2001.
2. K. Caird, "Integrating Substation Automation", *IEEE Spectrum*, Aug. 1997, pp. 64-69.
3. T.E. Dy-Liacco, "Control centers are here to stay," *IEEE Computer Appl. in Power*, Vol. 15, No. 4, Oct. 2002, pp. 18-23.
4. G. Deconinck, V. De Florio, R. Belmans, G. Dondossola, J. Szanto, "Experiences with integrating recovery strategies into a primary substation automation system," *Proc. of Int. Conf. on Dependable Systems and Networks (DSN-2003), Dependable Computing and Communications Symp.*, San Francisco, CA, Jun. 22-25, 2003, pp. 80-85.
5. G. Deconinck, V. De Florio, O. Botti: "Software-Implemented Fault Tolerance and Separate Recovery Strategies Enhance Maintainability," *IEEE Trans. Reliability*, Vol. 51, No. 2, Jun. 2002, pp. 158-165.

6. G. Deconinck, V. De Florio, R. Lauwereins, R. Belmans, "A Software Library, a Control Backbone and User-Specified Recovery Strategies to Enhance the Dependability of Embedded Systems," *Proc. 25th Euromicro Conf., Worksh. on Dependable Computing Systems*, Milan, Italy, Sep. 1999, pp. II 98-104.
7. V. De Florio, "A Fault Tolerance Linguistic Structure for Distributed Applications", *PhD thesis*, Katholieke Universiteit Leuven, Belgium, Oct. 2000.
8. D.K. Pradhan, "Fault-tolerant Computer System Design", *Prentice Hall*, Upper Saddle River, New Jersey, 1996.
9. V. De Florio, G. Deconinck, "REL: A Fault-Tolerance Linguistic Structure for Distributed Applications," *Proc. 9th IEEE Conf. and Workshop on Engineering of Computer-Based Systems (ECBS-2002)*, Lund, Sweden, Apr. 2002, pp. 51-58.
10. R. Gargiuli, P.G. Mirandola, *et al.*, "ENEL Approach to Computer Supervisory Remote Control of Electric Power Distribution Network," *Proc. 6th IEE Int. Conf. on Electricity Distribution (CIRED'81)*, Brighton (UK), 1981, pp. 187-192.
11. P. Veríssimo, L. Rodrigues, "Distributed Systems for System Architects," *Kluwer Academic Publishers*, Boston, 2001, 648p.
12. G. P. Nizzoli, G. Mazzini, "Map Discovery Procedures in Internet Protocol Version 6", *Proc. IEEE 10th Int. Conf. on software, telecommunications and computer networks (SOFTCOM 2002)*, Split, Croatia, Oct. 2002, pp. 204-208.
13. G. Mazzini, G.P. Nizzoli, P. Bergamo, "Measurements of Redundant Source-Routing," *Proc. IEEE 10th Int. Conf. on software, telecommunications and computer networks (Soft-COM2002)*, Split, Croatia, Oct. 2002, pp. 95-99.
14. R. Tirtea, G. Deconinck, V. De Florio, R. Belmans: "QoS monitoring at middleware level for dependable distributed automation systems," *Suppl.Proc. 13th Int. Symp. on Software Reliability Engineering (ISSRE-2002)*, Annapolis, Maryland, Nov. 2002, pp. 217-218.
15. R. Tirtea, G. Deconinck, V. De Florio, R. Belmans, "Using Resource Monitoring to Select Recovery Strategies," accepted for Reliability and Maintainability Symposium (*RAMS-2004*) (IEEE Reliability Soc.), Los Angeles, CA, USA, Jan. 26-29, 2004.
16. International Electrotechnical Commission, "IEC60300: Dependability Management", http://www.iec.ch.
17. C. Ghezzi, D. Mandrioli, A. Morzenti, "TRIO a Logic Language for Executable Specifications of Real-time Systems", *Journal of Systems and Software*, Jun. 1990.
18. S. Bernardi, "Building Stochastic Petri Net models for the verification of complex software systems," Ph.D. Thesis, University of Turin (Italy), Dept of Informatics, 2003.
19. S. Bernardi, S. Donatelli, J. Merseguer, "From UML Sequence Diagrams and StateCharts to analysable Petri Net models," *ACM Proc. 3rd Int. Worksh. on Software and Performance (WOSP02)*, Rome (Italy), July 2002, pp. 35-45.
20. S. Bernardi, S. Donatelli, "Building Petri net scenarios for dependable automation systems," *IEEE Proc. 10th Int. Workshop on Petri Nets and Performance Models (PNPM2003)*, Urbana-Champaign, Illinois (USA), Sep. 2003, pp. 72-81.
21. DepAuDE, "Dependability requirements in the developments of wide-scale distributed automation system: a methodological guidance," Deliverable D1.4, project IST-2000-25434 (available from www.depaude.org).
22. G. Dondossola, O. Botti, "System Fault Tolerance Specification: Proposal of a Method Combining Semi-formal and Formal Approaches," Proc. 3rd Int Conf. on Fundamental Approaches to Software Engineering (FASE 2000), LNCS 1783 (Springer), Berlin, Germany, Mar. 2000, pp. 82-96
23. F. Maestri. R. Meda, G.L. Redaelli, "Un ambiente di sviluppo di funzioni applicative strutturate per sistemi di automazione di impianti ENEL," *Automazione e strumentazione*, Dec. 1997); in Italian.
24. R. Meda, A. Bertani, P. Colombo, S. D'Imporzano, P. Perna, "Il Sistema di Protezione e Controllo della Cabina Primaria", ENEL internal report, Feb. 1999; in Italian.

25. E. Ciapessoni, F. Maestri *et al.*, "Partitioning of Hierarchical Automation Systems," *Proc. Euromicro Conf. on Real-time Systems*, Delft, The Netherlands, Jun. 2001, pp. 143-153.
26. A. Moro, "Traduttore delle reti ASFA," *Tesi di laurea*, Politecnico di Milano, Milan, Italy, 1998; in Italian.
27. Anonymous, "Editor Grafico di ASFA – Manuale Utente", *ENEL internal report*, ENEL SpA, Milan, Italy, 1995; in Italian.
28. G. Deconinck, O. Botti, F. Cassinari, V. De Florio, R. Lauwereins, "Stable Memory in Substation Automation: a Case Study," *Proc. 28th Ann. Int. Symp. on Fault-Tolerant Computing (FTCS)*, Munich, Germany, Jun. 1998, pp. 452-457.
29. Y. Huang, C.M.R. Kintala, "Software Fault Tolerance in the Application Layer", *chapter of* "Software Fault Tolerance", M. Lyu (Ed.), *John Wiley & Sons*, Mar. 1995.
30. M.R. Lyu (Ed.), "Handbook of Software Reliability Engineering", *McGraw-Hill*, New York, 1995.
31. Z.T. Kalbarczyk, R.K. Iyer, S. Bagchi, K. Whisnant, "Chameleon: A Software Infrastructure for Adaptive Fault Tolerance", *IEEE Trans. On Parallel and Distributed Systems*, Vol. 10, No. 6, Jun. 1999, pp. 560-579.
32. K.H. Kim, "ROAFTS: A Middleware Architecture for Real-time Object-oriented Adaptive Fault Tolerance Support", *Proc. HASE '98 (IEEE CS 1998 High-Assurance Systems Engineering Symp.)*, Washington, D.C., Nov. 1998, pp. 50-57.
33. R. Yansong, D. Bakken, T. Courtney, M. Cukier, D.A. Karr, P. Rubel, C. Sabnis, W.H. Sanders, R.E. Schantz, "AQuA: an adaptive architecture that provides dependable distributed objects," *IEEE Trans. on Computers*, Vol. 52, No. 1, Jan. 2003, pp. 31-50.
34. J.-C. Fabre, T. Pérennou, "A Metaobject Architecture for Fault-Tolerant Distributed Systems: The FRIENDS Approach", *IEEE Trans. on Computers* (Special issue on dependability of computing systems), Vol. 47, Jan. 1998, pp. 78-95.
35. G. Kiczales, J. des Rivières, D. G. Bobrow, "The Art of the Metaobject Protocol", *The MIT Press*, Cambridge, MA, 1991.
36. Object Management Group, Fault Tolerant CORBA, V3.0.3, Mar. 2004. Available from www.omg.org.
37. Object Management Group, Real-time CORBA, V2.0, Nov. 2003. Available from www.omg.org.
38. A.S. Gokhale, D.C. Schmidt, J.K. Cross, C. Andrews, S.J. Fernandez, B. Natarajan, N. Wang, C.D. Gill, "Towards Real-time Support in Fault-tolerant CORBA", *Proc. IEEE Workshop on Dependable Middleware-Based Systems*, Washington, D.C., Jun. 2002.
39. A. Coen-Porisini, M. Pradella, M. Rossi, D. Mandrioli, "A Formal Approach for Designing CORBA based Applications," *ACM Transactions on Software Engineering and Methodology (TOSEM)*, 12(2), Apr. 2003.
40. D. Powell, J. Arlat, L. Beus-Dukic, A. Bondavalli, P. Coppola, A. Fantechi, E. Jenn, C. Rabéjac, A. Wellings, "GUARDS: A Generic Upgradeable Architecture for Real-Time Dependable Systems, *IEEE Trans. On Parallel and Distributed Systems*, Vol. 10, No. 6, Jun. 1999, pp. 580-597.
41. B. Randell, J.-C. Laprie, H. Kopetz, B. Littlewood (Eds.), "ESPRIT Basic Research Series: Predictably Dependable Computing Systems", *Springer-Verlag*, Berlin, 1995.

A Dependable Architecture for COTS-Based Software Systems Using Protective Wrappers

Paulo Asterio de C. Guerra[1], Cecília Mary F. Rubira[1],
Alexander Romanovsky[2], and Rogério de Lemos[3]

[1] Instituto de Computação Universidade Estadual de Campinas, Brazil
{asterio,cmrubira}@ic.unicamp.br
[2] School of Computing Science, University of Newcastle upon Tyne, UK
alexander.romanovsky@ncl.ac.uk
[3] Computing Laboratory, University of Kent at Canterbury, UK
r.delemos@ukc.ac.uk

Abstract. Commercial off-the-shelf (COTS) software components are built to be used as black boxes that cannot be modified. The specific context in which these COTS components are employed is not known to their developers. When integrating such COTS components into systems, which have high dependability requirements, there may be mismatches between the failure assumptions of these components and the rest of the system. For resolving these mismatches, system integrators must rely on techniques that are external to the COTS software components. In this paper, we combine the concepts of an idealised architectural component and protective wrappers to develop an architectural solution that provides an effective and systematic way for building dependable software systems from COTS software components.

1 Introduction

A commercial off-the-shelf (COTS) software component is usually provided as a black box to be reused "as it is". Most of the time these components do not have a rigorously written specification, hence there is no guarantee that their description is correct (very often, it is ambiguous and incomplete). Moreover, these components may have faults, and the specific context in which they will be used is not known during their development. Once they are created, they can evolve over time through different versions. When an integrator builds a system out of COTS components, she/he can be forced to evolve the system whenever a new version of these COTS components is released. These new versions can be sources of new faults. When integrating such components into a system, solutions for meeting its overall dependability requirements should be envisaged at the architectural level, independently of the particular COTS versions. These solutions should ensure that the system delivers the service despite the presence of faults in the COTS component and how it interacts with other system components. In this paper, we focus on COTS software components that are integrated in a system at the application level and provide their services to other components and, possibly, use services provided by them. We assume that these application level software components are deployed in a reliable runtime environment that may include other COTS software components at the infrastructure level, such as operating systems, distribution middleware and component frameworks.

R. de Lemos et al. (Eds.): Architecting Dependable Systems II, LNCS 3069, pp. 144–166, 2004.

Research into describing software architectures with respect to their dependability properties has recently gained considerable attention [20,24,25]. In this paper, we focus on the architectural description of fault-tolerant component-based systems that provides an effective and systematic way for building dependable software systems from COTS software components. For that, we combine the concepts of an idealised architectural component [8], which is based on the idealised fault-tolerant component [2], and protective wrappers [15], known to be the most general approach to developing dependable software systems based on COTS components. While in previous work we have described the basis of the proposed approach [9,10], in this paper we elaborate on that work by discussing guidelines for specifying and implementing protective wrappers and by demonstrating our ideas using a case study.

The rest of the paper is organised as follows. In the next section, we briefly discuss background work on architectural mismatches, wrapper protectors, and the C2 architectural style. Section 3 describes the architectural representation of idealised fault-tolerant COTS, in terms of the idealised C2 component (iC2C), the idealised C2 COTS component (iCOTS), and the process of architecting fault-tolerant systems using iCOTS components. The case study demonstrating the feasibility of the proposed approach is presented in section 4. Related work on how to build dependable software systems based on COTS components is discussed in section 5. Finally, section 6 presents some concluding remarks and discusses future work.

2   Background

When integrating COTS components into a software system, the architect needs to develop glue code [18] that links various components together and includes new architectural elements, or *adaptors*, to resolve the different kinds of incompatibilities that may exist. A protector is a special kind of adaptor that deals with incompatibilities in the failure assumptions.

2.1   Architectural Mismatches and COTS Component Integration

Dealing with architectural mismatches [7] is one of the most difficult problems system integrators face when developing systems from COTS components. An *architectural mismatch* occurs when the assumptions that a component makes about another component or the rest of the system (ROS) do not match. That is, the assumptions associated with the service provided by the component are different from the assumptions associated with the services required by the component for behaving as specified [13]. When building systems from existing components, it is inevitable that incompatibilities between the service delivered by the component and the service that the ROS expects from that component give rise to such mismatches. These mismatches are not exclusive to the functional attributes of the component; mismatches may also include dependability attributes related, for example, to the component failure mode assumptions or its safety integrity levels.

We view all incompatibilities between a COTS component and the ROS as architectural mismatches. This, for example, includes internal faults of a COTS component that affect other system's components or its environment, in which case the failure assumptions of the component were wrong.

2.2 COTS Component Protectors

Component wrapping is a well-known structuring technique that has been used in several areas. In this paper, we use the term "wrapper" in a very broad sense, incorporating the concepts of wrappers, mediators, and bridges [6]. A *wrapper* is a specialised component inserted between a component and its environment to deal with the flows of control and data going to and/or from the wrapped component. The need for wrapping arises when (i) it is impossible or expensive to change the components when reusing them as parts of a new system, or (ii) it is easier to add new features by incorporating them into wrappers. Wrapping is a structured and a cost-effective solution to many problems in component-based software development. Wrappers can be employed for improving quality properties of the components such as adding caching and buffering, dealing with mismatches or simplifying the component interface. With respect to dependability, wrappers are usually used for ensuring properties such as security and transparent component replication.

A systematic approach has been proposed for using protective wrappers, known as *protectors*, that can improve the overall system dependability [15]. This is achieved by protecting both the system against erroneous behaviour of a COTS component, and the COTS component against erroneous behaviour of the rest of the system (ROS). As a protector has this dual role we call the interface between the COTS and the ROS the *protected interface*. The protectors are viewed as redundant software that detects errors or suspicious activity on a protected interface and executes appropriate recovery.

The development of protectors occurs during the assembly stage of the development process of a COTS-based system, as part of the system integration activities [15]. The approach consists of rigorous specification of the protector functionality, in terms of error detection and associated recovery actions, and in their integration into the software architecture. The protector error detection capabilities are specified in the form of *acceptable behaviour constraints* (ABCs) that ensure the normal behaviour of the protected interface. The protector recovery actions are specified in the form of exception handlers associated with the erroneous conditions that may arise in the protected interface. The protector specification is based on a set of *blueprints* and *safety specifications* that are produced during the earlier stages of the development process. A blueprint is a documented entity that specifies the overall architecture and external behaviour of a piece of software [3]. Safety specifications are derived from the system's safety requirements [5], which focus on reducing the risk associated with hazards and on limiting damage when an accident occurs. The general sources of information to be used in developing both ABCs and possible actions to be undertaken in response to their violations are the following:

1. The behaviour specification of COTS components as specified by the COTS's developers. This specification is materialized in the form of a *COTS blueprint* that is provided to the system designers as part of the COTS documentation.
2. The behaviour specification of a COTS component as specified by the system designers. This specification is materialized in the form of a *component blueprint* that is produced by the system designers during the specification phase of the system's development process. The component blueprint and the COTS blueprint must satisfy certain mutual constraints for the system design to be correct, but they will not be identical. E.g., the system designer's description requires the COTS compo-

nent to be able to react to a set of stimuli that is a subset of the set specified by the COTS's developers.

3. The description of the actual behaviour that the system designer expects from a COTS component (not necessarily approving it) based on previous experiences, i.e., he/she may know that it often fails in response to certain legal stimuli. The system designers describe this behaviour in an *annotated COTS blueprint.*

4. The behaviour specified for the ROS. This specification is materialized in a *system blueprint.*

5. The behaviour specification of the undesirable behaviour, especially unacceptable, of the component and the rest of the system, respectively, the *component safety specifications* and the *system safety specifications*. The system designer produces these during the specification stage of the development process.

The sources of information above allow the developer to formulate a number of statements describing the correct behaviour of the system (consisting in this case of the COTS component and of the ROS). The statements are expressed as a set of assertions on the states of input and output parameters. In addition to that, they may include assertions on the histories (sequences of calls) and assertions on the states of the system components.

2.3   The C2 Architectural Style

The C2 architectural style is a component-based style that supports large grain reuse and flexible system composition, emphasizing weak bindings between components [26]. In this style, components of a system are completely unaware of each other, as when one integrates various COTS components, which may have heterogeneous styles and implementation languages. These components communicate only through asynchronous messages mediated by connectors that are responsible for message routing, broadcasting and filtering. Interface and architectural mismatches are dealt with by means of wrappers that encapsulate each component.

In the C2 architectural style both components and connectors have a *top interface* and a *bottom interface*. Systems are composed in a layered style, where the top interface of a component may be connected to the bottom interface of a connector and its bottom interface may be connected to the top interface of another connector. Each side of a connector may be connected to any number of components or connectors.

There are two types of messages in C2: requests and notifications. *Requests* flow up through the system layers and *notifications* flow down. In response to a request, a component may emit a notification back to the components below, through its bottom interface. Upon receiving a notification, a component may react with the *implicit invocation* of one of its operations.

While in this section we have introduced a background on protectors and iC2C, in the next section we propose an architectural solution for turning COTS components into idealised fault-tolerant COTS components (iCOTS) by adding protective wrappers to them. Although in previous work we introduced the iCOTS concept [9, 10], in this paper we provide a detailed description of the iCOTS concept, a systematic description of the engineering steps to be used when applying the proposed solution, and a description of a case study used to evaluate this solution.

3   Idealised Fault-Tolerant COTS Component

Modern large scale systems usually integrate COTS components which may act as service providers and/or service users. Since, there is no control, or even full knowledge, over the design, implementation and evolution of COTS components, the evolutionary process of a COTS component should be considered as part of a complex environment, physical and logical, that might directly affect the system components. In order to build a dependable software system from untrustworthy COTS components, the system should treat these components as a potential source of faults. The overall software system should be able to support COTS components while preventing the propagation of errors. In other words, the system should be able to tolerate faults that may reside or occur inside the COTS components, while not being able to directly inspect or modify their internal states or behaviour.

In this paper we present the concept of an *idealised fault-tolerant COTS component*, which is an architectural solution that encapsulates a COTS component adding fault tolerance capabilities to allow it to be integrated in a larger system. These fault tolerant capabilities are related to the activities associated with error processing, that is, error detection and error recovery. The idealised fault-tolerant COTS component is a specialization of the idealised C2 Component (iC2C) [8] that is briefly described in the following section.

3.1   The Idealised C2 Component (iC2C)

The idealised C2 component (iC2C) is equivalent, in terms of behaviour and structure, to the idealised fault-tolerant component [2]; it was proposed to allow structuring of software architectures compliant with the C2 architectural style [26]. The C2 style was chosen for its orientation towards independent components that do not communicate directly. This makes it easier for the system developers to isolate critical components from the ROS.

Service requests and normal responses of an idealised fault-tolerant component are mapped as requests and notifications in the C2 architectural style. Interface and failure exceptions of an idealised fault-tolerant component are considered to be subtypes of notifications. In order to minimize the impact of fault tolerance provisions on the system complexity, we have decoupled the normal activity and abnormal activity parts of the idealised component. This has lead us to developing an overall structure for the iC2C that has two distinct components and three connectors, as shown in Figure 1.

The iC2C NormalActivity component implements the normal behaviour, and is responsible for error detection during normal operation and for signalling the interface and internal exceptions. The iC2C AbnormalActivity component is responsible for error recovery and for signalling the failure exceptions. For consistency, the signalling of an internal exception by an idealised fault-tolerant component is viewed as a subtype of notification, and, the "return to normal", flowing in the opposite direction, is viewed as a request. During error recovery, the AbnormalActivity component may also emit requests and receive notifications, which are not shown in Figure 1.

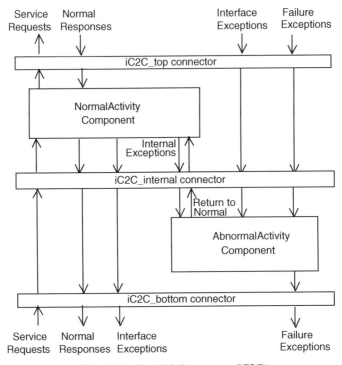

Fig. 1. Idealised C2 Component (iC2C).

The iC2C connectors are specialized reusable C2 connectors, which have the following roles:

1. The iC2C_bottom connector connects the iC2C with the lower components of a C2 configuration and serializes the requests received. Once a request is accepted, it queues new requests that are received until completion of the first request. When a request is completed, a notification is sent back, which may be a normal response, an interface exception or a failure exception.
2. The iC2C_internal connector controls message flow inside the iC2C, selecting the destination of each message received based on its originator, the message type and the operational state of the iC2C;
3. The iC2C_top connector connects the iC2C with the upper components of a C2 configuration.

The overall structure defined for the idealised C2 component is fully compliant with the component rules of the C2 architectural style. This allows an iC2C to be integrated into any C2 configuration and to interact with components of a larger system. When this interaction establishes a chain of iC2C components, the external exceptions raised by a component can be handled by a lower level component (in the C2 sense of "upper" and "lower") allowing hierarchical structuring.

3.2   Guidelines for Turning COTS into iC2C

In this section we show how the development of protectors can be included in the development process of a COTS-based software system. Typically, a COTS-based development process can be divided into six stages [4]: requirements, specification, provisioning, assembly (or integration), test and deployment. The requirements stage aims to identify the system's requirements. During the specification stage the system is decomposed in a set of components with specific responsibilities that interact to fulfil the system requirements. These components are instantiated during the provisioning stage. During this stage the system integrator decides if a component can be instantiated by an existing 'off-the-shelf' component, herein called a *COTS instance*, or if it will require an implementation effort, in which case it is called an *in-house instance*. During the assembly stage the system designer integrates COTS and in-house instances to build the whole system. This integration effort includes the development of glue code necessary to connect the various components, which include the specification and implementation of protectors. During the test stage the integrated system is tested and corrections may be made to ascertain that it fulfils its requirements and conforms to its specification. During the deployment stage the final system is installed in the user's environment.

The presented guidelines are applied to the provisioning and assembly stages of the development process. We assume that the following artefacts, as described in Section 2.2, have already been produced: (i) a system blueprint describing the initial software architecture and the system's safety specifications; and (ii) a set of component's blueprints specifying the components' interfaces and their safety specifications.

3.2.1   Steps for the Provisioning Stage

Step 1.   Develop a basic test plan for the component. This test plan should be based on the expected operational profile [11] of the component in the system being developed.

Step 2.   List candidate COTS components. One should obtain a list of candidate COTS software components that could be used to instantiate the provided interfaces specified in the component's blueprint.

For each candidate COTS component, execute steps 3 to 6, as below.

Step 3.   Consolidate COTS blueprint. One should obtain from the COTS vendor (or developer) the following information, which are consolidated in the COTS blueprint.

   a) The specification of the COTS provided interfaces, which is commonly referred to as the COTS API (Application Programming Interface).
   b) The specification of the COTS required interfaces, which is commonly referred as the COTS System Requirements.
   c) Information about known design faults in the COTS, which is usually found in sections called 'Known Bugs and Problems'.
   d) Any information that may give a "grey-box" view of the COTS, with selected details visible only [14]. Usually, this information may be found in technical articles and white papers from the COTS developers.

Step 4.   Test the COTS. One should test the COTS instance applying the basic test plan previously developed. The results obtained from these tests should be documented with information about:

a) The subset of the COTS interfaces (provided and required) activated during the tests.
b) The input domains covered by the tests.
c) The erroneous conditions detected and the observed COTS behaviour under those conditions.
d) Discrepancies between the behaviour specified in the COTS blueprint and its actual observed behaviour.

Step 5.   Enhance test coverage. One should revise the test plan and repeat the testing procedure until adequate test coverage is attained. Test coverage influences reliability, as higher test coverage is more likely to remove a greater number of software faults, leading to a lower failure rate and higher reliability [19]. The final tests should detect all known design faults in the COTS that can be activated under the component's expected operational profile. The test plan should also include test cases based on the "grey-box" view of the COTS.

Step 6.   Produce the annotated COTS blueprint. The annotated COTS blueprint consolidates the information obtained about the COTS actual behaviour. This annotated COTS blueprint is based on the COTS blueprint, the system's safety specifications and the results of the final tests and should include:

a) Detailed specifications of the actual behaviour of the interfaces that were activated during the tests, under both normal and erroneous inputs.
b) Specification of potentially dangerous conditions associated with the interfaces that were not activated during the tests.
c) Additional information that may be available from previous use of the same COTS instance.

Step 7.   Select COTS instance. If there are two or more candidate COTS instances being considered, select the one that fits best in the system. This selection is based on the information contained in the system blueprint and the various annotated COTS blueprints. For this selection, it may be necessary to develop alternate versions of the system blueprint adapted to limitations and requirements specific to each COTS instance. The result of this step is a revised system's blueprint with the version of the software architecture that includes the selected COTS instance wrapped by a protector (to be developed during the assembly stage).

Step 8.   Decide COTS integration. At this point, it should be decided between the system integration using the selected COTS instance or, alternatively, using a new component to be developed in-house.

3.2.2   Steps for the Assembly Stage

Step 9.   Classify erroneous conditions. One should define a set of generalised erroneous conditions that may arise in the protected interface. The erroneous (or dangerous) conditions specified in the annotated COTS blueprint (Step 6) are analyzed in view of the system's safety specification and classified according to how and in what extent they may affect the system's dependability requirements. For each resulting class it is defined a generalised exceptional condition.

Step 10. Specify acceptable behaviour constraints (ABCs) associated to the erroneous conditions. This specification is based on the information contained in the annotated COTS blueprint. The ABCs may include assertions on:

a) The domain of parameters and results of the requests that flow between the COTS instance and the ROS.

b) The history of messages exchanged through the interface.

c) Portions of the internal state of system's components that can be inspected by calling side-effect-free functions.

Step 11. Specify the desired system's exceptional behaviour. This exceptional behaviour defines the error recovery goals, which may depend on the type and severity of the errors detected. The main source of this specification is the system's safety specifications

Step 12. Allocate error recovery responsibilities. The system's exceptional behaviour specified in the preceding step is decomposed in a set of recovery actions assigned to specific components in the software architecture. Some of these responsibilities will be allocated to the protector associated to the selected COTS instance (Step 7). These recovery actions are also specified during this step.

Step 13. Refine the software architecture. This refinement decomposes the components involved with error processing (Step 11) into new architectural elements that will be responsible for error processing.

Step 14. Implement error detectors. The specified ABCs (Step 10) are implemented as the executable assertions encapsulated in two error detectors that act as message filters. The first error detector intercepts and monitors the service requests that flow from the ROS to the COTS and the corresponding results that flow back to the ROS. The second error detector intercepts and monitors the service requests that flow from the COTS to the ROS and the corresponding results that flow back to the COTS. The error detector intercepts these messages and verifies their associated assertions before delivering the message. When an ABC violation is detected the error detector raises an exception of a specific type associated with this ABC. The exception raised contains the pending message that, in this case, is not delivered to its recipient. Messages that do not cause an ABC violation are delivered to their recipients without change.

Step 15. Implement error handlers. The specified recovery actions (Step 12) are implemented in error handlers associated with the various exception types. These error handlers can be attached to the respective components of the architecture. This placement depends on the scope of the recovery action, which may vary from a single component instance to the whole system.

Step 16. Integrate the protectors. During this step, the COTS instances are integrated with their associated error detectors (Step 14) and errors handlers (Step 15) as specified by the refined software architecture (Step 13). The result of this step is a set of COTS instances in the form of iC2C.

Step 17. Integrate the system. During this step, the COTS instances are integrated with the in-house instances to produce the final system.

The integration of COTS instances in the form of iC2C into a C2 architectural configuration will be the topic of the next section. Such architectural configuration will contain iC2Cs for structuring in-house instances, and idealised C2 COTS component (iCOTS) for structuring COTS instances and their respective protective wrappers.

3.3 Idealised C2 COTS (iCOTS) Overall Architecture

A protective wrapper for a COTS software component is a special type of application-specific fault-tolerance capability. To be effective, the design of fault-tolerance capabilities must be concerned with architectural issues, such as process distribution and communication mode, that impact the overall system dependability. Although the C2 architectural style is specially suited for integrating COTS components into a larger system, its rules on topology and communication are not adequate for incorporating fault tolerance mechanisms into C2 software architectures, especially the mechanisms used for error detection and fault containment [8]. The idealised C2 fault-tolerant component (iC2C) architectural solution (section 3.1) overcomes these problems leveraging the C2 architectural style to allow such COTS software components to be integrated in dependable systems.

The idealised C2 COTS component (iCOTS) is a specialization of the iC2C that employs protective wrappers for encapsulating a COTS component. In our approach, the COTS component is connected to two specialized connectors acting as error detectors (Figure 2) to compose the NormalActivity component of the iCOTS. These detectors are responsible for verifying that the messages that flow to/from the COTS being wrapped do not violate the acceptable behaviour constraints specified for that system.

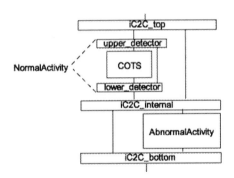

Fig. 2. Idealised C2 COTS (iCOTS) Overall Structure.

The lower_detector inspects incoming requests and outgoing responses (C2 notifications) from/to the COTS clients while the upper_detector inspects outgoing requests and incoming responses to/from other components providing services to the COTS. In the context of the overall diagram, the iC2C_bottom connector connects the iCOTS with the lower components of a C2 configuration, and serializes the requests received. The iC2C_internal connector controls message flow inside the iCOTS. The iC2C_top connector connects the iCOTS with the upper components of a C2 configuration.

When a constraint violation is detected, the detector sends an exception notification, which will be handled by the AbnormalActivity component, following the rules defined for the iC2C. Any of these detectors may be decomposed in a set of special purpose error detectors that, in their turn, are wrapped by a pair of connectors. For example, Figure 3 shows an upper_detector decomposed into a number of error

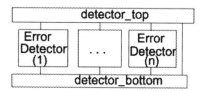

Fig. 3. Decomposition of a Detector.

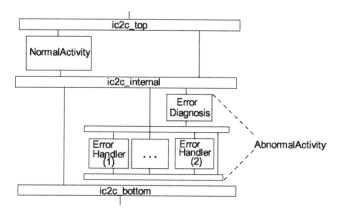

Fig. 4. Decomposition of the AbnormalActivity.

detectors. The detector_bottom coordinates error detection, and the detector_top connects the whole detector either to the COTS or to the iC2C top_connector.

The AbnormalActivity component is responsible for both error diagnosis and error recovery. Depending on the complexity of these tasks, it may be convenient to decompose it into more specialized components for error diagnosis and a set of error handlers, as shown in Figure 4. In this design, the ErrorDiagnosis component is able to react directly to exceptions raised by the NormalActivity component and send notifications to activate the ErrorHandlers or, alternatively, to stand as a service provider of requests sent by the ErrorHandlers.

4 Case Study

In this section, we present a case study that demonstrates the applicability of the iCOTS architectural solution when dealing with mismatches in the failure assumptions of COTS software components.

4.1 Problem Statement

Anderson et. al. [1] present the results of a case study in protective wrapper development [15], in which a Simulink model of a steam boiler system is used together with an off-the-shelf PID (Proportional, Integral and Derivative) controller. The protective wrappers are developed to allow detection and recovery from typical errors caused by unavailability of signals, violations of limitations, and oscillations.

The boiler system comprises the following components: the physical boiler, the control system and the rest of the system (ROS). In turn, the control system consists of PID controllers, which are the COTS components, and the ROS consisting of:

1. Sensors - these are "smart" sensors that monitor variables providing input to the PID controllers: the drum level, the steam flow, the steam pressure, the gas concentrations and the coal feeder rate.
2. Actuators - these devices control a heating burner that can be ON/OFF, and adjust inlet/outlet valves in response to outputs from the PID controllers: the feed water flow, the coal feeder rate and the air flow.
3. Boiler Controller - this device allows to enter the configuration set-points for the system: the steam load and the coal quality, which must be set up in advance by the operators.

The Simulink model represents the control system as three PID controllers dealing with the feed water flow, the coal feeder rate and the air flow. These three controllers output three variables: feed water flow (F_wf), coal feeder rate (C_fr) and air flow (Air_f), respectively; these three variables, together with two configuration set-points (coal quality and steam load) constitute the parameters which determine the behaviour of the boiler system. There are also several internal variables generated by the smart sensors. Some of these, together with the configuration set-points, provide the inputs to the PID controllers, in particular: bus pressure set-point (P_ref), O_2 set-point ($O2\_ref$), drum level (D_l), steam flow (S_f), steam pressure/drum (P_d), steam pressure/bus (P_b), O_2 concentration at economizer ($O2eco$), CO concentration at economizer ($Coeco$), and NOx concentration at economizer ($Noxeco$).

4.2   The Provisioning Stage

In this case study, we assume that the provisioning stage has been completed with the selection of a COTS PID Controller instance, as mentioned in Step 7 (Select COTS instance) of Section 3.2.1 (Steps for the Provisioning Stage). Anderson et. al. [1] summarise the available information describing the correct COTS component behaviour to be used in developing the protective wrappers. This document play the role of the annotated COTS blueprint mentioned in Step 6 (Produce the annotated COTS blueprint). Figure 5 shows the initial software architecture that is part of the system blueprint (Section 3.2). This architecture, which is based on the C2 architectural style, is organized in four layers: (i) the BoilerController component; (ii) the WaterFlow-Controller and CoalFeederController; (iii) the AirFlowController, which has as input the CoalFeederRate from the CoalFeederController; and (iv) the sensors and actuators required by the system. Table 1 specifies the operations provided by some key components that appear in Figure 5.

4.3   The Assembly Stage

The following paragraphs illustrate the assembly stage, starting from Step 9 of Section 3.2.2 (Steps for the Assembly Stage).

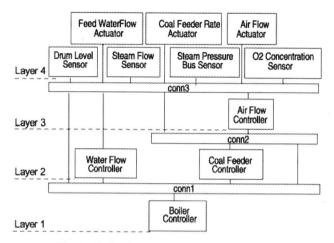

Fig. 5. C2 Configuration for the Boiler System.

Table 1. List of Operations.

Operation	Provider Component
readDrumLevel() : D_l	Drum Level Sensor
readSteamFlow() : S_f	Steam Flow Sensor
readBusPressure() : P_b	Steam Pressure Bus Sensor
readO2Concentration() : O2eco	O_2 Concentration Sensor
setFeedWaterFlow(F_wf)	Feed Water Flow Actuator
setCoalFeedRate(C_fr)	Cool Feeder Rate Actuator Air Flow Controller
setAirFlow(Air_f)	Air Flow Actuator
setConfiguration(P_ref, O2_ref)	Coal Feeder Controller Air Flow Controller

*Step 9.   Define a set of generalised erroneous conditions that may arise in the pro-
tected interface.* Three types of such erroneous conditions are considered: (i) unavailability of inputs/outputs to/from the PID controllers; (ii) violation of specifications of monitored variables; and (iii) oscillations in monitored variables.

*Step 10. Specify acceptable behaviour constraints (ABCs) associated to the errone-
ous conditions.* These ABCs are summarized in the second column of Table 2
(ABC to be checked).

Step 11. Specify the desired system's exceptional behaviour. Depending on the severity of the errors and on the specific characteristics of the system, two types of
recovery are used in the case study: raising an alarm and safe stop.

Step 12. Allocate error recovery responsibilities. The AirFlowController, Water-
FlowController and CoalFeederController components are responsible for error detection (ABCs violations). The BoilerController component is responsible
for error recovery, which may be either to sound an alarm or to shut down the
system, depending on the exception type.

Step 13. Refine the software architecture. The proposed solution applies the concepts of iCOTS and iC2C for structuring four components. The AirFlowController, WaterFlowController and CoalFeederController components are structured as iCOTS components that encapsulate a COTS instance (the COTS PID controller) wrapped by a protector. The BoilerController component is structured as an iC2C, to be provided as an in-house instance. Next we describe how we can build an iCOTS AirFlowController encapsulating a COTS PID controller wrapped by a protector. This solution equally applies to the WaterFlowController and CoalFeederController components.

Table 2. Error Detection Specifications.

Message Type	ABC to be checked	Exceptional Notification
Lower Detector		
Request setConfiguration (P_ref, O2_ref)	$0 <= O2\_ref <= 0.1$	InvalidConfigurationSetpoint
	corresponding notification must be received within a specified time interval	PIDTimeout
Request setCoalFeeder (C_fr)	$0 <= C\_fr <= 1$	InvalidCoalFeederRate
	check_oscillate(Air_f)	CoalFeederRateOscillating
	corresponding notification must be received within a specified time interval	PIDTimeout
Upper Detector		
Request setAirFlow(Air_f)	$0 <= Air\_f <= 0.1$	InvalidAirFlowRate
	check_oscillate(Air_f)	AirFlowRateOscillating
	corresponding notification must be received within a specified time interval	AirFlowActuatorTimeout
Notification from readO2Concentration()	$0 <= O2eco <= 1$	InvalidO2Concentration

Table 3. Summary of Exceptional Notifications.

Exception Notification	Generic Exception Type
PIDTimeout	NoResponse
AirFlowActuatorTimeout	(unavailability of inputs/ outputs to/from the PIDController)
InvalidConfigurationSetpoint*	
InvalidCoalFeederRate*	OutOfRange
InvalidO2Concentration	(violation of specifications of monitored variables)
InvalidAirFlowRate	
CoalFeederRateOscillating	Oscillation
AirFlowRateOscillating	(oscillations in monitored variables)
* Interface exceptions.	

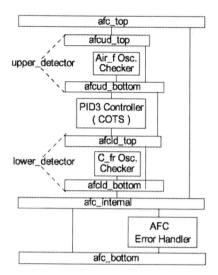

Fig. 6. Decomposition of the AirFlowController.

Figure 6 shows the internal structure of the iCOTS for the AirFlowController, based on the patterns shown in Figures 2 and 3. This solution equally applies to the WaterFlowController and CoalFeederController components.

The COTS PID controller is wrapped by a pair of error detectors (upper_detector and lower_detector) and inserted into an iC2C as its NormalActivity component. Both detectors use OscillatorChecker, which is responsible for checking whether oscillating variables revert to a stable state before a maximum number of oscillations. Table 2 specifies, for each detector: the message types to be inspected, their corresponding assertions that guarantee the acceptable behaviour constraints (Section 2.2), and the type of the exception notification that should be generated when a constraint is violated. Table 3 summarises these exception types, grouped by their generalised types. Two of these exception types are interface exceptions that are sent directly to the next lower level in the architectural configuration. The other exception types are internal exceptions, to be handled by the AFCErrorHandler. Thus, the AFCError-Handler propagates internal exceptions as failure exceptions of the generic type of the corresponding internal exception, using the mapping shown in Table 3. A PID-Timeout exception, for example, will generate a NoResponse failure exception.

The BoilerController component is responsible for:

1. Configuring the boiler system, sending setConfiguration requests when appropriate.
2. Handling interface exceptions of type InvalidConfigurationSetpoint, which may be raised in response of a setConfiguration request.
3. Handling failure exceptions of type NoResponse, OutOfRange or Oscillation, which may be raised by the three controllers (WaterFlowController, Coal-FeederController, AirFlowController).

The BoilerController component was structured as an iC2C to cope with fault-tolerance responsibilities, which are captured by items (2) and (3) above, in addition to its main functional responsibility, which is captured by item (1) above.

Figure 7 shows the resulting fault-tolerant architecture for this system, which is derived from the overall architectural configuration for the boiler system (Figure 5).

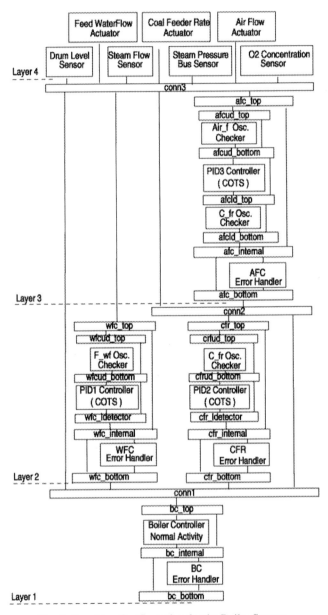

Fig. 7. Resulting Configuration for the Boiler System.

Each of its three controllers is structured as idealised C2 COTS (iCOTS) and the BoilerController as an idealised C2 component (iC2C). It is assumed that the sensors and actuators, as well as the connectors, do not fail. Figure 8 illustrates the flow of messages between the various components involved when a PIDTimeout exception occurs, after the BoilerController fails to configure the AirFlowController, which contains the COTS PID3Controller. When the AirFlowController bottom connector (afcld_bottom) detects that the AirFlowController is not responding, it raises an exception to AFCErrorHandler. Since AFCErrorHandler cannot cope with this exception type, it raises another exception to the BCErrorHandler that shuts down the whole system.

Step 14. Implement error detectors. During this and the following steps it was used an objected-oriented framework that provides a generic implementation for the key abstractions of the iC2C and iCOTS structuring concepts. Using this framework, the iCOTS lower and upper detectors are implemented as subclasses of, respectively, LowerDetectorAbst and UpperDetectorAbst. Figure 9 shows the main parts of the AfcLowerDetector class that implements the lower error detector associated with the AirFlowController component. In this code sample, the setConfiguration() and setCoalFeedRate() methods intercept the requests sent to the AirFlowController and check their associated ABCs, based on the specification shown in Table 2. When an assertion is violated an exception is raised by means of the raiseException() method, which is implemented by the abstract classes. Accepted requests are delivered to the AirFlowController that is connected to the wrappedNormal interface.

Step 15. Implement error handlers. Using the framework aforementioneto, the error handlers are implented as subclasses of AbnormalActivityAbst. Figure 10 shows the AFCErrorHandler class that implements the error handler associated with the AirFlowController. In this code sample, the handle() method is called when a failure exception is raised by one of the error detectors that wrap the AirFlowController. The exceptions raised are re-signalled with a more generic exception type according to the specifications shown in Table 3.

Step 16. Integrate the protectors. The following code snippet creates a component afc that encapsulates the AirFlowController and its associated error detectors and error handler, according to the iCOTS structuring. This new component is an iC2C instance composed by the basic AirFlowController wrapped by the two error detectors, acting as the iC2C normal activity component, and the error handler acting as the iC2C abnormal activity component.

```
Icomponent afc=new iC2C( new AfcWrappedNormal
                         ( new AirFlowController(),
                           new AfcLowerDetector(),
                           new AfcUpperDetector() ),
                          new AFCErrorHandler() );
```

Step 17. Integrate the system. The integration of the various components and connectors that are composed into the system is coded in the main() method of a StartUp class, based on the configuration shown in Figure7. The code snippet bellow illustrates this method body with: (i) the instantiation of component bc as an iC2C composed by the BoilerController component and its associated error handler; (ii) the instantiation of connector conn1; and (iii) the connection be-

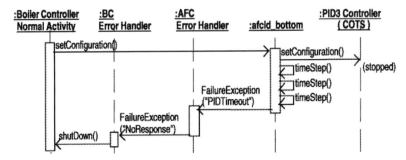

Fig. 8. UML Sequence Diagram for a PIDTimeout Exception.

tween the top interface of component bc and the bottom interface of connector conn1.

```
IComponent bc=new iC2C
        (new BoilerController(), new BCErrorHandler());
IConnector c1=new Conn1();
bc.connectTop(c1);
```

The resulting system was tested in a simulated environment that allowed us to inject different faults in the system. The final system passed all tests successfully. The system behaved as specified even in the presence of faults, aborting the erroneous operations and either stopping the system or activating an alarm.

A limitation of the case study is that it is based on a simulation of a boiler system, which does not allow an objective performance analysis. During execution time, the main overhead associated to a protector occurs when a service requested passes through a protected interface. This overhead is proportional to the number and complexity of the assertions encapsulated in the protectors. Assuming that this complexity should be much lower than the complexity of the services provided by the COTS, we may infer that the performance impact of the protective wrappers will be low. An ongoing experimental work in the DOTS[1] project is confirming this. The protector associated with the air flow controller, comprising its two error detectors with the eight ABCs and the associated error handler, required about a hundred lines of code. This additional code is added to the system in three new classes, which does not require any changes in the class that implements the base AirFlowController. An ongoing work is applying the proposed approach in a real world system and to more complex COTS software components.

5   Related Work

This section compares our approach with several relevant existing proposals. The main comparison criteria are the types of the components (application-level or middleware/OS level), fault tolerance (error detection and recovery) provided, type of the redundancy, the information used for developing error detection and recovery, phases of the life cycle (at which they are applied).

---

[1] Diversity with Off-The-Shelf Components Project, http://www.csr.ncl.ac.uk/dots/

```
public class AfcLowerDetector extends LowerDetectorAbst
  implements IConnector, IAirFlowController {
  private IAirFlowController wrappedNormal;
  private OscillatorChecker oscillatorChecker;
  public void setConfiguration
                  (double P_ref, double O2_ref) {
    if (O2_ref<0 || O2_ref>0.1)
      raiseException
        (new InvalidConfigurationSetpoint(O2_ref));
    try {wrappedNormal.setConfiguration(P_ref, O2_ref);
    } catch (TimeoutException e) {
      raiseException
        (new PIDTimeout("setConfiguration()"));
    } catch (AbortException e) { aborted(); }
  }
  public void setCoalFeedRate(double C_fr) {
    if (C_fr<0 || C_fr>1)
      raiseException(new InvalidCoalFeederRate(C_fr));
      if (oscillatorChecker.check_oscillate(C_fr))
        raiseException
          (new CoalFeederRateOscillating(C_fr));
      try {
        wrappedNormal.setCoalFeedRate(C_fr);
      } catch (TimeoutException e) {
        raiseException
          (new PIDTimeout("setCoalFeedRate()"));
      } catch (AbortException e) { aborted(); }
    } ...
```

Fig. 9. Implementation of the **AirFlowController**'s lower detector.

```
public class AFCErrorHandler
  extends AbnormalActivityAbst implements IComponent {
  public void handle(Exception exception) {
    try { throw exception; }
      catch (PIDTimeout e) {
      throw new NoResponse(e);
    } catch (AirFlowActuatorTimeout e) {
      throw new NoResponse(e);
    } catch (InvalidO2Concentration e) {
      throw new OutOfRange(e);
    } catch (InvalidAirFlowRate e) {
      throw new OutOfRange(e);
    } catch (CoalFeederRateOscillating e) {
      throw new Oscillation(e);
    } catch (AirFlowRateOscillating e) {
      throw new Oscillation(e);
    } catch (Exception e) {
      throw new FailureException(e); }
  }
```

Fig. 10. Implementation of the **AirFlowController**'s error handler.

Ballista [12] works with POSIX systems coming from several providers. The approach works under a strong assumption that the normal specification of the component is available, from which error detectors can be specified. In addition to this, the results of fault injection are used for the specification of error detectors. A layer between the applications and the operating system (OS), intercepting all OS calls as well as the outgoing results, implements this error detection. The recovery provided by this approach is very basic (blocking the erroneous calls) and is not application-specific.

A very interesting approach to developing protective wrappers for a COTS microkernel is discussed in [23]. The idea is to specify the correct behaviour of a microkernel and to make the protective wrapper check all functional calls (similar to Ballista, this approach cannot be applied for application-level COTS components that lack a complete and correct specification of the component's behaviour). Reflective features are employed for accessing the internal state of the microkernel to improve the error detection capability. In addition, the results of fault injection are used in the design of wrappers for catching those calls that have been found to cause errors of the particular microkernel implementation. A recent work [16] shows how recovery wrappers can be developed within this framework to allow for recovery after transient hardware faults, which is mainly based on redoing the recent operation.

Unfortunately these two approaches do not offer any assistance in developing fault tolerant system architectures. The Simplex framework (the best summary of this work performed in mid 90's can be found in [21]) proposes an architectural solution to dealing with the faults of the application-level COTS components. The idea is to employ two versions of the same component: one of them is the COTS component itself and another one is a specially-developed unit implementing some basic functions. The second unit is assumed to be bug free as it implements very simple algorithms. The authors call this analytical redundancy. The two units together form a safety unit in which only externally observable events of the COTS component are dealt with. The system architect is to implement a set of consistency constraints on the inputs to the COTS component and the outputs from it, as well as on the states of the device under control. This approach is oriented towards developing fault tolerant architectures of control systems. The disadvantage of this approach is that it is not recursive as it treats the whole control software as one unit and provides fault tolerance at only this level.

Rakic et. al. [17] offer a software connector-based approach to increasing the dependability of systems with components that evolve over time. The idea is to employ the new and the (several if available) old versions of a component to improve the overall system dependability. The authors put forward the idea of using a specialised multi-version connector allowing the system architect to specify the component authority for different operations: a version designated as authoritative will be considered nominally correct with respect to a given operation. The connector will propagate only the results from an authoritative version to the ROS and at the same time, log the results of all the multi-versioned components' invocations and compares them to the results produced by the authoritative version. This solution is mainly suitable for systems in which COTS components are to be upgraded (under the assumption that the interface of the old and new components remain unchanged) so there are several versions of a component in place.

6   Conclusions and Future Work

When building dependable systems from existing components, guarantees cannot be given on the system behaviour, if at least guarantees are not provided on the behaviour of its individual components. Since such guarantees are difficult to be obtained for individual COTS components, architectural means have to be devised for the provision of the necessary guarantees at the system level. The paper proposes an architectural solution to transform COTS components into idealised fault-tolerant COTS components by adding protective wrappers to them. We demonstrate the feasibility of the proposed approach using the steam boiler system case study, where its controllers are built reusing unreliable COTS components. Although we recognize that the proposed approach can result in incorporating repetitive checks into the integrated system, this is an unavoidable outcome considering the lack of guarantees provided by COTS components. For example, it might be the case that a COTS component has internal assertions checking the validity of an input parameter that is also checked by its protector, or other protectors associated with other COTS components. However, there are situations in which the system integrator can take care of this by coordinating development of fault tolerance means associated with individual components.

The protective wrappers are integrated in the architectural configuration as a set of new architectural elements that are dependent of a runtime environment, which is assumed to be reliable. The proposed approach also does not consider direct interactions between the COTS software component and human users. This implies that the proposed approach may not be effective for protecting COTS software components that either: (i) provide infrastructure services, such as operating systems, distribution middleware and component frameworks; or (ii) interacts intensively with human users, such as word processors.

The effectiveness of the proposed approach depends on the system designer's ability to anticipate the COTS behaviour when integrating it into a specific system, e.g. using the COTS usage profile. An approach for anticipating undesirable behaviour and, thus, increasing the protector's coverage factor for error detection is to perform integration tests of the COTS within the system being developed, prior to the specification of the protectors. These testing activities are the harder aspect in the development of the protectors, and they cannot be avoided. Our future work includes evaluating tools for automating these tests, which could be integrated in the protector's development process.

Although a single architectural style was used in the case study, software components in the C2 architectural style can be nevertheless integrated into configurations of other architectural styles of the independent components family [22], such as client/server and broker styles. This allows the idealised fault tolerant COTS (iCOTS) concept to be applied as a general solution in composing dependable systems from unreliable COTS components.

Acknowledgments

Paulo Asterio de C. Guerra is partially supported by CAPES/Brazil. Cecília Mary F. Rubira and Paulo Asterio de C. Guerra are supported by the FINEP/Brazil "Advanced Information Systems" Project (PRONEX-SAI-7697102200). Cecília Mary F. Rubira is also supported by CNPq/Brazil under grant no. 351592/97-0. Alexander Romanovsky is supported by EPSRC/UK DOTS and IST/FW6 RODIN Projects.

Special thanks go to Professor Brian Randell for many useful insights and suggestions.

References

1. T. Anderson, M. Feng, S. Riddle, A. Romanovsky. Protective Wrapper Development: A Case Study. In *Proc. 2nd Int. Conference on COTS-based Software Systems (ICCBSS 2003)*. Ottawa, Canada. Feb., 2003 M.H. Erdogmus, T. Weng (eds.). Lecture Notes in Computer Science Volume 2580 pp. 1-14 Springer-Verlag 2003,
2. T. Anderson, P. A. Lee. *Fault Tolerance: Principles and Practice*. Prentice-Hall, 1981.
3. S. Van Baelen, D. Urting, W. Van Belle, V. Jonckers, T. Holvoet, Y. Berbers, K. De Vlaminck. Toward a unified terminology for component-based development. WCOP Workshop, ECOOP 2000. Cannes, France. Available at:
   http://www.dess-itea.org/publications/ECOOP2000-WCOP-KULeuven.pdf
4. J. Chessman, J. Daniels. *UML Components: A Simple Process for Specifying Component-Based Software*. Addison-Wesley. 2001.
5. R. De Lemos, A. Saeed, T. Anderson. Analyzing Safety Requirements for Process-Control Systems. *IEEE Software*, Vol. 12, No. 3, May 1995, pp. 42--53.
6. R. DeLine. "A Catalog of Techniques for Resolving Packaging Mismatch". *Proc. 5th Symposium on Software Reusability (SSR'99)*. Los Angeles, CA. May 1999. pp. 44-53.
7. D. Garlan, R. Allen, J. Ockerbloom. Architectural mismatch: Why reuse is so hard. *IEEE Software*, 12(6):17--26, November 1995.
8. P. A.C. Guerra, C. M. F. Rubira, R. de Lemos. An Idealized Fault-Tolerant Architectural Component, in *Architecting Dependable Systems*. Springer-Verlag, Lecture Notes in Computer Science (LNCS). May, 2003. pp. 21-41.
9. P. A.C. Guerra, C. M. F. Rubira, A. Romanovsky, R. de Lemos. Integrating COTS Software Components Into Dependable Software Architectures. In. Proc. *6th IEEE International Symposium on Object-Oriented Real-Time Distributed Computing*. Hokkaido, Japan, 2003, pp. 139-142.
10. P. A.C. Guerra, C. M. F. Rubira, A. Romanovsky, R. de Lemos. A Fault-Tolerant Software Architecture for COTS-based Software Systems. In. Proc. *9th European Software Engineering Conference* held jointly with *10th ACM SIGSOFT International Symposium on Foundations of Software Engineering*. Helsinki, Finland, 2003, pp. 375-378.
11. D. Hamlet, D. Mason, D. Woit. Theory of System Reliability Based on Components. In Proc. *2000 International Workshop on Component-Based Software Engineering*. CMU/SEI. 2000.
12. P. Koopman, J. De Vale. Comparing the Robustness of POSIX Operating Systems. In *Proc. Fault Tolerant Computing Symposium (FTCS-29)*, Wisconsin, USA, 1999, 30-37.
13. P. Oberndorf, K. Wallnau, A. M. Zaremski. "Product Lines: Reusing Architectural Assets within an Organisation. *Software Architecture in Practice*. Eds. L. Bass, P. Clements, R. Kazman. Addison-Wesley. 1998. pp. 331-344.
14. F. Plasil and S. Visnovsky. Behavior Protocols for Software Components. In IEEE Transactions on Software Engineering, 28,11. 2002. pp. 1056-1076.
15. P. Popov, S. Riddle, A. Romanovsky, L. Strigini. On Systematic Design of Protectors for Employing OTS Items. In *Proc. 27th Euromicro Conference*. Warsaw, Poland, 4-6 September, IEEE CS, 2001. pp.22-29.
16. M. Rodriguez, J.-C. Fabre, J. Arlat. Wrapping Real-Time Systems from temporal Logic Specification. In *Proc. European Dependable Computing Conference (EDCC-4)*, 2002, Toulouse (France).

17. M. Rakic, N. Medvidovic. Increasing the Confidence in Off-The-Shelf Components: A Software Connector-Based Approach. *Proc. 2001 Symposium on Software Reusability (SSR'01). ACM/SIGSOFT Software Engineering Notes*, 26,3. 2001. pp. 11-18.
18. J.-G. Schneider, O. Nierstrasz. *Components, Scripts and Glue.* In: L. Barroca, J. Hall, P. Hall (Eds.) Software Architecture Advances and Applications. Springer-Verlag. 2000. pp. 13-25.
19. S. Sedigh-Ali, A. Ghafoor, R. A. Paul. Metrics and Models for Cost and Quality of Component-Based Software. In. Proc. *6th IEEE International Symposium on Object-Oriented Real-Time Distributed Computing.* Hokkaido, Japan, 2003.
20. D. Sotirovski. Towards Fault-Tolerant Software Architectures. In R. Kazman, P. Kruchten, C. Verhoef, H. Van Vliet, editors, *Working IEEE/IFIP Conference on Software Architecture*, pages 7--13, Los Alamitos, CA, 2001.
21. L. Sha. Using Simplicity to Control Complexity. *IEEE Software.* July/August, 2001. pp.20-28
22. M. Shaw, P. C. Clements. A Field Guide to Boxology: Preliminary Classification of Architectural Styles for Software Systems. In. Proc. *21st International Computer Software and Applications Conference.* 1997. pp. 6-13.
23. F. Salles, M. Rodriguez, J.-C. Fabre, J. Arlat. Metakernels and Fault Containment Wrappers. In *Proc. Fault Tolerant Computing Symposium (FTCS-29)*, Wisconsin, USA, 1999, 22-29.
24. T. Saridakis, V. Issarny. Developing Dependable Systems using Software Architecture. *Proc. 1st Working IFIP Conference on Software Architecture*, pages 83--104, February 1999.
25. V. Stavridou, R. A. Riemenschneider. Provably Dependable Software Architectures. *Proc. Third ACM SIGPLAN International Software Architecture Workshop*, pages 133--136. ACM, 1998.
26. R. N. Taylor, N. Medvidovic, K. M. Anderson, E. J. Whitehead Jr., J. E. Robbins, K. A. Nies, P. Oreizy, D. L. Dubrow. A Component- and Message-based Architectural Style for GUI Software. *IEEE Transactions on Software Engineering*, 22(6):390--406, June 1996.

A Framework for Reconfiguration-Based Fault-Tolerance in Distributed Systems

Stefano Porcarelli[1], Marco Castaldi[2], Felicita Di Giandomenico[1],
Andrea Bondavalli[3], and Paola Inverardi[2]

[1] Italian National Research Council, ISTI Dept., via Moruzzi 1, I-56124, Italy
{porcarelli,digiandomenico}@isti.cnr.it
[2] University of L'Aquila, Dip. Informatica, via Vetoio 1, I-67100, Italy
{castaldi,inverard}@di.univaq.it
[3] University of Firenze, Dip. Sistemi e Informatica, via Lombroso 67/A, I-50134, Italy
a.bondavalli@dsi.unifi.it

Abstract. Nowadays, many critical services are provided by complex
distributed systems which are the result of the reuse and integration of
a large number of components. Given their multi-context nature, these
components are, in general, not designed to achieve high dependability
by themselves, thus their behavior with respect to faults can be the most
disparate. Nevertheless, it is paramount for these kinds of systems to be
able to survive failures of individual components, as well as attacks and
intrusions, although with degraded functionalities. To provide control capabilities over unanticipated events, we focus on fault handling strategies,
particularly on system's reconfiguration. The paper describes a framework which provides fault tolerance of components based applications by
detecting failures through monitoring and by recovering through system
reconfiguration. The framework is based on Lira, an agent distributed infrastructure for remote control and reconfiguration, and a decision maker
for selecting suitable new configurations. Lira allows for monitoring and
reconfiguration at components and applications level, while decisions are
taken following the feedbacks provided by the evaluation of statistical
Petri net models.

1 Introduction

Dependability is becoming a crucial requirement of current computer and information systems, and it is foreseeable that its importance will increase in the
future at a fast pace. We are witnessing the construction of complex distributed
systems, for example in the telecommunication or financial domain, which are
the result of the integration of a large number of low–cost, relatively unstable
COTS (Commercial Off–The–Shelf) components, as well as of previously isolated
legacy systems. The resulting systems are being used to provide services which
have become critical in our everyday life. Since COTS and legacy components
are not designed to achieve high dependability by themselves, their behavior
with respect to faults can be the most disparate. Thus, it is paramount for these

R. de Lemos et al. (Eds.): Architecting Dependable Systems II, LNCS 3069, pp. 167–190, 2004.

kinds of systems to be able to survive failures of individual components, as well as attacks and intrusions, although with degraded functionalities.

The management of non functional properties in heterogeneous, complex component-based systems raises many issues to the application developers. Firstly, the management of such properties is difficult when the source code of the components is not available (*black box components*), since the developer has the limitation of using only the component's public API. Secondly, the heterogeneous environment, where components often implement different error detection and recovery techniques, without any or poor coordination among them, makes the composition of the non-functional properties a very difficult task. Moreover, a distributed application is exposed to communication and coordination failures, as well as to hardware or operating systems ones, that cannot be managed at component level but only at application level.

In order to provide fault tolerance of distributed component based applications, the system developer is forced to implement mechanisms which take into account the fault tolerance policies implemented by the different components within the system, and add the necessary coordination support for the management of fault tolerance at application level. Even if the creation of *ad hoc* solutions is possible and still very popular, some innovative approaches to face this problem have been recently proposed [1, 2].

In this paper we present a methodology and a framework for fault tolerance provision in distributed applications, created by assembling COTS and legacy components together with *ad hoc* application dependent components. The approach is based on monitoring the managed application to detect failures at component and operating system level, and on using dynamic reconfiguration for error recovery and/or for maintaining the system in a certain desirable state.

How to reconfigure the system is decided at run time, following a set of pre-specified reconfiguration policies. The decision process is performed by using online evaluation of a stochastic dependability model which represents the whole system. Such modeling activity depends on the specified policy, on the requirements of the application and on the system status at reconfiguration time. In order to represent the topology of the managed application, which may change dynamically, the model is created at run time by assembling a set of sub–models (building blocks). Before the evaluation, these sub–models are opportunely instantiated to represent the single parts of the system (such as components, hosts and connectors) and initialized with information collected at run time. When multiple reconfigurations are eligible, it seems reasonable in the context of fault tolerance provision to prefer the one that minimizes the error proneness of the resulting system.

The effectiveness of a reconfiguration policy depends on an accurate diagnosis of the nature of the unanticipated event, namely whether a hard, physical fault is affecting the system, or environmental adverse conditions are causing a soft fault which will naturally disappear in some time. However, it is out of the scope of this paper to address diagnosis issues, and we concentrate on reconfiguration only. Our proposed framework for fault tolerance provision is based on *Lira*, an infrastructure which monitors the system status and implements the reconfiguration strategy, enriched with a model based *Decision Maker*, which decides the most rewarding new reconfiguration for the managed application.

The paper is organized as follows. Section 2 introduces the reconfiguration based approach used for fault tolerance provision, while Section 3 describes the proposed framework. Sections 3.1 and 3.3 detail the different parts of the framework, with particular attention to the Lira reconfiguration infrastructure and the model based decision making process. Section 4 presents an illustrative example to show how the framework works, and Section 5 overviews related work. Finally, Section 6 summarizes the contribution of the paper.

2   A Reconfiguration Based Approach to Fault Tolerance

In the proposed approach the dynamic reconfiguration plays a central role: the managed system is reconfigured as a reaction to a specified event (for example, a detected failure) or as an optimization operation. A *reconfiguration* can be defined as "any change in the configuration of a software application" [3, 4]. Depending on where these changes occur, different kinds of reconfiguration are defined: a *component level reconfiguration* is defined as any change in the configuration parameters of single components, also called component re–parameterization, while an *architectural level reconfiguration* is any change in the application topology in terms of number and locations of software components [5–8].

The actuation of both kinds of reconfigurations should be performed in a coordinated way: if the components are self-contained and loosely coupled, a component level reconfiguration usually does not impact other components within the system; on the contrary, if there are many dependencies among components, or in the case of architectural reconfigurations which involve several components, a coordinator is necessary for a correct actuation of the reconfiguration process. The coordinator is in charge of considering both dependencies among components and architectural constraints in terms of application topology, in order to maintain the consistency within the system during and after the reconfiguration.

Many approaches to reconfiguration usually rely on a coordinator to manage the reconfiguration logics, and on a distributed framework for the reconfiguration actuation. Referring to Figure 1, the dependability aspects addressed in this paper are the selection (after a decision process) and actuation of a reconfiguration, while the detection of failures and diagnosis is left to specialized tools integrated in the reconfiguration infrastructure.

Our approach is divided in two phases: the *instrumentation phase* and the *execution phase*. The first one is performed before the deployment of the managed application and is in charge of instrumenting the framework with respect to the specific application. During this phase, the developer, looking at the managed application, identifies the critical events (e.g., the components failures) for which system reconfiguration is required, together with the related information that need to be monitored and collected. For each identified critical event, the developer specifies a set of alternative reconfiguration processes, to overcome

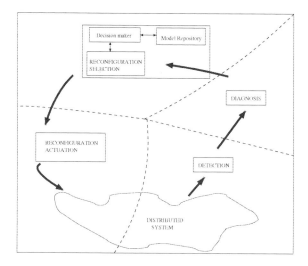

Fig. 1. Dependability Aspects

the event's effects. As an example of reconfiguration process, the developer may define the activation of a component on a different host, the re–connection of a client from its current server to another one, etc. It is important to notice that the definition of the reconfiguration processes depends on the reconfiguration capabilities of the involved components; the components are usually black boxes, thus allowing for reconfiguration only through their public APIs.

The second phase, instead, is performed after the deployment of the managed application, and represents the strategy used by the framework to provide fault tolerance on the managed application. During the execution phase the following operations are performed:

- **Monitoring of the managed system:** monitoring is necessary to collect information about the state of both components and deployment environment, and to detect the critical events within the system. Depending on the components, the critical events can be also notified by a tool which performs error detection and diagnosis.

- **Decision process:** as a reaction to one or more critical events, the system is reconfigured to restore its correct behavior. The decision process, performed by the *Decision Maker*, faces the problem of choosing the new configuration for the managed system, trying to take the most rewarding decision with respect to the detected failure and the current application state. In the presented approach the new configuration is chosen taking into account the feedbacks provided by the online evaluation of stochastic dependability models: in particular, the best one is the configuration which maximizes the health state of the system, as represented by a health function defined following the characteristics of the managed application.

– **Reconfiguration actuation:** once the new configuration is selected, a reconfiguration process places the managed system in that configuration. In this phase, the system which performs the reconfiguration must address several issues, such as the consistency of application data during the reconfiguration process, or the restoration of a correct state. Also in this case, the capability of ensuring consistency during the reconfiguration depends on the ability of the single application components to manage their internal state and, overall, on the degree of control provided to the developer for such management.

3   A Framework for Fault Tolerance Provision

This section describes the framework which implements the approach previously described. The framework is based on Lira [9–11], an infrastructure for component based application reconfiguration, enriched with decision making capabilities that allow the choice of the reconfiguration which better fits the actual state of the managed application. In the following, the different parts of the framework, and how they implement the proposed approach are described.

3.1   The Lira Infrastructure

Lira (Lightweight Infrastructure for Reconfiguring Applications) is an infrastructure to perform remote monitoring and reconfiguration at component and application level. Lira is inspired to the Network Management [12] in terms of reconfiguration model and basic architecture. The reconfiguration model of the Network Management is quite simple: a network device, such as a router or a switch, exports some reconfiguration variables through an Agent, which is implemented by the device's producer. These variables exported by the agent are defined in the MIB (Management Information Base) and can be modified using the *set* and *get* messages of SNMP (Simple Network Management Protocol) [12].

Using the same idea, in order to manage reconfiguration of software applications, software components play the role of the network devices: a component parameter that may be reconfigured is exported by an agent as a variable, or as a function. Following the architecture of SNMP, Lira specifies three architectural elements: (i) the **Agent**, that represents the reconfiguration capabilities of the managed software components, exporting the reconfigurable variables and functions; (ii) the **MIB** that contains the list of those variables and functions; and (iii) the **Management Protocol**, that allows the communication among the agents.

The Lira agents may be implemented either by the component developer, or by the application assembler: in the last case, the agents can export also functions that implement more complex reconfiguration activities, or variables that export the result of a monitoring activity performed by the agent on the managed component.

The agents can be hierarchically composed: so, it is possible to define agents managing a sub–system exactly like single components, thus allowing an easier

management of the reconfiguration at architectural level. The main advantage of
having a hierarchy of agents is the possibility of hiding the reconfiguration complexity behind the definition of a specialized higher level agent. Moreover, this
definition favours the scalability of the reconfiguration service, because a reconfiguration at application level is implemented like a reconfiguration at component
level. According to this hierarchical structure, in fact, an agent has manager
capabilities on the system portion under its own control, while it is a simple
actuator with respect to the higher level agents.

A Lira agent is a program that runs on its own thread of control, therefore
it is indipendent from the managed components and hosts.

There are four kinds of agents specialized in different tasks. The **Component Agents** (CompAgents) are associated to the software components, they
monitor the state of the component and implement the reconfiguration logics.
The agent–component communication is component dependent: if a component
is implemented in Java and distributed as a *.jar* file, the communication is implemented through *shared memory*. To avoid synchronization problems, the component must provide atomic access to the shared state. If the component provides
reconfiguration capabilities through *ad hoc* protocols, the agent is tailored to
perform this kind of communication.

The CompAgent manages the life–cycle of the component by exporting the
functions *start, stop, suspend, resume* and *shutdown*. The function *shutdown*
stops the component and kills the agent. For monitoring purpose, the CompA-
gent exports the predefined read–only variable $STATUS$, which maintains the
current state of the component (started, stopped, suspended). Like every agent,
the CompAgent is able to notify the value of a variable to its manager, addressed
by the variable $NOTIFYTO$: these variables are defined in every CompAgent
MIB.

Host Agents run on the hosts where components and agents are deployed.
They represent not only the run time support necessary for the installation and
activation of both agents and components, by exporting in their MIB the functions *install, uninstall, activate, deactivate*, but they also allow the monitoring
and reconfiguration of the software resources available on the host at operating system level. In fact, by exporting variables and functions associated to the
managed resources, the Host Agents allow the reconfiguration of the environment where the application is deployed. As well as the managed host resources,
the Host Agent maintains the lists of both installed and activated components,
making them available to the manager by exporting in the MIB the variables
$ACTIVE\_AGENTS$ and $INSTALLED\_AGENTS$.

The **Application Agent** is a higher level agent which controls a set of
components and hosts through the associated agents. This agent manages a sub–
system as an atomic component, hiding the complexity of reconfiguration and
increasing the infrastructure scalability. The application agent which controls the
whole system is called **Manager**. Figure 2 shows the different kinds of agents.

The higher level agents may be programmed by using an interpreted language: the *Lira Reconfiguration Language* [9], which provides a set of commands

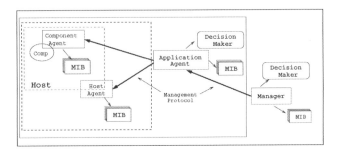

Fig. 2. Lira general architecture

for the explicit management of reconfiguration on component based applications. The language allows the definition of *proactive* and *reactive actions*: the first ones are continuously performed with a delay expressed in milliseconds, while the latter ones are performed when a specified notification is received by the agent. The reconfigurations performed on the managed components are specified in terms of remote setting of the exported variables or remote call of exported functions. A detailed description of the Lira Reconfiguration Language can be found in [9].

The **Management Protocol** is inspired to SNMP, with some necessary modifications and extensions. Each message is either a *request* or a *response*, as shown in Table 1:

Table 1. Management Protocol messages

request	response
SET(*var_name, var_value*)	ACK(*msg_text*)
GET(*var_name*)	REPLY(*var_name, var_val*)
CALL(*func_name, par_list*)	RETURN(*ret_value*)

Requests are sent by higher level agents to lower level ones and responses are sent backwards. There is one additional message, which is sent from agents to communicate an alert at upper level (even in the absence of any request):

NOTIFY(*variable_name, variable_value, agent_name*)

Finally, the **MIB** provides the list of variables and functions exported by the agent which can be remotely managed. It represents the agreement that allows agents to communicate in a consistent way, exactly like it happens in the network management. Note that also the predefined variables and functions that characterize the different agents (for example, the variable *STATUS* or the function *stop* in the CompAgent) are defined in the MIB, as detailed in [13].

3.2   Lira and the Proposed Approach

With respect to the previously defined approach, Lira provides the necessary infrastructural support for system monitoring and reconfiguration actuation.

In addition, it implements through the agents the interfaces with the external tools used within the framework, such as those for failures detection and for the stochastic models evaluation.

During the instrumentation phase, the developer creates the lower level (component and host) agents by specializing the Java classes of the Lira package. In particular, the host agents must specialize the functions for installation and activation of the components, making them working with the current component based application. Moreover, by using the Lira APIs, the developer defines the variables and functions for remote control and reconfiguration, that will be exported in the agent MIBs. Finally, the agents are programmed to perform local monitoring on the component, and to notify the manager when a critical event (such as a failure) is detected.

The Lira Manager (or Application Agent) implements the monitoring policies, usually specified as a set of *proactive actions*, the reconfiguration policies, usually implemented as a set of *reactive actions* performed when a particular event is received, and the reconfiguration processes, specified as functions implemented using the commands of the Lira Reconfiguration Language. For example:

```
proactive actions
begin
  stateMonitor: every 10000 do
    begin
      string healthState;
      healthState := read(A1, HEALTH_STATE);
      if (healthState = "down")
        then restartNode(N1);
      endif;
    end
end
```

specifies a monitoring activity in which, every 10000 milliseconds, the Manager checks the value of the variable HEALTH_STATE exported by the agent A1: if its value is *down*, the node N1 managed by the agent A1 is considered to be not working. In such a case, N1 is restarted, calling the local function restartNode. Note that this function can be exported by this agent (actually working as an application agent), making the *restartNode* reconfiguration available to the higher level agents.

In the example just presented, a single reconfiguration process (restarting the node) is specified. In our framework, instead, more sophisticated situations are accounted for, where the occurrence of a single or of a combination of critical events may trigger a number of possible reconfiguration processes, each one implemented by a Lira function. Then, the most rewarding one is selected after a decision process, and put in place by the Manager.

3.3   Decision Maker: General Issues

The decision maker (DM) takes decisions about system's reconfiguration, adopting a model-based analysis support to better fulfill this task. In presenting the decision maker subsystem, we outline the main aspects characterizing the overall decision process methodology as well as the involved critical issues.

Hierarchical Approach. Decisions can be taken at any level of the agents hierarchy as proposed by Lira and, consequently, the power of the reconfiguration is different. Resorting to a hierarchical approach brings benefits under several aspects, among which: i) facilitating the construction of models; ii) speeding up their solution; iii) favoring scalability; iv) mastering complexity (by handling smaller models through hiding, at one hierarchical level, some modeling details of the lower one). At each level, details on the architecture and on the status of components at lower levels are not meaningful, and only aggregated information is used. Therefore, information of the detailed model at one level is aggregated in an abstract model and used at a higher level. Important issues are how to abstract all the relevant information of one level to the upper one and how to compose the derived abstract models. In our framework the first, bottom level is that of a Component Agent. At this level, the Decision Maker can only autonomously decide to perform preventive maintenance, to prevent or at least postpone the occurrence of failures. An example of preventive maintenance is "software rejuvenation" [14]: software is periodically stopped and restarted in order to refresh its internal state. The second level concerns the Application Agent; the DM's reconfiguration capabilities span all software and hardware resources under its responsibility which encompass several hosts, and installation/activation of new components is allowed. At the highest level there is a Manager agent, which has a "global" vision of the whole system (by composing models representing such subsystems); therefore the DM at this level has the ability to perform an overall reconfiguration.

Composability. To be as general as possible, the overall model (at each level of the hierarchy) is achieved as the integration of small pieces of models (building blocks) to favor their composability. We define composability as the capability to select and assemble models of components in various combinations into a model of the whole system to satisfy specific user requirements [15]. Interoperability is defined as the ability of different models, connected in a distributed system, to collaboratively model a common scenario in order to satisfy specific user requirements. For us, the requirement is to make "good" decisions (in the sense explained later on); models of components are combined into a model of the whole system in a modular fashion and the solution is carried out on the overall model [16]. Interoperability among models in a distributed environment is not considered at this stage of the work.

For the sake of model composability, we are pursuing the following goals:

- To have a different building block model for each different type of components in the system. All these building blocks can be used as a pool of templates,
- For each component, to automatically (by the decision making software) instantiate an appropriate model from these templates, and
- At a given hierarchical level, to automatically link them together (by rules which are application dependent), thus defining the overall model.

Goodness of a Decision. The way to make decisions may be different, depending upon the referred hierarchical level. First of all it has to be defined how to judge the goodness of a decision: actually, the meaning of "good" decision strictly depends on the application domain and so cannot be stated in a general way. However, criteria to discriminate among decisions have to be well-stated since they drive the modeling as well as the decision process. The factors which contribute to make an appropriate decision are the rewards and the costs associated to a decision and its temporal scope. Indeed, costs/benefits balance has to be determined along all the interval from the time a reconfiguration is put in place to the next reconfiguration action. The solution of the overall model has to be carried out rather quickly to be usable. This is an open issue and, if not properly solved, will surely be a limiting factor to the practical utility of the on-line method. In general, to be effective, the time to reach the solution $(T_{Decision})$ and to put it in place $(T_{Actuation})$ has to be much shorter than the mean time between the occurrence of successive events requiring a reconfiguration action $(T_{NextRec})$. The parameter $T_{NextRec}$ may depend on the expected mean time to failure of system components, and on how severe the occurred failure is perceived by the application. Indeed, some failures may require system reconfiguration, while others may not. In general, the criterion for decision taking is a reward function which should account for several factors, including the time to take a decision, how critical is the situation to deal with, and the costs in terms of CPU time.

Suitability of the Modeling Approaches. An important issue in dependability modeling is the dependency existing among the system components, through which the state of one component is influenced or correlated to the state of others [17]. If it is possible to assume stochastic independence among failure and repair processes of components, the new reconfiguration scheme can be simply evaluated by means of combinatorial models, like fault tree. In case the failure of a component may affect other related components, state-space models are necessary. Since independence of failure events may be assumed only in restricted system scenarios, state-space models are more adequate approaches to model-based analysis in the general case. Therefore, in the proposed framework, each component is modeled with a simple Petri net which describes its forecasted behavior given its initial state. These models are put together and solved by the DM on the basis of the information collected from the subordinated agents.

Dynamic Solution. Another important issue to be considered is the dimension of the decision state-space problem. Considering systems which are the result of the integration of a large number of components, as we do in this work, it could be not feasible to evaluate and store offline all possible decision solutions for each case it may happen. These cases are determined by the combination of external environmental factors and internal status of the system (which are not predictable in advance or too many to be satisfactorily managed [18]) and by the topology of the system architecture which can vary along time. In this scenario, online decision making solutions have to be pursued. Although appealing, the online solution shows a number of challenging problems which require substantial investigations. Models of components have to be derived online and combined to get the model of the whole system. Thus, compositional rules and the resulting complexity of the combined model solution (both in terms of CPU time and in capability of automatic tools to solve such models) appear to be the most critical problems which need to be properly tackled to promote the applicability of this dynamic approach to reconfiguration.

3.4 Decision Maker: How It Works

In our approach a building block model is associated with each component. A simplified Stochastic Petri Net like model representing a generic building block model is shown in Figure 3. Error propagation effects can be taken into account by this model: e.g. a failure of a component may affect the status of another one. The model of Figure 3 represents only the possible states of a component, omitting all the details (which are implementation dependent) about the definition of the transitions from one state to another (which possibly depend on the status of other components). A token in the place Up means that the component is properly working. A token in one of places $D1... Dn$ means that the component is working in a degraded manner (e.g., in the case the component is hit by a transient fault which reduces its functionalities). The places F_{Crash}, F_{Value}, and $F_{Byzantine}$ [1] represent the possible ways a component may fail [19]. *Start* represents the initial state of a component involved in a reconfiguration, to indicate, e.g, that the component is performing installation, restarting, or attempting to connect to another one to be fully operative.

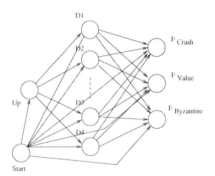

Fig. 3. General building block model

At each level of the decision making hierarchy, the DM has knowledge of the behavior of each system unit visible at the one-step lower level, in terms of the state of the corresponding building block model(s). To make an example, at the manager agent level, the DM has knowledge of the behavior of each component in

---

[1] It makes sense having a $F_{Byzantine}$ state only if the component is within a distributed environment and interacts with two or more components.

the system, each one seen as single system unit; in turn, at application agent level, the DM has knowledge of the behavior of each host involved in that application, again each one seen as a single system unit, and so on.

According to the depicted hierarchical reconfiguration process, when an event triggering a reconfiguration action at a certain level occurs, the DM at that level attempts the reconfiguration, if possible. In case it cannot manage the reconfiguration, it notifies the upper level DM about both the detected problem and its health status. In turn, the upper level DM receiving such request to trigger a reconfiguration, uses such health status information, together with those of the other system units under its control. After taking the decision on reconfiguration at a certain level, the decision is sent to the lower level agents which act as actuators on the controlled portion of the system. Therefore, upon the occurrence of a component failure, the initial states of each host and/or component is retrieved by the application agent by means of its subordinate host and/or component agents. Therefore, the states of any controlled component (provided by Lira) is used as *input* for the appropriate decision maker in the hierarchy. The building block models are then linked together through predefined compositional rules to originate the overall model capturing the system view at such hierarchical level. These compositional rules are applied online to each model component and possibly depend upon the marking of other components, the current topology of the system, and the topology of the system after a reconfiguration.

The information on the topology of the controlled network is stored in a data structure shared between the (application or manager) agent and the decision maker attached to it. The agent uses this information to put in place reconfigurations, while the decision maker uses it to build the online models for forecasting the health status of hosts and/or components participating to a given reconfiguration, and to compare different reconfiguration options. Since the topology of the network can change dynamically as consequence of faults or of a reconfiguration action, new pieces of Petri Nets, representing an host or component, can be changed/removed/added and linked to the overall model. Moreover, statistical dependencies among the different pieces of the overall model and their dynamic changes are captured.

As automatic tool for models resolution, we are using DEEM (DEpendability Evaluation of Multiple-phased systems) [20] which is a dependability modeling and evaluation tool specifically tailored for Multiple-phased systems (MPS). MPS are systems whose operational life can be partitioned in a set of disjoint periods, called "phases". DEEM relies upon Deterministic and Stochastic Petri Nets (DSPN) [21] as a modeling tool and on Markov Regenerative Processes (MRGP) for the analytical model solution. The analytical solution tool is suitable for decision-making purposes where predictability of the time to decision and of the accuracy of the solution are needed. Actually, the problem of reconfiguring a system can be seen as partitioned in multiple phases, as many as the steps needed for a given reconfiguration policy (e.g. reinstall and restart of a component, opening a new connection between two components).

In accordance with the models structure in DEEM, the model of the whole system is associated with a *phase net* model (PhN). The PhN synchronizes all the steps involved in the reconfiguration: it is composed by deterministic activities which fire sequentially whenever an event associated to a reconfiguration policy happens (see Figure 4). In the PhN only one token circulates and, in general, there exist as many different PhNs as the number of reconfiguration policies.

Fig. 4. General phase net model

Suppose for example that a unit has to be restarted. Initially the component is in state *Start* (see Figure 3), and, upon the firing of the transition of the phase net indicating the expiration of the restart time, the state of the component moves from *Start* to *Up*, or to one of the degraded states, or even to one of the failure states. Thus, decisions are affected by the following factors:

– The current topology of the system;
– The topology of the system after a reconfiguration has been undertaken;
– The steps provided for a reconfiguration policy;
– The current state of each host and/or component;
– The forecasted state of each host and component.

The DM decides the new reconfiguration by solving the overall model and gives back as *output* (to Lira) the *best reconfiguration action*. It is in charge of the Decision Maker to solve such overall composed model as quickly as possible to take appropriate decisions online identifying the most rewarding reconfiguration action among a pool of pre–defined options.

After taking the decision on reconfiguration at a certain level, the decision is sent to the lower level agents which act as actuators on the controlled portion of the system. Obviously, the correctness of the decisions depends on both the accuracy of the models and on its input parameters.

Since both the model-based evaluation and the reconfiguration processes depends on the specific application, the description on how the Decision Maker works cannot go in more details. In order to demonstrate how the proposed framework actually works, we introduce in the next Section a simple, but effective example, showing the different steps of the intended methodology.

4   A Simple Example: Path Availability in a Communication Network

A simple, but meaningful, scenario is the case of distributed computing where two peer–to–peer clients on the network are communicating. To prevent service interruption, it is necessary to provide an adequate level of paths redundancy among the clients involved in the communication. The network topology we assume consists of six hosts physically (wired) connected as shown in Figure 5a. For management purpose, we consider the network divided in two subnetworks Net_1 and Net_2, which contain the hosts $\{H_1, H_2\}$ and $\{H_3, H_4\}$ respectively. The hosts H_5 and H_6, where the clients are deployed, are not included in the managed network.

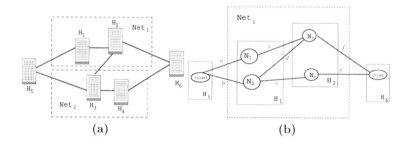

Fig. 5. Hosts physical connection (a) and the logical net (b)

Table 2. Available paths

Path	Route
1	a–N_1–c–N_3–f
2	a–N_1–c–N_3–d–N_2–e–N_4–g
3	b–N_2–e–N_4–g
4	b–N_2–d–N_3–f

A logical communication network composed by logical nodes connected through logical channels is installed on the managed hosts. The nodes N_1, N_2, N_3, N_4 connected through the channels a, b, c, d, e, f, g are deployed on the subnetwork Net_1, as shown in Figure 5b. These channels provide different choices for establishing the communication among the clients, as listed in Table 2.

As said before, the application is managed by the Lira infrastructure: each host H_i is controlled by a Host Agent HA_i, each subnetwork Net_i is controlled by an Application Agent AA_i, while the whole network is controlled by the Manager. The hosts H_5 and H_6 are considered outside the network, so they are not controlled by host agents.

The logical network is also controlled by the Lira agents. The Component Agents A_i control the logical nodes N_i, and they are managed by AA_1. AA_1 may decide to perform a reconfiguration if it has the necessary information, while it has to ask the general Manager when a global reconfiguration is needed and the local information is not enough. Figure 6 details the Lira management infrastructure.

During the instrumentation phase, the agents A_i and HA_j are programmed to export the enumerated variable *HEALTH_STATE*, which can assume the values *Up*, *Degraded*, and *Down*, corresponding to the health state of the managed

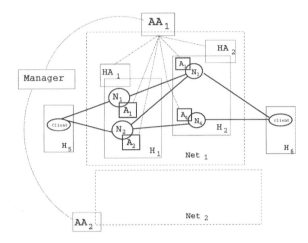

Fig. 6. Lira infrastructure for the controlled network

component or host. When this variable is *Down*, the agent is programmed to notify the Application Agent, which will trigger the decision process. The decision process consists in building the models representing the possible new configurations, in evaluating them using DEEM, and in deciding which reconfiguration must be performed to repair the system. During the decision process, only the reconfigurations that place the system in a consistent state are considered and evaluated: the Lira agents are in charge of controlling the application consistency during and after the reconfiguration. It is important to notice that also the costs of each reconfiguration process are considered during the decision process, to increase the accuracy of the taken decision.

For the proposed example, the paths redundancy can be used to improve the overall availability of the logical network. The goal of the framework is to keep *at least* two paths available between the clients involved in the communication. For the sake of simplicity, we consider that the manifestation of both a hardware fault (such as a wired connection's interruption or a damage in the physical machine) and a software fault (at operating system, application and logical communication level) has a fail-stop semantics, that is the component stops working.

4.1   Measure of Interest and Assumptions

We are interested in monitoring paths availability, so for a path to be available, all the nodes and links in the corresponding route must be available. Note that failures of a particular link or node may result in unavailability of more than one path. For example, if node N_3 fails, paths 1, 2, and 4 become unavailable. To evaluate which of these strategies is the most rewarding we define the "Probability of Failure" of the system as the probability that not even one path exists between the two clients involved in the communication. We analyze this measure both as instant-of-time and as interval-of-time, as function of the time to evaluate which reconfiguration has the lower probability of failure and the lower mean time to failure, respectively. Actually, the instant-of-time measure gives only a point-wise perception of the failure probability representing the distribution function of the failure probability. The interval-of-time measure weights point-wise values over a time interval giving an indication of the mean time to failure. Usually, neither one alone shows a satisfactory indicator and it is interesting to evaluate both of them.

We pursue an analytical transient analysis. The effectiveness of a reconfiguration strategy is studied during an interval of time starting from time T_0 to $T_{NextRec}$. T_0 represents the time at which a failure occurs and the system starts a reaction. $T_{NextRec}$ is the "temporal scope" of the reconfiguration and is an application dependent parameter. Actually, it is useless to test a reconfiguration option after time $T_{NextRec}$.

The framework is instantiated for this case study under the following assumptions:

- Failures occurrence follows an exponential distribution while the time to reinstall, restart or connecting to components follows a deterministic one;
- $T_{NextRec}$ is at least approximatively known;
- T_{Reconf} (that is, $T_{Decision} + T_{Actuation}$) is much less than $T_{NextRec}$ ($T_{Reconf} << T_{NextRec}$).
- No additional failures occur during the interval of time from T_0 to T_{Reconf}. Actually, this assumption is realistic when $T_{Reconf} << T_{NextRec}$.

4.2   Performing Reconfigurations

Reconfigurations can be triggered both at AppAgent and Manager Agent levels by their associated Decision Makers. Decisions are taken when a lower level agent notifies that its controlled component is failed. Moreover, to prevent failures of the agent itself, higher level agents proactively ask to the controlled agents for the value *HEALTH_STATE* with a frequency $T << T_{NextRec}$.

As an example of reconfiguration at the AppAgent level, let's suppose that the node N_3 is starting to work in a degraded manner: the associated agent A_3 notifies the variable *HEALTH_STATE* with the value *Degraded*. AA_1 receives the NOTIFY message, and it checks the path availability on the controlled network. Three reconfiguration options are here considered. First, accepting to continue working with node N_3 in a degraded state; this will be referred as "Reduced" later on. A second one is to restart N_3; in this case, the redundancy in terms of paths is temporarily reduced (see Figure 5). This will be referred as "Restart". The third can be to activate a new node N_5 on the host H_2, and to connect it to the client and to the nodes N_1 and N_2, creating new paths. It will be referred as "SetUp".

Obviously the different solutions have different costs in terms of probability of failure, which is the only metric considered in this example to take decisions. It is responsibility of the DM to select the best one.

4.3   Component Building Blocks and Phase Net

The components of the case study can be grouped in two categories: links and nodes. Thus, the corresponding building block models are defined (shown in Figure 7.a and Figure 7.b, respectively). They are quite similar. Each link and node have associated a corresponding Petri net model where only one token circulates. Let's start describing the model of a link, that can be easily generalized to explain that of a component. After an initial possible recovery or set up phase, a generic link X is supposed to be only in state Up or $Down$ (i.e. a token can be in place $ObjX\_Up$ or $ObjX\_Do$, respectively). When the exponential transition $ObjX\_UpToDo$ fires, the link X fails.

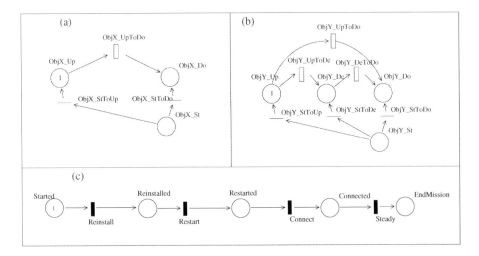

Fig. 7. Building blocks for links (a) and nodes (b), and general phase net model (c)

Place $ObjX\_St$ may hold a token only for a while at initial time T_0. A token is in this place if link X, as consequence of system reconfiguration, has to be newly setup or restarted because of a previous failure. From place $ObjX\_St$, a token may move in places $ObjX\_Up$ or $ObjX\_Do$ through the instantaneous transitions $ObjX\_StToUp$ or $ObjX\_StToDo$, to represent the transition of the link X in state Up or $Down$, respectively. This allows accounting for a probability of success/failure of the set-up of a new link or of the recovery operation of an old link. Moreover, the time to complete set-up or recovery, through instantaneous transitions $ObjX\_StToUp$ or $ObjX\_StToDo$, depends on the kind of operation. Actually, such transitions are enabled by the Phase Net which emphasizes the length of possible phases following a reconfiguration.

Components are modelled similarly to links. A generic component is shown in Figure 7.b. The only difference is that the possible states of a component include also "Degraded". Thus, place $ObjY\_De$ has been added, together with the exponential transitions $ObjY\_DeToDo$ and $ObjY\_UpToDe$ and the instantaneous transition $ObjY\_StToDe$ to connect such place to the rest of the net. This model works analogously to the model of a link, with the difference that a node in the "Up" state goes through "Degraded" before becoming "Down".

A possible Phase Net is shown in Figure 7.c, where a token in place $Started$ sequentially moves to place $Reinstalled$, $Restarted$, $Connected$, and then in place $EndMission$.

These DSPN models are specified through the Stochastic Reward Net (SRN) formalism [22]. Beside the general characteristics of SRN, this formalism provides *enabling functions* and *rate/probability functions*[2] which allow to decide, in a marking-dependent fashion, both when a transition is enabled and the rate/probability associated with the firing of such transition. This way, the evolution of a submodel can be dependent on the marking of another one, without explicit and visible links among them. Moreover, the SRN formalism considers the specification and evaluation of the measure of interest as an integral part of the model: reward rates are associated to the states of the models. From this point of view, the tool DEEM we are using allows, also, to i) embed variable parameters in the rate/probability functions, ii) specify the measure of interest in terms of complex reward functions, and iii) to solve the model at varying value of some values of the user-defined variable parameters and/or the time at which the solution is carried out.

In order to clarify how the proposed modeling approach works, Figure 8 shows the overall composed model instantiated for the "Restart" strategy. Similar considerations hold for the other strategies. The model of Figure 8 is achieved by combining together the models of links and components (on the basis of their respective building block models shown in Figure 7), according to the network topology of Figure 5b and the "Restart" strategy.

The "Restart" strategy prescribes that the faulty node N_3 be restarted. In Figure 8 the initial marking of each submodel is indicated by a "1" in the corresponding place. Initially a token is in place $Reinstalled$ of the Phase Net (actually the component to be restated is already installed). The initial state of all components (apart the faulty node N_3 and the links c, d, and f connected to it) are initially set according to their $HEALTH\_STATE$ variables (monitored by Lira). The initial marking of node N_3 and its connected links are $ObjN_3\_St$ and $ObjX\_St$ (for $X = c$, d, and f), respectively. The instantaneous transitions $ObjN_3\_StToUp$, $ObjN_3\_StToDe$, and $ObjN_3\_StToDo$ for node N_3 are enabled only after the firing of the transition $Restart$ of the Phase net Model. This synchronization among the involved models is achieved by associating to these transitions the enabling functions "$MARK(Reistalled)==0$" (the function $MARK(Place\_Name)$ returns the marking of place $Place\_Name$). Similar considerations hold for the instantaneous transitions $ObjX\_StToUp$ and $ObjX\_StToDe$ (for $X = c$, d, and f). The probability functions of these transitions have to be assigned taking into account that the sum of the probabilities associated to all instantaneous activities connected to the same place have to

---

[2] Rate functions are associated to timed transitions, while probability functions to instantaneous transitions.

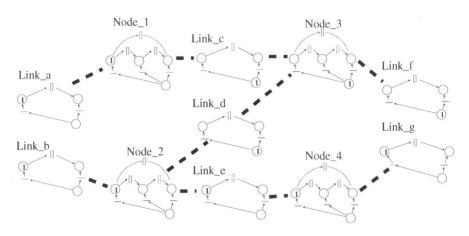

Fig. 8. Overall model for the "Restart" reconfiguration

be one. In the proposed simple example, numerical values have been associated to these probabilities (see Section on setting for numerical evaluation later on). However more complex marking-dependent expression can be assigned, if appropriate.

Notice that the whole model is composed by a set of submodels whose structure is known in advance. In this way, given the building block templates, a set of interdependence rules (which can be derived from the topology of the system or explicitly defined) and the relevant dependability parameters (such as the failure rates and the probabilities involved in the building blocks), the overall model is built automatically by the decision maker and solved by the tool DEEM.

The measure of interest "failure probability" previously introduced is also simply defined and evaluated upon the Petri net model. For example, the failure probability of path 1 of Table 2 is specified as in the following expression:

$$(1\text{-}MARK(Obja\_StToDo)) * (1\text{-}MARK(ObjN_1\_StToDo)) *$$
$$(1\text{-}MARK(Objc\_StToDo)) * (1\text{-}MARK(ObjN_3\_StToDo)) *$$
$$(1\text{-}MARK(Objf\_StToDo)).$$

where each factor represents the probability that the corresponding link or node is operative. In this example, a relatively simple figure of merit has been identified for the analysis. However, the SRN formalism is powerful enough to allow defining and evaluating also performability measures, where dependability factors can be weighted with performance factors and costs.

4.4   Numerical Evaluation

In this Section, the settings for the numerical evaluation and the obtained results are shown. The failure rates of the system components (assuming they are in state "Up") are listed in Table 3, in terms of models transition rates.

Table 3. Default parameters

Parameter	Value	Comments
Observation time interval $T_{NextRec}$	(1200 min) 20 hours	-
Rate of transition $ObjY\_UpToDe$	1e-05 1/min.	for $Y = N_1, N_2, N_3, N_4$
Rate of transition $ObjY\_DeToDo$	1e-04 1/min.	for $Y = N_1, N_2, N_3, N_4$
Rate of transition $ObjY\_UpToDo$	1e-06 1/min.	for $Y = N_1, N_2, N_3, N_4$
Rate of transition $ObjX\_UpToDo$	1e-05 1/min.	for $X = a, b, c, d, e, f, g$

Table 4. Strategy "Restart"

Parameter	Value
Component restart time $T_{Restart}$	0.1 min.
Probability that $N3$ restart is successful p_RestUp_N3	0.75
Probability that $N3$ restart is partially successful p_RestDe_N3	0.15
Probability that $N3$ restart fails p_RestDo_N3	0.10

Table 5. Strategy "Set-up"

Parameter	Value	Comments
Component reinstall time $T_{Reinstall}$	0.1 min.	-
Component connection time $T_{Connect}$	0.05 min.	-
Prob. $N3$ reinstall is successful p_ReinUp_N3	0.90	-
Prob. $N3$ reinstall is partially successful p_ReinDe_N3	0.08	-
Prob. $N3$ reinstall fails p_ReinDo_N3	0.02	-
Prob. the new link connection is successful p_ConnUp_X	0.95	for $X = c, d, f$
Prob. the new link connection fails p_ConnDo_X	0.05	for $X = c, d, f$

As consequence of a failure affecting node N_3 the three possible reconfigurations "Reduced", "Restart" and "Set-up" have been evaluated considering the values listed in Table 3, Table 4 and Table 5, respectively. The overall model is almost the same for all the three cases: they change only for their initial marking, enabling conditions and the values of some parameters, as shown in the Tables.

Figure 9 shows the comparison among the different strategies in terms of the failure probability. The instant-of-time measure of the failure probability is the unreliability of the system. The case when all components are "Up" is referred as "Perfect" in the Figure and it represents a lower bound for the failure probability. It is interesting to observe that at varying of time the best strategy changes: the strategy that minimizes the failure probability is initially the "Reduced" strategy (up to 4 hours), and, then, the best one becomes "SetUp". This suggests that the choice of the "best" reconfiguration depends also on the mission time for the system, as dictated by the application.

5   Related Work

Recently, several approaches and frameworks to manage non functional properties in component based applications have been proposed in the literature.

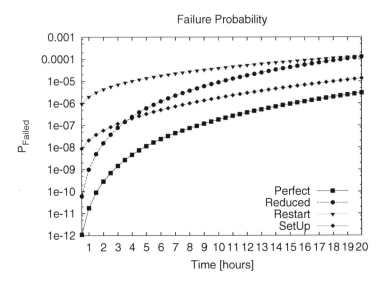

Fig. 9. Comparison among different choices

In [2], Knight et al. present *Willow*, an architecture for enhancing survivability of critical information systems. Willow is designed to detect *local* and *complex faults* by means of monitoring features, and to react to the failures by dynamically reconfiguring the managed system. The broad and complete management of reconfiguration in terms of component dependencies, conflicting policies, global data and state consistency, makes Willow a suitable framework for survivability provision of large scale distributed applications. However, the Willow framework results quite heavy and appropriate for applications composed by hundreds of thousands components. For usual distributed systems, where components are in the order of tens, this framework can be too expensive to instrument and deploy, and many of its functionalities may remain unused.

In [1, 23] Garlan et al. present an approach to dependability and performance management based on *monitoring, interpretation* and *reconfiguration*, where the Software Architecture plays a central role. The Software Architecture of the managed system is specified in terms of components and connectors using Acme [24]. Then, the architectural model is enriched by using the runtime information provided by the *gauges* and finally it is evaluated by using AcmeStudio. If the current architecture violates the specified constraints, it is dynamically modified by the framework. In order to react to the detected failures, a set of *repair strategies* are associated to a constraint violation, while a set of *tactics* is carried out to actually repair the managed system. The tactics rely on some *adaptation operators*, defined by the developer within the framework taking into account the actual reconfiguration capabilities of the managed components. This last approach is very similar to our reconfiguration based approach: in fact, the abstraction of data performed by the gauges is provided in Lira by a hierarchy of agents, while the repair strategies and tactics are defined using the reconfiguration operators provided by the Lira Reconfiguration Language. In Lira, the higher level agents must be programmed to explicitly manage the architectural constraints, a task performed in [1] by the AcmeStudio tool by simply defining the architectural family in Acme ADL. In general, the instrumentation phases of both approaches depend on the complexity of the managed applications: for systems where the types of components are limited in number and the architecture is not extremely complex, the framework proposed in this paper should be instrumented quicker than the other.

With respect to the decision making process, both the approaches proposed in [1] and in [2] do not provide a way to choose the new system configuration specifically created for the optimization of dependability properties, namely fault tolerance. The choice of the tactics in [1] and the *postures* in [2] which place the system in a new configuration are not driven by dependability concerns: in fact, they are just chosen among a set of the possible ones which repair the system. In our approach, instead, among the possible reconfigurations it is chosen the one that places the system in a more healthy state, taking into account the feedbacks provided by the evaluation of Stochastic Timed Petri Nets built at run time to represent the current topology and state of the managed systems.

6   Conclusions

This work has proposed a framework for reconfiguration-based fault tolerance in distributed systems. It integrates Lira, a light-weight infrastructure for reconfiguring applications, with a model–based Decision Maker. On the basis of the monitoring activity carried on by the Lira agents, the Decision Maker performs system reconfiguration in presence of components malfunctions. It resorts to an on-line evaluation of the different available reconfiguration strategies in order to select the most profitable one, in accordance with some predefined optimization criteria. Building block models for the different typology of system components (namely, node and link), capturing the correct/faulty behavior of the components they are associated to, are instantiated on line and connected to reflect the current system configuration.

Since the evaluation process and the system reconfiguration are application dependent, the methodology is firstly described in a very general way, then it is detailed using a simple case study. Managing the communication between two clients in a peer–to–peer network, we have shown how the system is monitored and reconfigured to maintain the communication capabilities, and overall how the framework is able to take online decisions by dynamically setting up and solving stochastic models from available general building blocks.

Applying reconfigurations which adapt to evolving systems structures is highly attractive nowadays, and methodologies pursuing such objective are therefore very appealing. The work we have presented constitutes a relevant initial step in this direction. However, at the current stage of definition, a number of open issue and possibly limiting factors are left unresolved, and further investigations are necessary. The identification of appropriate compositional rules to dynamically build up the overall system model, of the criteria to base the re-configuration selection process on and, primarily, of the necessary features to manage the complexity of the model solution in order to make the on-line evaluation a feasible approach, are among the most challenging problems still under investigations.

In addition, to provide an effective means to fault tolerance in critical systems, the Lira infrastructure itself has to be made fault–tolerant. Another possible research direction is to improve error diagnosis capabilities of each agent, to better calibrate system reconfiguration.

Acknowledgments

This work has been partially supported by the Italian Ministry for University, Science and Technology Research (MIUR), project "Strumenti, Ambienti e Applicazioni Innovative per la Societa' dell'Informazione, SOTTOPROGETTO 4".

References

1. Garlan, D., Cheng, S.W., Schmerl, B.: Increasing System Dependability through Architecture-based Self-repair. In: Architecting Dependable Systems. Springer-Verlang (2003)
2. Knight, J.C., Heimbigner, D., Wolf, A.L., Carzaniga, A., Hill, J., Devanbu, P., Gertz, M.: The Willow Architecture: Comprehensive Survivability for Large-Scale Distributed Applications. In: International Conference of Dependable Computer and Systems (DSN02), Washington DC (2002)
3. Kramer, J., Magee, J.: Dynamic Configuration of Distributed System. IEEE Transaction of Software Engineering **SE** (1985) 424–436
4. Kramer, J., Magee, J.: The Evolving Philosophers Problem: Dynamic Change Management. IEEE Transactions on Software Engineering **16** (1990) 1293–1306
5. Young, A.J., Magee, J.N.: A Flexible Approach to Evolution of Reconfigurable Systems. Proc. of IEE/IFIP Int. Workshop on Configurable Distributed Systems (1992)
6. Magee, J.: Configuration of Distributed Systems. In Sloman, M., ed.: Network and Distributed Systems Management. Addison-Wesley (1994)
7. Kramer, J., Magee, J.: Analysing Dynamic Change in Software Architectures: A Case Study. Proc. 4th Int. Conf. on Configurable Distributed Architecture (1998) 91–100
8. Wermelinger, M.: Towards a Chemical Model for Software Architecture Reconfiguration. Proceedings of the 4th International Conference on Configurable Distributed Systems (1998)
9. Castaldi, M., De Angelis, G., Inverardi, P.: A Reconfiguration Language for Remote Analysis and Application Adaptation. In Orso, A., Porter, A., eds.: Proceedings of Remote Analysis and Measurement of Software Systems. (2003) 35–38
10. Castaldi, M., Carzaniga, A., Inverardi, P., Wolf, A.: A Light-weight Infrastructure for Reconfiguring Applications. In Westfechtel, B., van der Hoek, A., eds.: Software Configuration Management, ICSE Workshops SCM 2001 and SCM 2003 Toronto, Canada, and Portland, OR, USA. Volume 2649 of Lecture Notes in Computer Science., Springer (2003)

11. Castaldi, M., Costantini, S., Gentile, S., Tocchio, A.: A Logic-based Infrastructure for Reconfiguring Applications. Technical report, University of L'Aquila, Department of Computer Science (2003) To appear in LNAI, Springer.
12. Rose, M.T.: The Simple Book: An Introduction to Networking Management. Prentice Hall (1996)
13. Castaldi, M., Ryan, N.D.: Supporting Component-based Development by Enriching the Traditional API. In: Proceedings of Net.Object Days 2002 - Workshop on Generative and Component-based Software Engineering, Erfurt, Germany (2002) 44–48
14. Huang, Y., Kintala, C., Kollettis, N.: Software rejuvenation: Analysis, module and applications. In: Proc. of 25th Int. Symposium on Fault-Tolerance Computing (FTCS-25), , Pasadena, CA, USA (June 1995)
15. Petty, M.D., Weisel, E.W.: A Composability Lexicon. In: Proceedings of the Spring 2003 Simulation Interoperability Workshop, Orlando FL, USA (2003)
16. Betous-Almeida, C., Kanoun, K.: Stepwise Construction and Refinement of Dependability Models. In: IEEE International Conference on Dependable Systems and Networks, Washington D.C, USA (2002)
17. Siewiorek, D.P., Swarz, R.S.: Reliable Computer System - Design and Evaluation. 3 edn. Digital Press (2001)
18. Chohra, A., Porcarelli, S., Di Giandomenico, F., Bondavalli, A.: Towards Optimal Database Maintenance in Wireless Communication System. In: 5th World Multi-Conference on Systemics, Cybernetics and Informatics, (SCI2001), Orlando, Florida (2001)
19. Powell, D.: Failure Mode Assumptions and Assumption Coverage. In Laprie, J., Randell, B., Kopetz, H., Littlewood, B., eds.: Predictably Dependable Computing Systems. Springer Verlag (1995) 3–24
20. Bondavalli, A., Mura, I., Chiaradonna, S., Filippini, R., Poli, S., Sandrini, F.: DEEM: a Tool for the Dependability Modeling and Evaluation of Multiple Phased Systems. In: Proc. of Dependable Systems and Networks, New York, USA (2000)
21. Marsan, M.A., Chiola, G.: On Petri Nets with Deterministic and Exponentially Distribuited Firing Times. In: LNCS. Volume 266. Springer Verlang (1987) 132–145
22. Muppala, A.K., Ciardo, G., Trivedi, K.S.: Stochastic reward nets for reliability prediction. Communications in Reliability, Maintenability and Serviceability **1** (1994) 9–20
23. Garlan, D., Schmerl, B., Chang, J.: Using Gauges for Architecture-Based Monitoring and Adaptation. In: Proceedings of Working Conference on Complex and Dynamic Systems Architecture, Brisbane, Australia (2001)
24. Garlan, D., Monroe, R., Wile, D.: Acme: Architectural Description of Component-Based Systems. In Leavens, G.T., Sitaraman, M., eds.: Foundations of Component-Based Systems. Cambridge University Press (2000) 47–68

On Designing Dependable Services
with Diverse Off-the-Shelf SQL Servers

Ilir Gashi, Peter Popov, Vladimir Stankovic, and Lorenzo Strigini

Centre for Software Reliability, City University,
Northampton Square, London EC1V 0HB, UK
{I.Gashi,V.Stankovic}@city.ac.uk
{Ptp,Strigini}@csr.city.ac.uk
http://www.csr.city.ac.uk

Abstract. The most important non-functional requirements for an SQL server are performance and dependability. This paper argues, based on empirical results from our on-going research with diverse SQL servers, in favour of diverse redundancy as a way of improving both. We show evidence that current data replication solutions are insufficient to protect against the range of faults documented for database servers; outline possible fault-tolerant architectures using diverse servers; discuss the design problems involved; and offer evidence of the potential for performance improvement through diverse redundancy.

1 Introduction

'Do not put all eggs in the same basket', 'Two heads are better than one' summarise the intuitive human belief about the value of redundancy and diversity as a means of reducing the risk of failure. We are more likely to trust the results of our complex calculation if a colleague has arrived independently at the same result. In this regard, Charles Babbage was probably the first person to advocate using two computers - although by computer he meant a person [1].

In many cases, e.g. in team games, people with diverse, complementary abilities signify a way of improving the overall team performance. Every football team in the world would benefit from having an exceptional player such as Ronaldo[1]. A good team is one in which there is a balance of defenders, midfielders and attackers because the game consists of defending, play making and, of course, scoring. Therefore, a team of 11 Ronaldos has little chance of making a good team.

High performance of computing systems is often as important as the correctness of the results produced. When a system performs various tasks, optimising the performance with respect to only one of them is insufficient; good response time must be achieved on different tasks, similarly to how a good team provides a balanced performance in defence, midfield and attack. When both performance and dependability are taken into account, there is often a trade-off between the two. The balance chosen will depend on the priorities set for the system. In some cases, improving performance has a higher priority for users than improving dependability. For instance, a timely,

---

[1] At the time of writing the Brazilian footballer Ronaldo is recognised as one of the best forwards in the world.

R. de Lemos et al. (Eds.): Architecting Dependable Systems II, LNCS 3069, pp. 191–214, 2004.
© Springer-Verlag Berlin Heidelberg 2004

only approximately correct response is sometimes more desirable than one that is absolutely correct but late.

The value of redundancy and diversity as a means of tolerating faults in computing systems has long been recognised. Replication of hardware is often seen as an adequate mechanism for tolerating 'random' hardware faults. If hardware is very complex, however, e.g. VLSI chips, and hence design faults are likely, then diverse redundancy is used as a protection against hardware design faults [2]. For software faults as well, non-diverse replication will fail to detect, or recover from, all those failures that do not produce obvious symptoms like crashes, or that occur in identical ways on all the copies of a replicated system, and at each retry of the same operations. For these kinds of failures, diverse redundancy (often referred to as 'design diversity') is required. The assumptions about the failure modes of the system to be protected dictate the choice between diverse and non-diverse replication.

Diverse redundancy has been known for almost 30 years [3] and is a thoroughly studied subject [4]. Many implementations of the idea exist, for instance recovery blocks [3], N-version programming [5] and self-checking modular redundancy [6].

Over the years, diverse redundancy has found its way to various industrial applications [7]. Its adoption, however, has been much more limited than the adoption of non-diverse replication. The main reason has been the cost of developing several versions of software to the same specification. Also, system integration with diverse versions poses additional design problems, compared to non-diverse replication [8], [4], [9].

The first obstacle – the cost of bespoke development of the versions - has been to a large extent eliminated in many areas due to the success of standard products in various industries and the resulting growth in the market for off-the-shelf components. For many categories of applications software from different vendors, compliant with a particular standard specification, has become an affordable commodity and can be acquired off-the-shelf[2]. Deploying several diverse off-the-shelf components (or complete software solutions) in a fault-tolerant configuration is now an affordable option for system integrators who need to improve service dependability.

In this paper we take a concrete example of a type of system for which replication can be (and indeed has been) used – SQL servers[3]. We investigate whether design diversity is useful in this domain from the perspectives of dependability and performance.

Many vendors offer support for fault-tolerance in the form of server 'fail-over', i.e. solutions with replicated servers, which cope with crashes of individual servers by redistributing the load to the remaining available servers. Despite the relatively long history of database replication [10], effort on standardisation in the area has only started recently [11]. Fail-over delivers some improvement over non-replicated servers although limited effectiveness has been observed in some cases [12]. Fail-over can

---

[2] The difference between commercial-off-the-shelf (COTS) and just off-the-shelf (e.g. freeware or open-source software) is not important for our discussion despite the possible huge difference in cost. Even if the user is to pay thousands for a COTS product, e.g. a commercial SQL server, this is a tiny fraction of the development cost of the product.

[3] Although many prefer relational Databases Management System (RDBMS), we instead use the term SQL server to emphasise that Structured Query Language (SQL) will be used by the clients to interact with the RDBMS.

be used as a recovery strategy irrespective of the type of failure (not necessarily "fail-stop" [13]). However its known implementations assume crash failures, as they depend on detecting a crash for triggering recovery.

The rest of the paper is organised as follows. In Section 2 we summarise the results of a study on fault diversity of four SQL servers [14] which run against the common assumptions that SQL servers fail-stop and failures can be tolerated simply by roll-back and retry. In Section 3, we study the architectural implications of moving from non-diverse replication with several replicas of the same SQL server to using diverse SQL servers, and discuss the main design problems that this implies. We also demonstrate the potential for diversity to deliver performance advantages and compensate for the overhead created by replication, and in Section 4 we present preliminary empirical results suggesting that these improvements can indeed be realised with at least two existing servers. This appears to be a new dimension of the usefulness of design diversity, not recognised before. In Section 5 we review some recent results on data replication. In Section 6 we discuss some general implications of our results. Finally, in Section 7 some conclusions are presented together with several open questions worth addressing in the future.

2 A Study of Faults in Four SQL Servers

Whether SQL servers require diversity to achieve fault tolerance depends on how likely they are to fail in ways that would not be tolerated by non-diverse replication. There is little published evidence about this. First, we must consider *detection*: some failures (e.g. crashes) are easily detected even in a non-diverse setting. A study using fault injection [15] found that 2% of the bugs of Postgres95 server violated the fail-stop property (i.e., they were not detected before corrupting the state of the database) even when using the transaction mechanism of Postgres95. 2% is a high percentage for applications with high reliability requirements. The other question is about *recovery*. Jim Gray [16] observed that many software-caused failures were tolerated by non-diverse replication. They were caused by apparently non-deterministic bugs ("*Heisenbugs*"), which only cause failures under circumstances that are difficult to reproduce. These failures are not replicated when the same input sequence is repeated after a rollback, or applied to two copies of the same software. However, a recent study of fault reports about three open-source applications (including MySQL) [17] found that only a small fraction of faults (5-14%) were triggered by transient conditions (probable Heisenbugs).

We have recently addressed these issues via a study on *fault diversity* in SQL servers. We collected 181 reports of known bugs reported for two open-source SQL servers (PostgreSQL 7.0 and Interbase 6.0[4]) and two commercial SQL servers (Microsoft SQL 7.0 and Oracle 8.0.5). The results of the study are described in detail in [14]. Here we concentrate on the aspects relevant to our discussion.

---

[4] Made available as an open-source product under this name by Borland Inc. in 2000. The company reverted to closed development for subsequent releases. The product continues to be maintained as an open source development under a different name - "Firebird".

1.C

194   Ilir Gashi et al.

2.1   SQL Servers Cannot Be Assumed to 'Fail-Stop'

Table 1 summarises the results of the study. The bugs are classified according to the characteristics of the failures they cause, as different failure types require different recovery mechanisms:

Engine Crash failures: crashes or halts of the core engine.

Incorrect Result failures: not engine crashes, but incorrect outputs: the outputs do not conform to the server's specification or to the SQL standard.

Performance failures: the output is correct, but observed to carry an unacceptable time penalty for the particular input.

Other failures.

Table 1. A summary of the study with reported bugs for 4 SQL servers. The first 6 rows represent the observations after running the bug scripts. Each shaded column represents the results of running bug scripts on the server for which the bugs were reported, while the non-shaded columns represent the results of running the scripts on the other three servers. The last 6 rows represent a classification of the observed failures.

			Interbase	PostgreSQL	Oracle	MSSQL	PostgreSQL	Interbase	Oracle	MSSQL	Oracle	Interbase	MSSQL	PostgreSQL	MSSQL	Interbase	Oracle	PostgreSQL
Total Scripts			55	55	55	55	57	57	57	57	18	18	18	18	51	51	51	51
Script cannot be run (Functionality Missing)			n/a	23	20	16	n/a	32	27	24	n/a	13	13	12	n/a	36	32	31
Further Work			n/a	5	4	6	n/a	2	0	0	n/a	1	1	2	n/a	3	7	2
Total scripts run			55	27	31	33	57	23	30	33	18	4	4	4	51	12	12	18
No failure observed			8	26	31	31	5	23	30	31	4	4	4	3	12	11	12	12
Failure observed			47	1	0	2	52	0	0	2	14	0	0	1	39	1	0	6
Types of failures	**Poor Performance**		3	0	0	0	0	0	0	0	1	0	0	0	6	0	0	0
	Engine Crash		7	0	0	0	11	0	0	0	3	0	0	0	5	0	0	0
	Incorrect Result	Self-evident	4	0	0	1	14	0	0	1	3	0	0	0	10	0	0	6
		Non-self-evident	23	1	0	1	20	0	0	1	7	0	0	1	17	1	0	0
	Other	Self-evident	2	0	0	0	2	0	0	0	0	0	0	0	1	0	0	0
		Non-self-evident	8	0	0	0	5	0	0	0	0	0	0	0	0	0	0	0

We also classified the failures according to their detectability by a client of the database servers:

Self-Evident failures: engine crash failures, cases in which the server signals an internal failure as an exception (error message) and performance failures.

Non-Self-Evident failures: incorrect result failures, without server exceptions within an accepted time delay.

[14] shows that the fraction of reported faults causing crash failures varies across servers from 13% (MS SQL) to 21% (Oracle and PostgreSQL). These are small per-

centages, despite crashes being *easy to detect* and thus likely to get reported [14]. More than 50% of the faults cause failures with incorrect but seemingly legal results, i.e. a client application will not normally detect them. In other words, an assumption that either a server will process a query correctly or the problem will be detected is *flatly wrong.* Any replication scheme that tolerates server crashes only does not provide any guarantee against these failures – the incorrect results may be simply replicated. Although our results do not show how likely non-self-evident *failures* are - the percentages above are based on *fault* counts - the evidence in [14] seems overwhelming against assuming (until actual failure counts are available) that 'fail-stop' failures are the main concern to be resolved by replication.

2.2   Potential of Design Diversity for Detecting/Diagnosing Failures

Table 2 gives another view on the reported bugs of the 4 SQL servers: what would happen if 1-out-of-2 fault-tolerant SQL servers were built using these 4 SQL servers.

Table 2. Potential of diverse pairs of servers for tolerating the effects of the reported bugs in our sample. *IB* stands for Interbase, *PG* for PostgreSQL, *OR* for Oracle and *MS* for MS SQL.

Pairs of servers	Number of bug scripts run	Failure Observed (in at least one server)	One out of two servers failing		Both servers failing		
			Self-evident	Non-Self-evident	Non–Detectable	Detectable	
						Self-evident	Non-Self-evident
IB + PG	62	43	17	25	1	0	0
IB + OR	62	29	8	21	0	0	0
IB + MS	69	35	11	21	2	1	0
PG + OR	64	30	13	16	0	0	1
PG + MS	76	46	18	21	1	6	0
OR + MS	71	14	7	7	0	0	0

What we want to find out is how many of the coincident failures are *detectable* in the 2-version systems. We define:

Detectable failures: Self-Evident failures or those where servers return different incorrect results (the comparison algorithm must be written to allow for possible differences in the representation of correct results). All failures affecting only one out of two (or up to n-1 out of n) versions are detectable.

Non-Detectable failures: the two (or more) servers return identical incorrect results.

Replication with identical servers would only detect the self-evident failures: crash failures, failures reported by the server itself and poor performance failures. For all four servers, less than 50% of faults cause such failures. Instead, with diverse pairs of servers many of the failures are detectable. All the possible two-version fault-tolerant configurations detect the failures caused by at least 94% of the faults.

3   Architecture of a Fault-Tolerant Diverse SQL Server

3.1   General Scheme

Studying replication protocols is not the focus of this paper. Data replication is a well-understood subject [10]. A recent study compared various replication protocols in terms of their performance and the feasibility of their implementation [18]. One of the oldest replication protocols, 'Read once write all available (ROWAA)' [10] comes out as the best protocol for a very wide range of scenarios. In ROWAA, read operations are on just one copy of the database (e.g. the one that is physically nearest to the client) while write operations must be replicated on all nodes. An important performance optimisation for the updates is executing the update statements only once and propagating the updates to the other nodes [10]. This may lead to a very significant improvement; with up to a fivefold reduction in execution time of the update statements [19], [20]. However, these schemes would not tolerate non-self-evident failures that cause incorrect updates or return incorrect results by select queries. For the former, incorrect updates would be propagated to the other replicas and for the latter, incorrect results would be returned to the client. This deficiency can be overcome by building a fault-tolerant server node ("FT-node") from two or more diverse SQL servers, wrapped together with a "middleware" layer to appear to each client as a single SQL server and to each of the SQL servers as a set of clients, as shown in Fig. 1.

Fig. 1. Fault-tolerant server node (FT-node) with two or more diverse SQL servers (in this case two: *SQL Server 1 and SQL Server 2*). The *middleware* "hides" the servers from the clients (*1 to n*) for which the data storage appears as a single SQL server.

Some design considerations about this architecture follow.

The middleware must ensure connectivity with the clients and the multiple servers. The connectivity between the clients and the middleware can implement a "standard" API, e.g. JDBC/ODBC, or some proprietary API. The middleware communicates with the servers using any one of the connectivity solutions available for the chosen servers (with server independent API, e.g. JDBC/ODBC, or the server proprietary API).

The rest of Section 3 deals with other design issues in this fault-tolerant design:

– synchronisation between the servers to guarantee data consistency between them;
– support for fault-tolerance for realistic modes of failure via mechanisms for:
  – error detection;
  – error containment;
  – state recovery
– "replica determinism": dealing with aspects of server behaviour which would cause inconsistencies between database replicas even with identical sequences of queries;

- translation of the SQL queries coming from the client to be "understood" by diverse SQL servers which use different "dialects" of the SQL syntax;
- "data diversity": the potential for improving fault tolerance through expressing (sequences of) client queries in alternative, logically equivalent ways;
- performance effects of diversity, which depending on the details of the chosen fault-tolerance scheme may be negative or positive.

3.2 Fault Tolerance Strategies

This basic architecture can be used for various forms of fault-tolerance, with different trade-offs between degree of replication, fault tolerance and performance [21].

We can discuss separately various aspects of fault tolerance:

- *Failure detection and containment.* Self-evident server failures are detected as in a non-diverse server, via server error messages (i.e. via the existing error detection mechanisms inside the servers), and time-outs for crash and performance failures. Diversity gives the additional capability of detecting non-self-evident failures by comparing the outputs of the different servers. In a FT-node with 3 or more diverse versions, majority voting can be used to choose a result and thus mask the failure to the clients, and identify the failed version which may need a recovery action to correct its state. With a 2-diverse FT-node, if the two servers give different results, the middleware cannot decide which server is in error: it needs to invoke some form of manual or automated recovery. The middleware will present the failure to the client as a delay in response (due to the time needed for recovery), or as a self-evident failure (crash - a "fail-silent" FT-node; or an error message - a "self-checking" FT-node). The voting/comparison algorithm will need to allow for "cosmetic" differences between equivalent correct results, like padding characters in character strings or different numbers of digits in the representations of floating point numbers.
- *Error recovery.* As just described, diversity allows for more refined diagnosis (identification of the failed server). This improves availability: the middleware can selectively direct recovery actions at the server diagnosed as having failed, while letting the other server(s) continue to provide the service. State recovery of the database can be obtained in the following ways:
  - via standard backward error recovery, which will be effective if the failures are due to Heisenbugs. To command backward error recovery, the middleware may use the standard database transaction mechanisms: aborting the failed transaction and replaying its queries may produce a correct execution. Alternatively or additionally, checkpointing [22] can be used. At regular intervals, the states of the servers are saved (by database "backup" commands: e.g., in PostgreSQL the pg_dump command). After a failure, the database is restored to the state before the last checkpoint and the sequence of (all or just update) queries since then is replayed to it;
  - additionally, diversity offers ways of recovering from Bohrbug-caused failures, by essentially copying the database state of a correct server into the failed one (similarly to [23]). Since the formats of the database files differ between the servers, the middleware would need to query the correct server[s] for their database contents and command the failed server to write them into the corresponding records in its database, similar to what is proposed in [11]. This would be

expensive, perhaps to be completed off-line, but a designer can use multi-level recovery, in which the first step is to correct only those records that have been found erroneous on read queries.

To increase the level of data replication a possibility is to integrate our FT-node scheme with standard forms of replication, like ROWAA, possibly with the optimisation of writes [10]. One could integrate these strategies into our proposed middleware, or for simplicity choose a layered implementation (possibly at a cost in terms of performance) in which our fault-tolerant nodes are used as server nodes in a standard ROWAA protocol. However, a layered architecture using, say, 2-diverse FT-nodes may require more servers for tolerating a given number of server failures.

3.3 Data Consistency Between Diverse SQL Servers

Data consistency in database replication is usually defined in terms of 1-copy serialisability between the transaction histories executed on the various nodes [10]. In practical implementations this is affected by:

- the order of delivery of queries to the replicas
- the order in which the servers execute the queries, which in turn is affected by:
  - the execution plans created for the queries
  - the execution of the plans by the execution engines of the servers, which are normally non-deterministic and may differ between the servers, in particular with the concurrency control mechanism implemented.

Normally, consistency relies on "totally ordered" [24] delivery of the queries by reliable multicast protocols. For the optimised schemes of data replication, e.g. ROWAA, only the updates are delivered in total order to all the nodes. Diverse data replication would also rely on the total ordering of messages.

In terms of execution of the queries the difference between non-diverse and diverse replication is in the execution plans, which will be the same for replicas of the same SQL server, but may differ significantly between diverse SQL servers. This may result in significantly different times to process the queries. If many queries are executed concurrently, identical execution plans across replicas do not guarantee the same order of execution, due to for example multithreading. The allocation of CPU time to threads is inherently non-deterministic. In other words, non-determinism must be dealt with in both non-diverse and diverse replication schemes. The phenomenon of inconsistent behaviour between replicas that receive equivalent (from some viewpoint) sequences of requests is not limited to database servers [25] and there are well known architectural solutions for dealing with it [26]. Empirically [27], we repeatedly observed data inconsistency even with replication of the same SQL server.

To achieve data consistency, i.e. a 1-copy serialisable history [10] across replicas, the concurrent execution of modifying transactions needs to be restricted. Two extreme possible scenarios can be exploited to deal with non-determinism in SQL servers, and apply to both non-diverse and diverse SQL servers:

- non-determinism does not affect the combined result of executing concurrent transactions: for instance, the transactions do not "clash". No concurrent transactions attempt modifications of the same data. If this is the case, all possible subhistories, which may result from various orders of executing the transactions concurrently, are identical and thus 1-copy serialisability across all the replicas (no

matter whether diverse or non-diverse) will be guaranteed despite the possibly different orders of execution of the transactions by the different servers;
- non-determinism is eliminated with respect to the modifying transactions by executing them one at a time. Again, 1-copy serialisability is achieved [27]. This regime of serialisability may be limited to within each individual database, thus allowing concurrency between modifying transactions executed on different databases.

Combinations of these two are possible: concurrent transactions are allowed to execute concurrently, but if a "clash" is detected, all transactions involved in the clash are rolled back and then serialised according to some total order [24].

3.4 Differences in Features and SQL "Dialects" Between SQL Servers

3.4.1 Missing and Proprietary Features
With two SQL standards (SQL-92 and SQL-99 (SQL 3)) and several different levels of compliance to these, it is not surprising that SQL servers implement many different variants of SQL. Most of the servers with significant user bases guarantee SQL-92 Entry Level of compliance or higher. SQL-92 Entry Level covers the basic types of queries and allows in many cases the developers to write code which requires no modification when ported to a different SQL server. However some very widely used queries are not part of the Entry Level, e.g. the various built-in JOIN operators [28]. Triggers and stored procedures [29] are another example of very useful functionality, used in many business databases, which are not part of SQL-92 (surprisingly they are not yet supported in MySQL, one of the most widely used SQL servers).

In addition vendors may introduce proprietary extensions in their products. For example Microsoft intends to incorporate .NET in "Yukon", their new SQL server [30].

3.4.2 Differences in Dialects for Common Features
In addition to the missing and proprietary features, there are differences even in the dialect of the SQL that is common among servers. For instance the example below shows differences in the syntax for outer joins between the SQL dialects of three servers which we used in experiments with diverse SQL servers [27] (Oracle uses a non-standard syntax for outer joins):

ORACLE 8.0.5
```
select items.number
    from items, orders
    where items.number = orders.item_number (+)
    group by items.number
    having items.number < 20000
    order by items.number desc
```

MS SQL 7.0 and INTERBASE 6.0
```
select items.number
    from items
    left outer join orders on items.number =
    orders.item_number
    group by items.number
    having items.number < 20000
    order by items.number desc
```

Although the difference in the syntax is marginal, Oracle 8.0.5 will not parse the standard syntax. Significant differences exist between the syntax of other SQL constructs, e.g. stored procedures and triggers. For instance, Oracle's support for SQLJ for stored procedures differs slightly from the standard syntax.

3.4.3 Reconciling the Differences Between Dialects and Features of SQL Servers

Standardisation is unlikely to resolve the existing differences between the SQL dialects in the foreseeable future, although there have been attempts to improve interoperability by standardising "persistent modules" [29] (also called "stored procedures" in most major SQL servers or "functions" in PostgreSQL). However, some vendors still undermine standardisation by adding proprietary extensions in their products.

To use replication with diverse SQL servers, the differences between the servers must be reconciled. Two possibilities are:

– requiring the client applications to use the SQL sub-set which is common to all the SQL servers in the FT-node, and reconciling the differences between the dialects by implementing "translators" that translate the syntax used by the client applications to the syntax understood by the respective servers. Such "translators" can become part of the replication middleware (Fig 1). One may:
  – require the client applications to use ANSI SQL to work with the middleware, which will contain translators for all SQL dialects used in the FT-node;
  – allow the clients to use the SQL dialect of their choice (e.g. the dialect of a specific SQL server or ANSI SQL), to allow legacy applications written for a specific SQL server to be "ported" and run with diverse replication.
– expressing some of the missing SQL features through equivalent transformation of the client query to query(ies) supported by the SQL servers used in the FT-node (see 3.6).

In either case, translation between the dialects of the SQL servers is needed. Translation is certainly feasible. Surprisingly, though, we could not find off-the-shelf tools to assist with the translation even though "porting" database schema from one SQL server product to another is a common practice.

3.5 Replica Determinism: The Example of DDL Support

The differences between SQL servers also affect the Data Definition Language (DDL), i.e., the part of SQL that deals with the metadata (schema) of a database. The DDL does not require special attention with non-diverse replication: the same DDL statement is just copied to all replicas. We outline here an aspect of using DDL which may lead to data inconsistency: *auto numeric fields*.

SQL servers allow the clients to simplify the generation of unique numeric values by defining a data type, which is under the direct control of the server. These unique values are typically used for generating keys (primary and secondary) without too much overhead on the client side: the client does not need to explicitly provide values for these fields when inserting a new record. Implementations of this feature differ between servers (Identity() function in MS SQL, generators in Interbase, etc.), but this is not a serious problem. The real problem is that the different servers specify different behaviours of this feature when a transaction is aborted within which unique numbers were generated. In some servers, the values generated in a transaction that was rolled back are "lost" and will never appear in the fields of committed data. Other servers keep track of these "unused" values and generate them again in some later transactions, which will be committed. This difference affects data consistency across different SQL servers. The inconsistencies thus created must be handled explicitly, by the middleware [27], or by the client applications by not using auto fields at all.

This is just one case of diversity causing violations of *replica determinism* [31]; others may exist, depending on the specific combination of diverse servers.

3.6 Data Diversity

Although diversity can dramatically improve error detection rates it does not make them 100%, e.g. our study found four bugs causing identical non-self-evident failures in two servers.

To improve the situation, one could use the mechanism called "data diversity" by Ammann and Knight [32] (who studied it in a different context). The simplest example of the idea in [32] would refer to computation of a continuous function of a continuous parameter. The values of the function computed for two close values of the parameter are also close to each other. Thus, failures in the form of dramatic jumps of the function on close values of the parameter can not only be detected but also corrected by computing a "pseudo correct" value. This is done by trying slightly different values of the parameter until a value of the function is calculated which is close to the one before the failure. This was found [32] to be an effective way of masking failures, i.e. delivering fault-tolerance. Data diversity thus can help not only with error detection but with recovery as well, and thus to tolerate some failures due to design faults without the cost of design diversity.

Data diversity seems applicable to SQL servers because most queries can be "re-phrased" into different, but logically equivalent [sequences of] queries. There are cases where a particular query causes a failure in a server but a *re-phrased* version of the same query does not. Examples of such queries often appear in bug reports as "*workarounds*". The example below is a bug script for PostgreSQL v7.0.0, producing a non-self-evident failure (incorrect result) by returning one row instead of six.

```
create table employee (name varchar(10) not null, age
integer, salary float, deptname varchar(10), manager
varchar(10), primary key(name));
The following data exists in the table:
```

Name	Age	Salary	Deptname	Manager
Mike	28	1500.00	Shoe	Edna
Sally	42	877.50	Toy	Ted
Georgia	22		Book	
Ted		2615.73	Toy	Malcolm
Edna	39	2000.00	Shoe	Malcolm
Malcolm	50	2750.00	Admin	

```
CREATE VIEW avg_int AS SELECT AVG(salary) AS avg_sal
FROM employee;
CREATE VIEW average AS SELECT employee.name, em-
ployee.salary, avg_int.avg_sal, (salary-avg_sal) as
sal_diff FROM employee, avg_int;
```

```
SELECT * FROM average;

name  | salary | avg_sal  | sal_diff
------+--------+----------+----------
 Mike |   1500 | 1948.646 | -448.646
```

A workaround exists which is based on using a TEMP (temporary) table instead of a view (in this case to hold the average salaries). The same table schema definition and data given above are used together with the code below, and then the result is correct.

```
/* This is the temporary table*/
SELECT AVG(salary) AS avg_sal INTO TEMP TABLE avg_int
FROM employee;

/* This view is same as above. */
CREATE VIEW average AS SELECT employee.name, em-
ployee.salary, avg_int.avg_sal, (salary-avg_sal) as
sal_diff FROM employee, avg_int;

SELECT * FROM average;
name    | salary | avg_sal  | sal_diff
--------+--------+----------+----------
Mike    |   1500 | 1948.646 |  -448.646
Sally   |  877.5 | 1948.646 | -1071.146
Georgia |        | 1948.646 |
Ted     |2615.73 | 1948.646 |   667.084
Edna    |   2000 | 1948.646 |    51.354
Malcolm |   2750 | 1948.646 |   801.354
                             (6 rows)
```

Data diversity could be implemented via an algorithm in the middleware that re-phrases queries according to predefined rules. For instance, one such rule could be to break-up all complex nested SELECT queries so that the inner part of the query is saved in a temporary table, and the outer part then uses the temporary table to generate the final result[5].

Data diversity can be used *with* or *without* design diversity. In the case of databases it would be attractive alone as it would for instance allow applications to use the full set of features of an SQL server, including the proprietary ones. Architectural schemes using data diversity are similar to those using design diversity. For instance, Amman and Knight in [32] describe two schemes, which they call "retry block" and "n-copy programming", which can also be used for SQL servers. The "retry block" is based on backward recovery. A query is only re-phrased if either the server "fail-stops" or its output fails an acceptance test. In "n-copy programming", a copy of the query as issued by the client is sent to one of the servers and re-phrased variant[s] are sent to the others; their results are voted to mask failures. The techniques for error detection and state recovery would also be similar to the design diversity case (Section 3.2). In the "retry block" scheme (backward error recovery), applied to one of

---

[5] Re-phrasing algorithms can also be part of the translators for the different SQL dialects. A complex statement which can be directly executed with some servers but not others may need to be re-phrased as a logically equivalent sequence of simpler statements for the latter.

the servers, a failed transaction would be rolled back, and the rephrased queries executed from the rolled-back state thus obtained. In the "n-copy programming" scheme,
the state of a server diagnosed to be correct would be copied to the faulty server (forward error recovery). Another possibility is not to use "re-phrasing" unless diverse
replicas produce different outputs with no majority. Then, the middleware could abort
the transaction and replay the queries, after "re-phrasing" them, to all or some of the
servers. Fig. 2 shows, at a high level, an example of architecture using both data diversity and design diversity with SQL servers. This example assumes a combination
of "N-version programming" and "n-copy programming", with a single voter in the
middleware.

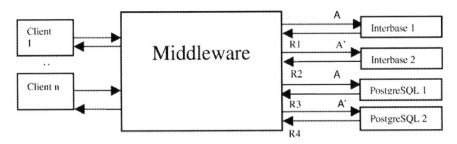

Fig. 2. A possible design for a fault-tolerant server using diverse SQL servers and data diversity. The original query (*A*) is sent to the pair {*Interbase 1*, *PostgreSQL 1*}, the re-phrased
query (*A'*) is sent to the pair {*Interbase 2*, *PostgreSQL 2*}. The *middleware* compares/votes the
results in one of the ways described in Section 3.2 for solutions without data diversity.

A designer would choose a combination of design diversity and data diversity as a
trade-off between the conflicting requirements of dependability, performance and
cost. At one extreme, combining both design and data diversity and re-phrasing all
those queries for which re-phrasing is possible would give the maximum potential for
failure detection, but with high cost.

3.7 Performance of Diverse-Replicated SQL Servers

Database replication with diverse SQL servers improves dependability, as discussed
in the previous sections. What are its implications for system performance? In Fig. 3
we sketch a timing diagram of the sequence of events associated with a query being
processed by an FT-node which includes two diverse SQL servers.

Processing every query will involve some synchronisation overhead. To "validate"
the results of executing each query, the middleware should wait for responses from
both servers, check if the two responses are identical and, in case they differ, initiate
recovery. We will use the term "pessimistic" for this regime of operation. If the response times are close, the overhead due to differences in the performance of the
servers (shown in the diagram as dashed boxes) will be low. If the difference is significant, then this overhead may become significant. If one of the servers is the *slower
one on all queries*, this slower server dictates the pace of processing. The service
offered by the FT node will be as fast as the service from a non-replicated node implemented with the slower server, provided the extra overhead due to the middleware
is negligible compared to the processing time of the slower server. If, however, the

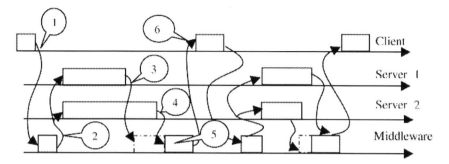

Fig. 3. Timing diagram with two diverse servers and middleware running in pessimistic regime. The meaning of the *arrows* is: *1* – the client sends a query to the middleware; *2* – the middleware translates the request to the dialects of the servers and sends the resulting queries, or sequences of queries, to the respective servers; *3* – the faster response is received by the middleware; *4* – the slower response is received by the middleware; *5* – the middleware adjudicates the two responses; *6* – the middleware sends the result back to the client or if none exists initiates recovery or signals a failure.

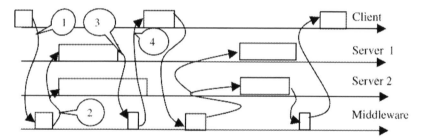

Fig. 4. Timing diagram with two diverse servers and middleware running in optimistic regime. The meaning of the *arrows* is: *1* – the client sends a query to the middleware, *2* – the middleware translates the request to the dialects of the servers and sends the resulting queries, or sequences of queries, to the respective servers; *3* – the fastest response is received by the middleware; *4* - the middleware sends the response to the client.

slower response may come from either server, the service provided by the FT-node will be slower than if a non-replicated node with the slower server was used. This slow-down due to the pessimistic regime is the cost of the extra dependability assurance.

Many see performance (e.g. the server's response time) as the most important non-functional requirement of SQL servers. Is diversity always a bad news for those for whom performance is more important than dependability? Fig. 4 depicts a scenario, referred to as the "optimistic" regime. For this regime the only function of the middleware is to translate the client requests, send them to the servers and as soon as the first response is received, return it back to the client.

Therefore, if the client is prepared to accept a higher risk of incorrect responses diversity can, in principle, improve performance compared with non-diverse solutions.

How does the optimistic regime compare in terms of performance (e.g. response time) with the two diverse servers used? If one of the servers is faster on *every* query, diversity with the optimistic regime does not provide any improvement compared with the faster server. If, however, the faster response comes from different servers depending on the query, then the optimistic regime will give a faster service than the faster of the two servers (provided the overhead of the middleware is not too high compared with the response times of the servers).

The faster response for a query may come from either server (as shown in Fig. 4). A similar effect is observed when accepting the faster response between those of two or more *identical* servers. Similarly, in mirrored disk configurations one can take advantage of the random difference between the physical disks' response times to reduce the average response time on reads [33]. What changes with diverse servers is that they may *systematically differ* in their response times for different types of transactions/queries, yielding a greater performance gain. The next section shows experimental evidence of this effect.

4 Increasing Performance via Diversity

4.1 Performance Measures of Diverse SQL Servers

We conducted an empirical study to assess the performance effects of the pessimistic and optimistic regimes using two open-source SQL servers, PostgreSQL 7.2.4 and Interbase 6.0 (licenses for commercial SQL servers constrain the users' rights to publish performance related results).

For this study, we used a client implementing the TPC-C industry-standard benchmark for on-line transaction processing [34]. TPC-C defines 5 types of transactions: *New-Order, Payment, Order-Status, Delivery* and *Stock-Level* and sets the probability of execution of each. The specified measure of throughput is the number of *New-Order* transactions completed per minute (while all five types of transactions are executing). The benchmark provides for performance comparisons of SQL servers from different vendors, with different hardware configurations and operating systems.

We used several identical machines with different operating systems: Intel Pentium 4 (1.4 GHz), 640MB RAMBUS RAM, Microsoft Windows 2000 Professional for the client(s) and the Interbase servers, Linux Red Hat 6.0 for the PostgreSQL servers. The servers ran on four machines: 2 replicas of Interbase and two replicas of PostgreSQL. Before the measurement sessions, the databases on all four servers were populated as specified by the standard.

The client, implemented in Java, used JDBC drivers to connect to the servers. We ran two experiments with different loads on the servers:

Experiment 1: A single TPC-C client for each server;

Experiment 2: 10 TPC-C clients for each server, each client using one of 10 TPC-C databases managed by the same server, so that we could measure the servers' performance under increased load while preserving 1-copy serialisability.

Our objective of the study was not just to repeat the benchmark tests for these servers, but also to get preliminary indications about the performance of an FT-node using diverse servers, compared to one using identical servers and to a single server. Our measurements were more detailed than the ones required by the TPC-C standard.

We recorded the response times for each individual transaction, for each server. We were specifically interested in comparing two architectures:

- two *diverse servers* concurrently process the same stream of transactions (Fig. 1) translated into their respective SQL dialects: the smallest possible configuration with diverse redundancy.
- a reference, non-diverse architecture in which two *identical servers* concurrently process the same stream of transactions.

All four servers were run concurrently, receiving the same stream of transactions from the test harness, which produced four copies of each transaction/query. The overhead that the test harness introduces (mainly due to using multi-threading for communication with the different SQL servers) is the same with and without design diversity.

Instead of translating the queries into the SQL dialects of the two servers on the fly, the queries were hard-coded in the test harness. The comparison between the two architectures is based on the *transaction response times*, neglecting all extra overheads that the FT-node's middleware would introduce. This simplification may somewhat distort the results, but also allows us to compare the potential of the two architectures, and to look at possible trade-offs between dependability and performance, without the effects of the detailed implementation of the middleware.

We compare the performance of the two servers with each other and with the two regimes, pessimistic (Fig. 3) and optimistic (Fig. 4). The performance measure we calculated for the pessimistic regime represents the upper bound of the response time for this particular mix of transactions while performance measure for the optimistic regime represents the lower bound.

We used the following measures of interest:

- mean transaction response times for all five transaction types (Fig. 5)
- mean response times per transaction of each type (Fig. 6).

With *two identical SQL servers* (last two server pairs in Fig. 5), the difference between the mean times is minimal, within 10%. The mean times under the optimistic and pessimistic regimes of operation remain very close (differences of <10% for Interbase and <15% for PostgreSQL). Interbase is the faster server, being almost twice as fast as PostgreSQL, for this set of transactions.

When we combine *two diverse SQL servers* we get a very different picture. Now the optimistic regime can deliver dramatically better performance than the faster server, Interbase. The mean response time is almost 3 times shorter than for Interbase alone (compare the first two bars for the first four pairs). When the pessimistic regime is used, the value of the mean response time is larger than the respective value of the slower server, PostgreSQL, but the slow down is within 40% of PostgreSQL's mean response time - the cost of the improved dependability assurance.

In order to understand why a diverse pair is so different from a non-diverse pair we looked at the individual transaction types. The mean response times of the five transaction types individually are shown in Fig. 6. The figure indicates that the servers "complement" each other in the sense that when Interbase is slow (on average) to process one type of transaction PostgreSQL is fast (*New-Order* and *Stock-Level*) and vice versa (*Payment*, *Order-Status* and *Delivery*). This illustrates why a diverse pair outperforms a non-diverse one so much when the optimistic regime is used, and why it is worse than the slower server when the pessimistic regime is used (Fig. 5).

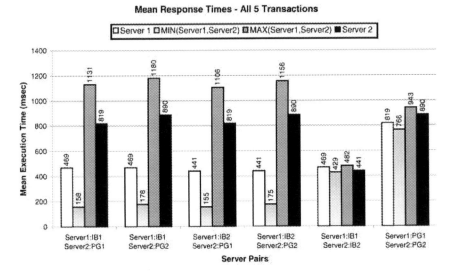

Fig. 5. Mean response time for all five transaction types over 10,000 transactions for two repli-cas of Interbase 6.0 and two of PostgreSQL 7.2.4. The X-axis lists the servers grouped as pairs (*Server 1 and Server 2*). Each server may be of type Interbase (*IB*) or PostgreSQL (*PG*). For each of the 6 server pairs the vertical bars show: – the mean response times of the individual servers and the mean response times calculated for the two regimes of operation of an FT-node (optimistic and pessimistic).

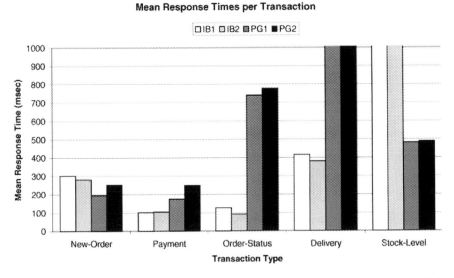

Fig. 6. Mean response times by two replicas of Interbase 6.0 and PostgreSQL 7.2.4 for all five transactions. The X-axis lists the transaction types (*New-Order, Payment, Order-Status, Deliv-ery and Stock-Level*). The Y-axis gives the values of the mean response time in milliseconds for each of the servers (*IB1, IB2, PG1 and PG2*) for a particular transaction type.

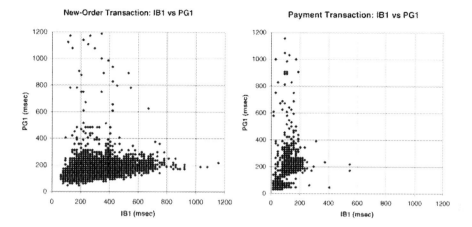

Fig. 7. Response times for the *New-Order* and *Payment* transactions. Every *dot* in the plots represents the response times of two servers for an *instance* of the respective transaction type. If the times were close to each other most of the dots would be concentrated around the unit slope (observed for the pairs of identical servers, IB1 vs IB2 and PG1 vs PG2). If the dots are mostly below the slope, Interbase is slower (as with the *New-Order*). If the dots are concentrated above the unit slope – PostgreSQL is slower (as with the *Payment*). Similar results were obtained for the other three diverse server pairs.

In addition to the mean execution times, we have calculated the percentage of the faster responses coming from either Interbase or PostgreSQL for each transaction. For three transaction types the situation is clear-cut. Interbase is always the faster server for *Order-Status* and *Delivery* transactions, while PostgreSQL is always the faster for *Stock-Level* transactions. For *New-Order* and *Payment* transactions instead, the server that is faster on average does not provide the faster response for each individual transaction. Consider the pair {IB1, PG1}. For *New-Order* transaction, PG1 is faster than IB1 on 81.2% of the transactions but slower on 15.6% (3.2% of the response times were equal). The situation is reversed for *Payment* transactions: 77.2% of the faster responses come from IB1, 15.3% from PG1. This fluctuation is further revealed in Fig. 7. Both observations confirm that diverse servers under the optimistic regime would have performed better (for this transaction mix and load) than a pair of identical servers.

This pattern of the two SQL servers "complementing" each other was also observed in *Experiment 2* under increased load with 10 TPC-C clients. During this experiment the servers were "stretched" so much that the virtual memories of the machines were exhausted. Similarly to the observations of *Experiment 1*, when *two identical servers* are used the difference between the mean response times is minimal, within 10%, and the difference between the mean response times of the optimistic and pessimistic regime remain less than 10% for both servers. Again Interbase is the faster server.

The mean response times when *two diverse servers* are considered under the optimistic regime are around four times shorter than for Interbase alone. Under the pessimistic regime, the mean response time is of course larger than the value of the slower server (on average), PostgreSQL, but the slow down is within 60% of PostgreSQL's mean response time (it was 40% in *Experiment 1*, when a single client was used).

4.2 Design Solutions for the Optimistic Regime

Under the optimistic regime, diversity offers better performance than each of the diverse SQL servers used. Various design solutions are possible, with different trade-offs between dependability and performance. We discuss two in more detail, for an FT-node with two or more servers:

Non fault-tolerant solution: For each query, the middleware forwards the first response to the client and discards all later responses. The performance gain depends on whether, by the time the middleware relays a query to the servers, all servers have finished processing the previous query[6]. If the slowest server is still processing the previous query, there are two options:

- the middleware waits until the slowest server completes (aborting the query is not an option because it will compromise data consistency); this delay may seriously limit the performance gain given by the optimistic regime;
- the middleware forwards each query, of a transaction, immediately to those servers that are done processing the previous one, but buffers it for servers that are not. If the middleware only behaves like this within transactions, while on commits of transactions it, inevitably, waits for the slowest server, 1-copy serialisability is preserved.

The transport delays and the client's own processing delays are the two key factors, which decide how much time will be gained using the optimistic regime. The transport delays are implementation-specific and likely to be significant in multi-tier systems. Similarly, the client's own delay is application specific. For interactive applications, it is very likely to be significant.

Fault-tolerant solution: The middleware optimistically forwards the first response to the client, and keeps a copy to compare with later responses when they arrive. If they differ, it initiates recovery. This is easily accomplished within a transaction: the transaction is rolled back, and the client is notified just as for any other transaction rollback decided by a server. This optimistic fault-tolerant scheme will be almost as fast as discarding the late responses, except in the presumably rare case of discrepancy between the servers' responses. The previous considerations about the impact of transport delays and of the client's processing delays still apply.

5 Related Work

Replicated databases are common, but most designs are not suitable for diverse redundancy. We have referred in the previous section to some of the standard solutions [10], [11], [19], [22] and [20].

Recent surveys exist of the mechanisms for eager replication of databases [35], and for the replication mechanisms (mainly lazy replication) implemented in various SQL

---

[6] This happens if the sum of the transport delay to deliver the fastest response to the client, the client's own processing time to produce the next query, and the transport delay to deliver the next query to the middleware is longer than the extra time needed by the slower server to complete query processing. In this case, both (or all) servers will be ready to take the next query and the race between them will start over.

servers [36]. The Pronto protocol [37] attempts to reduce the negative effects of lazy replication using ideas typical for eager replication. One of its selling points is that it can be used with off-the-shelf SQL servers, but it is unclear whether this includes diverse servers. A potential problem is the need to broadcast the SQL statement from the primary to the replicas. The syntax of SQL statements varies between SQL servers, as discussed in Section 3.

A relevant discussion of the various ways of implementing database replication with off-the-shelf SQL servers is in [38]. Three forms are discussed, treating the SQL servers as black, white or grey boxes. All commercial vendors of SQL servers use the white-box approach, where a suite necessary for replication is added to the code of the non-replicated server. The black-box and the grey-box approaches are implemented in the form of middleware on top of the existing SQL servers. The black-box approach, like the design solutions discussed here, uses the standard interfaces of the servers and its main advantage is applicability to a wide range of servers. The grey-box approach, implemented in [39] and [40], assumes that the servers provide services specifically to assist replication.

Comparisons of various replication protocols from the point of view of their performance and feasibility are presented in [18], [19].

The problem of on-line recovery is scrutinised in [41] and [24] and cost-effective solutions are proposed.

6 Discussion

The fault diversity figures (presented in Section 2) point to a serious potential gain in reliability from using a fault tolerant SQL server built from two or more off-the-shelf servers. There are limitations to what can be speculated from the bug reports alone, because these do not address the *frequency* of the failures caused. The actual failure reports would be more informative, especially if the vendors used automatic failure reporting mechanisms. An even better analysis could be obtained if these mechanisms gave indications about the users' usage profile as proposed in [42]. However such detailed dependability information is difficult to obtain from the vendors. Based on the evidence of fault diversity presented in Section 2, using a diverse fault-tolerant server would already appear a reasonable and relatively cheap precautionary decision (even without good predictions of its effects) for a user that had: serious concerns about dependability (e.g., interruptions of service or undetected incorrect data being stored are very costly); client applications using mostly the core features common to multiple off-the-shelf products (for instance a user who required portability of applications); modest throughput requirements for database updates which make it easy to accept the synchronisation delays of a fault-tolerant server.

We have provided a more detailed discussion of the fault diversity results in [14].

Data diversity has been proposed as a possibility to detect failures that would otherwise be un-detectable in some diverse server replication settings. We have provided examples of this in Section 3.6. The possible benefits of this approach could be its relatively lower cost (especially if OTS re-phrasing software becomes available) in comparison with design diversity, and also that it can be used with or without design diversity allowing for various cost-dependability trade-offs.

In Section 4 we presented the results from our experiments on the performance of two open-source SQL servers. We estimated the likely performance effect of diversity under optimistic and pessimistic regime of operation.

The *Quality of service* provided by a database server can be defined to include both performance and dependability. Clients with conflicting needs may benefit from design diversity according to their own priorities because an FT-node can apply different regimes for different databases or different clients. When performance is top priority the optimistic regime can be used, possibly even in the non-fault-tolerant variation, which discards the slower responses. In many practical cases this is likely to produce significant improvement. At the other end of the spectrum, when dependability is top priority, the pessimistic regime with a fully featured middleware for fault-tolerance will provide significantly improved dependability assurance. Several intermediate solutions are possible with different trade-offs between performance and dependability. The optimistic regime can be used together with functionality for fault-tolerance using the responses from all servers as discussed in Section 4.2.

7 Conclusions

Most users of SQL servers see performance as the most critical requirement. Dependability, although important, is often assumed not to be a problem, and users who seek to improve it are apparently satisfied with redundant solutions meant to tolerate crash failures only.

We have argued that non-diverse replication is a limited solution, since many server failures are non-self-evident and cannot be tolerated by non-diverse replication. We have shown evidence of this problem from our "fault diversity" measurements. To provide extended protection against non-self-evident failures, we have argued in favour of using diverse SQL servers and outlined a range of possible architectural solutions.

We have presented some encouraging empirical results which suggest that diversity can improve the performance of a fault-tolerant server. To the best of our knowledge, similar results have not been reported before. This possibility is due to the fact that different SQL server may "complement" each other, as we have established empirically for Interbase and PostgreSQL: one of the server is systematically faster in processing some types of transactions while the other server is faster processing other types of transactions. This is similar to the intuitive idea of forming teams of individuals who have different skills, which is an accepted view in various areas. Diversity can improve both aspects of the service provided by the SQL servers, dependability and performance.

We have outlined some design problems in implementing middleware for diverse SQL servers. However, the technical benefits of having such a solution for data replication could be significant. There remain open questions worth studying in the future:

- the work on fault diversity can be extended by finding out whether the same proportion of crash/non-crash failures will be observed with later versions of the servers, or even including other servers e.g. DB2, MySQL, etc.
- evidence of actual failure diversity (or lack thereof) in actual use is also to be sought. We are currently running experiments to assess statistically the actual reliability gains. We have so far run a few million queries on a configuration with

three off-the-shelf SQL servers (Interbase, Oracle and MSSQL), with various loads without failures. We plan to continue these experiments for more complete test loads

- demonstrating the feasibility of automatic translation of SQL queries from, say ANSI/ISO SQL syntax to the SQL dialect implemented by the deployed SQL servers.
- empirical evaluation of whether the "optimistic" regime, discussed in Section 4, is practicable for a range of widely used clients;
- implementing configurable middleware, deployable on diverse SQL servers, to allow the clients to request quality of service in line with their specific requirements for performance and dependability, is a possibility for future work

Acknowledgement

This work was supported in part by the Engineering and Physical Sciences Research Council (EPSRC) of the United Kingdom through the Interdisciplinary Research Collaboration in Dependability (DIRC) and the DOTS (Diversity with Off-The-Shelf Components) projects. We wish to thank Peter Bishop for comments on an earlier version of this paper.

References

1. Babbage, C., *On the Mathematical Powers of the Calculating Engine (Unpublished manuscript, December 1837)*, in *The Origins of Digital Computers: Selected Papers*, B. Randell, Editor, 1974, Springer, pp. 17-52.
2. Traverse, P.J., *AIRBUS and ATR System Architecture and Specification*, in *Software diversity in computerized control systems*, U. Voges, Editor, 1988, Springer-Verlag, pp. 95-104.
3. Randell, B. *System Structure for Software Fault-Tolerance*, in *International Conference on Reliable Software, Los Angeles, California, April 1975, (in ACM SIGPLAN Notices, Vol. 10, No. 6, June 1975)*, 1975, pp. 437-449.
4. Lyu, M.R., ed. *Software Fault Tolerance*. Trends in Software Series. 1995, Wiley
5. Avizienis, A. and J.P.J. Kelly, *Fault Tolerance by Design Diversity: Concepts and Experiments*, IEEE Computer, 1984, 17(8): pp. 67-80.
6. Laprie, J.C., et al., *Definition and Analysis of Hardware-and-Software Fault-Tolerant Architectures*, IEEE Computer, 1990, 23(7): pp. 39-51.
7. Voges, U., ed. *Software diversity in computerized control systems*. Dependable Computing and Fault-Tolerance series, ed. A. Avizienis, H. Kopetz, and J.C. Laprie. Vol. 2. 1988, Springer-Verlag: Wien.
8. Avizienis, A., et al. *The UCLA DEDIX System: A Distributed Testbed for Multiple-Version Software*, in *Proc. of 15th IEEE International Symposium on Fault-Tolerant Computing (FTCS-15)*, 1985, Ann Arbor, Michigan, USA, IEEE Computer Society Press, pp. 126-134.
9. Pullum, L., *Software Fault Tolerance Techniques and Implementation*, 2001, Artech House.
10. Bernstein, P.A., V. Hadzilacos, and N. Goodman, *Concurrency Control and Recovery in Database Systems*, 1987, Reading, Mass.: Addison-Wesley.
11. Sutter, H., *SQL/Replication Scope and Requirements document*, in *ISO/IEC JTC 1/SC 32 Data Management and Interchange WG3 Database Languages*, 2000, pp. 7.

12. Kalyanakrishnam, M., Z. Kalbarczyk, and R. Iyer. *Failure Data Analysis of LAN of Windows NT Based Computers*, in *Proc. of 18th Symposium on Reliable and Distributed Systems (SRDS '99)*, 1999, Lausanne, Switzerland, pp. 178-187.
13. Schneider, F., *Byzantine generals in action: Implementing fail-stop processors*, ACM Transactions on Computing Systems, 1984, 2(2): pp. 145-154.
14. Gashi, I., P. Popov, and L. Strigini. *Fault diversity among off-the-shelf SQL database servers*, in *Proc. of Inter. Conf. on Dependable Systems and Networks (DSN'04)*, 2004, Florence, Italy, IEEE Computer Society Press: to appear.
15. Chandra, S. and P.M. Chen. *How fail-stop are programs*, in *Proc. of 28th IEEE International Symposium on Fault-Tolerant Computing (FTCS-28)*, 1998, IEEE Computer Society Press, pp. 240-249.
16. Gray, J. *Why do computers stop and what can be done about it?*, in *Proc. of 5th Symp. on Reliability in Distributed Software and Database Systems (SRDSDS-5)*, 1986, Los Angeles, CA, USA, IEEE Computer Society Press, pp. 3-12.
17. Chandra, S. and P.M. Chen. *Whither Generic Recovery from Application Faults? A Fault Study using Open-Source Software*, in *Proc. of Inter. Conf. on Dependable Systems and Networks (DSN 2000)*, 2000, NY, USA, IEEE Computer Society Press, pp. 97-106.
18. Jimenez-Peris, R., et al., *Are Quorums an Alternative for Data Replication?*, ACM Transactions on Database Systems, 2003, 28(3): pp. 257-294.
19. Jimenez-Peris, R., et al. *How to Select a Replication Protocol According to Scalability, Availability and Communication Overhead*, in *Proc. of Int. Symp. on Reliable Distributed Systems (SRDS)*, 2001, New Orleans, Louisiana, IEEE Computer Society Press, pp. 24 -33.
20. Kemme, B. and G. Alonso. *Don't be lazy, be consistent: Postgres-R, A new way to implement Database Replication*, in *Proc. of Int. Conf. on Very Large Databases (VLDB)*, 2000, Cairo, Egypt.
21. Anderson, T. and P.A. Lee, *Fault Tolerance: Principles and Practice (Dependable Computing and Fault Tolerant Systems, Vol 3)*, 2nd Revised ed, 1990, Springer- Verlag.
22. Gray, J. and A. Reuter, *Transaction processing : concepts and techniques*, 1993, Morgan Kaufmann.
23. Tso, K.S. and A. and Avizienis. *Community Error Recovery in N-Version Software: A Design Study with Experimentation*, in *Proc. of 17th IEEE International Symposium on Fault-Tolerant Computing (FTCS-17), Pittsburgh, Pennsylvania, July 6-8 1987*, 1987, pp. 127-133.
24. Jimenez-Peris, R., Patino-Martinez, and G. Alonso. *An Algorithm for Non-Intrusive, Parallel Recovery of Replicated Data and its Correctness*, in *Proc. of 21st IEEE Int. Symp. on Reliable Distributed Systems (SRDS 2002)*, 2002, Osaka, Japan, pp. 150-159.
25. Poledna, S., *Replica Determinism in Distributed Real-Time Systems: A Brief Survey*, Real-Time Systems Journal, 1994, 6: pp. 289-316.
26. Powell, D., *Delta-4: A Generic Architecture for Dependable Distributed Computing*, Springer-Verlag Research Reports ESPRIT, 1992, Springer-Verlag.
27. Popov, P., et al. *Software Fault-Tolerance with Off-the-Shelf SQL Servers*, in *Proc. of 3rd International Conference on COTS-based Software Systems, ICCBSS'04*, 2004, Redondo Beach, CA USA, Springer: to appear.
28. Gruber, M., *Mastering SQL*, 2000, SYBEX.
29. Melton, J., *(ISO-ANSI Working Draft) Persistent Stored Modules (SQL/PSM)*, 2002, http://www.jtc1sc32.org/sc32/jtc1sc32.nsf/Attachments/9611E99B3901802188256D95005 B0184/$FILE/32N1008-WD9075-04-PSM-2003-09.PDF
30. Microsoft, *SQL Server "Yukon"*, 2003, http://www.microsoft.com/sql/yukon/productinfo/default.asp
31. Poledna, S., *Fault-Tolerant Real-Time Systems: The Problem of Replica Determinism*, 1996, Kluwer Academic Publishers.
32. Ammann, P.E. and J.C. Knight. *Data Diversity: an Approach to Software Fault-Tolerance*, in *Proc. of 17th IEEE International Symposium on Fault-Tolerant Computing (FTCS-17)*, 1987, Pittsburgh, Pennsylvania, USA, IEEE Computer Society Press, pp. 122-126.

33. Chen, P.M., et al., *Raid: High-Performance, Reliable Secondary Storage,* ACM Computing Surveys, 1994, 26(2): pp. 145-185.
34. TPC, *TPC Benchmark C, Standard Specification, Version 5.0.,* 2002, http://www.tpc.org/tpcc/
35. Weismann, M., F. Pedone, and A. Schiper. *Database Replication Techniques: a Three Parameter Classification,* in *Proc. of 19th IEEE Symposium on Reliable Distributed Systems (SRDS'00),* 2000, Nurnberg, Germany, IEEE Computer Society Press, pp. 206-217.
36. Vaysburd, A. *Fault Tolerance in Three-Tier Applications: Focusing on the Database Tier,* in *Proc. of 18th IEEE Symposium on Reliable Distributed Systems (SRDS'99),* 1999, Lausanne, Switzerland, IEEE Computer Society Press, pp. 322-327.
37. Pedone, F. and S. Frolund. *Pronto: A Fast Failover Protocol for Off-the-shelf Commercial Databases,* in *Proc. of 19th IEEE Symposium on Reliable Distributed Systems (SRDS'00),* 2000, Nurnberg, Germany, IEEE Computer Society Press, pp. 176-185.
38. Jimenez-Peris, R. and M. Patino-Martinez, *D5: Transaction Support,* 2003, ADAPT Middleware Technologies for Adaptive and Composable Distributed Components, pp. 20.
39. Patino-Martinez, M., R. Jimenez-Peris, and G. Alonso. *Scalable Replication in Database Clusters,* in *Proc. of International Conference on Distributed Computing, DISC'00,* 2000, Springer, pp. 315-329.
40. Jimenez-Peris, R., et al. *Scalable Database Replication Middleware,* in *Proc. of 22nd IEEE Int Conf on Distributed Computing Systems,* 2002, Vienna, Austria, pp. 477-484.
41. Kemme, B., A. Bartoli, and O. Babaoglu. *Online Reconfiguration in Replicated Databases Based on Group Communication,* in *Proc. of Int. Conf. on Dependable Systems and Networks (DSN 2001),* 2001, Goteborg, Sweden, IEEE Computer Society Press, pp. 117-126.
42. Voas, J., *Deriving Accurate Operational Profiles for Mass-Marketed Software,* 2000, http://www.cigitallabs.com/resources/papers/

A Model and a Design Approach
to Building QoS Adaptive Systems

Paul D. Ezhilchelvan and Santosh Kumar Shrivastava

School of Computing Science, Newcastle University, UK

Abstract. This chapter addresses the task of building Internet-based service provisioning systems where the quality of services (QoS) provided should not be perturbed due to changes in execution environments and user requirements. Specifically, it presents a system architecture and identifies a model appropriate for developing distributed programs that would implement the system. The model abstracts the network performance and dependability guarantees typically offered by the Internet service providers and is termed the *probabilistic asynchronous* model. The protocols for this model are shown to be derivable from those developed for the well-known classical models, namely: the synchronous and the asynchronous models. A protocol for reliable broadcast is derived from a synchronous protocol, together with QoS management algorithms. The system architecture prescribes the role of QoS management algorithms to be: feasibility evaluation on QoS requests from the end users, and adapting system protocols in response to changes in the environments.

1 Introduction

A software architecture is typically described in terms of components (a component characterises a unit of computation), connectors (a connector characterises a unit of interaction), and a configuration (that describes the composition of a set of components via connectors). Services provided by a component are used by other components via connectors. Components and connectors can be either primitive or complex. A complex connector is a connector that is built from a set of connectors and components. A complex connector can be seen as the middleware that comprises a set of services for hosting components and their interoperation (e.g., CORBA). We examine here some fundamental issues on how middleware (from now on referred to as system) can be designed to host components capable of providing services to users that demand specified levels of Quality of Service (QoS) such as availability and timeliness.

A system's ability to maintain the QoS level desired by a user can be perturbed by several factors. An example can be a new user requesting services with some specified QoS or an existing user issuing dynamically a request for an enhanced level of QoS. In these occasions, the system has to be able to evaluate if the request can be met without jeopardising the QoS commitments already in force for other users. Thus, it should essentially evaluate the feasibility of QoS provisioning and, where and if possible, adapt itself when QoS perturbs are encountered. In essence, it needs to be *QoS adaptive* in nature. The adaptation can range from adjusting the operational parameters (e.g., reducing the level of redundancy) to, at the extreme end, deploying additional resources such as computational capacity, bandwidth and storage.

R. de Lemos et al. (Eds.): Architecting Dependable Systems II, LNCS 3069, pp. 215–238, 2004.
© Springer-Verlag Berlin Heidelberg 2004

There are many QoS attributes that can be generally associated with a system; *latency*, *throughput*, and *reliability* are common ones and will be the focus of this chapter. Intuitively, the end-to-end QoS (e.g., latency) offered at the system level, and seen by the end user, is an aggregation (of some sort) over the QoS offered by the various subsystems that make up the system. A subsystem provides certain services to other (consumer) subsystems, by making use of the services provided to it by some other (producer) subsystems. (The end-user is the ultimate consumer.) When a consumer subsystem requests an enhanced QoS requirement, a QoS adaptive subsystem either adapts its operations to accommodate the request or evaluates the enhanced QoS which one or more producer subsystems need to provide if the consumer request has to be satisfied. The request cannot be met if a producer subsystem cannot support the enhanced QoS. At the bottom-end of this producer-consumer chain are the subsystems that directly manage the resources themselves: communication subsystems (CS), operating systems (OS) and storage systems (SS).

It is thus obvious that building a QoS adaptive system requires that it must be feasible to dynamically evaluate the QoS guarantees which the resourceful subsystems – CS, OS and SS – can offer for a given set of higher level requirements. Of these three resourceful subsystems, the service providers normally own computational resources, operating systems and storage systems. Furthermore, the techniques for evaluating latency, throughput and failure rates of OS (real-time OS in particular) and SS under a given operational environment are well known. However, the situation will be different with the CS if it operates on a best-effort basis over the Internet. In such an environment, the application related message traffic needs to compete for bandwidth and survive router congestions, and the CS cannot therefore offer meaningful QoS guarantees. This means that there must be means to reserve bandwidth and accord priority to traffic flows so that the CS can also be QoS aware. The task of building an Internet based, QoS adaptive system thus becomes solving a design problem which involves

i. formulating a *model*, specifically a network communication model, that accurately characterises an environment that is realisable in practice as well as supportive of building a QoS adaptive system; and,

ii. generating a design solution that consists of logical modules which are structured as per an *architecture* and implemented by *protocols* whose performance can be influenced as per some *algorithms* in order to achieve QoS adaptation.

The contributions of this chapter are to address in detail each of these aspects, namely, the model, the architecture, and the protocols and algorithms. Approaches to distributed system designs have thus far assumed two broad classes of computational and communication models: *synchronous* and *asynchronous*. In the synchronous model, processing and communication delays are bounded by known constants. Considering the synchronous model requires that the resources be adequately provided for a system load anticipated at the design time and that the run-time load never exceeds, nor be ever allowed to exceed, what has been anticipated. It is shown to be appropriate for designing hard real time systems embedded in well-characterised environments (e.g., MARS system [22]). For our purposes, this would mean that the service provider owns and controls all resources (including the network) and the system blocks new service requests if there is an apparent risk that the load may exceed an assumed threshold. Such a system will be uneconomical to run in the service provisioning context and cannot scale beyond the private network onto the Internet.

Best-effort traffic over the Internet, as mentioned earlier, involves contention for bandwidth and surviving congestion in en-route routers. It is therefore not possible to derive bounds on message communication delays. Moreover, a school of opinion in the literature advocates that the Internet traffic pattern is accurately captured only by self-similar processes [25]. As per self-similar network traffic, arrivals are concentrated (i.e., occur in batches) irrespective of the smallness of granularity of the observation time. This aspect runs counter to the notion of processes being rescaled in time so that the resulting coarsified processes lose dependence and take on the properties of an independent and identically distributed (i.i.d.) sequence of random variables. Consequently, self-similar processes are not amenable to a tractable analysis necessary for deriving probabilistic distributions of latency and throughput. The underlying cause for this difficulty is the breakdown of Markovian assumptions, and also the lack of moments (e.g., an infinite mean) of a self-similar process.

These observations led researchers to considering the second model, the asynchronous model, wherein the delays are finite but no assumption can be made on the ability to deduce delay bounds or delay distribution. A system design based on the asynchronous model can therefore guarantee only eventual correctness, leaving QoS considerations as an after-thought.

We believe that the QoS provisioning, like many dependability attributes (like security), should not be achieved effectively as an add-on feature, but rather should be made a core objective of the design process. This then makes the availability of a QoS-aware and scaleable CS, an essential requirement. Developments in network service provisioning indicate that Internet Service Providers (ISPs) help meet this requirement. ISPs offer to their customers QoS guarantees on the end-to-end network performance based on elegant resource management models for the Internet (see [15] for example). For example, the AT&T managed Internet service – a leading ISP – offers 99.99% network availability, a *monthly average* latency of 60 milliseconds (within the US), and a packet loss rate of less than 0.7%. We will therefore assume that the CS of the QoS adaptive system to be built is provided by an ISP together with well-defined network performance guarantees.

Note that the QoS guarantees offered by the ISPs (even to the high-end users) are not deterministic, as regarded within the synchronous model; rather they are *probabilistic* in nature. Note also that when the network is not guaranteed to be 100% loss-less and 100% available, a message may have to retransmitted and may therefore take an arbitrary amount of time – a feature of the asynchronous model.

Section 2 will focus on presenting a *model* that characterises the environment considered for building a QoS adaptive system, the *system architecture* as per which the subsystems get structured and interact, and the *subsystem architecture* identifying the internal structure of a subsystem and *the requirements* which *the protocols* and *algorithms* of a subsystem need to meet. Our computation and communication model will be termed the *probabilistic asynchronous* model, and will include an abstract representation of the QoS guarantees offered by the ISPs. We also compare and contrast our model against other known models. The system architecture presented next will echo the principles of design composability [22]: an efficient and modular construction of a QoS adaptive system requires that its subsystems are built to be QoS adaptive as well. The subsystem architecture that follows will identify the following requirements: the probabilistic asynchronous protocols of a subsystem must be designed with configurable parameters; and, they should be associated with algorithms with which the protocol parameters can be appropriately set in order that the subsystem can maintain the desired QoS level.

The next three sections are devoted to convincing the reader that our proposed approach to building a QoS adaptive system is feasible and realistic. To this end, we consider the task of building a QoS adaptive group communication (middleware) system. We show that the probabilistic asynchronous protocols with configurable parameters *can be derived* for various subsystems from the rich set of protocols developed for asynchronous and synchronous models in Sections 3 and 4, respectively. In section 3, we consider protocols for various subsystems, such as reliable multicast [3, 18] consensus, non-blocking atomic commit [16], and indicate how their derivation can be done. Section 4 focuses on one particular subsystem (reliable multicast) and presents a complete derivation of a protocol for the probabilistic asynchronous model from a synchronous protocol. Section 5 presents the derivation of algorithms, or more specifically a set of expressions, for setting the parameters of the protocol derived in Section 4. Section 6 examines the related work in the literature, and identifies many directions for future research; Section 7 concludes the chapter.

2   The Model and a Design Framework

2.1   Probabilistic Asynchronous (PA) Model

The system is made up of nodes that communicate using the communication subsystem (CS). A node or any process hosted within it functions correctly until and unless it crashes. A node (or a process) that does not crash is said to be correct. To present the probabilistic asynchronous model, PA model for short, we will assume a global clock which is not accessible to processes.

Processing Delays: Within a correct node, any task that is scheduled to be executed at time t, will be executed at $t + \pi$ where π is a random variable with some known distribution.

Storage Delays: When a correct process initiates a storage request (for storing or retrieving of data) at time t, the request will be correctly processed at $t + \sigma$, where σ is a random variable with some known distribution.

Transmission Delays: If a correct process i sends a message m to another correct process j at time t, then

- m is delivered to j (i.e., m arrives at the buffer of j) with some probability 1-q (m may be lost in transmission with probability q).
- if m is not lost, it is delivered at $t + \delta$ where δ is a random variable with some known distribution.

If the distributions of π, σ, and δ are uniform with some known mean and $q = 0$, then the PA model refers to the well-known synchronous model which permits upper bounds on π, σ, and δ to be determined with certainty; a violation of this bound is to be regarded as a failure of either the sending node or the receiving node. Thus, the synchronous model is a special case of the PA model. This means that any PA protocol designed for any given delay distribution and for a non-zero q should run correctly in a synchronous system when the delay distribution is uniform and $q = 0$. Conversely, if a problem is unsolvable in a synchronous system, then it cannot be solved in the PA model.

The asynchronous model considers the bounds on the delays π, σ, and δ to be finite; neither the bounds nor the delay distributions can be known with certainty. For example, any bound on delays, however judiciously deduced, is vulnerable to being violated with unknown probabilities. The PA model, on the other hand, assigns probabilities or *coverage* to quantification of delay bounds. The PA model also differs in two ways from the two deterministic models over the treatment of message/packet loss. First, the losses are considered to be independent, though in reality they are likely to be correlated. This is abstracted for two reasons: it leads to a tractable performance analysis and the loss probability guaranteed by commercial ISPs is usually very small (about 1%).

Suppose that process i sends message m to process j a finite number of times, say k times, there is a small probability (q^k) that m is not delivered to j. Whereas, in the synchronous and the asynchronous models, the probability of a transmission failure with k, $k > 1$, attempts is assumed to be nil for some finite k. This assumption is often referred to as the bounded degree omission failures, and implies an underlying assumption that the losses are transient in nature and do not affect a flow between a given pair of processes permanently. The bound k is regarded to be known and unknown in the synchronous and asynchronous models respectively. Furthermore, in these deterministic models, it is usual to abstract the redundant transmissions necessary to mask losses within the '*send*' operation and to denote the over-all end-to-end transmission delay as δ. The '*send*' operation in the PA model however refers to a single, non-redundant transmission. Thus, if q^k in the PA model is taken to be zero for some k and the delay distributions be unknown and with finite support, then the PA model becomes the asynchronous model. Table 1 summarises these observations on k and δ.

The timed asynchronous (TA) model [10] assumes a fail-aware service on top of an asynchronous CS. This service discards messages delivered by the asynchronous CS, if the messages are delayed by more than a threshold which is a fail-aware service parameter. Consequently, the CS of the TA model becomes much similar to that of the synchronous model (see Table 1) except for a non-zero loss probability that can be much higher than q of the PA model due to the filtering by the fail-aware service.

Table 1. Relative Comparison of the Models.

MODELS / PARAMETERS	Synchronous	Asynchronous	Timed Asynchronous	Probabilistically Asynchronous
Bound on successive transmission losses, k	Known	Finite and Unknown	Finite and Unknown	Random variable on $[0, \infty]$
End-to-end delay for a '*sent*' message, δ	Has a known bound	Has a finite and unknown bound	Has a known bound, if message not lost nor discarded by fail-aware	Random variable on $[0, \infty]$ with known distribution, if message not lost
Processing and Storage delays, π and σ	Have known bounds	Have finite and unknown bounds	Have finite and unknown bounds	Random variables on $[0, \infty]$ with known distribution

2.2   A Framework for Building a QoS Adaptive System

The model characterises the behaviour of subsystems CS, OS and SS which manage respectively the capacity to communicate, process and store information. These subsystems are collectively denoted as S_0 in figure 1. For a QoS adaptive system to be feasible, S_0 must export a QoS management interface in addition to the traditional service interface. Using this interface, a higher-level subsystem S_1 can request S_0 whether a specified distribution for each of the delay variables (π, σ, δ) and a specified loss probability (q) can be supported; this in turn would help determine whether a given set of requirements on processing, storage and bandwidth capacities additionally needed to support an end user requirement can be met. If the request for a specified distribution for each of the delay variables cannot be supported, S_0 may respond with the delay distributions which it can currently support.

Each subsystem S_i, $i \geq 1$, will have two components: service component ($service_i$) and QoS management component (qos_i).

- $service_i$ implements a specified service tolerating at most ϕ node crashes;
- qos_i evaluates the delay and throughput distributions of $service_i$ as a function of such distributions offered by $service_{i-1}$. (The throughput offered by S_0 is $(1-q)$ times the message sending rate, if a buffered message is received by the destination process instantly.) qos_i will also take into account the overhead that $service_i$ would incur given the size of input from the higher level.

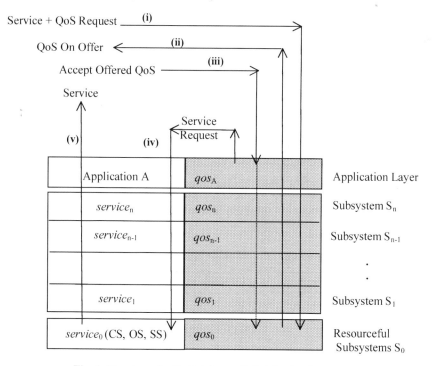

Fig. 1. Structure of a Fault-tolerant QoS Adaptive System.

At the top of the stack are the application (A) and its QoS manager (qos_A). When a user submits a request with the required (probabilistic) delay and throughput guarantees (interaction (i) in figure 1), the application QoS manager qos_A computes and passes down the QoS guarantees expected of S_n to qos_n. The qos_n computes the guarantees expected of S_{n-1} so that the guarantees required by qos_A can be met. The guarantees expected of S_{n-1} are passed down to qos_{n-1}.

The QoS feasibility evaluation thus travels down to S_0 which computes if it can maintain the necessary mean and the variance of delay distributions for the overall resource requirement. If it is possible, then the user request will be accepted; else, S_0 returns the mean and variance it can sustain and the reverse computations are made by successive qos_i upwards (interaction (ii) in the figure). The user is then informed of the QoS guarantees the system can offer.

Structure of a Subsystem

Suppose that a user request is accepted for a set of given QoS metrics. Each qos_i, $i \geq 1$, records the QoS requirements that $service_i$ needs to meet (interaction (iii) in Figure 1). The service request is submitted to the application whose execution invokes various $service_i$ (interaction (iv) in Figure 1). The (fault-tolerant) protocols and programs that implement a $service_i$ must be designed with configurable parameters (which can be regarded as 'QoS control knobs'). The qos_i needs to set appropriate values for these parameters so that the $service_i$ can meet its QoS obligations to $service_{i+1}$ (interaction (vi) in Figure 2). This parameter setting and the feasibility analyses carried out prior to accepting the user request will require that qos_i be equipped with algorithms to evaluate the performance of $service_i$ in terms of these parameters. Specifically, qos_i should be able to evaluate the QoS metrics offered by $service_i$ for a given set of parameter values (e.g., latency for a given level of redundancy) and *vice versa*, and also derive the parameter values from the QoS guarantees from $service_{i-1}$ below (e.g., the level of redundancy for a given loss probability) and *vice versa*. The necessary algorithms are contained in a module called the *qos evaluator* within qos_i, denoted in figure 2 as $qosE_i$.

Developing algorithms for $qosE_i$ to evaluate the QoS metrics offered by $service_i$ for a given set of parameter values (and *vice versa*), will involve stochastic modelling and predicting the performance of $service_i$. Tractable performance predictions often warrant approximations to be taken and we would propose that such approximations tend to underestimate the actual performance. This means that $service_i$ will tend to perform better than predicted by $qosE_i$, offering a better QoS to $service_{i+1}$ than qos_{i+1} is expecting. The system will thus have an inherent tendency not to fail on the end-to-end QoS promised to the user.

It is possible that the QoS guarantees agreed by the ISP are violated for a prolonged period. These violations can lead to various higher level subsystems being unable to meet their QoS obligations. So, a requirement for each qos_i is to monitor the QoS offered by $service_{i-1}$ to $service_i$, and attempt to re-adapt the protocols of $service_i$

so that $service_i$ still maintains its QoS guarantees to $service_{i+1}$. The monitoring module of qos_i, denoted in figure 2 as $qosM_i$, monitors $service_{i-1}$ (interaction (vii) in figure 2) and extracts QoS metrics which are passed to $qosE_i$ (interaction viii). When the discrepancy between the assumed and reported metrics is beyond a threshold, $qosE_i$ attempts to re-set the appropriate protocol parameters of $service_i$.

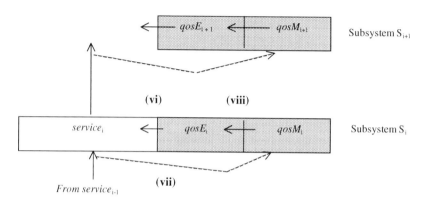

Fig. 2. The Structure of a Subsystem.

In summary, the protocols and programs of $service_i$ must be designed with parameters that can be used to influence the performance of $service_i$; $qosE_i$ must contain algorithms or expressions characterising the relationship between the choice of parameters and the resulting QoS metrics of $service_i$; and, $qosM_i$ must contain algorithms to monitor the services provided by $service_{i-1}$ to $service_i$ and to determine the QoS metrics of $service_{i-1}$. In the next two sections, we will address the first issue of developing protocols for building a QoS adaptive middleware system. Specifically, we will indicate that the PA model middleware protocols with configurable parameters can be derived from the rich set of synchronous and asynchronous middleware protocols in the literature. The last two issues will be addressed in Section 5.

3   QoS Enabled Middleware Protocol Derivation

We have earlier noted that the classical synchronous model is a special case of the PA model, with an implication that any problem that is unsolvable in the former is also not solvable in the PA model. We will therefore restrict our protocol derivation efforts to the domain of middleware services available in a synchronous, fault-tolerant system. We have also noted that the PA model with assumptions on q and finite support distributions becomes a special case of the asynchronous model. Thus, the PA middleware service protocols can, in theory, be derived from the (deterministic) asynchronous protocols, if the latter do exist for a given service. In this section, we will describe how protocol derivation can be accomplished. To this end, we will first focus on the timing aspects of a service specification in the synchronous, asynchronous and PA models. It is fair to claim that the synchronous model specification of a given service, when expressed in the asynchronous and PA models, can differ only in the timing aspects and all other aspects must remain the same. This claim will be explained and be exemplified shortly.

Among the asynchronous protocols published in the literature, we will make use of the ones based on failure detectors, FD for short [5], as they conveniently separate the time-related issues from time-free ones. The former are abstracted within FDs, leaving the protocols themselves time-free and deterministic. This separation of temporal concerns allows an appropriate FD-based protocol to be used in the PA model relatively unchanged, provided that the required failure detector is implemented in the PA model. We identify three useful failure detectors for our purpose and propose their PA implementation. Thus, deriving a PA service protocol amounts to choosing an appropriate FD-based asynchronous protocol and implementing that FD.

3.1 Models and Service Specifications

It is not unusual to state synchronous service specifications with reference to nodes' clocks which are assumed to be synchronised within some known bound ε. A node's synchronised clock is the local approximation of a global time base; in what follows, we will assume that if nodes' clocks are assumed to be synchronised in a specification, then clocks are perfectly synchronised, i.e., $\varepsilon = 0$. In other words, the synchronous specifications we consider have time expressed with reference to a global (and reliable) time base.

The timing aspect of a synchronous service specification usually runs as follows: if a specified event happens at one process at time t, then another (specified) event must occur at a correct process at t', $t' \leq t + \Delta$, where Δ is a known constant. In the asynchronous specification of the same service, Δ is finite but unknown: the second (specified) event must occur at a correct process *eventually*. In the PA model, Δ is bounded by D with probability r_D that can be estimated in advance. Below we present the specifications of four well-known middlware services in the three models; the timing aspects shown within brackets in normal, bold, and underlined fonts refer to the synchronous, asynchronous, and PA models, respectively.

Clock Synchronisation Service

A clock is said to be correct if its host node is correct and its running rate does not differ from that of the global reference clock by an amount whose magnitude is bounded by a small known constant κ. At any global time t,

- *Precision:* The absolute difference between the readings of any two correct clocks will be within ε, (where ε is a small known constant) (**where ε is finite but unknown**) (<u>where ε is bounded by E with probability r_E that can be estimated in advance</u>), and

- *Accuracy:* The absolute difference between the reading of a correct clock and that of the global reference clock will be within β, (where β is a small, known constant) (**where β is finite but unknown**) (<u>where β is bounded by B with probability r_B that can be estimated in advance</u>).

Atomic Commit Service

Among a set of n > 2 processes that are known to each other, one process is designated as the General [26] and others as Lieutenants (which are only crash prone). The General is to broadcast a value at time t (that is known to the Lieutenants) (**that is unknown to the Lieutenants**) (that is known to the Lieutenants with a certainty that can be estimated in advance).

- *Termination*: every correct process decides at $t + \Delta$ (where Δ is a known constant) (**where Δ is finite but unknown**) (where Δ is bounded by D with probability r_D that can be estimated in advance)
- *Validity*: If the General is correct and broadcasts value v, then all correct processes decide on v
- *Unanimity*: all correct processes decide on the same value (even if the General crashes at or before t)
- *Uniform Integrity*: every process decides at most once (i.e., a process that decides, decides irreversibly).

Consensus Service

In a set of n > 2 processes that are known to each other, each process is to propose a value by time t (that is known) (**that is unknown**) (that is known with certainty that can be estimated in advance).

- *Termination*: every correct process decides on some value by $t + \Delta$ (where Δ is a known constant) (**where Δ is finite but unknown**) (where Δ is bounded by D with probability r_D that can be estimated in advance),
- *Validity*: If a process decides on value v, then some process proposed v,
- *Unanimity*: no two correct processes decide differently, and
- *Uniform Integrity*: every process decides at most once.

Reliable Broadcast Service

In a set of n > 2 processes that are known to each other, any process can broadcast a message at any time. We will use 'delivery of m' to refer to the event of a reliable broadcast service process supplying a received m to the application.

- *Termination*: if a correct process broadcasts a message m at time t, then all correct processes deliver m by time $t + \Delta$ (where Δ is a known constant) (**where Δ is finite but unknown**) (where Δ is bounded by D with probability r_D that can be estimated in advance)
- *Unanimity*: if a correct process delivers a message m at time t then all other correct processes deliver m by time $t + \Sigma$ (where Σ is a known constant) (**where Σ is finite but unknown**) (where Σ is bounded by S with probability u_S that can be estimated in advance), and
- *Uniform Integrity*: every process delivers any given message m at most once.

A closer look at the asynchronous specification of the clock synchronization service indicates that the underlying problem is indeed a non-problem: consider two correct clocks which, at time t_0, are within ε_0 of each other, and within β_0 with respect to the global reference clock; since the clocks are physical devices, the values of ε_0 and β_0 will have to be finite (which need not be known); left undisturbed, the clocks will have at any time t, $\varepsilon = \varepsilon_0 + 2\kappa(t-t_0)$ and $\beta = \beta_0 + \kappa(t-t_0)$. The values of ε and β will also have to be finite since the bound (κ) on clock drift rates is small and finite.

We refer the reader to Cristian's probabilistic protocol [9] which meets the PA specification of the clock service. Cristian also describes how the core aspects of his design relate to, and are enhancements over, those of the well-known synchronous protocols. Improvements over [9] are claimed in [1].

3.2 Failure Detectors and Suspectors

We have observed that a class of synchronous problems can reduce to non-problems when their specifications are adopted to the asynchronous model. For the remaining set of problems, one could obtain at most three classes of detector-based asynchronous protocols which can solve their asynchronous versions. We will denote these protocol classes as C1, C2 and C3 and distinguish them by the kind of failure detectors [5] they employ:

- perfect failure detectors (C1 protocols),
- eventually strong failure detectors (C2 protocols), and
- failure suspectors (C3 protocols)

The failure suspector of a node monitors the operational status of remote processes and regularly reports its suspicions to the local process. Its suspicions need not be accurate and may change with time; for example, after having suspected a remote process to be crashed, a suspector may later suspect that process to be operative. However, it is not a trivial component and the suspector of a correct node has the following *completeness* property:

- If a remote process is crashed, there is a time after which the suspector permanently suspects the crashed process.

Failure detectors encapsulate failure suspectors and, additionally, detectors of a given type are an abstract representation of certain requirements imposed on, or desired of, the communication subsystem behaviour. Two types of detectors are of interest here.

A perfect failure detector of a correct node inherits the *completeness* property (of the failure suspector it encapsulates) and also satisfies the following *strong accuracy* property:

- No correct process is ever suspected.

An eventually strong failure detector has the *completeness* property and the following *eventual weak accuracy* which is expressed in a context of distributed processes monitoring each other's operative status:

- There is a time after which some correct process is never suspected by the suspector of any correct process

Chandra and Toueg, who first defined the above two and two other classes of failure detectors, also prove that a failure detector of any other class is strictly weaker than a perfect failure detector [5](since the latter can be reduced to the former). Furthermore, it is obvious that a failure suspector that can make any number of mistakes is strictly weaker than an eventual strong failure detector. This 'strictly weaker than' relation is transitive and is denoted as $\rightarrow$ in figure 2 which indicates how the detectors and suspectors of our interest are related.

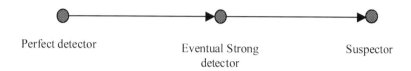

Perfect detector   Eventual Strong   Suspector
                                               detector

Fig. 3. Relationship between the Detectors.

The relation depicted in figure 3 implies that if a problem is solvable with a failure suspector then it can be solved with a perfect or eventual strong failure detector and such solutions are implementable if the failure detector can be built; similarly, if solvable with an eventual strong failure detector, then a solution with a perfect failure detector is also possible. Certain services, such as the atomic commit, require the perfect failure detector as the minimum requirement. Such services can only be solved by C1 type protocols. For certain other services, such as the consensus, the eventual strong failure detector is known to be the minimum requirement [6]. These services can have C1 or C2 type protocols. Services, such as reliable broadcast, uniform reliable broadcast, and causal broadcast, can be solved just with failure suspectors, and their solutions can therefore be of any type.

3.3 PA Implementations of Suspectors and Detectors

The FD-based protocols of types C1, C2, and C3 are deterministic and time-free: a protocol process responds to receiving a message or to receiving an output from the FD. Two mechanisms are needed to make these protocols work in the PA model satisfying the PA versions of their respective service specifications: the probability of service not being provided decreases with time.

- A PA version of the FD needs to be used, and
- A mechanism is needed to maximise the probability that a correct process receives the message sent by another correct process.

The second mechanism caters for the asynchronous model characteristic that the correct processes can send messages to each other successfully (i.e., with the delivery probability being 1). This mechanism and the FDs can be implemented using heart-beat messages.

Heart-Beats: Every message sent by the protocol process is stored in the disk. A *gossiper* process periodically broadcasts the history of sent messages stored in the disk, with period set as a parameter; it also requests for a retransmission if a heart-beat message received indicates that a sent message is found not received locally; and, it re-transmits the messages requested by remote processes. The more number of times a sent message is gossiped (before being garbage collected from the disk), the larger is the probability that all correct processes receive that message; similarly, the more frequently it is gossiped, i.e., the smaller the gossip period chosen, the larger is the probability that all correct processes receive that message by a given time.

Failure Suspectors: They are the easiest ones to implement as they are allowed to make mistakes in an arbitrary manner. However, we propose that they are implemented judiciously by taking advantage of the known delay distributions of the PA model so that the mistake rate is small. For example, when message transmission delays are exponentially distributed with mean d, the transmission delay between a source and a destination is less than η with a probability α (that can be made reasonably close to 1) if $\eta = -d\ ln(1-\alpha)$.

A simple timeout-based implementation of suspectors can be achieved as follows. Suppose that the *gossiper* process of each node transmits a 'heart-beat' message once every τ time (measured as per the respective local clock). If a heart-beat message is not received from an unsuspected process j within $(\tau+\eta)$ time, then the suspector of process i suspects process j; if a heart-beat message is received from a suspected process, the suspicion is reversed.

Eventual Strong Failure Detector: Using an algorithm similar to the failure suspector, Chen *et.al.*, implement a failure detector with configurable QoS properties [7]. With known delay distributions of the PA model, one can set appropriate parameters to obtain the accuracy necessary and implement a detector that meets the specifications of eventual strong failure detector with the desired probability.

Perfect Failure Detectors: They cannot be implemented within an asynchronous or a PA system; an external observer who can accurately determine the operative status of processes is needed. However, by adding the following delay assumption into the PA model, we can obtain an implementation:

- *Crash-recovery delay*: a crashed process resumes functioning after a delay which is a random variable with known distribution.

The above assumption requires that a crashed node is re-booted and the pre-crash states are available in a crash-proof store. Since a crashed node recovers and its gossiper process resumes broadcasting heart-beats, a crash need not be suspected by any other process. Thus, the perfect failure detector effectively has to neither suspect nor reverse its suspicions; i.e., it is an empty module that makes no output at all.

4   Derivation of a Reliable Broadcast Protocol

In this section, we consider a protocol [13] that implements reliable broadcast service in a synchronous system and derive its PA version. The derivation will also incorporate efficiency measures for reducing message overhead and these measures will be clearly indicated. For brevity, we will present the synchronous protocol in a slightly altered form to the original, but this does not alter the fundamentals.

4.1   The Synchronous Protocol

The message communication, invoked by the *send(m)* operation, can experience a uniformly distributed delay on $(0, 2d)$, i.e., with mean d. We assume that a perfect failure detector is available. Such a failure detector can be easily constructed since the delays are bounded by $2d$: if a heart-beat does not arrive for every ($\tau+4d$) time, the source process must have crashed.

A process that wishes to initiate a reliable broadcast of message m executes the primitive *RBcast(m)* and is denoted as the *originator* of m. The protocol has two features to attain reliability against process crashes resulting in a partial broadcast.

a) The execution of *RBcast(m)* comprises two invocations of a *broadcast(m)* operation. Each of these invocations concurrently sends m once to each destination process.

b) The responsibility for invoking *broadcast(m)* initially rests with the *originator* of the message, but may devolve to other processes as a consequence of the *originator* crashing.

These features can be described as *Redundancy* and *Responsiveness*, respectively. *Redundancy* of the protocol is expressed by two parameters:

• the integer $\rho = 1$ specifies the level of redundancy; the originator of m makes $\rho +1$ attempts to broadcast m (if operative); these attempts are numbered 0 and 1.

• the interval between consecutive broadcasts is of fixed length, $\eta = d$.

Responsiveness: If the originator of a message crashes during its redundant broadcast attempt, the destination processes respond by taking over the broadcasting responsibility upon themselves. To facilitate this takeover, each copy of a message, m, has fields *m.copy*, *m.originator* and *m.broadcaster*; these specify the number of the current broadcast attempt (0 or 1), the index of the originating process, and the index of the process that actually broadcasts the message m, respectively. The values of *m.originator* and *m.broadcaster* will be different if a destination process carries out the broadcasting of m.

When a destination process receives a message m for the first time, it delivers m; if *m.copy* = 0, it must be prepared to become a broadcaster of m if necessary. It waits to receive *m.copy* = 1; while waiting if its failure detector suspects *m.broadcaster*, then it executes *RBcast(m)*.

The protocol tolerates the crash of the originator and any number of destination processes: a correct destination process that delivers m either carries out *RBcast(m)* or receives *m.copy* = 1; in the latter case, *m.broadcaster* did not crash while broadcasting *m.copy* = 0 and every other correct process must deliver m. Further, if the originator is correct, only two broadcasts are carried out and every correct destination can deliver m within $2d$ which is the optimal worst-case latency for a deterministic reliable broadcast protocol.

4.2 A Simple Derivation

We will first derive a probabilistic protocol by simply replacing the perfect failure detector of the synchronous protocol with the PA version that relies on the additional assumption that a crashed process recovers (see subsection 3.3). The following observations can be made on the resulting protocol:

• The number of complete[1] broadcasts carried out will be two – both by the originator, since no destination process ever suspects an originator crash; this means that a

---

[1] A broadcast is incomplete when interrupted by a crash of the broadcaster; the claim of two complete broadcasts assumes that broadcast completion is instantly recorded in the broadcaster's stable store.

correct destination may not receive m directly from the originator process with probability no smaller than q^2.

- The gossiper process plays a role in increasing the probability that m is delivered to all correct destination processes.
- The latency distribution will be influenced by the probability that (i) the originator crashes while broadcasting $m.copy = 0$ and the recovery delay distribution; and (ii) a crashed destination process recovers before the gossiper of the originator node discards m.

The crash-recovery assumption and the dependency of latency distribution on the recovery delays may be inappropriate in many practical contexts. Moreover, this assumption is needed only because we use the PA version of the perfect failure detector. Recall that the reliable broadcast problem is also solvable (in the asynchronous model) just with a failure suspector. So, in what follows, we derive a probabilistic protocol using a PA version of a failure suspector which does not require a crashed node to recover. In this derivation, we will also incorporate adaptive measures by letting ρ be chosen appropriately rather than restricting it to two, and efficiency measures by (i) suspecting failures using the broadcast messages in addition to heart-beats, and (ii) adding a third feature (called the *Selection*). It is assumed that the numbering of processes implies a '*seniority*' ordering: process i is said to be `more senior' than process j if $i<j$.

4.3   A Practical Probabilistic Protocol

This protocol has three features which are designed to assure high probability of success at a tolerable cost in message traffic:

a) The execution of *RBcast(m)* comprises more than one invocation of a *broadcast(m)* operation. Each of these invocations concurrently sends the message m once to each destination.
b) The responsibility for invoking *broadcast(m)* initially rests with the originator of the message, but may devolve to another process, and then to another, in consequence of crashes, message losses or excessive delays.
c) In the event of such a devolution, a decision procedure attempts to select exactly one process to take over the broadcasting responsibilities.

The last feature is termed as the *Selection* while the first two are as *Redundancy* and *Responsiveness* as before.

Redundancy. The redundancy of the protocol is controlled by two configurable parameters:

- The integer, ρ, now specifies the level of redundancy desired; the originator of a message makes $\rho + 1$ attempts to broadcast it (if operative); these attempts are numbered $0,1, .. , \rho$; typically, $\rho \geq 1$.
- The interval between consecutive broadcasts is of fixed length, η; that length is chosen to be as small as possible, but sufficiently large to make any dependencies between consecutive broadcasts negligible.

One way of choosing η is to require that the transmission delay between a source and a destination is less than η with a given probability, α (reasonably close to 1).

In the case of exponentially distributed delays with mean d, η is given by $\eta = -d \ln (1 - \alpha)$.

Responsiveness. Every process that receives a message, m, such that $m.copy = k < \rho$, must be prepared to become a broadcaster of m if necessary. It does so by setting a timeout interval of length $\eta + \omega$, with some suitable value of ω (η is the interval between consecutive broadcasts, while ω - another protocol parameter - accounts for differences in transmission delays or 'jitter'). If a copy $k+1$ of m arrives from the broadcaster of copy k before the timeout expires, then all is well with that broadcaster; the receiver process sets a new timeout of $\eta + \omega$ for the next copy (if there is one). Otherwise, the receiver suspects that the process $m.broadcaster$ has crashed while broadcasting copy k of m, and that it is the only process to have received any copy of m. It therefore prepares to appoint itself as a broadcaster of copies $k, k+1, .., \rho$.

However, $m.broadcaster$ may not in fact have crashed; copy $k+1$ of m may just be delayed unduly or lost; moreover, even if $m.broadcaster$ has crashed, this receiver may not be the only process that has observed the crash. In order to avoid multiple receivers becoming broadcasters unnecessarily, a further random wait, ζ, uniformly distributed on $(0,\eta)$, is added to the timeout interval $\eta + \omega$. If a copy number k or higher is not received before the expiration of ζ, this receiver appoints itself as a broadcaster. Otherwise it sets a new timeout of $\eta + \omega$.

Selection. The protocol guards against multiple self-appointed broadcasters (an efficiency measure). It requires that any broadcaster with index i, whose latest broadcast has been of copy k of the message, should relinquish its broadcasting role in any of the following circumstances:

- Process i receives a message m such that $m.copy = k$ and either $m.broadcaster < i$ or $m.broadcaster = m.originator$. That is, a more senior process has assumed the duties of broadcaster, or the originator has not in fact crashed.
- Process i receives a message m such that $m.copy > k$. This would happen if process i has missed one or more copies of m, and now learns that another broadcaster is closer to completing the protocol.

Suppose that a process which abandoned its broadcasting role and has set a timeout expecting a copy, say, k, from a given broadcaster. It will have to reset that timeout if either copy k is received later from a broadcaster more senior to the current broadcaster or from the originator, or copy $k+1$ or higher is received from any broadcaster. This is necessary because when the first broadcaster receives the message which this process just received, it would relinquish its broadcasting role.

The purpose of these provisions is to avoid unnecessary broadcasts and hence message traffic, while ensuring that $\rho + 1$ copies of each message are broadcast. The idea is that when any broadcaster crashes, all receivers that timeout on $\eta + \omega + \zeta$ will briefly become broadcasters, but after that only one is most likely to continue broadcasting, at intervals of length η. That process will be a receiver process if the originator has crashed or its messages suffer excessive delays. A detailed pseudo-code description of the reliable multicast protocol executed by the process i is shown in Figure 4, where the variables max_recd_i, $leader_i$, and $last\_own\_bcast_i(m)$ denote the number of the largest copy of the message received, the index of the broadcaster from which the next copy is expected, and the copy number of m which the process i broadcasted when it last acted as a self-appointed broadcaster respectively.

Referring to Figure 4, an execution of *RBCast(m)* involves the originator setting the fields *m.originator* and *m.sequenceNo* and, as described earlier, making $(\rho + 1)$ invocations of *broadcast(m)* with *m.copy* increasing from $0, 1, .., \rho + 1$. The primitive *broadcast(m)* sets the *m.broadcaster* field and concurrently sends m to all other processes in the group. The protocol for delivering a reliable multicast message is *RMDeliver()*, and is structured into two concurrently executed parts. The first part handles a received message and the second part the expiry of timeout $(\eta + \omega)$. A received message calls for one or more of the following three actions:

- New m. Variables are initialised and m is delivered.
- $m.copy = \rho$. Blocks any future occurrence of the third action (described next), by setting $max\_recd_i(m)$ to ∞ (*MaxInt*). Note that a new m can have $m.copy = \rho$ if earlier copies are lost or excessively delayed.
- Change of $leader_i(m)$. The received m indicates one of the circumstances (described earlier) in which the process i needs to either relinquish its broadcasting role or change the broadcaster from which the next copy is expected. A new timeout $(\eta + \omega)$ is set after $max\_recd_i(m)$ and $leader_i(m)$ are updated.

When timeout $(\eta + \omega)$ for m expires, an additional timeout ζ is set, during which a message with appropriate copy number from any broadcaster is admissible. So, $leader_i(m)$ is set to *MaxInt* (line 21). If no such message is received, process i appoints itself as a broadcaster and sets up a thread *Broadcaster(m)*. The thread *Broadcaster(m)* broadcasts m only if the process i remains to be the broadcaster (i.e., $leader_i(m) = i$) as per selection rule; otherwise, it dies.

5   QoS Evaluation and Monitoring

The qos_i for a *service_i* has two modules: QoS evaluator ($qosE_i$) and QoS monitor ($qosM_i$) (see figure 2). Here, we will present algorithms that implement $qosE$ and $qosM$ for a reliable broadcast service implemented by the protocol of Section 4. The algorithms for $qosE$ are expressions that evaluate, in terms of protocol parameters, the *eventual delivery probability* and the probability distributions of two delays: *latency* and *relative latency*.

Eventual Delivery: An invocation of *RBcast(m)* delivers m to all correct destination processes with a probability which can be made arbitrarily close to 1.

Latency Bound: The interval between an invocation of *RBcast(m)* and the first instant thereafter when all correct destination processes have received m, does not exceed a given latency bound, D, with a probability, r_D, which can be evaluated in advance.

Relative Latency Bound or Skew: The instants when m arrives for the first time at every operative destination process are within an interval of a given length, S, with a probability, u_S, which can also be evaluated in advance.

```
RBCast(m)
  begin
    m.originator ← i; m.SequenceNo ← seq_number;
    m.copy←0;
    repeat (r +1)   times
      {broadcast(m);wait(h);m.copy ← m.copy+1;}
end
RMDeliver()
begin
  cobegin // message-handling part
    receive(m);
    if new(m) then {
      max_recd_i(m)← m.copy; leader_i(m)← m.broadcaster;
      last_own_bcast_i(m)← -1; deliver(m);
    }// m is delivered (once)
    if (m.copy = r) then { max_recd_i(m)←MaxInt;}
    if(m.copy > max_recd_i(m)) or ((m.copy = max_recd_i(m)
      and (m.broadcaster = m.originator) or
        (m.broadcaster < leader_i(m))) then {
        max_recd_i(m)← m.copy; leader_i(m)←m.broadcaster;
      set timeout for η+ω;}
  coend
  cobegin
    // timeout-triggered, timer-driven part
    timeout(m)➡{
      leader_i(m)←MaxInt; wait(ζ);
        if (leader_i(m) = MaxInt) then {
        leader_i(m) ¨ i; create_thread Broadcaster(m)};}
    }
  coend
end
- - - - - - - - - - - - - - - - - - - - - - - - - - - - - - - - - - - - - - - - - -
Broadcaster(m)
begin
while((max_recd_i(m) < r) and (leader_i(m) = i))
    do {
      m.copy←max{last_own_bcast_i(m)+1, max_recd_i(m)};
      broadcast(m); max_recd_i(m)← m.copy;
      last_own_bcast_i(m)← m.copy; wait(ζ);
}
die; // the thread dies.
end
```

Fig. 4. Pseudo-code description of the protocol.

Note that the eventual delivery probability is r_D as $D \rightarrow \infty$. In what follows, we will be concerned with deriving only the delay distributions. We will make the following approximation. In estimating r_D, the originating process is assumed not to crash. This is not unreasonable because it will generally be a pessimistic approximation: if the originator crashes at some point after broadcasting copy 0 but before broadcasting copy ρ, some of the processes that receive a copy of m will make at least one broadcast themselves. Thus, the number of broadcasters and hence the probability of eventual delivery will increase. Of course it is possible that the originator crashes during broadcast 0, and no operative process receives any copy of m; we consider the probability of that event to be negligible.

Latency. Let ξ be the random variable representing the execution time of a $send(m)$ operation, i.e., the transmission time of a message from a given source to a given destination. The probability, $h(x)$, that such an operation *does not* succeed within time x, is equal to

$$h(x) = q + (1 - q)P(\xi > x), \tag{1}$$

where q is the probability that the message is lost. By definition, $h(x) = 1$ if $x \le 0$.

Since the originator makes its kth broadcast at time $k\eta$ ($k = 0, 1, .., \rho$), the probability, g_D, that a *given destination* does not receive any of the $\rho + 1$ copies within time D,

is given by $g_D = \prod_{k=0}^{\rho} h(D - k\eta)$. So, the probability, r_D, that every destination

receives at least one copy of the message within an interval of length D is equal to

$$r_D = (1 - g_D)^{n-1}. \tag{2}$$

A user requirement, stated in terms of a success probability R and latency D, is achievable if the probability evaluated by (2) satisfies $r_D \ge R$; otherwise it is not achievable. In the latter case, the value of r_D is returned as the possible alternative for R and also the smallest D' such that $r_{D'} \ge R$ as the possible alternative latency for the desired R.

Relative Latency. Suppose now that at a given moment, t, a given process, p_i (different from the originator), receives copy number k of the message. Of interest is the probability, $u_k(S)$, that all other processes will receive at least one copy of the message with relative latency S, i.e., before time $t+S$.

The implication of p_i receiving copy number k is that the originator has started broadcasting no later than at time $t-k\eta$ in the past, and has issued at least k broadcasts. Consider a given process, p_j, different from the originator and from p_i as well. The probability, $g_k(S)$, that p_j will not receive any of those k copies before time $t+S$ is no

greater than $g_k(S) = \prod_{m=0}^{k} h(S + m\eta)$, where $h(x)$ is given by (1).

In addition, if $k<\rho$, p_j may receive copies k, $k+1$, .. , ρ, from p_i, in the event of the originator crashing. Those latter broadcasts would be issued at times $t+\eta+\omega+\zeta$, $t+2\eta+\omega+\zeta$,.., $t+(\rho-k+1)\eta+\omega+\zeta$, assuming that no other process starts broadcasting. Since ζ is uniformly distributed on $(0,\eta)$, we can pessimistically replace ζ by η. The probability, $\tilde{g}_k(S)$, that p_j will not receive any of the messages from p_i before time $t+S$ is thus approximated by $\tilde{g}_k(S) = \prod_{m=1}^{\rho-k+1} h(S-(m+1)\eta - \omega)$, where $\tilde{g}_\rho(S) = 1$ by definition; also, $h(x)=1$ if $x \leq 0$.

Thus, a pessimistic estimate for the conditional probability, $u_k(S)$, that all other processes will receive at least one copy of the message with relative latency S, given that a given process has received copy number k, is given by

$$u_k(S) = [1 - g_k(S)\tilde{g}_k(S)]^{n-2}.$$ (3)

A pessimistic estimate for the conditional probability, $u_k(S)$, that all other processes will receive at least one copy of the message with relative latency S, given that a given process has received any copy, is obtained by taking the smallest of the above probabilities:

$$u_S = \min(u_0(S), u_1(S), \dots, u_\rho(S))$$ (4)

A user requirement stated in terms of a desired success probability U and relative latency S, is achievable if $u_S \geq U$. If $u_S < U$ then the value of u_S is returned as the possible alternative for U, and also the smallest S' such that $u_{S'} \geq U$ as the possible alternative skew for the desired U.

5.1 QoS Monitoring and Subsequent Adaptation

As the reliable broadcast service sits on top of the CS, its QoS monitor component *qosM* should monitor the performance of the CS. If the performance of CS is observed to be slow, with the mean delay larger than guaranteed, then the *qosE* of receiver processes can set smaller values for the parameters η and ω. This will have the effect of those receiver processes that have received some copy of *m* timing out on the broadcaster sooner i.e., suspecting the broadcaster very prematurely (see figure 4); consequently, each timed-out receiver will initially try to act as the broadcaster and this will maximise the chances of a receiver that has not received any copy of *m*, to receive some copy of *m* quickly from one of the processes acting as the broadcaster. If, on the other hand, the CS performs faster than guaranteed, the *qosE* of receiver processes can set larger values for η and ω, which will have the opposite effect: only the originator of *m* (if operative) is very likely to broadcast *m* which is sufficient in better conditions and also reduces the message overhead. The simulation results reported in [11] confirm these QoS adaptive aspects of the protocol.

QoS monitoring is an active topic of research and we will here point to various ways in which *qosM* module can be realised. It should be noted that a *qosM* module could be a sophisticated distributed subsystem in its own right. For example, EdgeMeter [27] is a distributed meter system designed to monitor QoS of traffic of IP networks. Metric collection is central to QoS monitoring and is concerned with gathering statistical information about the performance of a service. A good discussion of the advantages and limitations of existing techniques for metric collection is presented in [8]. The metric collector component (MeCo) can be realised as one or more pieces of software possibly in combination with some hardware components. Referring to figure 2, the MeCo for $qosM_{i+1}$ can be realised by deploying it within $qosM_{i+1}$ (service consumer instrumentation), or within $service_i$ (provider instrumentation) or somewhere in the path between the provider, S_i and the service consumer, S_{i+1}.

6 Related Work

From the known synchronous and asynchronous middleware protocols, we have derived protocols for the probabilistic model. Similar attempts can be found in the literature. The timed asynchronous (TA) protocols are claimed to have been designed through a stepwise refinement of the problem specification initially expressed in the synchronous model with no crashes [24]. This reinforces our earlier observation (Table 1) that the TA model can be seen as the synchronous model with non-zero message loss probability. Deriving probabilistic (PA) protocols from TA ones, we believe, will only be of theoretical interest. The fail-aware service can be viewed as a QoS monitor on CS (i.e., a part of $qosM_1$ in figure 2) which additionally discards messages that do not conform to a range of QoS metrics. The TA system uses the fail-aware service to identify QoS-wise bad periods and brings the system environment to a fail-safe state if necessary. We believe that a similar fail-safe mechanism can be achieved by monitoring the QoS offered to an end user.

Hermant and Le Lann demonstrate that certain abstractions within deterministic asynchronous protocols (such as FDs) are closely linked to the tuneable performance of low-level subsystems (such as CS), and they can be 'bound' to the synchronous model with the desired coverage during system implementation [19]. This then leads them to establish a thesis that the asynchronous model design approach combined with binding-at-implementation is better suited to building real-time applications. We have taken a view that, for the Internet-based service-provisioning applications, the coverage be made explicit in terms of QoS probabilities and that the CS is constantly being tuned by the ISP at run-time to meet the negotiated coverage. So, any protocol binding can be done at the design time itself. The overlay approach of Verissimo and Casimiro [28] is another example of design-time binding.

The approach of setting appropriate parameters for the desired system behaviour is long known. A classical example is the TCP congestion control by adapting the window size in the sliding window protocol. The challenges in this approach are deriving protocols with configurable parameters and, more so, developing algorithms, such as the linear-increase and multiplicative-decrease algorithm for TCP congestion control [21], that help choose the right parameter values at the right occasions. Both these challenges are addressed in sections 4 and 5 for a reliable broadcast protocol. A complementary approach pursued in [20] is to support selection of an appropriate protocol from a protocol suite for the current execution environment.

An observation which is gaining widespread acceptance is that the FD protocols and also their close cousins – virtually synchronous protocols – cannot scale while maintaining throughput simultaneously. It was borne out of a variety of experiments by Gupta et. al. who also provide informed explanations for it [17]. These explanations are of interest here as we propose to derive PA protocols from the FD-based ones. The central argument for the non-attainability of a scalable throughput is as follows. While it is common to model a correct process operating continuously in the steady state, events such as page faults, according low scheduling priority, etc., can cause a process to suspend its operation (i.e., to go to 'sleep') for a while. As the number of processes increases, the probability of at least one process being in sleep mode at any given instance of time, rises to a significant level. Since the asynchronous protocols offer deterministic guarantees, correct processes need to retain each message until all processes have acknowledged it. With at least one process being slow at any given time, the buffers can easily overflow causing high loss rates.

PA protocols, however, offer only probabilistic guarantees and can well avoid suffering from this phenomenon to a considerable extent, and go on to offer a scalable throughput. The RBcast(m), for example, broadcasts m only for ρ times and the gossiper process afterwards retains the sent messages only for a bounded number of gossip rounds (see subsection 3.3). Thus, the protocol should not suffer from one or more processes being asleep at any time. We suspect, on the other hand, that the ζ–timer introduced as an efficient measure (see *Selection* in subsection 4.3) may suffer from the effect of a low probability event becoming a significant one due to increase in system size. This ζ–timer mechanism traces its origin to the *random assessment delay* (RAD) of the SRM protocol [14] which is a best-effort reliable multicast protocol. Gupta et. al., observe that the RAD is ineffective as the size increases and offers smaller throughput than what can be achieved without it, and advocate *randomised gossip* [2] as a solution to achieve scalable throughput. One could achieve an efficient scalable measure by adopting this technique, for example, by designing a self-appointed broadcaster to broadcast message m only to a subset of randomly selected receivers.

Exploiting such randomisation techniques will be our future work. We also note here that the stochastic analysis of such randomised gossip protocols seen in the literature may not be sufficient for building QoS adaptive subsystems. For example, the evaluation of latency distribution of [2] is done in terms of gossip rounds, rather than in global time. This is also true of randomised consensus protocols (e.g., [4, 12]): the probability of termination is shown to approach 1 as the rounds increase. QoS analysis will additionally require evaluating latency distributions.

7   Concluding Remarks

We have examined some fundamental issues on how middleware can be designed to host components capable of providing services to users that demand specified levels of QoS. The probabilistic model we have chosen characterises a practical environment for building an Internet based, QoS-adaptive system. We have termed it as the probabilistic asynchronous model to indicate that the delays may not be bounded with absolute certainty, but can be done in probabilistic terms. The model is compared against the classical models. The appropriateness of our model for the purposes of building the desired system has also been identified.

The system architecture we have presented identifies the interactions between the subsystems, and between the modules of a given subsystem. Two classes of modules and their design requirements have thus been made obvious: a set of protocols that implement system services and a set of algorithms that help adapt these protocols and thereby the QoS offered by the system. The interface between these two types of modules consists of the parameters exported by the service protocols. Thus, the design challenges are two-fold: developing protocols with configurable parameters and performance evaluation based on stochastic modelling with approximations (if necessary) that would help choose the right parameters for the desired QoS.

Based on the features of the probabilistic asynchronous model, we have claimed that protocols for this model can be derived from those developed for the synchronous and the asynchronous models. This amounts to exposing the possibilities of 'design reuse' in building a QoS adaptive system. This derivability claim is then substantiated by deriving a reliable broadcast protocol, which implements a basic service in a middle system. We have not attempted to generalise the task of performance evaluation for a general class of protocols. It is not easy since performance evaluation will very much depend on the nature of the protocol being evaluated and its outcome on the approximations that may be taken to keep the analysis tractable. The performance evaluation of a simple reliable broadcast protocol, presented in Section 5, highlights these difficulties and challenges. We have recommended that the approximations, if taken, are preferred to have a bias for performance under-estimation.

Acknowledgements

This work is part-funded by the UK EPSRC under grants GR/S02082/01, GR/S63199/01 and the European Union Project IST-2001-34069: TAPAS (Trusted and QoS Aware Provision of Application Services). Discussions with, and clarification provided by, Professor Isi Mitrani were extremely useful. We thank the reviewers for their many suggestions, also Ms Ferrari and Mr Di Ferdinando for their help in formatting the final version.

References

1. Arvind K. Probabilistic Clock Synchronisation in Distributed Systems. *IEEE Transactions in Parallel and Distributed Systems*, 5(5):475-487, May 1994.
2. Birman K. et. al. Bimodal Multicast. *ACM Transactions on Computer Systems*, 17(2):41-88, May 1999.
3. Birman K and Joseph T. Reliable Communication in the Presence of Failures. *ACM Transactions on Computer Systems*, 5(1): 47-76, February, 1987.
4. Bracha G. and Toueg S. Asynchronous consensus and Broadcast Protocols, in the *Journal of the ACM*, 32: 824 – 840, Oct. 1985.
5. Chandra T D and Toueg. Unreliable Failure Detectors for Reliable Distributed Systems, *Journal of the ACM*, 43(2): 225-267, 1996.
6. Chandra T D, Hadzilacos V and Toueg. The weakest Failure Detector for Solving Consensus, *Journal of the ACM*, 43(4), pp. 685 - 722, 1996.
7. Chen W, Toueg S and Aguilera M K. On the Quality of Service of Failure Detectors, IEEE Transactions on Computers, 51: 561-580, May 2002.
8. Cherkasova L., Fu Y., Tang W. and Vahdat A. Measuring and Characterizing End-to-End Internet Service Performance. *ACM Transactions on Internet Technology*, 3(4), Nov 2003.
9. Cristian F. Probabilistic Clock Synchronisation. *Distributed Computing*, 3(3):146-158, 1989.

10. Cristian F and Fetzer C. The Timed Asynchronous Distributed System Model, In *IEEE Transactions on Parallel and Distributed Systems*, 10 (6): 642-57, June 1999.
11. Di Ferdinando A., Ezhilchelvan P. D. and Mitrani I. Performance Evaluation of a QoS-Adaptive Reliable Multicast Protocol. *Technical Report CS-TR-833*, School of Computing Science, University of Newcastle. April 2004.
12. Ezhilchelvan P D, Mostefaoui A and Raynal M. Randomized Multivalued Consensus. In the proceedings of the fourth International IEEE Symposium on Object oriented Real-time Computing (ISORC), pp. 195-201, May 2001.
13. Ezhilchelvan P D and Shrivastava S K. *rel/REL*: A Family of Reliable Multicast Protocols for Distributed Systems, *Distributed Systems Engineering*, 6:323 – 331, 1994.
14. Floyd S. *et. al.* A reliable Multicast Framework for Light-Weight Sessions and Application Level Framing. *SIGCOMM Computer Communications Review*, 25(4): 342-356, Oct 1995.
15. Gibbens R. *et. al.* Fixed Point Models for the end-to-end performance analysis of IP Networks. *In Proceedings of the thirteenth ITC Specialist Seminar: IP Traffic Measurement Modelling and Management,* September 2000, Montrey, USA.
16. Guerraoui R. Revisiting the relationship between Non-blocking Atomic Commitment and Consensus. *In Proceedings of the Ninth International Workshop on Distributed Algorithms*, Springer-Verlag, September 1995.
17. Gupta I, Birman K and Van Renesse R. Fighting Fire with Fire: Using a Randomised Gossip to Combat Stochastic Scalability Limits. *Quality and Reliability Engineering International* 18:165-184, 2002.
18. Hadzilacos V. and Toueg S. Fault-Tolerant Broadcasts and Related Problems. In *Distributed Systems*, (Ed.) S Mullender, Addison-Wesley, 1993, pp. 97-146.
19. Hermant J-F. and Le Lann G. Fast Asynchronous Consensus in Real-Time Distributed Systems. *IEEE Transactions on Computers,* 51(8):931-944, August 2002.
20. Hiltunen M. *et. al.* Real-Time Dependable Channels: Customising QoS Attributes for Distributed Systems. *IEEE Trans. on Parallel and Distributed Systems*, 10(6):600-612, June 99.
21. Jacobson V. Congestion Avoidance and Control. In the *proceedings of the SIGCOMM symposium*, pp. 314-332, August 1988.
22. Kopetz H. Real-Time Systems: Design Principles for Distributed Embedded Applications. Kluwer Academic Publishers, 1997, ISBN 0-7923-9894-7
23. Miley M. Reinventing Business: Application Service Providers. *ORACLE Magazine*, December 2000, pp. 48-52.
24. Mishra S., Fetzer C. and Cristian F. The Timewheel Group Communication System. *IEEE Transactions on Computers,* 51(8): 883-889, August 2002.
25. Park K and Willinger W. *Self-Similar Network Traffic and Performance Evaluation*. John Wiley & Sons, 2000, ISBN 0-471-31974-0.
26. Pease M., Shostak R. and Lamport L. Reaching Agreement in the Presence of Faults. *Journal of the ACM*, 27(2):228-234, April 1980.
27. Pias M. and Wilbur S. EdgeMeter: Distributed Network metering, In *Proceedings of the IEEE Openarch 2001 conference*, Anchorage, Alaska, Apr. 2001.
28. Verissimo P and Casimiro A, The Timely Computing Base Model and Architecture, *IEEE Transaction on Computing Systems*, 51(8): 916-930, August 2002.

Quantifiable Software Architecture
for Dependable Systems of Systems

Sheldon X. Liang[1], Joseph F. Puett III[2], and Luqi[1]

[1] United States, Naval Postgraduate School
833 Dyer Road, Monterey 93940, USA
{xliang,luqi}@nps.navy.mil
[2] United States Military Academy
West Point, NY 10996, USA
joseph.puett@us.army.mil

Abstract. Software architecture is a critical aspect in the successful development and evolution of dependable systems of systems (DSoS), because it provides artifactual loci around which engineers can reason, construct, and evolve the software design to provide robustness and resilience. Quantifiably architecting DSoS involves establishing a consensus of attributes of dependability (from different stakeholders' perspectives) and translating them into quantifiable constraints. Unfortunately, there are few established approaches for quantifiably architecting such systems with dependability concerns considered at the architectural level. This paper presents a quantifiable architectural approach for evolving hybrid systems into DSoS so that the attributes of dependability can be justifiably translated into constraints and attached to architectural artifacts. Furthermore, it provides a means of quantitatively assessing these characteristics throughout the DSoS development/evolution process. Basically, this approach strengthens system composition in combination with explicit architecting and quantifiable constraints attached to the subsequent artifacts so as to improve the dependability of the intended systems through design inspection via static checking at the architectural level and dynamic monitoring at runtime.

1   Introduction

Architecture is recognized as a critical aspect in the successful development and evolution of Dependable Systems of Systems (DSoS), because it provides artifactual loci around which engineers can reason, construct, and evolve the software design to provide robustness and resilience. In general, DSoS comprise a set of distributed quality systems (or subsystems) which collaborate via internal or external communications mechanisms and are characterized as providing dependable services through concurrent execution. The quantifiable architecting approach aims to emphasize composing a dependable "system of systems" from highly autonomous component systems by reusing existing dependable legacy components. The approach of building dependability into the architectural design seeks to reduce cost and increase the quality of the developed software product. The central idea is that dependable architectures in large, complex, evolvable systems will provide their users with a reasonable assurance that the system will deliver the services promised. Quantifiably architecting DSoS in-

R. de Lemos et al. (Eds.): Architecting Dependable Systems II, LNCS 3069, pp. 241–265, 2004.

volves establishing a consensus of dependability attributes (from different perspectives) and translating them into quantifiable constraints. This provides an effective solution of associating various perspectives with attributes of dependability [1-5]. For instance, a customer and/or analyst will have a particular view of dependability attributes; a designer has a particular view of quantifiable constraints to be met by specific architectural artifacts, while an implementer has a particular view of semantic characteristics bound to segments of code. Although these views are addressed in different development strata (or stages), semantic consistency among them is required to facilitate the quantitative assessment of quality attributes through reasoning analysis, formal verification, deadlock detection, and thread scheduling [6-11].

The difficulties in engineering DSoS are further exacerbated by requirements uncertainty, dynamic organizational structures (and concerns), and the requirement for rapid application development. Three crucial aspects are involved: 1) accurately identifying all customer requirements, 2) resolving customer requirement conflicts within the context of different customer perspectives, and 3) verifying and monitoring that the resulting system satisfies customer intent (and if not, correcting the requirements and the system).

While measurable attributes reflecting different aspects of dependability are addressed in various specification techniques and approaches, e.g., rapid prototyping, model checking, as well as runtime monitoring [8,9,10], the lack of a quantifiable architectural framework (QAF) to incorporate current techniques into architectural design is a crucial problem [3-5]. New modeling methods and related design patterns are needed to associate quality attributes with architectural artifacts so that quantifiable software architecture can be transitionally built throughout the software development processes.

1.1   Contributions

This chapter provides a quantifiable architectural approach for evolving hybrid systems into DSoS. The approach, beginning with rapid system prototyping, provides fundamentals for modeling architecture, assessing the dependability impact of design decisions before coding begins, and monitoring dependability attributes at runtime after a quantifiable architecture framework (QAF) has been automatically generated. The model involved in this approach defines compositional patterns [3-4] with which quantifiable constraints are associated so that a set of rules (patterns) is provided to govern system composition based on the subsequent architectural artifacts.

From the view of point of various stakeholders' concerns the quantifiable architecting technique treats dependability at three developmental strata: the acquisition of dependability attributes at computational requirements level, the attachment of quantifiable constraints at the compositional architecture level, and the monitoring of semantic characteristics at the componential derivation level.

Also the approach provides a rational for translating typical constraints such as timing constraints, synchronous coordination and architectural features, into semantic characteristics bound to the auto-generated QAF as fundamental basis for quantitative assessment of DSoS and architecture-based system evolution. Thus, dependability attributes become effectively and practically computable for validation and verification purposes, such as static checking at architectural level and dynamic monitoring at runtime.

Because successful systems are in a constant state of change, achieving these contributions in the face of this change is particularly challenging for DSoS development. This approach seeks to maintain the assurance of dependability as the system evolves. It strengthens system composition in combination with explicit architecting and quantitative assessment techniques that enable parts of the assurance to be based on properties of the architecture that are invariant with respect to system requirements changes. The quantifiable architecting approach will reduce the amount of recertification effort required after each requirement change, while assuming that the change is within the envelope of these invariants. It is recognized that safety is a holistic property, rather than a 'sum of parts' [12-14]. Quantifiable software architecture can be used to additionally address synergistic effects and emergent behavior within the overall safety case.

1.2   Related Work

A number of techniques, frameworks and approaches have emerged to address the problems in engineering quality systems. These efforts include rapid system prototyping [6-8], software architectures [12-20], and component techniques [21-23]. All of these focus on composing software systems from coarser-grained components, while some also take advantage of using the quality attributes associated with performance, time-criticality, and concurrent execution.

Rapid system prototyping has traditionally been useful to effectively capture computational requirements [6]. It seeks to provide a rapid response to customer's concerns. More specifically, timing constraints, representing quality attributes, are bound to essential activities and information flows between them. Subsequently, a static scheduling algorithm is employed to validate that specified timing constraints are feasible on a given hardware configuration. However, because of the significant differences between the final system and the prototype, a real product system can seldom be sufficiently assured through static scheduling validation of the prototype [3-5].

Component techniques assume a homogeneous architectural environment in which all components adhere to certain implementation constraints (e.g., design, packaging, and runtime constraints). These constraints are imposed on the component's evolution, with little concern for mapping dependability to executable facilities [3, 15, 16].

Software architecture approaches typically separate computation (components) from interaction (connectors) in a system. Undoubtedly, both connectors and components provide suitable loci where quality attributes could be explicitly addressed and implemented. However, the current level of understanding and support for connectors has been insufficient, particularly at the implementation language level, so that connectors are often considered to be explicit at the level of architecture, but intangible in the system implementation [3, 15, 16]. Several sources have recommended the use of architecture views [1-2]. They specify how architecture should be represented, but do not provide a process for developing the specific artifacts that are used in the representation [2, 3].

Another relatively new approach is to use UML extensions to model software architecture [17, 25]. UML provides a variety of useful capabilities to the software designer, including multiple, interrelated design views (perspectives), a semiformal semantics expressed as a UML meta model, and an associated language for expressing formal logic constraints on design elements. While UML is expressive in certain areas of architectural design, it is deficient in others. In particular, UML lacks direct support for modeling and exploiting architectural styles, explicit software connectors, and local and global architectural constraints. UML also has deficiencies in use case architectural modeling and system decomposition for requirement specification [25, 26].

The lack of a definitive architectural artifact synthesis poses a challenge to those who are responsible for developing architectures that satisfy the differing perspectives of stakeholders. Some software research groups have set their focus on developing a procedure; for instance, the structured analysis approach and object-oriented approach for software design [2, 27], and the object-oriented model for interoperability via wrapper-based translation [20]. However, none of these procedures support quantifiable and explicit treatment of architecting and system composition.

1.3   Organization

Section 2 of this chapter outlines a quantifiable architectural approach with emphasis on the conceptual context where the perspective-based modeling techniques reside. Section 3 discusses the core model of the approach, the dependable composition model (DCM), and the associated compositional patterns to which quantifiable constraints are attached; the related formalization and examples are also discussed to fulfill the compositional pattern. Section 4 discusses the application of DCM in building substantial interconnections and further investigates three views of dependability assurance at architectural level. Using an example, section 5 illustrates the synthesized approach, highlights the automated transitions between multiple perspective models, and demonstrates how compositional evolution is achieved by deriving a composite system from simple homogeneous compositions and complex heterogeneous compositions. Section 6 outlines the conclusion with a discussion of the impacts of the approach in quantifiably architecting DSoS and lists some directions for further research.

2   An Overview

The quantifiable architectural approach described here is broadly designed for conceptual contexts that deal with multiple perspectives from various stakeholders. It assumes typical stages of software life cycle processes [24] and employs a perspective-based synthesis procedure.

2.1   Conceptual Context

Fig. 1 depicts the conceptual context for multiple perspective models in the quantifiable architectural approach. A system's multiple perspectives from particular stakeholders (e.g., customer, analyst, designer, assessor, implementer), are mapped into a collection of software life cycle activities including requirement analysis, architectural design and quantitative assessment, and application implementation.

Each of these activities is associated with a set of engineering heuristics and intellectual judgments (the cloud callouts). Three development strata are formed, where the quantifiable architecture is positioned in the central stratum (shaded area) that

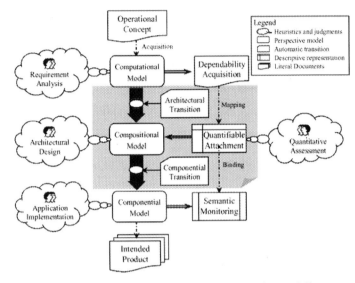

Fig. 1. Conceptual context for multiple perspective modeling.

incorporates architectural design and quantitative assessment leading towards the quantifiable software architecture as a whole.

More specifically, since architectural design aims to develop a common vehicle for communication among systems' stakeholders and is the arena in which conflicting goals and requirements are mediated [1-4], this central strata answers crucial questions on how to consistently engineer a system with multiple perspective models and how to quantifiably formulate architectural artifacts so that they are capable of automatic manipulation by CASE tools.

2.2   Perspective-Based Modeling

Quantifiably architecting DSoS inevitably involves establishing consensus from various stakeholders – addressing their particular concerns and then anchoring the design on architectural elements that deliver promised dependable services.

Computational Requirements

The computational perspective accounts for the users' concerns and represents the computational activities and information flows of the DSoS. The computational perspective accomplishes the operational concept, that is, what activities are needed and how their interactions are associated with workflows, networking, and plans necessary to support the users' operations [1-2]. The computational model, derived from the prototyping model [6, 8], is specified by capturing conceptual components (C_c), interconnections (I_{int}), and dependability attributes ($Attr$) associated with components and interconnections, i.e.,

$$P_{computation} = [C_c, I_{int}, Attr\,(C_c, I_{int})] \qquad \text{Def-1}$$

Regarding components, the focus is on systematic decomposition reasoning out component granularity and computational responsibility. The former is used for handling logically packaged complexity related to the hierarchy at which the constraints are implemented, while the latter is embodied as (distributed) collaborations, (configurable) missions, (computable) functions, and (executable) tasks. Granularity is an important factor for constructing complex systems because well-grained components help not only to increase productivity but also to improve understandability, reliability and maintainability.

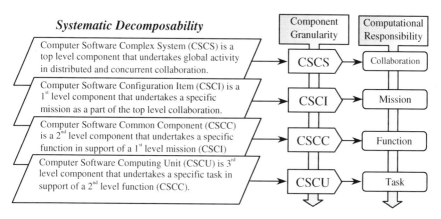

Fig. 2. Computational responsibility schema and related features.

Fig. 2 illustrates the computation-responsibility schema, which defines the systematic decomposition of computational properties. As the system is hierarchically decomposed, levels of granularity establish levels of computational responsibility (component). Moreover, the interconnections only represent communications between components, not the way one component interacts with another.

Compositional Architecture

The compositional perspective accounts for the system architects' concerns. It deals with the rules (patterns) and their quantifiable constraints governing the interactions among components. The interconnections from the computational perspective are further refined by well-modeled architectural artifacts. A dependable compositional model is developed by generalizing conceptual components into roles ($C_c \Rightarrow R$). These roles serve in the context of a particular collaboration of component to accomplish a particular larger purpose, and by specifying their interaction $(R_o - ^S/_P \rightarrow R_i)$[1] via architectural styles (S) while complying with communication protocols (P), with constraints ($Cons$) attached to these factors, i.e.,

$$P_{composition} = [C_c \Rightarrow R, R_o - ^S/_P \rightarrow R_i, Cons (R, S, P)] \qquad \text{Def-2}$$

---

[1] $R_o - ^S/_P \rightarrow R_i$ represents the producer (Output) role R_o interacts with the consumer (Input) role R_i via architectural style S, while complying with communication protocol P.

With respect to interconnections, the focus is on architectural composition[2] related to interactive heterogeneity and compositional coupling. The former precisely determines for each particular interaction the way diverse components interact with others, while the latter is used to control flexible configuration and inherent complexity. Dependability attributes from the computational perspective are mapped to quantifiable constraints[3] and are attached to three specified factors for precisely-refined interconnections.

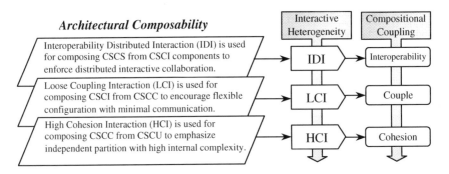

Fig. 3. Compositional coupling and related features.

Fig. 3 depicts the composition-coupling schema, introduced for architectural composition. Moreover, the interconnections are refined here as interactions between interactive roles via architectural styles while complying with communication protocols.

Componential Derivation

The componential perspective accounts for the implementers' concerns. It defines the physical components and their instantiated topological connectivity used to carry out the computational activities and the derivational evolution of those components from the composition model. The roles that undertake specific responsibility in the compositional architecture are realized by physical components. A componential model is exploited by capturing derivation of physical components from the related roles $(R \triangleright C_p)$[4]; instances of components are glued to specific roles $(C_p \twoheadrightarrow R)$[5]; and finally, characteristics (**Chr**) bound to concrete components, styles and protocols, i.e.,

$$P_{component} = [R \triangleright C_p, (C_p \twoheadrightarrow R_o) \overset{S}{-}/_p \to (R_i \twoheadleftarrow C_p), Chr (C_p, S, P)] \qquad \text{Def-3}$$

---

2   Architectural composition refers to hierarchical composition; i.e., an entire architecture becomes a single component in another larger architecture.

3   There exist mapping relationships between attributes and constraints. E.g., safety refers to real time constraints, so safety requirements could be mapped to constraints attached to architectural artifacts.

4   $R \triangleright C_p$ represents an extension from a role to a component in terms of subtyping. The R provides a plug-compatible interface for interaction and a behavioral template for computation, while the C_p serves as the role and will be considered as a behavioral subtype of related role by overriding the templates

5   $C_p \twoheadrightarrow R_o$ represents dynamic binding where the instance of the component is glued to a specific role under support of the run-time mechanism

Regarding the relationships between roles and components, the focus is on derivational evolution referring to topological connectivity and componential functionality. The former emphasizes the relationships between architectural roles and autonomous components, while the latter refers to the derivational functionality from the related role. As is common, roles in the architectural context undertake specific responsibility through interconnections [3-4]; the derived component provides dependable services.

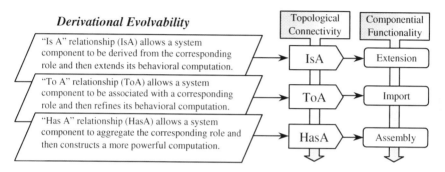

Fig. 4. Componential functionality and related features.

Fig. 4 illustrates the component-functionality schema, introduced for derivational evolution of componential functionality. The evolution from the role to component is demonstrated by treating a component as a behavioral subtype of the related role. Further, the roles are architectural elements of the system and are treated as wrappers of functional components. Thus, derived components inherit the architectural properties and constraints with functional extension.

Quantitative Assessment

The quantifiable perspective, responsible for addressing assessor's concerns, deals with validation and verification of system design. This refers to acquisition of dependability attributes, the attachment of constraints to architectural artifacts, the application of constraints in the design, and the construction and evolution of the constraints throughout the DSoS development. The modeling method captures the mapping from dependability requirements to quantifiable constraints $(D_r \leftrightarrows Q_c)$[6], and supplies the quantifiable attachment of the constraints to the essential factors of the dependable composition model $Q_c \rightsquigarrow DCM\ (R,S,P)$[7], i.e.,

$$P_{\text{quantification}} = [D_r \ \leftrightarrows Q_c,\ Q_c \rightsquigarrow DCM\ (R,S,\ P)] \qquad \text{Def-4}$$

With respect to the dependability requirements (conceptual view), the focus is on the mapping from dependability attributes to quantifiable constraints attached to architectural artifacts (quantifiable view) for static checking at the architectural level. The constraints are further treated as semantic characteristics for dynamic monitoring

---

[6] $(D_r \leftrightarrows Q_c)$ represents the mapping between dependability requirements and quantifiable constraints from computational perspective to compositional perspective.

[7] $Q_c \rightsquigarrow DCM\ (R,S,P)$ represents the attachment of quantifiable constraints to the dependable compositional model referring to interactive roles **R**, architectural styles **S**, and communication protocols **P**.

at runtime (semantic view). In this context quantifiable constraints must be effectively and practically computable. Static checking provides a means of assessing the quality impact of design decisions before coding begins, while dynamic monitoring provides feedback on the impact that various software architecture and design choices have on the quantifiable architectural framework – a framework that is automatically generated for quantitative assessment and system evolution.

Attributes	mapping	Constraints	binding	Artifacts
• Availability • Reliability • Safety • Integrity • Confidentiality • Maintainability		• Consistency • Compatibility • Granularity • Heterogeneity • Real time • Synchronization • Quality of Service		• Role • Style • Protocol

Fig. 5. Constraint attachment on compositional artifacts.

Fig. 5 illustrates the constraints-to-artifact schema, introduced for dependability acquisition and the related handling methods at the architectural level. The term "attachment" represents the acquisition of dependability attributes, the attributes mapping to quantifiable constraints, and the handling (binding) method in the design, construction, and evolution of DSoS.

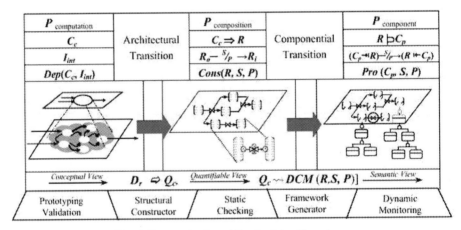

Fig. 6. Perspective-based Synthesizing Procedure.

2.3   Perspective-Based Synthesis

Fig. 6 illustrates a perspective-based synthesis throughout a software development process. Four perspectives defined by Def-1, 2, 3, and 4 are combined to support the quantifiable architecting approach: perspective transitioning, quantitative analysis and tool assisted treatment. The quantifiable architectural framework is generated by exploiting supportive architectural facilities [3-4]. The componential transition is developed by exploiting the derivational relationships between roles (under the framework) and components using an object-oriented approach.

The transitions between the three strata provide the refinement from one item to the other, step by step. For instance, (1) C_c → (2) $C_c \Rightarrow R$ → (3) $R \models C_p$: first, conceptual components are identified from operational concept as the system is decomposed; second, exact roles are extracted from conceptual components in the architectural context; and third, physical components evolve from the roles within the quantifiable architectural framework. During these transitions, designers and/or implementers are only concerned with the architectural decisions and componential refinement while employing supportive architectural facilities [3-4, 17, 28].

3   Dependable Composition Model (DCM)

The dependable composition modeling method is used to develop the quality-intensive architecture (or quantifiable software architecture) of the DSoS.

3.1   Definition of Dependable Composition

A dependable composition model (DCM) promoting system composition refers to three kinds of artifacts within the architectural context: interactive roles, architectural styles, and communication protocols [3-4].

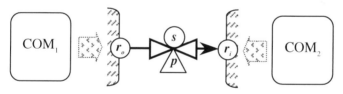

Fig. 7. Interconnection specified by DCM.

Fig. 7 shows a simple example where two components that undertake specific responsibilities; one adopts a producer role (r_o) and the other a consumer role (r_i). The architectural style (s) specifies how r_o interacts with r_i, while the communication protocol (p) provides a communication channel for the information transportation during the interaction.

Compositional Patterns
Generally, a DCM defines the compositional patterns that provide a set of rules governing interactions between components and associating quantifiable constraints with the artifacts. With emphasis on the non-functional features, such factors as roles, styles, and protocols and their dependable semantics are identified and then applied to develop a set of reusable architectural facilities known as dependable composers.

A well defined model should provide a means for reasoning about desired properties in specification and manipulation by CASE tools. The DCM supports the architecture construction through the auto-generation of a quantifiable architectural framework, and facilitates design inspection through static checking at architectural level, and dynamic monitoring at runtime.

Relational Composition

For the convenience of discussion, consider three sets of typical elements involved in the composition:

$R = \{$	$S = \{$	$P = \{$
Caller, Definer,	Explicit-invocation,	Message-passing,
Announcer, Listener,	Published-Subscriber,	Event-broadcast
Outflow, Inflow,	Pipe-filter,	Dataflow-stream,
Source, Repository,	Repository-centric,	Sampled-stream
Reader, Writer, ...	Blackboard, ...	Shared-data, ...
$\}$	$\}$	$\}$

Where R is the set of interactive roles undertaking specific responsibility in an architectural context, S is the set of architectural styles specifying the way one role interacts with the other, and P is the set of communication protocols defining the means by which interaction information is transported.

Formally, a composition C is a tuple $< r_o, s, p, r_i >$, where $r_o, r_i \in R, s \in S, p \in P$. Further, regardless of the restrictions on these elements, the C can be defined as an interaction between two roles via a style, while complying with a protocol, written as: $r_o{-}^s/_p{\rightarrow}r_i$. Therefore, the Cartesian product R x S x P x R enumerates all possible compositions:

$$C(R, S, P) = \{ \, r_o{-}^s/_p{\rightarrow}r_i \, | \, r_o, r_i \in R, s \in S, p \in P \, \} \qquad \text{Def-5}$$

However, it is worth noting that real compositions of these elements have restrictions. For instance, the architectural style *Pipeline* permits a direct interaction between roles (*Outflow* and *Inflow*), while the role *Announcer* cannot normally interact with *Inflow* unless an adaptor is applied. A functional operator *Grw*(), treating the role as a Generalized Role Wrapper, is introduced to represent the application of restrictions and constraints on the roles [3-4]. Therefore, dependable compositions DC will be defined as the relation of the Cartesian product of compositions with constraints justifiably attached to the factors:

$$DC(R, S, P)=\{Grw(r_o){-}^s/_p{\rightarrow}Grw(r_i) \, | \, r_o, r_i \in R, s \in S, p \in P, Ct(\, r_o, s, p, r_i)\} \quad \text{Def-6}$$

Both Def-5 and 6 can be seen as the refinement of Def-2, but Def-6 actually strengthens the interaction betweens *specific* roles via a *specific* architectural style while complying with a *specific* communication protocol. The *Grw* restricts how the interacting roles should comply with the architectural style and communication protocol; e.g., *Grw* (**Outflow**) $-^{\text{pipeline}}/_{\text{dataflow}} \rightarrow$ *Grw* (**Inflow**) suitably represents a dependable composition.

3.2   Formalizations of Compositional Pattern

To formally apply specific restrictions and/or constraints to the role, an abstract class is used to implement the generalized role wrapper (*Grw*).

Functionality and Non-functionality

The *Grw* of an abstract class involves at least two aspects (non-functional and functional) to support quantifiable architecting. In terms of non-functionality, a *Grw* provides adherence to restricted, plug-compatible interfaces for interaction; in terms of functionality, the *Grw* defines behavioral templates for computation. The component serving as a role will be considered as a behavioral subtype of related *Grw* by specifying, refining or overriding the behavioral templates. Obviously, the *Grw* is responsible for addressing issues related to communication and compatibility during interactions, while the derived component addresses issues related to computation and functionality.

Rational Considerations

A set of formal descriptive methods is introduced to state what kinds of modeling features and functions are needed in the description. Surveying current architectural description languages [13, 16-18], the following considerations are adopted in establishing DCM formalizations:

- **Types:** treating architecture entities as types enhances reusability with complex concepts (such as roles, styles and protocols) simplified.
- **Interfaces:** the interfaces enable proper connectivity of components and their communication in an architectural context. They also enable an engineer or a software tool to reason about how well-formed the configuration is.
- **Semantics:** processing semantics support analyses of component interactions, consistent refinements across strata of abstraction, and enforcement of interconnection and communication constraints.
- **Constraints:** quantifiable constraints (e.g., consistency, compatibility, timing constraints, etc.) are specified to ensure attachment to roles, styles and protocols.
- **Evolution:** element derivation, using subtyping, inheritance, and refinement, maximizes the reusability of architectural entities.
- **Hierarchical Composition and Configuration:** this ensures an entire architecture becomes a single component in another, larger architecture.

Table 1 gives the descriptive structures that support the DCM formalization with two types of explicit architectural building blocks: the composer and the component. A set of Ada-like notations is exploited to create the descriptive formalizations. Of practical consideration, these formalizations can be easily mapped to the modules and related programming mechanisms of various object-oriented programming languages (OOPLs), such as Ada95, C++, and Java [3-4, 17, 28].

Basically, componential computation of wrapped roles and interactive collaboration of semantic behavior are described in Communicating Sequential Process (CSP) [29] or in CSP-based form. Quantifiable constraints are appropriately bound to the related segment of code by providing synchronous coordination with asynchronous control transits and timing constraints that can be monitored at runtime.

3.3   Dependable Composer

The DCM defines the compositional patterns and dependable composers are exploited to fulfill these patterns. In contrasting dependable composers and connectors [13-15],

Table 1. Descriptive structure for architectural entities.

	Composer		Component
1	**composer** DCM **is generalized** -- generic parameters	1,5 2	**component** COM **is** [*Derivable relation*]<grw> **port**
	style as ...;		... --computing states and service operations:
	protocol as ...;		... --some computing states
5	**role** R_1 **is** [*Derivable relation*] <grw>		... --some are overridden from wrapped role
2	**port**		... --some are refined and extended
	... -- data status & service operations	3	**computation**
3	**computation**		... --autonomous behavior including
4	... -- autonomous behavior and semantics	4	... --control constraints
	end R_1;		... --scheduling & synchronous coordination
	role R_2 **is ... end** R_2;		... --asynchronous task scheduling
	collaboration $(P : R_1; C : R_2)$	6	**configuration**
	... -- collaborative behavior and semantics		... -- hierarchical decomposition
	end DCM;		**end** COM;

1. **composer** and **component** define architectural entities as types
2. **port** specifies interfaces including computing states and service operations
3. **computation** states the behavioral computation with specified semantics
4. constraints will adhere to the semantic formulation
5. option of *derivational relation* reflects the evolution between the Grw and the component
6. **configuration** provides a means for hierarchical composition from a lower level of components

a connector is an ideal entity that is considered to be explicit at the level of architecture, but intangible in the system implementation [17-18]. A dependable composer is an actual entity that refers to generalized role wrappers (abstract classes), the architectural style, the communication protocol, and the behavioral collaboration between roles.

A dependable composer, introduced to fulfill compositional patterns, encapsulates multiple roles of Grw's (interacting with each other), the architectural style, the communication protocol, and the behavioral collaboration between roles.

Pipeline – A Typical Composer

Table 2 describes a typical example of the *Pipeline* composer. This composer exhibits excellent architectural features (e.g., asynchronous communication, loose component coupling, and data buffering). The related componential derivation and configuration also appear in the same example. In order to establish reusable generalization, *Pipeline* defines two generic parameters: the transported *Data* type (a basic item for dataflow) and a flexible buffer *Size* (100 by default).

Constraints and Semantics

In Table 2, both **synchronized** and **abstract** procedures are introduced to support synchronous coordination of interactive communication and abstract behavioral template of functional derivation, respectively. Synchronized procedures (*Output* and *Input*) employ execution guards to coordinate concurrent synchronization, while the abstract template is overridden by the derived components. Regarding the timing constraints [6, 8], these are treated as semantic characteristics and bound to the CSP-based semantic description. The role of *Outflow* is subject to a maximum execution time (MET) while *Inflow* is subject to a maximum response time (MRT). Both of the quantitative attributes MET(100) and MRT(100) are bound to asynchronous control

Table 2. Composer and Architectural Configuration.

```
composer Pipeline is generalized
   type Data is private;
   Size : Integer : = 100;
style as   <#pipe-filter#>;
protocol as   <#dataflow-stream#>;
role Outflow is
port
   procedure Output(d: Data) is synchronized;
   procedure Produce(d: Data) is abstract;
computation
      Produce (d); *[ Output (d) → Produce (d) ◇ MET (100) →exception; ]
end Outflow;
role Inflow is
port
   procedure Input(d: Data) is synchronized;
   procedure Consume(d: Data) is abstract;
computation
   *[ Input (d)→ Consume (d) ◇ MRT(100) →exception; ]
end Inflow;
collaboration (P : Outflow; C : Inflow)
   P•Produce(d);
   *[ P•Output(d)→ P•Produce(d) ▯ C•Input(d) → C •Consume (d) ]
end Pipeline;

composer My-Pipe is specialized Pipeline (Data =>Adt, Size =>300);
component Producer   is new My_Pipe.Outflow ...   end Producer;
component Consumer is new My_Pipe.Inflow   ...   end Consumer;

component CONFIG-COM is
port
      Source    :   component Producer;
      Sink      :   component Consumer;
computation   ...
configuration
      Source –{My_Pipe}→ Sink;
      My_Pipe•Collaboration(Source, Sink);
      ... -- Roles are glued with the instances of producer & consumer
      ... -- Instances assigned to play roles are concurrently executed
      ... -- Source keeps producing data and then outputs them
      ... -- Sink keeps inputting data and then consumes them
end CONFIG-COM;
```

transits for runtime monitoring. The symbol "◇" represents an asynchronous operation: when producing data for interaction with the *sink* role, the *Outflow* must be synchronized within an MET(100) otherwise, an exception is triggered.

In the descriptive configuration, *Source* –{My_Pipe}→ *Sink* represents topological connectivity by specifying how *Source* interacts with *Sink* via a *My_Pipe* composer, which implements the interconnection. In this case, this also guides the configuration so that *Source* is glued to the *Outflow* role, while *Sink* to the *Inflow* role, as described as My_Pipe.Cpllaboration (Source, Sink).

4   Quantifiable Architecting via a DCM

As previously discussed, the two issues of software architecture (computation and interaction) are suitably characterized as formalized factors (role, style, and protocol) in a DCM. Using a DCM to quantifiably architect DSoS becomes practical with the support of a reusable dependable composer library.

4.1   Substantial Interconnections

It used to be that the architecture of a software system was annotated as "box-line-box" diagrams, where lines inadequately attempted to represent complex relationships between components (boxes) [13-15]. Over time, this annotation has become much richer, for instance, the use of Architecture Description Languages (ADLs) has greatly improved the expressiveness of software architectures. Developing quantifiable software architecture via the DCM continues in this vein. The DCM makes the interconnections among components substantial with dependable composers, which is embodied by the following four aspects:

- **Dependable entities** can be employed to build an additional interconnection among components, provided the components share the same architectural style.
- **Heterogeneous forms** or representations need to be integrated in order to provide coherent communication during interaction between components.
- **Topological connectivity** establishes a connected configuration graph of components and composers. It simplifies the interconnections by leveraging the employed composers.
- **Quantifiable constraint attachment** to the architectural artifacts provides dependability attributes to the DSoS.

An explanation of the first three of these aspects immediately follows; the fourth aspect referring to system dependability analysis is discussed later in this section.

Interconnection via Dependable Composers
After establishing the computational model [6] (the computational perspective derived from prototyping model), the next step is to employ suitable composers to realize the related interconnections by analyzing the roles (roles components adopt to accomplish a larger purpose) in the architectural context [3-4]. The DCM defines compositional patterns that are fulfilled as dependable composers (entities). The dependable composers are employed to build the interconnection with quantifiable constraints concretely attached for static checking and dynamic monitoring.

Communication via Heterogeneous Representation
Heterogeneous representations reflect information transportation during an interaction between a producer role and a consumer role. When the *Outflow* role interacts with the *Inflow* role via the *Pipeline* composer, it is not necessary to establish a heterogeneous representation for the communication between these two roles. This is mainly because both roles share the same architectural style and communication protocol. Heterogeneous representation is needed only when a component is adopting different roles in order to interact with other components. In such cases, it is necessary to unify the data representation so that multiple communication channels can be built with several components that are accepting the interactions. The object-oriented model for interoperability (OOMI) [20] has solved this problem by employing a wrapper-based translator. Similarly, the *Grw* in a dependable composer provides the best architectural entity for recording and accounting for representational differences.

Configuration via Topologic Connectivity

Topological connectivity is an important architectural aspect that simplifies the inter-connections between components by employing dependable composers. Because of asymmetric interaction, a producer role could interact with one or more consumer roles and vice versa. For the sake of convenience, two generic roles *producer* and *consumer*, are introduced to discuss topologic connectivity. The producer producing data interacts with the consumer consuming data when data is transported through a specific communications channel. In terms of producer and consumer (with emphasis on how to employ composers to interconnect components) topologic connectivity includes the following types:

- **Unique (1~1):** a producer is allowed to interact with a consumer via a composer.
- **Fork (1~N):** a producer is allowed to interact with one or more consumers via a composer.
- **Merge (N~1):** several producers are allowed to interact with a consumer via a composer.
- **Heterogeneity:** multiple producers are allowed to interact with multiple consumers via various composers of different architectural styles.
- **Hierarchy:** interactions between a producer and a consumer are located on differ-ent architectural levels, while a subsystem of a lower architecture can be config-ured as an entire component.

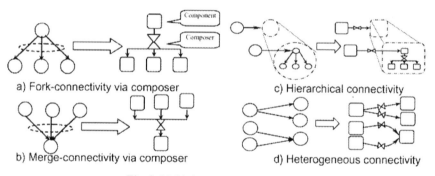

a) Fork-connectivity via composer

b) Merge-connectivity via composer

c) Hierarchical connectivity

d) Heterogeneous connectivity

Fig. 8. Multiple types of connectivity.

The examples in Fig. 8 depict how to use composers to fulfill various types of topologic connectivity. The left portion represents a computational prototyping model (graph), where the bubble represents an operation or process and the directed edge represents a dataflow. The right portion of each figure depicts the interconnections among components when using composers. Fig. 8 a) and b) illustrate typical *Fork* and *Merge* connectivity.

Hierarchical connectivity (shown in Fig. 8 c)) depicts an entire component which is implemented by a subsystem of a lower architecture. It allows interaction between the internal components at the lower level of the architecture and interaction with external components at the higher level of architecture.

Heterogeneous connectivity results from the interconnections of components with various architectural styles. The styles will determine the identity of roles and the selection of communication protocols. In this case, various composers of different styles are employed to promote heterogeneous interactions, as shown in Fig. 8 d). As an example, consider a given *Producer* which simultaneously serves as both *Publisher* (role) of **Event** and as *Outflow* (role) of **dataflow**, and interacts with a *Subscriber* via a *Pub-Sub* composer, and with an *Inflow* via the *Pipeline* composer. A similar situation can occur with the *Consumer*. So, heterogeneity, in terms of roles, means the same component adopts more than one role.

4.2   System Dependability Analysis

The quantifiable architecting approach treats software dependability at three developmental strata. Three views of system dependability analysis are developed to support the quantitative assessment of dependability with emphasis on architectural artifacts. This assessment includes the acquisition of dependability attributes, static checking of quantifiable constraints, and dynamic monitoring of semantic characteristics.

Conceptual View for Dependability Acquisition

The conceptual view refers to the global requirements of dependability and is focused on the computational perspective. The notation of dependability is broken down into six fundamental attributes: *availability, reliability, safety, confidentiality, integrity* and *maintainability* [3-5]. This view of fundamental attributes implies following concerns about a dependable system:

- **Availability:** how to create a system operational when needed.
- **Reliability:** how to keep a system operating correctly when used.
- **Safety:** how to ensure a system is operated without danger.
- **Confidentiality:** how to ensure a system's information safe from unauthorized disclosure.
- **Integrity:** how to ensure information is free of unauthorized modification when used.
- **Maintainability:** how to develop a system that is easy to maintain.

  Although precise definitions of these terms have been developed over a period of many years, some aspects of dependability are not completely intuitive. For instance, a communications system needs high availability but can suffer some unreliability; an aircraft system needs high safety but can suffer some lower availability. While it is desirous that such systems maximize all aspects of dependability, in practice it is seldom possible to do so. Therefore, a careful tradeoff must be considered which optimally maximizes the overall dependability of the DSoS.

  This view refers to precise identification of dependability attributes, recognition of threats produced by faults, and clarification of means by which faults are removed during requirement analysis.

Quantifiable View for Static Checking

The quantifiable view refers to quantifiable constraints or measurable attributes that are translated from the conceptual view, and is focused on the compositional perspective. The constraints are attached to architectural artifacts and are mapped into *consistency, compatibility, granularity, heterogeneity, timing constraints*, and *synchronous control*, etc. This view provides a formalized foundation and is based on which static checking techniques are applied to the architectural (specification) artifacts, such as reasoning analysis, validation and verification (V&V), deadlock detection, thread scheduling, and so forth.

The quantifiable view is responsible for attaching constraints to architectural factors, such as roles, styles and protocols, and then static checking can be done at the architectural level, on the basis of formalized descriptions discussed previously. The following rules are examples regarding how to check quantifiable constraints attached to architectural artifacts:

- A specific role can only interact with another (consistency)
- Interactive roles should be consistent with architectural style (consistency)
- Gluing several components to a role that serves as multiple responsibilities (compatibility)
- Hierarchical composition is done from well-grained components via composers (granularity)
- Components are running on the distributed environment via a specific protocol (granularity)
- There is heterogeneous interaction of components serving in several roles (heterogeneity)
- A component interacts with one via pub-sub and with the other via pipeline (heterogeneity)
- Maximum execution times are specified for a consumer computation (timing constraints)
- Latency of communication protocols are related to potential starvation (timing constraints)
- Synchronization between concurrent entities ensures proper functioning (synchronization).
- Provide rendezvous of the producer role with the consumer role (synchronous control)

Semantic View for Dynamic Monitoring

With emphasis on the componential perspective, the semantic view embodies how constraints from the quantifiable view are treated as semantic characteristics bound to segments of code. The semantic characteristics are bound to roles' behavioral computation, referring to the architectural style and communication protocol. This view drives the automated architectural framework generation with a semantic description bound to crucial segments of code so that semantic characteristics become effectively and practically computable for dynamic monitoring at runtime.

Although semantic characteristics (such as synchronous coordination, maximum execution time) semantically restrict a concurrent producer and consumer in their behavior, it is still a challenge to generate a quantifiable architectural framework with bounded semantic characteristics. For example, consider a role as an element of architecture -- how the role would pass on its semantic behavior to the derived component requires assisted tool support. Obviously, hand coding is not practical or effective.

The semantic view is responsible for driving the automatic architectural framework generation and infusing semantic characteristics associated with the crucial segments of code. The following example illustrates how dynamic monitoring is done. For a distributed system that emphasizes a safety-critical service, the idea is to translate the attributes of safety into timing constraints. This may be embodied as an instant reply of a particular component, under a given request, within an MET (maximum execution time), or as a dataflow communication between components performed within an affordable LATENCY [6, 8]. An MET requires that the computation (that a role undertakes) must be executed within a specific amount of time. The LATENCY constrains the maximum delay during data transportation associated with the protocol.

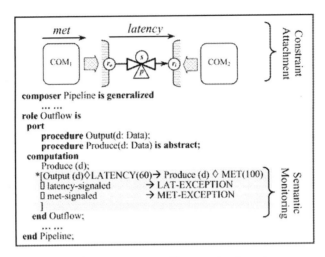

Fig. 9. The composer with constraints bound.

Fig. 9 illustrates that timing constraints are attached to the composer (referring to the role, style and protocol) and then actually bound to the computational behavior of *Produce* and *Output* as semantic characteristics. Two typical timing constraints are involved: MET and LATENCY [6, 8]. This example illustrates the dynamic monitoring of correctness assurance [9-10] by specifying the semantics. Since procedure *Output* is implicated in the communication protocol from the composer, we associate LATENCY(60) with it. Once the communication of *Output*(d) is beyond the latency constraint, the asynchronous control will set 'latency-signaled' and abort current communication execution, and then raise LAT_EXECPTION. Similarly, we associate MET(100) with procedure *Produce* (d) and related exception is MET_EXCEPTION.

5   Demonstration

The example presented in this section demonstrates the effectiveness of the quantifiable architecting effort when exposing and molding multiple perspective issues in the perspective-based synthesizing procedure. It also illustrates the power of compositional evolution in building a more complex heterogeneous composer based on existing composers.

5.1   Computational Prototyping Model

In this section, the computational prototyping model starts with a simple control system. A prototyping system description language PSDL [8] is used to model the operational concept of the control system into the computational model. The model in PSDL consists of a hierarchically structured set of definitions for operators (components) and abstract data streams (interconnections). Each definition has a specification part for black-box descriptions and an optional implementation part for clear-box descriptions. The clear-box description contains a network of operators and streams that is represented by a direct graph.

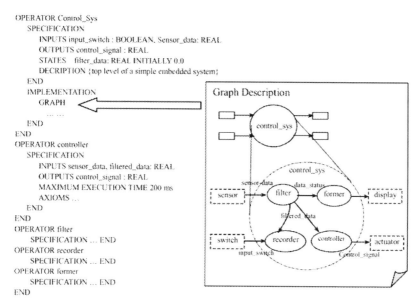

```
OPERATOR Control_Sys
    SPECIFICATION
        INPUTS input_switch : BOOLEAN, Sensor_data: REAL
        OUTPUTS control_signal : REAL
        STATES  filter_data: REAL INITIALLY 0.0
        DECRIPTION {top level of a simple embedded system}
    END
    IMPLEMENTATION
        GRAPH
        .. ...
    END
END
OPERATOR controller
    SPECIFICATION
        INPUTS sensor_data, filtered_data: REAL
        OUTPUTS control_signal : REAL
        MAXIMUM EXECUTION TIME 200 ms
        AXIOMS ...
    END
END
OPERATOR filter
    SPECIFICATION ... END
OPERATOR recorder
    SPECIFICATION ... END
OPERATOR former
    SPECIFICATION ... END
END
```

Fig. 10. Computational Models in PSDL.

Fig. 10 shows the computational model comprising two portions: a textual description and a graphical description. The former provides rigorously formalized description suitable for manipulation by CASE tools, while the latter presents the description as a visual graph suitable for human understanding. The model is presented on two hierarchy levels: the first comprises the specification of operator (component) Control_Sys, and the second comprises its implementation part, which contains a graph showing the decomposition of the system into subsystems. Top-level component Control_Sys is embedded in an environment comprising a simple *switch* served by some human operator, an external *sensor* providing signals at relatively regular intervals, a *display* that shows the status for human monitoring, and an *actuator* that manipulates the behavior of the controlled technical process. The more detailed behavior of these system components lies outside the scope of this discussion.

5.2   Automated Transitions

Perspective-based modeling of DSoS inevitable faces significant challenges in establishing continuity between the different models of each system that make up the "system of systems." Accordingly this approach employs two kinds of transitions (architectural and componential) to bridge the gaps between these multiple models.

Architectural Transitions

The architectural transition plays a paramount role in ensuring the development and evolution of the DSoS. Using the architectural transition designers construct substantial interconnections between computing activities with composers as a system is broken into a set of activities and associated information flows. For the DSoS, each node of a subsystem undertaking a computing activity could be executed concurrently, and collaborated via internetworking communications.

The left side of Fig. 11 illustrates a simplified computational model derived from that shown in Fig. 10. Two composers are employed to realize the transitioning architecture: *Pipeline* (dataflow) and *Pub_Sub* (an event-based invocation). The external interconnections (e.g., I_1, I_2, O_1, and O_2) naturally belong to the higher level component, e.g., CSCI (Computer Software Configuration Item). Our focus is on the internal interconnections (d_{12}, d_{13}, d_{14}). Suppose d_{13} and d_{14} have the same architectural style (e.g., *event-based*) and d_{12} has another style (e.g., *dataflow*). This implies the use of a 'unique' (1~1) and 'fork' (1~2) topology type to establish the topologic connectivity for the subsystem.

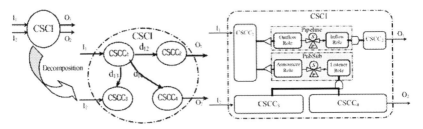

Fig. 11. Transitioning Procedure and Hierarchical Composition.

With respect to heterogeneity and hierarchy, $CSCC_1$ serves both the *Announcer* and *Output* roles in the context of *dataflow* and *event-based*, which means it interacts with the other three components via heterogeneous architectural styles. Further, the CSCI configuration embodies a hierarchical composition from decomposed components and heterogeneous interactions among them. That is, $CSCC_1$, $CSCC_2$, $CSCC_3$, and $CSCC_4$ are configured as an entire architecture that forms a single component CSCI in another, larger architecture.

Componential Transitions

With dependable composers chosen to establish interconnections among components, it becomes relatively straight forward to derive the physical components from the associated *Grws* through subtyping and refinement. These components serve specific roles in the architectural context of a particular collaboration to accomplish a particular larger purpose. From an object-oriented standpoint, the physical component is treated as a behavioral subtype of the related *Grw*, so that the component can be derived directly from it. Multiple inheritances will be naturally considered because they provide a means by which a component that services multiple roles within the architectural context can be derived from one more *Grw*. The component $CSCC_1$ is such a component and is derived from both *Outflow* and *Announcer*.

Table 3 illustrates an architectural transition and a componential transition from the computational model, through the compositional model, to the componential model. Typical OO class relationships such as *association, generalization, aggregation*, and *adaptation* [27-28] effectively support the transition. Multiple inheritances belonging to *generalization* (in terms of class relationships) are the powerful mechanism that supports componential transition in the stage of componential derivation.

Table 3. Descriptive Architectural Entities.

```
--- <Composer Definitions> ---                  --- <Component Definitions> ---
composer Pipeline is generalized                with Pipeline, PubSub;
    type Data is private;                       component CSCC₁ is new Outflow, Announcer
    Size : Integer : = 100;                          ... -- derived from two roles via multiple inheritance
style as  <#pipe-filter#>;                       end CSCC₁;
protocol as  <#dataflow-stream#>;                component CSCC₂ is new Inflow   ...   end CSCC₂;
role Output is                                   component CSCC₃ is new Listener  ...   end CSCC₃;
    ...                                          component CSCC₄ is new Listener  ...   end CSCC₄;
end Output;
role Input is                                    --- <Component Configuration > ---
    ...                                          component CSCI is
end Input;                                       port
collaboration(O: Outflow; I: Inflow)                PI    : composer Pipeline;
    ...                                             PS    : composer PubSub;
end Pipeline;                                        C₁    : component CSCC₁;
                                                     C₂    : component CSCC₂;
composer PubSub is ...                               C₃    : component CSCC₃;
role Announcer is  ...  end Announcer;               C₄    : component CSCC₄;
role Listener is                                 computation
    ...                                             ...
end Listener;                                    configuration
collaboration(A: Announcer; L: Listener)            C₁ –{PL}→ C₂;   PL.collaboration (C₁, C₂);
    ...                                             C₁ –{PS }→ C₃,C₄;PS.collaboration (C₁, {C₃, C₄})
end PubSub;                                       end CSCI;
```

Table 4. Compositional Evolution of Composer.

```
composer Pipe-Pub is     ...
    role Ann-Out is new Pipeline.Outflow,
                        PubSub.Announcer
    port
        procedure Produce (Data d) is overridden;
        procedure Prepare (Event e) is overridden;
        ... ...
    computation
        Produce (d); Prepare (e);
      *[ Output (d)      → Produce(d) ◊ latency(100) →exception;
        [] Broadcast(e) → Prepare(e) ◊ latency(200) →exception;
        ]
    end Ann-Out;
    role PP-Inflow is new   Pipeline.Inflow
        ...
    end PP-Inflow;
    role PP-Listener is new   PubSub.Listener
        ...
    end PP-Listener;
collaboration
    ... ...
end Pipe-Pub;
```

5.3   Compositional Evolution

When a component needs to adopt two or more roles and each role has its specific architectural style (e.g., a component is required to simultaneously adopt *Outflow* (*Pipeline*) and *Announcer* (*Pub_Sub*)), heterogeneous interactions arise (see Table 3). Is it possible to get compositional evolution from several existing composers and to form a new heterogeneous composer? The answer is yes.

Compositional evolution specifically refers to the heterogeneity and the hierarchy of system composition. The former is embodied in constructing a new composer from existing composers of different architectural styles, while the latter treats a subsystem of lower architecture as an entire component in another, larger architecture. As an example assume there are two existing composers: *Pipeline* with *Outflow/Inflow* roles, and *Pub_Sub* with *Announce/Listener* roles. A new composer can be derived from both as described by Table 4. Obviously, the new composer is created with three roles: *Ann_Out*, *Listener*, and *Inflow*. With respect to hierarchic composition, the **configuration** in a component can be directly used to form an entire component.

This illustrates that compositional evolutions from existing composers provide an effective means to construct more complex and more powerful composers to ensure the architecture is composable and evolvable.

6 Conclusion

Quantifiably architecting DSoS provides a promise of faster, better, cheaper software systems, because the approach provides a means for analyzing system designs with respect to quantifiable constraints [3, 12, 19]. Indeed, a premise of quantifiable software architecture is that quantifiable constraints – and our ability to reason about them – are attached to compositional patterns. These patterns are actually interactive roles, architectural styles and communication protocols in the DCM [3-4]. While there has been much written on how to develop and annotate software architecture, there has been comparatively little work on providing quantifiable architectural techniques for early resolution of the differing perspectives of the stakeholders. Traditional architectural processes specify how architectures should be represented but do not provide techniques or tools for developing early artifacts that can be used to identify and resolve issues in the description, and quantitative assessment. In order to consistently engineer DSoS, this quantifiable architectural approach provides a procedure (with tool support) that uncovers perspective concerns of various stakeholders, increases the effectiveness of designed inspection techniques such as requirements validation, static checking, and dynamic monitoring of desired properties. This approach addresses three crucial aspects: 1) accurately identifying various customer requirements and determining their impact to the required architecture of the system, 2) mapping customer dependability attributes into quantifiable constraints within multiple associated perspectives , and 3) verifying and monitoring if the resulting system architecture satisfies customer intent (and if not, correcting the requirements and the system architecture).

Because this approach can be used to structurally map and quantitatively assess dependability attributes that are translated into quantifiable constraints attached to the invariant architectural artifacts, it will significantly reduce the amount of recertification effort required after each requirement change, and increase dependability assurance at the architectural level. The approach illustrates that with reusable architectural facilities and associated tools support, the quantifiable architecture with multiple perspectives can be used to identify and resolve conflicting stakeholder perspectives, and effective support the engineering of DSoS.

References

1. IEEE Standard Board, Recommended Practice for Architectural Description of Software-Intensive Systems (IEEE-std-1471 2000), September 2000.
2. Alexander, H., et el: C4ISR Architectures: I. Developing a Process for C4ISR Architecture Design. Systems Engineering, John Wiley and Sons, Inc., Vol. 3 (4), 2000, pp 225.

3. Liang, X., Puett, J., Luqi: Perspective-based Architectural Approach for Dependable Systems, ICSE'03, Proc. of Workshop on Software Architecture for Dependable Systems, May 3, 2003, Portland, OR, USA, pp. 1-6

4. Liang, X., Puett, J., Luqi: Synthesizing Approach for Perspective-based Architecture Design, Proc. of 14th IEEE International workshop on Rapid System Prototyping, Jun. 9-11, 2003, San Diego, CA, USA, pp. 218-225.

5. Avizienis, A., Laprie, J., Randell, B.: Fundamental Concepts of Dependability, Research Report N01145, LAAS-CNRS, April 2001. http://citeseer.nj.nec.com/489854.html

6. Luqi, Qiao, Y., Zhang, L.: Computational Model for High-Confidence Embedded System Development, Monterey workshop 2002, Venice, Italy, Oct 7-11, 2002, pp 285-303.

7. Kordon, F., Mounier, I., Paviot-Adet E., Regep, D.: Formal verification of embedded distributed systems in a prototyping approach, Proc. of the International Workshop on Engineering Automation for Software Intensive System Integration , Monterey, June 2001

8. Luqi, Berzins, V., Yeh, R.: A Prototyping Language for Real-Time Software, IEEE TSE, Vol. 14(10), Oct 1988, pp 1409-1423.

9. Clarke, E., Kurshan R.: Computer-Aided Verification, IEEE Spectrum, 33(6), 1996, pp 61-67

10. Kim, M., Lee, I., Sammapun, U., Shin, J., Sokolsky, O.: Monitoring, Checking, and Steering of Real-Time Systems, 2nd International Workshop on Run-time Verification. Copenhagen, Denmark, July 26, 2002

11. Luqi, Liang, X., Brown, M.: Formal Approach for System Safety Analysis and Assessment via an Instantiated Activity Model, Proc. of 21st International System Safety Conference, August 4-8, 2003, Ottawa, Canada, pp. 1060-1069.

12. Bate, I., Kelly, T.: Architectural Considerations in the Certification of Modular Systems, Proceedings of the 21st International Conference on Computer Safety, Reliability and Security 2002 / September 10 - 13, 2002, Lecture Notes In Computer Science, Springer-Verlag   London, UK, pp: 321 - 333

13. Shaw, M., Garlan, D.: Software Architecture: Perspectives on an Emerging Discipline. Prentice Hall, Inc., 1996.

14. Andrew P.: Systems Integration and Architecting: An Overview of Principles, Practices, and Perspectives, System Engineering, John Wiley and Sons, Inc., 1998.

15. 15.Mehta, N., Medvidovic, N.: Towards a Taxonomy of software Connectors. Proc. ICSE, Limerick Ireland, 2000.

16. 16.Medvidovic, N., Taylor: A classification and comparison framework for software architecture description languages. IEEE Transactions on Software Engineering, 2000, 26(1), pp 70-93.

17. Medvidovic, N., et el: Modeling Software Architectures in the Unified Modeling Language, ACM Transaction on Software Engineering and Methodology Vol. 11(1), 2002.

18. Liang, X., Wang, Z.: Event-based implicit invocation decentralized in Ada, SIGAda Ada Letters, Vol. 22(1), March 2002, pp 11-16.

19. Wallnau, K., Stafford, J., Hissam, S., Klein, M.: On the Relationship of Software Architecture to Software Component Technology, Proc. of the 6th Workshop on Component-Oriented Programming (WCOP6), in conjunction with the Europea Conference on Object-Oriented Programming (ECOOP), Budapest, Hungary, 2001

20. Young, P.: Use of Object-Oriented Model for Interoperability in Wrapper-based Translator fro Resolving Representational Differences between Heterogeneous Systems, Monterey Workshop'01, Monterey, California, USA, 2001, pp 170-177.

21. Sessions, N.: COM and DCOM, Microsoft's Vision for Distributed Objects. John Wiley & Sons, Inc., NY, 1997.

22. OMG/ISO Standard, CORBA: Common Object Request Broker Architecture, http://www.corba.org/.

23. Sun Microsystems, Inc. Java 2 Enterprise Edition Specification v1.2. http://java.sun.com/j2ee/.

24. ISO/IEC 12207 Software Life Cycle Processes, http://www.12207.com/

25. Egyed, A., Medvidovic, N.: Extending Architectural Representation in UML with View Integration, Published in Proceedings of the 2nd International Conference on the Unified Modeling Language (UML), Fort Collins, CO, October 1999, pp. 2-16

26. 26.Glinz, M.: Problems and Deficiencies of UML as a Requirements Specification Language, Proceedings of the Tenth International Workshop on Software Specification and Design (IWSSD'00), November 5-7, 2000, San Diego, pp. 11-22.

27. Lee, W., et el: Synthesizing Executable Models of Object Oriented Architectures. Proc. Formal Methods in Software Engineering & Defense Systems. Adelaide, Australia, 2002.

28. Liang, X., Zhang, L., Luqi: Automatic Prototype Generating via Optimized Object Model,, SIGAda Ada Letters, Vol 23 (2), June 2003, pp. 22-31.

29. Hoare, C.: Communicating Sequential Process, London: Prentice-Hall International, UK, LTD., 1985.

Dependability Modeling
of Self-healing Client-Server Applications

Olivia Das and C. Murray Woodside

Department of Systems and Computer Engineering
Carleton University, Ottawa, K1S 5B6, Canada
{odas,cmw}@sce.carleton.ca

Abstract. Proliferation of large and complex fault-tolerant distributed applications has stimulated the use of separate management components for automatic detection of software and hardware failures and for reconfiguration. This paper describes an analytical model, called the Dependable-LQN model, for evaluating combined performance and dependability attributes of client-server applications that now include these additional management components and their interactions. It also constructs and analyzes a model for a large-scale Air Traffic Control system in order to demonstrate the model's capability in evaluating large systems.

1 Introduction

The Dependable Layered Queueing Network (Dependable-LQN) model is a performability model (i.e. a combined performance and dependability model) for fault-tolerant distributed applications with a layered software architecture and with an overlaid architecture for failure detection and reconfiguration. The model considers the failures and repairs of its application and management components and the management connections, and the application's layered failure dependencies, together with the application performance. It combines Fault-Tolerant Layered Queueing Networks (FTLQN) [4] and the Model for Availability Management Architecture (MAMA) [5]. FTLQN in turn adds dependability related components and attributes to the Layered Queueing Network (LQN) model [11], which is a pure performance model.

In performability modeling, a common approach is to use a Markov reward model [17], [20] in which the dependability aspects of the system are represented by a continuous-time Markov chain with a reward rate, which is a performance measure, associated to each of the states of the Markov chain. A higher-level specification of these models, called Stochastic Reward Nets [2], is sometimes used to specify the problem in a concise fashion and the underlying Markov chain is generated automatically. These models are inappropriate for modeling large systems since they lead to generation, storage and solution of infeasibly large state spaces.

The Dependable-LQN modeling approach used in this paper can be seen as an extension of the Dynamic Queueing Network (DQN) approach [12], [13] that is based on Markov reward models. They both consider a hierarchy of models: a higher level availability model representing the failure and repair behaviour of components and a

R. de Lemos et al. (Eds.): Architecting Dependable Systems II, LNCS 3069, pp. 266–285, 2004.
© Springer-Verlag Berlin Heidelberg 2004

set of lower level performance models, one for each structural state in the availability model. In the DQN model, a parameterized queueing network is used to model the performance aspects and a Generalized Stochastic Petri Net is used to describe the availability aspects. The calculations are done by converting the DQN model to a Markov reward model. In the Dependable-LQN model the performance aspects are described by a *layered queueing network* which can model the logical software resources and which treats the hardware and the software uniformly. Further, the Dependable-LQN model uses an AND-OR-NOT graph for capturing the dependability aspects and it avoids the generation or solution of large Markovian models.

Dependable-LQN has a slight resemblance to a multilevel framework by Kaaniche et. al. [14] for modelling Internet-based applications. They present four levels: user, function, service and resource levels. However, these levels are fixed and represent layers of abstraction, while this work introduces application-dependent layers of servers.

The architectural design of an application could be specified using a design model, e.g. in UML [18]. Some work has reported on the translation of UML models to different dependability models. [19] considers conversion of UML models to dynamic fault trees while [16] considers transformation of UML models to Timed Petri nets. In a similar way, UML models can also be used to capture architectural designs considered in this work and they could eventually be transformed to a Dependable-LQN model. This work however does not address this transformation.

Our previous work defined the model in [5] and gave an efficient algorithm for evaluating dependability in [8]. This paper describes its application to a substantial system for Air Traffic Control.

An Air Traffic Control (ATC) system [3], [1], [9] is a large-scale complex distributed system which demands high availability and high performance. Its software architecture plays a key role in achieving its quality requirements. We consider the architecture described in [3], which describes an en route system to control aircraft from soon after takeoff until shortly before landing. The end users in the model are the air traffic controllers. It has a layered software architecture with one subsystem depending on another for services and it uses a separate management architecture for automatic failure detection and recovery. It is an important case study for us because the Dependable-LQN model perfectly fits the choice for modeling such a complicated and large system.

The goal of this paper is to demonstrate the use of the Dependable-LQN model on a substantial system with strong requirements for performance and dependability. It also describes the use and scalability of a tool [6] that takes the layered software description and the management component interactions as input and solves the model analytically to generate results.

The paper is organized as follows. Section 2 describes the Dependable-LQN modeling concepts. Section 3 briefly describes the solution strategy for solving the model. Section 4 describes the model for one sector of an ATC en route system. Section 5 discusses the results obtained for the model in Section 4. Section 6 concludes the paper.

2 The Dependable-LQN Model

A Dependable-LQN model combines two parts:

- a Fault-Tolerant Layered Queueing Network (FTLQN) submodel for describing the layered software architecture
- a Model for Availability Management Architecture (MAMA) submodel for describing the fault management architecture

This section first describes the assumed failure behaviour for system components and then it describes the submodels, FTLQN and MAMA, that comprises the Dependable-LQN model.

2.1 Failure Behaviour of a Single Independent Component

Individual components fail and are repaired independently, with a failure state governed by the Markov chain in Fig. 1. It has two states, a working state W and a failed state F. The failure rate is λ and the repair rate is μ.

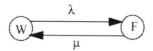

Fig. 1. Markov model for each component.

The services offered by these components may fail due to service dependencies, even though the component itself has not failed. These dependencies are described by FTLQN model, which is described next.

2.2 First Part of the Dependable-LQN Model: FTLQN Model

An FTLQN model [4] extends the Layered Queueing Network (LQN) [11] performance model by specifying the strategies to be used in case of failures and by adding redundant components and availability related parameters to it.

Fig. 2 shows the graphical notations used for an FTLQN model. The notations are defined in more detail below.

Fig. 3 illustrates an example of an FTLQN model showing a layered console application. There are seven *tasks* (i.e. concurrent operating system processes), "Console", "Application Server", "Console Server", "Log Server", "Database-A", "Database-B" (backup for "Database-A") and "Data Server". Each task runs on its own *processor*. The task "Application Server" creates a report which involves reading from the database, requesting some kind of application data from the "Data Server" and then logging the report to the "Log Server". Tasks have one or more *entries* which are service handlers embedded in them (for instance, "Data Server" has "Get Application Data" and "Get Console Data"). A *service request* has a single target server if there is no server redundancy, or it may have a set of redundant target servers with a policy on how to use them.

The different redundancy policies supported for a service request are:

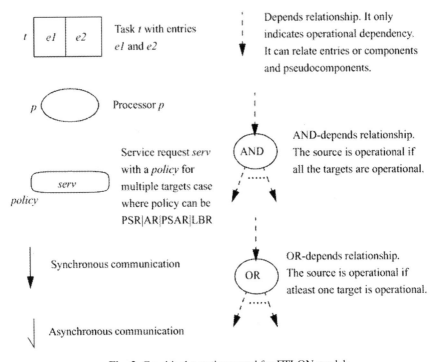

Fig. 2. Graphical notations used for FTLQN models.

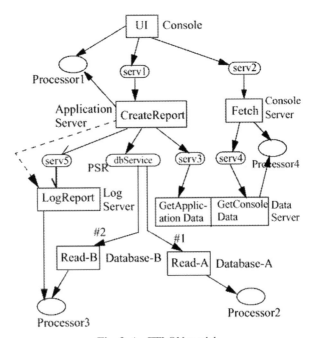

Fig. 3. An FTLQN model.

- Primary-Standby Redundancy (PSR), with requests sent only to the primary target. When the primary fails, one of the standbys (next in priority) will become the primary and the requests are rerouted to the new primary.
- Active Redundancy (AR), with requests replicated and sent to all the working target servers.
- Load-Balanced Redundancy (LBR), with requests equally divided among all the working target servers.

In Fig. 3, "dbService" is a service requested by the entry "Create Report" for reading from the database. It has a PSR policy where the priority of the target servers are labelled "#n" on the arcs going out from the service to the servers (smaller n denotes higher priority). These service requests are synchronous, so the sender is blocked until the receiver replies. (The LQN model [11] and thus the FTLQN model also, assume that requests between tasks do not form a cycle; such a cycle could induce mutual waiting and deadlock.)

Asynchronous service requests can also be accommodated, where a client does not block after sending a request to a server. In Fig. 3, "serv5" represents an asynchronous service request. In contrast to a synchronous service request where the failure of a client directly depends on the failure of the servers, an asynchronous service request does not add any failure dependencies. In order to add additional failure dependencies that are not represented by service-based dependencies, another abstraction called a *depends* relationship can exist between any two entries. The depends relationship may exist from an entry to a single entry, or to multiple entries with "AND" or "OR" relationships. For example, the entry "CreateReport" fails if the logging mechanism fails even though the communication is asynchronous, indicated by a dotted arrow from the entry "CreateReport" to the entry "LogReport". "AND" and "OR" types have been used in Section 4.

The performance parameters for the FTLQN model are the mean total demand for execution on the processor by each entry and the mean number of requests for each interaction. The availability related parameters for this model are the failure and repair rates for each component (either a task or a processor) of the application. The performance measures are usually associated with the tasks that only originate requests (e.g. "Console" task), also called *reference tasks*.

The FTLQN model shows the policy for redundant servers but the decision about where to forward the request is made by the fault management sub-system (not visible in this model) based on its knowledge of the state of the application components. This resolution of requests gives different *operational configurations* of the application. For example, in Fig. 3 if all the tasks are operational, then the configuration is the system as shown, but with Database-B, and its service requests (labelled #2) removed as they are not used. The probabilities of the operational configurations now depend on the fault management architecture, and on management subsystem failures, as well as on the application. The next section describes the management components, their connections and how they are related to the application components.

2.3 Second Part of the Dependable-LQN Model: MAMA Model

The MAMA model describes fault management architectures based on the manager-agent model described in [15]. A separate architectural model is introduced for management because the relationships of the parts are entirely different. This is seen in the different connector types representing different types of interactions.

The MAMA model considers four classes of components: *application tasks*, *agent tasks*, *manager tasks* and the *processors* hosting them. They are connected using three different classes of connector:

- *Alive-watch* connector: This connector is used between two components in cases where the destination component must be able to detect whether the source component is alive or not. This may be achieved by periodic polls or "i-am-alive" messages. Usually, the source of this connector is a manageable application component.

- *Status-watch* connector: In cases where a destination component must know about the liveness of the source component and also must collect failure data about other components in the system that has been gathered by the source component, this connector is used. An example would be a connector from an agent task to a manager task.

- *Notify* connector: This connector is used for cases where the source component must send or forward reconfiguration commands to its sub-ordinate destination component (for example, a manager sending commands to an agent or an agent forwarding a command to an application task) or must convey management information to its peer (for example, a manager sending information about the domain it manages to another manager).

These connectors are typed according to the information they convey, in a way which supports the analysis of knowledge of the system status at different points in the management system.

Upon occurrence of a failure or repair of a task or a processor, the occurrence is first captured via *alive-watch* or *status-watch* connections and the information propagates through *status-watch* and *notify* connections, to managers which initiate system reconfiguration. Reconfiguration commands are sent by *notify* connections.

It is required by the analysis, that if a task watches a remote task, then it also watches the processor executing the remote task, so it can differentiate between a task failure and a processor failure.

Fig. 4 shows the graphical notation used in this work for MAMA components and connectors.

Fig. 5 shows a MAMA model for a centralized management architecture for the application of Fig. 3, with agents ag1-ag4 running on the processors p1-p4. m1 is the single manager task that indirectly manages all the application tasks through the agents and directly monitors the processors.

The failure assumptions about the management components are the same as for application components, and can include the connectors between them as well. Failure and repair rates are provided for each components and connector.

The management architecture influences the *fault coverage* of the system, where the fault coverage is the ability of the system to recover. This is because the system's knowledge about failures in order to recover from them depends on the management architecture and also on the status of its components. For example, if the central manager (shown in Fig. 5) is failed when the task "Database-A" fails, then the task "ApplicationServer" (shown in Fig. 3) would not know about this failure and it would not switch to the backup task "Database-B", even if "Database-B" is working. This

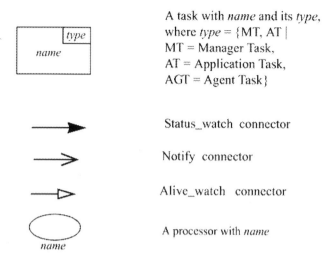

A task with *name* and its *type*,
where *type* = {MT, AT |
MT = Manager Task,
AT = Application Task,
AGT = Agent Task}

Status_watch connector

Notify connector

Alive_watch connector

A processor with *name*

Fig. 4. Graphical notations used for MAMA models.

effect of management architecture and its failures is taken into account in the model analysis strategy, which is described next.

3   Dependable-LQN Model Solution

A Dependable-LQN model can be solved to obtain the mean of any performance measure, averaged over failure states and the probability that a system has failed. It can also be solved for transient measures, for example, the expected throughput at time t.

The general strategy of the analysis is to compute the performance for each reachable *operational configuration* that has different choices of alternative targets for requests and combine it with the probability of each configuration occurring, to find the measures. Each operational configuration is a pure Layered Queueing Network (LQN) performance model [11], which can be solved for different performance measures by the LQNS tool [11], based on extended queueing approximations.

The complete model solution has been described in the paper [8]. It has following steps (as shown in Fig. 6):

1. convert the MAMA model into a directed graph, called a Knowledge Propagation Graph and then apply minpath generation algorithms to the graph to obtain the connectivity information;
2. create an AND-OR-NOT graph, called a Fault-Propagation graph, using the FTLQN model and the connectivity information from the knowledge propagation graph;
3. using the Fault-Propagation graph, determine the set of all the distinct operational configurations;
4. compute the probability of each operational configuration by generating and solving a non-coherent fault tree [10] (this is a fault tree with NOT gates).

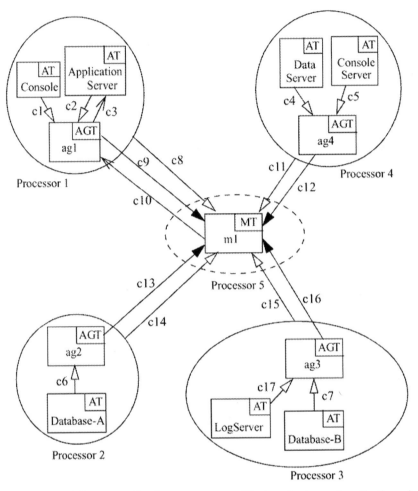

Fig. 5. MAMA model for a centralized management architecture for layered application of Fig. 3.

5. compute the reward for each operational configuration by generating and solving an ordinary Layered Queueing Network performance model [11].
6. combine the rewards using the probabilities of configurations, to obtain the performability measures.

The complexity of the overall analysis is dominated by the number of operational configurations generated in step 3, which depends on the number of replicated services in the system.

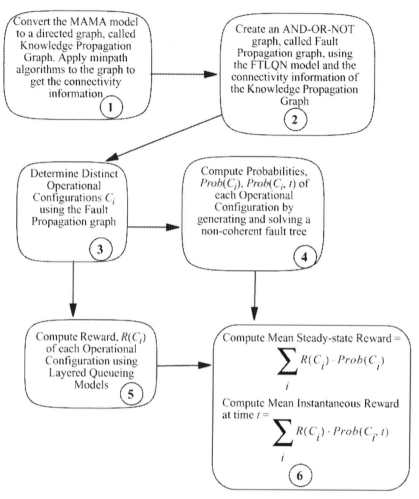

Fig. 6. General strategy for Dependable-LQN model solution. $Prob(C_i)$ and $Prob(C_i, t)$ are the probabilities of the operational configuration C_i in steady-state and at time t respectively. $R(C_i)$ is the reward associated with each C_i.

4   Dependable-LQN Model of an ATC En Route System

An airspace controlled by a single ATC facility is administratively divided into sectors. For example, US airspace is serviced by 20 facilities, with up to 118 sectors per facility. Each facility receives aircraft surveillance and weather data from radars and communicates with other external subsystems such as other en route facilities. Inside each facility, air traffic services are divided among four subsystems: *Surveillance Processing Service* (that receives radar data and correlates it with individual aircraft tracks) is provided by the Radar subsystem directly connected to radars, *Flight Plan Processing and Conflict Alert Service* is provided by the Central subsystem, *Display Service* (which displays aircraft position information obtained from radars and allows inputs from air traffic controllers to modify flight plan data or change display format) is hosted by the Console subsystem, and *Monitoring Service* (which provides the monitoring and control service for other ATC services ensuring their availability policies) is hosted by the Monitor and Control subsystem. There are up to four consoles allocated for handling each sector. Fault-tolerance is achieved by software server groups. For example, there are up to four Display Management load-balanced redundant servers per sector, three primary/standby active redundant Surveillance Processing servers, and two primary/ standby Flight Plan Management servers.

All the three redundant Surveillance Processing servers receive the raw radar data from the radars in parallel, however only the primary server sends the processed radar data to the Display Management servers running in the consoles. A Primary-Standby Active Redundancy (PSAR) policy models this case.

Fig. 7 shows some parts of a Dependable-LQN model based loosely on the description in [3]. Each dotted bubble represents a process group which is replicated; the redundant components are not shown. The communications with replicas is performed transparently by a process-to-process session manager (P2PSM) in each host (not shown here).

Some failure dependencies are implicit in the server request-reply dependencies. Others have been made explicit with a *depends* relationship, for instance that "display radar data" depends on "process radar data", even though the communications is asynchronous. This is an OR dependency on the three radar processing replicas, since any one is sufficient.

The fault management architecture depends on a *group availability management* server (gSAM) on each processor which monitors all the software servers in its own processor and also monitors the other processors in its software server group. In MAMA terms, the gSAM servers maintain an *alive-watch*. This is supported by three redundant name servers which maintain a list of primary host processors for each server group. When a failure of a software server occurs in its processor, a gSAM server notifies other gSAM servers in its own group. Similarly, the failure of a processor is detected by the other gSAM servers in a group. Whenever a failure is detected, the gSAM server notifies the name servers which in turn notify the relevant P2PSM's so that they can retarget their service requests.

Fig. 8 shows a portion of the MAMA model for Fig. 7, including one replica of the Monitor and Control subsystem. The redundant servers are not shown here.

Fig. 9 shows the interactions among the gSAM servers in the central subsystem group containing two replicas. The interactions among the gSAM servers in other groups are similar to this one and are not shown here.

5   Numerical Results

This section analyzes the Dependable-LQN model of the ATC system which is described in Section 4. The model is parameterized (subsection 5.1) and the average throughput and average response time is computed (subsection 5.2). The impact of failures of management components on system availability is found (subsection 5.3), and the most and least sensitive components (subsection 5.4). Optimal replication of

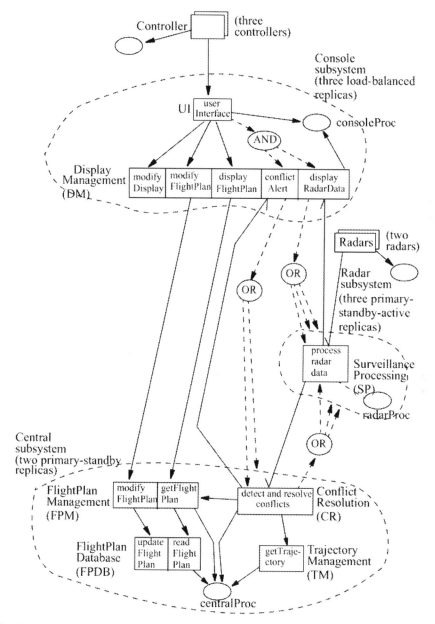

Fig. 7. A Dependable-LQN model for an ATC en route system. Redundant server groups are not shown here. The dotted boundary indicates one replica of a replicated subsystem.

the name server, which is one of the managers, is considered in subsection 5.5 for a given level of availability of the management components. Replication of unreliable agents is considered in subsection 5.6, with its effect on overall system reliability.

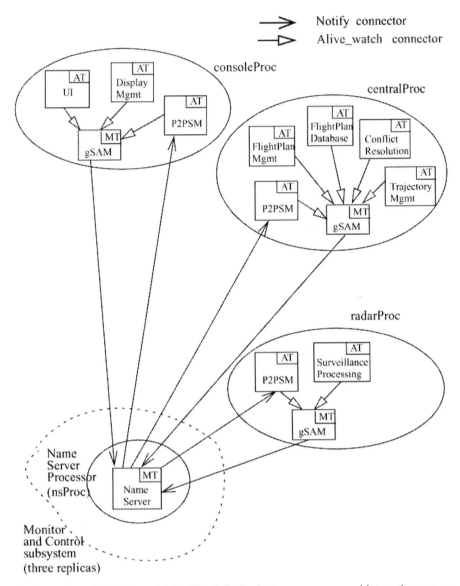

Fig. 8. Portion of MAMA model for Fig. 7. Redundant server groups and interactions among the gSAM servers in a group are not shown here.

5.1 Parameterizing the Model

In order to obtain numerical results, we need to select parameter values for the failure and repair rates of the components, CPU execution demand for the entries and the mean number of service requests made from one entry to another per call. The parameter values used here were invented for purposes of demonstration.

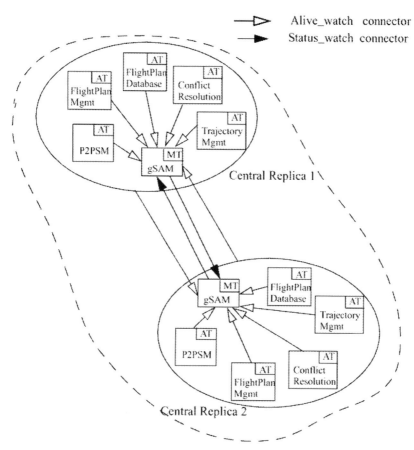

Fig. 9. Portion of MAMA model for Fig. 7 showing interactions among the gSAM servers in a group of two replicas of the central subsystem.

The mean time to failure (MTTF) and mean time to repair (MTTR) for all the processors are 1 year and 2 days respectively so that their steady-state availability is approximately 0.99455. The MTTF and MTTR for all the tasks except the gSAM servers are 30 days and 1 hour respectively so that their steady-state availability is approximately 0.99861. For the gSAM servers, the MTTF is 15 days and MTTR is 1 hour so that their availability is approximately 0.99723. The tasks "Controller", "Radars" and their associated processors are assumed to be fully reliable.

The execution demand for the entries of tasks "UI" and "DisplayManagement" are assumed to be 0.01 seconds, of tasks "FlightPlanManagement" and "FlightPlanData-base" are assumed to be 0.02 seconds, of task "SurveillanceProcessing" is assumed to be 0.5 seconds and of tasks "ConflictResolution" and "TrajectoryManagement" are assumed to be 0.001 seconds. The CPU demand for all the entries of the P2PSM tasks (not shown in Fig. 7) are assumed to be 0.00001 seconds. On average, the entry "userInterface" makes 1 call to "modifyDisplay", 1 call to "modifyFlightPlan" and 2 calls to "displayFlightPlan", per invocation. When the rest of the entries are invoked they make 1 request (on average) to each entry they call.

5.2 Results

The model for a sector (as illustrated in Fig. 7, 8 and 9) has 13 processors and 38 tasks (including the P2PSM and gSAM tasks), i.e. 51 components. There are 114 connectors in the MAMA model. Applying the Dependable-LQNS tool [6], we obtain:

Number of Operational Configurations	: 14
Number of nodes generated in Knowledge Propagation graph	: 98
Number of nodes generated in Fault Propagation graph	: 714
Average Throughput of the Controller task	: 1.5376 requests/sec
Average response time of the Controller task	: 1.951 seconds
Probability that all the three "userInterface" entries are working (there are two operational configurations for this case)	: 0.947714
Probability that two "userInterface" entries are working (there are six operational configurations for this case)	: 0.035460
Probability that one "userInterface" entry is working (there are two operational configurations for this case)	: 0.000246
System availability	: 0.983416
Model solution time	: 76.18 seconds

5.3 Effect of Management Component Failures on System Availability

In order to see the effect of the management component failures on system availability, we varied the availability (from 0.99 to 1) for all the management components and observed the effect on system availability. The management components include the name servers and their associated processors, and the gSAM servers.

Fig. 10 shows the system availability as a function of the availability of management components. From this figure, it can be seen that the system availability increases linearly with the availability of management components. It increases up to 0.9869 where the management components are assumed fully reliable. If the system availability requirement is greater than 0.9869, then this result suggests that solely increasing the management component availabilities would not achieve the goal, it would require change in the application component availabilities and their replication strategies.

5.4 Sensitivity Analysis of System Availability

In order to see which component is the strongest determinant of the system availability, we decreased the availability of the components in turn by 10 percent and observed the effect on the predicted system availability.

The sensitivity of the predictions to a ten-percent change in the availabilities is shown in Table 1. The system availability is most sensitive to the availabilities of the processors and the gSAM servers of the Central subsystem. A ten-percent decrease for gSAM servers in the Radar processors has a negligible effect on system availability. This is because the knowledge (propagated through the management architecture) of the Surveillance Processing servers running on the Radar processors are not critical to the retargettable services of the system.

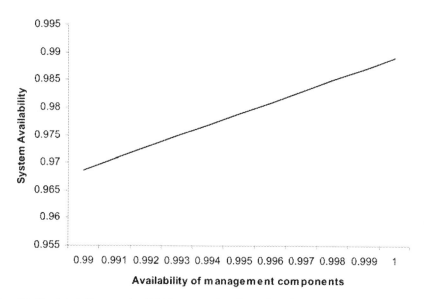

Fig. 10. Predicted System Availability as a function of availabilities of the management components.

The sensitivity results suggest that it would be better to upgrade the availability of the processors and the gSAM servers of the Central subsystem than any other component, to increase the system availability.

5.5   Optimal Replication Number for Name Servers

For a given system availability goal, we would like to answer questions such as: whether replication of name servers (and their associated processors) would help to achieve that goal and if yes, how many replicas would be needed.

We varied the availability of the NameServer and its associated processor, nsProc, and observed its effects on the system availability for different numbers of replicas. Table 2 summarizes the results. From row 1 of this table, we see that when the NameServer and its processor are fully available, the system availability is 0.983417. This suggests that if the system availability requirement is greater than this, then replicating the NameServer would not achieve it. Let us suppose that the requirement is 0.9832. Then, from row 2 to 5 of the table, it can be seen that

- if the availabilities of NameServer and nsProc are 0.99, then three replicas are needed to meet the goal
- if the availabilities of NameServer and nsProc are 0.999 or if they are same as assumed in Section 5.1, then two replicas are needed to meet the goal
- if the availabilities of NameServer and nsProc are 0.9999, then one replica would suffice

Table 1. Sensitivity of System Availability to availabilities of components.

Parameter	System Availability	% change in System Availability
No change, i.e. Original Model	0.983416	
10% decrease in availability of either {consoleProc1, consoleProc2, consoleProc3, Console1-gSAM, Console2-gSAM, Console3-gSAM}	0.981828	-0.1615 %
10% decrease in availability of either {centralProc1, centralProc2, Central1-gSAM, Central2-gSAM}	0.885075	-9.999938 %
10% decrease in availability of either {radarProc1, radarProc2, radarProc3, SP1, SP2, SP3, Radar1-P2PSM, Radar2-P2PSM, Radar3-P2PSM}	0.98341	-6.101×10^{-4} %
10% decrease in availability of either {nsProc1, nsProc2, nsProc3, NameServer1, NameServer2, NameServer3}	0.983412	-4.067×10^{-4} %
10% decrease in availability of either {UI1, DM1, UI2, DM2, UI3, DM3, Console1-P2PSM, Console2-P2PSM, Console3-P2PSM}	0.983408	-8.135×10^{-4} %
10% decrease in availability of either {FPM1, FPDB1}	0.982741	-0.068638 %
10% decrease in availability of either {CR1, TM1, FPM2, CR2, FPDB2, TM2, Central1-P2PSM, Central2-P2PSM}	0.982742	-0.068537 %
10% decrease in availability of either {Radar1-gSAM, Radar2-gSAM, Radar3-gSAM}	0.983416	no change

5.6 Effect of Replication of Unreliable Agents (i.e. the gSAM servers) on System Availability

In this section, we replicate the gSAM servers to see their effect on system availability. In section 5.4, we have seen that the agents (i.e. the gSAM servers) in the Central subsystem are highly sensitive components. Here, the gSAM server is replicated in all three processors of the Central subsystem to observe its effect on the system availability for different number of NameServers. Fig. 11 shows part of the

MAMA model for the Central subsystem group with replicated gSAM servers. Table 3 summarizes the results. From the table, we see that in both cases, with one or two NameServers, the replication of gSAM servers in the Central subsystem has increased the system availability by 0.554 %.

Table 2. System Availability for different number of NameServer replicas.

Availability of NameServer	Availability of nsProc	System Availability for 1, 2, and 3 replicas of NameServer and its associated processor, nsProc		
		1	2	3
1.0	1.0	0.983417	0.983417	0.983417
0.99	0.99	0.963847	0.983027	0.983409
0.9945504 (same as in section 5.1)	0.9986142 (same as in section 5.1)	0.976703	0.983371	0.983416
0.999	0.999	0.981451	0.983413	0.983417
0.9999	0.9999	0.983221	0.983417	0.983417

Table 3. System availability with or without replicated gSAM servers.

Number of NameServers	System Availability without replicated gSAM servers in Central subsystem	System Availability with replicated gSAM servers in Central subsystem (as shown in Fig. 11)
1	0.976703	0.982117
2	0.983371	0.988823

6 Conclusions

The use and scalability of the Dependable-LQN model and its analysis tools have been demonstrated on an example of an Air Traffic Control system, to determine its performability and reliability measures. This is a system of full industrial scale, and the analysis was carried out in reasonable times, just over one minute per evaluation. A number of important design issues were investigated.

In general the complexity of the analysis is exponential (from the algorithms used for minpaths generation from the Knowledge Propagation graph, and for operational configurations determination from the Fault Propagation graph), however clearly the

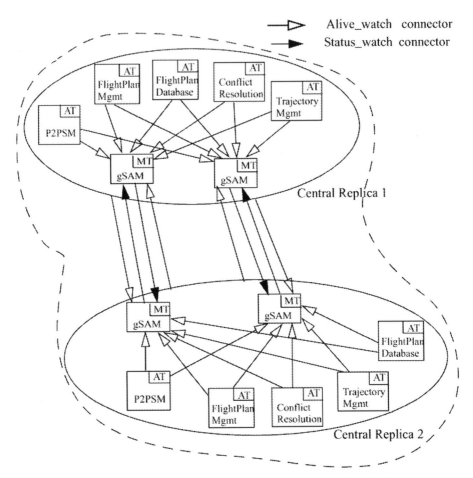

Fig. 11. Part of the MAMA model showing the interactions in the Central subsystem group. There are two replicas of gSAM servers in each processor.

time for substantial cases is not excessive. The number of distinct operational configurations found was not excessive (just 14 in the basic case). The analysis of the Fault Propagation graph did put stress on the storage requirements of the Aralia tool [10], used to determine the probability of the operational configurations.

The Dependable-LQN model has some limitations. First, the performance model is solved in steady state only. Steady state performability measures are then computed from steady state component availability; transient and cumulative measures for medium time-scales could in principle be found from transient component availabilities. Transient and cumulative measures at short time scales that involve short-term performance transients would require a different model. Second, the model captures the layered service dependencies for service failure, but it assumes independent failures for the components. Some forms of dependency can be modeled by abstract "failure dependency factors" as described in [4], however this does not capture all kinds of statistical dependencies. Third, the model assumes that each component undergoes repair which is independent of other components. It can easily be extended to model repair dependencies, for example, a shared repair facility, by constructing a Markov submodel for the set of components that share a repair facility, instead of for a single component. Fourth, the model assumes constant failure rates for the components. An extension of the model to incorporate aging (i.e. increasing failure rate) for components and the effect of software rejuvenation has been outlined in [7].

Acknowledgments

This research was supported by a scholarship from Nortel Networks, and by the Natural Sciences and Engineering Research Council of Canada.

References

1. Bass, L., Clements, P., Kazman, R.: Software Architecture in Practice. Addison-Wesley, 1998.
2. Ciardo, G., Blakemore, A., Chimento, P. F., Muppala, J. K., Trivedi, K. S.: Automated Generation and Analysis of Markov Reward Models using Stochastic Reward Nets. In Linear Algebra, Markov Chains and Queueing Models, C. Meyer and R. J. Plemmons (eds.), Springer-Verlag, 1993.
3. Cristian, F., Dancey, B., Dehn, J.: Fault-Tolerance in Air Traffic Control Systems. ACM Transactions on Computer Systems, 14(3), August 1996, 265-286.
4. Das, O., Woodside, C. M.: Evaluating layered distributed software systems with fault-tolerant features. Performance Evaluation, 45 (1), 2001, 57-76.
5. Das, O., Woodside, C. M.: Modeling the coverage and effectiveness of fault-management architectures in layered distributed systems. IEEE International Conference on Dependable Systems and Networks (DSN 2002), June 2002, 745-754.
6. Das, O., Woodside, C. M.: Dependable LQNS: A Performability Modeling Tool for Layered Systems. IEEE International Conference on Dependable Systems and Networks (DSN 2003), San Francisco, California, USA, June 2003, 672.
7. Das, O., Woodside, C. M.: The Influence of Layered System Structure on Strategies for Software Rejuvenation. Sixth International Workshop on Performability Modeling of Computer and Communication Systems (PMCCS-6), Monticello, Illinois, USA, Sept. 2003, 47-50.
8. Das, O., Woodside, C. M.: Computing the Performability of Layered Distributed Systems with a Management Architecture. ACM Fourth International Workshop on Software and Performance (WOSP 2004), Redwood City, California, USA, Jan 2004, 174-185.
9. Debelack, A. S., Dehn, J. D., Muchinsky, L. L., Smith, D. M.: Next generation air traffic control automation. IBM Systems Journal, 34(1), 1995, 63-77.
10. Dutuit, Y., Rauzy, A.: Exact and Truncated Computations of Prime Implicants of Coherent and non-Coherent Fault Trees within Aralia. Reliability Engineering and System Safety, 58, 1997, 127-144.
11. Franks, G., Majumdar, S., Neilson, J., Petriu, D., Rolia, J., Woodside, C. M.: Performance Analysis of Distributed Server Systems. In Sixth International Conference on Software Quality (6ICSQ), Ottawa, Ontario, 1996, 15-26.
12. Haverkort, B. R.: Performability modelling using DYQNTOOL+. International Journal of Reliability, Quality and Safety Engineering, 1995, 383-404.

13. Haverkort, B. R., Niemegeers, I. G., van Zanten, P. V.: DYQNTOOL: A performability modelling tool based on the Dynamic Queueing Network concept. In Proc. of the 5th Int. Conf. on Computer Perf. Eval.: Modelling Techniques and Tools, G. Balbo, G. Serazzi, editors, North-Holland, 1992, 181-195.
14. Kaaniche, M., Kanoun, K., Martinello, M.: A User-Perceived Availability Evaluation of a Web based Travel Agency. IEEE International Conference on Dependable Systems and Networks (DSN 2003), June 2003, 709-718.
15. Kreger, H.: Java management extensions for application management, IBM Systems Journal, 40(1), 2001, 104-129.
16. Majzik, I., Pataricza, A., Bondavalli, A.: Stochastic Dependability Analysis of System Architecture Based on UML Models. In Architecting Dependable Systems, LNCS 2677, R. de Lemos, C. Gacek and A. Romanovsky Ed., Springer-Verlag, 2003, 219-244.
17. Meyer, J. F.: On evaluating the performability of degradable computing systems. IEEE Trans. on Computers, 29(8), Aug. 1980, 720-731.
18. Object Management Group: Unified Modeling Language, http://www.uml.org/.
19. Pai, G.J., Dugan, J.B.: Automatic Synthesis of Dynamic Fault Trees from UML System Models. Proc. of the IEEE International Symposium on Software Reliability Engineering, (ISSRE), Nov. 2002.
20. Trivedi, K. S., Muppala, J. K., Woolet, S. P., Haverkort, B. R.: Composite Performance and Dependability Analysis. Performance Evaluation, 14, 1992, 197-215.

Multi-view Software Component Modeling for Dependability

Roshanak Roshandel and Nenad Medvidovic

Computer Science Department
University of Southern California
Los Angeles, CA 90089-0781, USA
{roshande,neno}@usc.edu

Abstract. Modeling software components from multiple perspectives provides complementary views of a software system and enables sophisticated analyses of its functionality. A software component is traditionally modeled from one or more of four functional aspects: interface, static behavior, dynamic behavior, and interaction protocol. Each of these aspects helps to ensure different levels of component compatibility and interoperability. Existing approaches to component modeling have either focused on only one of the aspects (e.g., interfaces in various IDLs) or on well-understood combinations of pairs of aspects (e.g., interfaces and their associated pre- and post-conditions in static behavior models). We advocate that, in order to accrue the true benefits of component-based software development, one needs to model all four aspects of components. In such a case, ensuring the consistency among the multiple views becomes critical. We offer an approach to modeling components using a fourview perspective (called the Quartet) and identify the points at which the consistency among the models must be maintained. We outline the range of possible intra-component, inter-model relationships, discuss their respective advantages and drawbacks, and motivate the specific choices we have made in our on-going research on ensuring the dependability of software systems from an architectural perspective.

Keywords: Software architecture, software component, dependability, reliability, the Quartet

1 Introduction

Component-based software engineering has emerged as an important discipline for developing large and complex software systems. Software components have become the primary abstraction level at which software development and evolution are carried out. We consider a software component to be any self-contained unit of functionality in a software system that exports its services via an interface, encapsulates the realization of those services, and possibly maintains transient internal state. In the context of this paper, we further focus on components for which information on their interface and behavior may be obtained. In order to ensure the desired properties of component-based systems (e.g., dependability attributes such as

R. de Lemos et al. (Eds.): Architecting Dependable Systems II, LNCS 3069, pp. 286–304, 2004.

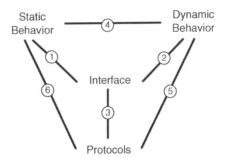

Fig. 1. Software Model Relationships within a Component.

correctness, compatibility, interchangeability, and functional reliability), both individual components and the resulting systems' architectural configurations must be modeled and analyzed.

The role of components as software systems' building blocks has been studied extensively in the area of software architectures [18,23,30]. In this paper, we focus on the components themselves. While there are many aspects of a software component worthy of careful study (e.g., modeling notations [6,18], implementation platforms [1,3], evolution mechanisms [15,17]), we restrict our study to an aspect of dependability only partially considered in existing literature: internal consistency among different models of a component. We consider this aspect from an architectural modeling perspective, as opposed to an implementation or runtime perspective.

The direct motivation for this paper is our observation that there are four primary functional aspects of a software component: (1) *interface*, (2) *static behavior*, (3) *dynamic behavior*, and (4) *interaction protocol*. Each of the four modeling aspects represents and helps to ensure different characteristics of a component. Moreover, the four aspects have complementary strengths and weaknesses. As detailed in Section 3, existing approaches to component-based development typically select different subsets of these four aspects (e.g., interface and static behavior [15], or interface and interaction protocol [31]). At the same time, different approaches treat each individual aspect in very similar ways (e.g., modeling static behaviors via pre- and post-conditions, or modeling interaction protocols via finite state machines, or FSM).

The four aspects' complementary strengths and weaknesses, as well as their consistent treatment in literature suggest the possibility of using the four modeling aspects in concert. However, what is missing from this picture is an understanding of the different relationships among these different models in a single component. Figure 1 depicts the space of possible intra-component model relationship clusters. Each cluster represents a range of possible relationships, including not only "exact" matches, but also "relaxed" matches [32] between the models in question. Of these six clusters, only the pair-wise relationships between a component's interface and its other modeling aspects have been studied extensively (relationships *1*, *2*, and *3* in Figure 1).

This paper suggests an approach to completing the modeling space depicted in Figure 1. We discuss the extensions required to commonly used modeling approaches for each aspect in order to enable us to relate them and ensure their compatibility. We also discuss the advantages and drawbacks inherent in modeling all four aspects (referred to as the Quartet in the remainder of the paper) and six relationships shown in Figure 1. This paper represents a starting point in a much larger study. By addressing all the relationships shown in Figure 1 we eventually hope to accomplish several important long-term goals:

- enrich, and in some respects complete, the existing body of knowledge in component modeling and analysis,
- suggest constraints on and provide guidelines to practical modeling techniques, which typically select only a subset of the quartet,
- provide a comprehensive functional basis for quantifying software dependability attributes such as architectural reliability,
- provide a basis for additional operations on components, such as retrieval, reuse, and interchange [32],
- suggest ways of creating one (possibly partial) model from another automatically, and
- provide better implementation generation capabilities from thus enriched system models.

The rest of the paper is organized as follows. In Section 2 we introduce a simple example that will be used throughout the paper to clarify concepts. Section 3 provides an overview of existing approaches to component modeling techniques and introduces the Quartet in more detail. Section 4 demonstrates our specific approach to component modeling using the Quartet and provides details of each modeling perspective. Section 5 discusses the relationships among the four modeling aspects shown in Figure 1 by identifying their interdependencies. In Section 6 we discuss the implications of our approach on dependability of software systems. Finally, Section 7 discusses our on-going research and future directions.

2 Example

Throughout this paper, we use a simple example of a robotic rover to illustrate the introduced concepts. The robotic rover, called SCRover, is designed and developed in collaboration with NASA's Jet Propulsion Laboratory, and in accordance with their Mission Data System (MDS) methodology. To avoid unnecessary complexity, we discuss a simplified version of the application. In this paper, we focus on SCRover's "wall following" behavior. In this mode, the rover uses a laser rangefinder to determine the distance to the wall, drives forward while maintaining a fixed distance from that wall, and turns both inside and outside corners when it encounters them. This scenario also involves sensing and controlled locomotion, including reducing speed when approaching obstacles.

The system contains five main components: *controller, estimator, sensor, actuator,* and a *database*. The sensor component gathers physical data (e.g., distance from the wall) from the environment. The estimator component accesses the data and passes them to the controller for control decisions. The controller component issues

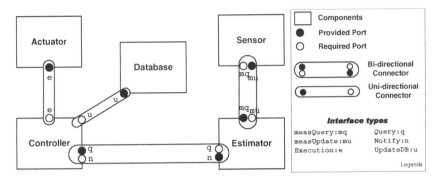

Fig. 2. SCRover's Software Architecture.

commands to the actuator to change the direction or speed of the rover. The database component stores the "state" of the rover at certain intervals, as well as when a change in the values happens. Figure 2 shows a high-level architecture of the system in terms of the constituent components, connectors, and their associated interfaces (ports): the rectangular boxes represent components in the system; the ovals are connectors; the dark circles on a component correspond to interfaces of services *provided* by the component/connector, while the light circles represent interfaces of services *required* by the component To illustrate our approach, we will specifically define the static and dynamic behavioral models and protocols of interactions for the Controller component in Section 4.

3 Component Modeling

Building good models of complex software systems in terms of their constituent components is an important step in realizing the goals of architecture-based software development [18]. Effective architectural modeling should provide a good view of the structural and compositional aspects of a system; it should also detail the system's behavior. Modeling from multiple perspectives has been identified as an effective way to capture a variety of important properties of component-based software systems [6,7,12,14,20]. A well known example is UML, which employs nine diagrams (also called views) to model requirements, structural and behavioral design, deployment, and other aspects of a system. When several system aspects are modeled using different modeling views, inconsistencies may arise.

Ensuring consistency among heterogeneous models of a software system is a major software engineering challenge that has been studied in multiple approaches, with different foci. Due to space constraints, we discuss a small number of representative approaches here. In [10] a model reconciliation technique particularly suited to requirements engineering is offered. The assumption made by the technique is that the requirements specifications are captured formally. In [5,11] a formal solution to maintaining inter-model consistency is presented that is more directly applicable at the software architectural level. One criticism that could be levied at these approaches is that their formality lessens the likelihood of their adoption. On the other hand, in [8,13] more specialized approaches for maintaining consistency among UML diagrams are offered. While their potential for wide adoption is aided by their focus on UML, these approaches may be ultimately harmed by UML's lack of formal semantics.

In this paper, we address similar problems to those cited above, but with a specific focus on multiple functional modeling aspects of a single software component. We advocate a four-view modeling technique, called *the Quartet*. Using the Quartet, a component's structural, behavioral (both static and dynamic), and interaction properties may be described and used in the analysis of a software system that encompasses the component. The Quartet also has the potential to provide a basis for generating implementation-level artifacts from component models. In the rest of this section, we will first motivate the four component aspects. We will then discuss existing techniques for modeling each aspect. We will use this discussion as the basis for studying the dependencies among these models and implications of maintaining their interconsistency in Sections 4 and 5.

3.1 Introducing the "Quartet"

Traditionally, functional characteristics of software components have been modeled predominantly from the following four perspectives:
1. *Interface* models specify the points by which a component interacts with other components in a system.
2. *Static behavior* models describe the functionality of a component discretely, i.e., at particular "snapshots" during the system's execution.
3. *Dynamic behavior* models provide a continuous view of *how* a component arrives at different states throughout its execution.
4. *Interaction protocol* models provide an *external* view of the component and how it may legally interact with other components in the system.

3.2 Existing Approaches to the Quartet

Interface modeling. Component modeling has been most frequently performed at the level of interfaces. This has included matching interface names and associated input/ output parameter types. Component interface modeling has become routine, spanning modern programming languages, interface definition languages (IDLs) [19,21], architecture description languages (ADLs) [18], and general-purpose modeling notations such as UML. However, software modeling solely at this level does not guarantee many important properties, such as interoperability or substitutability of components: two components may associate vastly different meanings with identical interfaces.

Static Behavior Modeling. Several approaches have extended interface modeling with static behavioral semantics [1,15,22,32]. Such approaches describe the behavioral properties of a system at specific snapshots in the system's execution. This is done primarily using invariants on the component states and pre- and post-conditions associated with the components' operations. Static behavioral specification techniques are successful at describing what the state of a component should be at specific points of time. However, they are not expressive enough to represent *how* the component arrives at a given state.

Dynamic Behavior Modeling. The deficiencies associated with static behavior modeling have led to a third group of component modeling techniques and notations. Modeling dynamic component behavior results in a more detailed view of the component and *how* it arrives at certain states during its execution. It provides a continuous view of the component's internal execution details. While this view of component modeling has not been practiced as widely as interface or static behavior modeling, there are several notable examples of it. For instance, UML has adopted a StateChart-based technique to model the dynamic behaviors of its conceptual components (i.e., Classes). Other variations of state-based techniques (e.g., FSM) have been used for similar purposes (e.g., [9]). Finally, Wright [3] uses CSP to model dynamic behaviors of its components and connectors.

Interaction Protocol Modeling. The last category of component modeling approaches focuses on legal protocols of interaction among components. This view of modeling provides a continuous *external* view of a component's execution by specifying the allowed execution traces of its operations (accessed via interfaces). Several techniques for specifying interaction protocols have been developed. These techniques are based on CSP [3], FSM [31], temporal logic [1], and regular languages [24]. They often focus on detailed formal models of the interaction protocols and enable proofs of protocol properties. However, some may not scale very well, while others may be too formal and complex for routine use by practitioners.

Typically, the static and dynamic component behaviors and interaction protocols are expressed in terms of a component's interface model. For instance, at the level of static behavior modeling, the pre- and post-conditions of an operation are tied to the specific interface through which the operation is accessed. Similarly, the widely adopted protocol modeling approach [31] uses finite-state machines in which component interfaces serve as labels on the transitions. The same is also true of UML's use of interfaces specified in class diagrams for modeling event/action pairs in the corresponding StateCharts model. This is why we chose to place *Interface* at the center of the diagram shown in Figure 1.

4 Our Approach

The approach to component modeling we advocate is based on the concept of the Quartet introduced in Section 3. We argue that a complete functional model of a software component can be achieved only by focusing on all four aspects of the Quartet. At the same time, focusing on all four aspects has the potential to introduce certain problems (e.g., large number of modeling notations that developers have to master, model inconsistencies) that must be carefully addressed. While we use a particular notation in the discussion below, the approach is generic such that it can be easily adapted to other modeling notations. In this section, we focus on the conceptual elements of our approach, with limited focus on our specific notation used.

Component models are specified from the following four modeling perspectives:[1]

```
Component_Model:
    (Interface,
     Static_Behavior,
     Dynamic_Behavior,
     Interaction_Protocol);
```

4.1 Interface

Interface modeling serves as the core of our component modeling approach and is extensively leveraged by the other three modeling views. A component's interface has a type and is specified in terms of several *interface elements*. Each interface element has a direction (+ or -), name (method signature), a set of input parameters, and possibly a return type (output parameter). The direction indicates whether the component *requires* (+) the service (i.e., operation) associated with the interface element or *provides* (-) it to the rest of the system. In other words:

```
Interface:
    (Type,
     {Interface_Element});

Interface_Element:
    (Direction,
     Method_signature,
     {Input_parameter},
     Output_parameter);
```

In the context of the SCRover example discussed in Section 2, the *Controller* component exposes four interfaces through its four ports: *e*, *u*, *q*, and *n*, correspond to *Execution*, *UpdateDB*, *Query*, and *Notification* interface types, respectively (recall Figure 2). Each of these interfaces may have several interface elements associated with it. These interface elements are enumerated in Figure 3, for instance

```
Controller:
u:  -updateSpeed(val: SpeedType):Boolean;
q:  +getWallDist():DistanceType;
```

where *updateSpeed()* is an interface element required by the *Controller* component. Its input parameter *val* is of user-defined type *SpeedType* and returns a *Boolean* indicating a successful change of speed operation. On the other hand, *getWallDist()* is provided by the controller component, has no parameters, and returns a value of type *DistanceType*.

---

[1] Concise formulations are used throughout this section to clarify our definitions and are not meant to serve as a formal specification of our model.

4.2 Static Behavior

We adopt a widely used approach for static behavior modeling [15], which relies on first-order predicate logic to specify functional properties of a component in terms of the component's *state variables*, *invariants* (the constraints associated with the state variables), *interfaces* (as modeled in the interface model), *operations* (accessed via interfaces) and their corresponding *pre-* and *post-conditions*. In other words:

```
Static_Behaviors:
    ({State_Variable},
     Invariant,
     {Operation});

State_Variable:
    (Name,
     Type);

Invariant:
    (Logical_Expression);

Operation:
    ({Interface_Element},
     Pre_Cond,
     Post_Cond);

Pre/Post_Cond:
    (Logical_Expression);
```

A partial static behavior specification of SCRover example's *Controller* component is depicted in Figure 3.

4.3 Dynamic Behavior

A dynamic behavior model provides a continuous view of the component's internal execution details. Variations of state-based modeling techniques have been typically used to model a component's internal behavior (e.g., in UML). Such approaches describe the component's dynamic behavior using a set of *sequencing constraints* that define legal ordering of the operations performed by the component. These operations may belong to one of two categories: (1) they may be directly related to the interfaces of the component as described in both interface and static behavioral models; or (2) they may be internal operations of the component (i.e., invisible to the rest of the system such as private methods in a UML class). To simplify our discussion, we only focus on the first case: publicly accessible operations. The second case may be reduced to the first one using the concept of *hierarchy* in StateCharts: internal operations may be abstracted away by building a higher-level state-machine that describes the dynamic behavior only in terms of the component's interfaces.

A dynamic model serves as a conceptual bridge between the component's model of interaction protocols and its static behavioral model. On the one hand, a dynamic model serves as a refinement of the static model as it further details the internal behavior of the component. On the other hand, by leveraging a state-based notation, a dynamic model may be used to specify the sequence by which a component's operations get executed. Fully describing a component's dynamic behavior is essential

Controller (Interface)

```
Ports:
  prov: {q:Query}
  req: {n:Notify, u:UpdateDB, e:Execution}
Interfaces:
  u: updateSpeed(val:SpeedType):Boolean;
  u: updateDirection (val:Direction);
  u: updateBatteryMode (val:BattMode);
  u: updateAll (val:AllTypes);
  u: setDefaults();
  ...
  e: executeSpeedChange (val:newSpeed);
  e: executeDirChange (val:newDir);
  n: notifyDistChange():DistType;
  n: notifySpeedChange():SpeedType;
  q: getWallDist():DistanceType;
  ...
```

```
Interface types
  e: Execution
  q: Query
  n: Notify
  u: UpdateDB
  ...
```

Controller (Static Behavior)

```
Operations:
 op_updateSpeed{
   v:SpeedType
   speedVal:STATE_VARIABLE;
   preCond: {v <> speedVal}
   postCond: {~speedVal <> speedVal}
   mapped_interfaces: {updateSpeed}
 }
 op_getWallDist{
   preCond: {dist >0}
   postCond: {result=dist}
   mapped_interfaces: {getWallDist}
 }
 op_updateAll{
   v:AllType
   allVal:STATE_VARIABLE;
   preCond: {v <> allVal}
   postCond: {~allVal <> allVal}
   mapped_interfaces: {updateAll}
 }
 op_notifyDistChange{
   postCond: {result=newDist}
   mapped_interfaces: {notifyDistChange}
 }
 op_setDefaults{
   preCond: {dist > 100}
   postCond: {~speed > 100 AND dir = 0}
   mapped_interfaces: {setDefaults}
 }
 op_executeSpeedChange{
   preCond: {val <> speed}
 }
```

```
StateVariable:
  mode:Integer;
  dist:DistanceType;
  speed:SpeedType;
  dir:DirType;
Invariant:
  { 0 ≤ mode ≤ 3 //off=0, on=1, halt=2,
 failure=3
    0 ≤ dist }
```

Fig. 3. Partial View of the *Controller* component's Interface and Static Behavior.

in achieving two key objectives. First, it provides a rich model that can be used to perform sophisticated analysis and simulation of the component's behavior. Second, it can serve as an important intermediate level model to generate implementation level artifacts from the architectural specification.

Existing approaches to dynamic behavior modeling employ an *abstract* notion of component state. These approaches treat states as entities of secondary importance, with the transitions between states playing the main role in behavioral modeling. Component states are often only specified by their name and set of incoming and outgoing transitions. We offer an extended notion of dynamic modeling that defines a state in terms of a set of variables maintained by the component and their associated

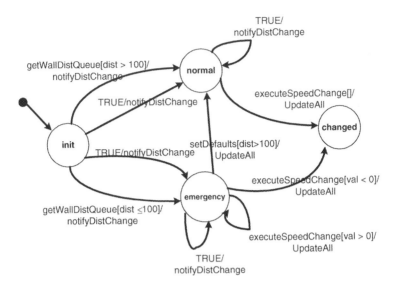

Controller (Interaction Protocols)

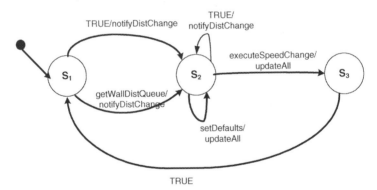

Fig. 4. Partial View of *Controller* Component's Dynamic Behavior (top)
and Interaction Protocol (bottom)

invariants. These invariants constrain the values of and dependencies among the variables [28]. As examples of this extension to the definition of states consider the invariants associated with *Normal* and *Emergency* states in the top diagram of Figure 4 (the details of state invariants are actually omitted from the diagram itself for clarity).

```
Normal_inv: (0 ≤ dir < 360) AND (0 < speed < 500}
Emergency_inv: (100 < speed < 200) AND (dir = 0) AND (dist ≤ 100)
```

In summary, our dynamic behavior model consists of a set of initial states and a sequence of guarded transitions from an origin to a destination state. Furthermore, a state is specified in terms of constraints it imposes over a set of a component's state variables. In other words,

```
Dynamic_Behavior:
    (InitState,
     {State:(Direction)Transition->State});
State:
    (Name,
     Variables,
     Invariant);
Transition:
    (Label,
     {Parameter},
     Guard);
Guard:
    (Logical_Expression);
```

A model of the *Controller* component's dynamic behavior is depicted in the middle portion of Figure 4. Note that the transitions are decorated with the StateCharts' event/action pairs. We omit further discussion of actions in this paper since their usage is not critical to the paper's argument.

4.4 Interaction Protocols

Finally, we adopt the widely used notation for specifying component interaction protocols, originally proposed in [23]. Finite state semantics are used to define valid sequences of invocations of component operations. Since interaction protocols are concerned with an "external" view of a component, valid sequences of invocations are specified irrespective of the component's internal state or the pre-conditions required for an operation's invocation. A simple interaction protocol for the *Controller* component is shown in the bottom portion of Figure 4. Our notation specifies protocols in terms of a set of initial states, and a sequence of transitions from an origin state to a destination.

```
Interaction_Protocol:
    (InitState,
     {State:(Direction)Transition->State});
State:
    (Name);
Transition:
    (Label,
     {Parameter});
```

5 Relating Component Models

Modeling complex software systems from multiple perspectives is essential in capturing a multitude of structural, behavioral, and interaction properties of the system under development. The key requirement for ensuring that dependable systems will result from this process is to maintain the consistency among the different system models [5,8,10,11,13]. We address the issue of consistency in the context of functional component modeling based on the Quartet technique.

In order to ensure the consistency among the models, their inter-relationships must be understood. Figure 1 depicts the conceptual relationships among these models. We categorize these relationships into two groups: syntactic and semantic. A *syntactic* relationship is one in which a model (re)uses the elements of another model directly and without the need for interpretation. For instance, interfaces and their input/output parameters (as specified in the interface model) are directly reused in the static behavior model of a component (relationship *1* in Figure 1). The same is true for relationships *2* and *3*, where the dynamic behavior and protocol models (re)use the names of the interface elements as transition labels in their respective FSMs.

Alternatively, a *semantic* relationship is one in which modeling elements are designed using the "meaning" and interpretation of the other elements. That is, specification of elements in one model *indirectly* affects the specification of elements in a different model. For instance, an operation's pre-condition in the static behavior model specifies the condition that must be satisfied in order for the operation to be executed. Similarly, in the dynamic behavior model, a transition's guard ensures that the transition will only be taken when the guard condition is satisfied. The relationship between a transition's guard in the dynamic behavior model and the corresponding operation's pre-condition in the static behavior model is semantic in nature: one must be interpreted in terms of the other (e.g., by establishing logical equivalence or implication) before their (in)consistency can be established. Examples of this type of relationship are relationships *4* and *5* in Figure 1.

In the remainder of this section we focus in more detail on the six relationships among the component model Quartet depicted in Figure 1.

5.1 Relationships *1*, *2*, and *3* — Interface vs. Other Models

The interface model plays a central role in the design of other component models. Regardless of whether the goal of modeling is to design a component's interaction with the rest of the system or to model details of the component's internal behavior, interface models will be extensively leveraged.

When modeling a component's behaviors from a static perspective, the component's operations are specified in terms of interfaces through which they are accessed. As discussed in Section 4, an interface element specified in the interface model is mapped to an operation, which is further specified in terms of its pre- and post-conditions that must be satisfied, respectively, prior to and after the operation's invocation.

In the dynamic behavior and interaction protocol models, activations of transitions result in changes to the component's state. Activation of these transitions is caused by internal or external stimuli. Since invocation of component operations results in changes to the component's state, there is a relationship between these operations' invocations (accessed via interfaces) and the transitions' activations. The labels on these transitions (as defined in Section 4) directly relate to the interfaces captured in the interface model.

The relationship between the interface model and other models is syntactic in nature. The relationship is also unidirectional: all interface elements in an interface model may be leveraged in the dynamic and protocol models as transition labels; however, not all transition labels will necessarily relate to an interface element. Our (informal) discussion provides a conceptual view of this relationship and can be used as a framework to build automated analysis support to ensure the consistency among the interface and remaining three models within a component.

5.2 Relationship *4* — Static Behavior vs. Dynamic Behavior

An important concept in relating static and dynamic behavior models is the notion of *state* in the dynamic model and its connection to the static specification of component's *state variables* and their associated *invariant*. Additionally, operation *pre- and post-conditions* in the static behavior model and *transition guards* in the dynamic behavior model are semantically related. We have extensively studied these relationships in [28] and identified the ranges of all such possible relationships. The corresponding concepts in the two models may be equivalent, or they may be related by logical implication. Although their equivalence would ensure their inter-consistency, in some cases equivalence may be too restrictive. A discussion of such cases is given below.

Transition Guard vs. Operation Pre-condition. At any given state in a component's dynamic behavior model, multiple outgoing transitions may share the same label, but with different guards on the label. In order to relate an operation's pre-condition in the static model to the guards on the corresponding transitions in the dynamic model, we first define the *union guard (UG)* of a transition label at a given state. UG is the disjunction of all guards G associated with outgoing transitions that carry the same label:

$$UG = \bigvee_{i=1}^{n} G_i$$

where n is the number of outgoing transitions with the same label at a given state, and G_i is the guard associated with the ith transition.

As an example in Figure 4, the dynamic model is designed such that different states (*Normal* and *Emergency*) are going to be reachable as destinations of the *getWallDist()* transition depending on the distance of the encountered obstacle (*dist* variable in the transition guards). In this case at state *Normal* we have:

$$UG_{getWallDist} = (dist > 100) \text{ OR } (0 < dist \leq 100)$$

Clearly, if UG is equivalent to its corresponding operation's pre-condition, the consistency at this level is achieved. However, if we consider the static behavior model to be an abstract specification of the component's functionality, the dynamic behavioral model becomes the concrete realization of that functionality. In that case, if UG is stronger than the corresponding operation's pre-condition, the operation may still be invoked safely. The reason for this is that UG places bounds on the operation's (i.e., transition's) invocation, ensuring that the operation will never be invoked under circumstances that violate its pre-condition; in other words, UG should imply the corresponding operation's pre-condition. This is the case for the *getWallDist()* operation in the rover's *Controller* component.

State Invariant vs. Component Invariant. The state of a component in the static behavior specification is modeled using a set of state variables. The possible values of these variables are constrained by the *component's invariant*. Furthermore, a component's operations may modify the state variables' values, thus modifying the state of the component as a whole. The dynamic behavior model, in turn, specifies internal details of the component's states when the component's services are invoked. As described in Section 3, these states are defined using a name, a set of variables, and an invariant associated with these variables (called *state's invariant*). It is crucial to define the states in the dynamic behavior state machine in a manner consistent with the static specification of component state and invariant.

Once again, an equivalence relation among these two elements may be too restrictive. In particular, if a state's invariant in the dynamic model is stronger than the component's invariant in the static model (i.e., state's invariant implies component's invariant), then the state is simply bounding the component's invariant, and does not permit for circumstances under which the component's invariant is violated. This relationship preserves the properties of the abstract specification (i.e., static model) in its concrete realization (i.e., dynamic model) and thus may be considered less restrictive than equivalence. A simple case is that of state *Normal* and its invariant in the *Controller* component. Relating the component invariant and the invariant of state *Normal*, we have:

$\text{Normal}_{inv}: (0 \leq \text{dir} < 360) \text{ AND } (0 < \text{speed} < 500) \text{ AND } (\text{dist} > 100)$

$\text{Controller}_{inv}: (0 \leq \text{dir} < 360) \text{ AND } (0 < \text{speed} < 1000) \text{ AND } (\text{dist} \geq 0);$

$\text{Normal}_{inv} \Rightarrow \text{Controller}_{inv}$

For more discussion on these, and a study of other possible relationships, see [28].

State Invariants vs. Operation Post-Condition. The final important relationship between a component's static and dynamic behavior models is that of an operation's post-condition and the invariant associated with the corresponding transition's destination state. For example, in Figure 3, the post-condition of the *setDefaults()* operation is specified as:

$\text{setDefaults}_{post}: (\text{speed} > 100) \text{ AND } (\text{dir} = 0)$

while state *Normal* is a destination state for *setDefaults()* and we have:

$\text{Normal}_{inv}: (0 \leq \text{dir} < 360) \text{ AND } (0 < \text{speed} < 500) \text{ AND } (\text{dist} > 100)$

In the static behavior model, each operation's post-condition must hold true following the operation's invocation. In the dynamic behavior model, once a transition is taken, the state of the component changes from the transition's origin state to its destination state. Consequently, the state invariant constraining the destination state and the operation's post-condition are related. Again, the equivalence relationship may be unnecessarily restrictive. Analogously to the previous cases, if the invariant associated with a transition's destination state is stronger than the corresponding operation's post-condition (i.e., destination state's invariant implies the corresponding operation's post-condition), then the operation may still be invoked safely. As an example consider the specification of state *Normal* and operation *setDefaults()* shown above. Clearly, the appropriate implication relationship does not exist. The *setDefaults()* operation may assign the value of the variable *speed* to be greater than 500, which would, in turn, negatively affect the component's dependability.

5.3 Relationship 5 — Dynamic Behavior vs. Interaction Protocols

The relationship between the dynamic behavior and interaction protocol models of a component is semantic in nature: the concepts of the two models relate to each other in an indirect way.

As discussed in Section 3, we model a component's dynamic behavior by enhancing traditional FSMs with state invariants. Our approach to modeling interaction protocols also leverages FSMs to specify acceptable traces of execution of component services. The relationship between the dynamic behavior model and the interaction protocol model thus may be characterized in terms of the relationship between the two state machines. These two state machines are at different granularity levels however: the dynamic behavior model details the internal behavior of the component based on both internally- and externally-visible transitions, guards, and state invariants; on the other hand, the protocol model simply specifies the externally-visible behavior of the component, with an exclusive focus on transitions. Examples of the two models are shown in Figure 4.[2]

Our goal here is not to define a formal technique to ensure the equivalence of two arbitrary state machines. This would first require some calibration of the models to even make them comparable. Additionally, several approaches have studied the equivalence of StateCharts [4,16,31]. Instead, we provide a more pragmatic approach to ensure the consistency of the two models. We consider the dynamic behavior model to be the concrete realization of the system under development, while the protocol of interaction provides a guideline for the correct execution sequence of the component's interfaces. For example, consider again models of the *Controller* component specified in Figure 4. Assuming that the interaction protocol model demonstrates *all* the valid sequences of operation invocations of the component, it can be deduced that the multiple consecutive invocation of *setDefaults()* are permitted. However, based on the dynamic model, only one such operation is possible. Consequently, the dynamic and protocol models are not equivalent. Since, the *Controller* component's dynamic behavior FSM is less general than its protocol FSM, some legal sequences of invocations of the component are not permitted by the component's dynamic behavior FSM. This, in turn, directly impacts the component's dependability.

---

[2] Recall that in our example, the dynamic model is only specified at the level of external operations. Adding internal operations to the model increases the granularity gap between the dynamic and protocol models.

5.4 Relationship 6 — Static Behavior vs. Interaction Protocol

The interaction protocol model specifies the valid sequence by which the component's interfaces may be accessed. In doing so, it fails to take into account the component's internal behavior (e.g., the pre-conditions that must be satisfied prior to an operation's invocation). Consequently, we believe that there is no direct conceptual relationship between the static behavior and interaction protocol models. Note, however, that the two models are related indirectly via a component's interface and dynamic behavior models.

6 Implications of the Quartet on System-Level Reliability

The goal of our work is to support modeling architectural aspects of complex software systems from multiple perspectives and to ensure the inter- and intra-consistency among these models. Such consistency is critical in building dependable software systems, where complex components interact to achieve a desired functionality. Dependability attributes must therefore be "built into" the software system throughout the development process, including during the architectural design phase. This paper has presented a first step in this direction. We have restricted our focus in the paper to software components alone. However, the Quartet enables a natural progression toward system-wide modeling and analysis: a configuration of software components in a system's architecture is "tied together" via the components' interface and interaction protocol models; the remaining two models of each component are abstracted away from other components.

Several existing approaches (e.g., [3,31]) have demonstrated how protocols can be leveraged to assess a system's architecture-level (functional) consistency. This paper is part of our ongoing research in quantifying, measuring, and consequently ensuring architecture-level dependability of software systems. Specifically, our ongoing work on architecture-level reliability estimation of software systems directly leverages the analyses results obtained from the Quartet modeling, and applies those results to a stochastic model to estimate component-level reliability [25,26]. Our stochastic reliability model is applicable to early stages of development when the implementation artifacts are unavailable and the exact execution profile of the system is unknown. Furthermore, we use these results to estimate the overall system-level reliability in a compositional manner. A series of concurrent state machines, each representing an individual component's interaction protocol, are used to build an augmented Markov model. We believe that our approach could be directly applied to other dependability attributes that are probabilistic in nature (e.g., availability).

7 Conclusion and Future Work

In this paper, we argued for a four-view modeling approach, referred to as *the Quartet*, that can be used to comprehensively model structural, static and dynamic behavioral, and interaction properties of a software component. We also discussed the conceptual dependencies among these models, and highlighted specific points at which consistency among them must be established and maintained in the interest of ensuring the component's dependability. While the discussion provided in this paper has been semi-formal, we believe that it provides a promising starting point for formalization and development of related modeling and analysis tools. Such tools are likely to alleviate a common criticism levied at an approach such as ours: practitioners will be reluctant to use it in "real" development situations because it requires too much rigor and familiarity with too many notations. We believe such a criticism to be misplaced for several reasons. First, this approach does not require formality and rigor beyond what an average computer science undergraduate must become familiar with: FSM and first-order predicate logic. Second, the experience of UML has shown that practitioners will be all too happy to adopt multiple notations if those notations solve important problems. Third, the potential for automated system specification, model inter-consistency analysis, and implementation in our view should outweigh any perceptions of difficulty in adopting the Quartet. Finally, this approach still allows developers to select whatever subset of the Quartet they wish, but should give them an understanding of how incorporating additional component aspects is likely to impact their existing models. In fact, we have recently begun using three of the four Quartet models (interface, static behavior, and protocol) to calculate system reliability at the architectural level [25,26].

The ideas discussed in this paper were inspired by our previous work, in which we integrated support for modeling static and dynamic system behaviors at the architectural level [27]. We are currently reengineering and extending this tool support using an extensible XML-based ADL [29]. Our long-term goal is to use this tool support in formalizing the component modeling framework introduced in this paper, and to provide an extensible basis for modeling and ensuring the consistency among interacting and interchangeable components in large-scale software systems.

References

1. Aguirre N., Maibaum T.S.E., "A Temporal Logic Approach to Component Based System Specification and Reasoning", in *Proceedings of the 5th ICSE Workshop on Component-Based Software Engineering*, Orlando, FL, 2002.
2. America P. "Designing an Object-Oriented Programming Language with Behavioral Subtyping", *Lecture Notes in Computer Science*, vol. 489, Springer-Verlag, 1991.
3. Allen R., Garlan D., "A Formal Basis for Architectural Connection", *ACM Transactions on Software Engineering and Methodology*, 6(3):213–249, 1997.
4. Ashar P., Gupta A., Malik S., "Using complete-1-distinguishability for FSM equivalence checking", *ACM Transactions on Design Automation of Electronic Systems*, Vol. 6, No. 4, pp 569-590, October 2001.
5. Balzer R., "Tolerating Inconsistency", in *Proceedings of 13th International Conference on Software Engineering (ICSE-13)*, Austin, Texas, 1991.
6. Booch G., Jacobson I., Rumbaugh J. "*The Unified Modeling Language User Guide*", Addison-Wesley, Reading, MA.

7. Dias M., Vieira M., "Software Architecture Analysis based on Statechart Semantics", in *Proceedings of the 10th International Workshop on Software Specification and Design, FSE-8*, San Diego, USA, November 2000.

8. Egyed, A. "Scalable Consistency Checking between Diagrams - The ViewIntegra Approach," in *Proceedings of the 16th IEEE International Conference on Automated Software Engineering*, San Diego, CA, 2001.

9. Farías A., Südholt M., "On Components with Explicit Protocols Satisfying a Notion of Correctness by Construction". in *Proceedings of Confederated International Conferences CoopIS/DOA/ODBASE* 2002.

10. Finkelstein A., Gabbay D., Hunter A., Kramer J., and Nuseibeh B., "Inconsistency Handling in Multi-Perspective Specifications", *IEEE Transactions on Software Engineering*, 20(8): 569-578, August 1994.

11. Fradet P., Le Métayer D., Périn M., "Consistency checking for multiple view software architectures", in *Proceeding of ESEC / SIGSOFT FSE 1999*.

12. Hofmeister C., Nord R.L., and Soni D., "Describing Software Architecture with UML" In *Proceedings of the TC2 First Working IFIP Conference on Software Architecture (WICSA1)*, San Antonio, TX, February 22-24, 1999.

13. Hnatkowska B., Huzar Z., Magott J., "Consistency Checking in UML Models", in *Proceedings of Fourth International Conference on Information System Modeling (ISM01)*, Czech Republic, 2001.

14. Krutchen, P.B. "The 4+1 View Model of Architecture", *IEEE Software 12*, pp. 42 - 50, 1995.

15. Liskov B. H., Wing J. M., "A Behavioral Notion of Subtyping", *ACM Transactions on Programming Languages and Systems,* November 1994.

16. Maggiolo-Schettini A., Peron A., and Tini S., "Equivalence of Statecharts", *In Proceedings of CONCUR '96*, Springer, Berlin, 1996

17. Medvidovic N., Rosenblum D.S., and Taylor R.N.,"A Language and Environment for Architecture-Based Software Development and Evolution." In *Proceedings of the 21st International Conference on Software Engineering*, Los Angeles, CA, May 16-22, 1999.

18. Medvidovic N., Taylor R.N., "A Classification and Comparison Framework for Software Architecture Description Languages", *IEEE Transactions on Software Engineering*, January 2000.

19. Microsoft Developer Network Library, *Common Object Model Specification*, Microsoft Corporation, 1996.

20. Nuseibeh B., Kramer J., and Finkelstein A., "Expressing the Relationships Between Multiple Views in Requirements Specification", in *Proceedings of the 15th International Conference on Software Engineering (ICSE-15)*, Baltimore, Maryland, USA, 1993.

21. Object Management Group, *The Common Object Request Broker: Architecture and Specification*, Document Number 91.12.1, OMG, December 1991.

22. *The Object Constraint Language (OCL)*, http://www-3.ibm.com/software/ad/library/standards/ocl.html.

23. Perry D.E., and Wolf A.L., "Foundations for the Study of Software Architectures", ACM SIGSOFT Software Engineering Notes, 17(4): 40-52, October 1992.

24. Plasil F., Visnovsky S., "Behavior Protocols for Software Components", *IEEE Transactions on Software Engineering* 28(11), pp. 1056–1076, November 2002.

25. Roshandel R., "Calculating Architectural Reliability via Modeling and Analysis" (Qualifying Exam Report), *USC Technical Report Number USC-CSE-2003-516*, December 2003.

26. Roshandel R., "Calculating Architectural Reliability via Modeling and Analysis", In the *proceedings of the Doctoral Symposium of the 26th International Conference on Software Engineering*, (to appear), Scotland, UK, 2004.

27. Roshandel R., Medvidovic N., "Coupling Static and Dynamic Semantics in an Architecture Description Language", in *Proceeding of Working Conference on Complex and Dynamic Systems Architectures,* Brisbane, Australia, December 2001.

28. Roshandel R., Medvidovic N., "Relating Software Component Models", *USC Technical Report Number USC-CSE-2003-504,* March 2003.

29. Roshandel R., van der Hoek A., Mikic-Rakic M., Medvidovic N., "Mae - A System Model and Environment for Managing Architectural Evolution", Submitted *to ACM Transactions on Software Engineering and Methodology (In review),* October 2002.

30. Shaw M., Garlan D., "Software Architecture: Perspectives on an Emerging Discipline". Prentice-Hall, 1996.

31. Yellin D.M., Strom R.E., "Protocol Specifications and Component Adaptors," *ACM Transactions on Programming Languages and Systems,* Vol. 19, No. 2, 1997.

32. Zaremski A.M., Wing J.M., "Specification Matching of Software Components", *ACM Transactions on Software Engineering and Methodology,* 6(4):333–369, 1997.

A Dependable Open Platform for Industrial Robotics – A Case Study

Goran Mustapić[1], Johan Andersson[1], Christer Norström[2], and Anders Wall[2]

[1] ABB Automation Technology Products, Robotics
Hydrovägen 10, SE-721 68, Västerås Sweden
{goran.mustapic,johan.x.andersson}@se.abb.com
[2] Dept. of Computer Science and Engineering, Mälardalen University
PO Box 883, SE-721 23 Västerås Sweden
{christer.norstrom,anders.wall}@mdh.se

Abstract. Industrial robots are complex systems with strict real time, reliability, availability, and safety requirements. Robot controllers are the basic components of the product-line architecture of these systems. They are complex real time computers which control the mechanical arms of a robot. By their nature, robot controllers are generic and open computer systems, because to be useful, they must be programmable by end-users. This is typically done by using software configuration parameters and a domain and vendor-specific programming language. For some purposes, this may not be sufficient. A means of adding low-level software extensions to the robot controller, basically extending its base software platform is needed when, for example, a third party wants to add a completely new sensor type that is not supported by the platform. Any software platform evolution in this direction introduces a new set of broad quality issues and other concerns. Dependability concerns, especially safety, reliability and availability, are among the most important for robot systems. In this paper, we use the ABB robot controller to show how an architecture transformation approach based on quality attributes can be used in the design process for increasing the platf openness.

1 Introduction

The demands of industry for safety at work and 50.000 hours of mean time between failures (MTBF) require the hardware and software of industrial robot systems to be of very high quality. Industrial robot systems consist of one or more mechanical units, e.g. robot arms that can carry different tools, electrical motors, a robot controller (computer hardware and software), and clients (see Figure 1). Clients are used for on-line and off-line programming of the robot controller.

The software of the ABB robot controller discussed in this paper can be divided into: *platform software*, *application* and *configuration software*. The variations between different products within the product line are currently accomplished through the configuration and application software while the platform software is fixed. The focus of this article is on increasing the number of variation points in the software system through the design of an open software platform architecture for the robot controller. Unless explicitly stated otherwise, *system* in this context is the software

R. de Lemos et al. (Eds.): Architecting Dependable Systems II, LNCS 3069, pp. 307–329, 2004.
© Springer-Verlag Berlin Heidelberg 2004

system of the robot controller, and *platform*, the software platform of the robot controller. The software platform is the basis for the product-line architecture and its role is similar to that of a domain-specific operating system. One of the differences between the two is that the platform is less flexible with respect to extension and its share in the responsibility for the final system properties is greater than that of an OS.

According to [9], components in open systems do not depend on a single administrative domain and are not known at design time. As a measure of openness, we use the diversity of the platform extensions and the layer-level in the layered software architecture, in which extensions can be included in the platform. Increasing openness in the platform means, at the same time, that it is possible to increase the number of variations within the product line. An example would be to introduce functionality not available from the base system manufacturer, e.g. new type of sensor in the system. With a closed platform, it is only the development organization responsible for the platform that can add low-level extensions to the system.

When designing the platform for a product line, there are many, varied architectural level aspects that must be considered. Some are of a technical nature, e.g. defining what type of new functionality should be supported and defining the open platform architecture. In addition, many other related non-technical aspects, organizational, business and processes issues are involved. Even though, in this paper, we focus on the technical aspects, each of those different aspects is important. One of the main technical challenges in designing an open platform is in increasing its openness without jeopardizing the quality of the final system. Consequently, all precautions must be taken to maximize the positive contribution of extensions to the platform, and to minimize any negative side effect on the behavior of the final system. As Bosch says [4], "the qualities of the product-line architecture are not relevant in themselves, but rather the way these qualities translate to the software architecture of the products that are a part of the product line". More specifically, we focus on the following technical aspects of the problem we have described:

- systematic analysis and modeling of the open platform quality constraints, the first step in architectural design, and
- we show how a combination of the fault prevention means and architectural transformations can be used when designing the open platform. The results from the previous step are used for evaluation of the design decisions.

The paper is divided into seven sections. Section 2 begins with a short description of the ABB Robotic System and robot controller, the subject of this case study. In Section 3, we define *platform openness*. The design approach that we use in this case study is motivated and described in Section 4. In Section 5 we analyze and model the constraints, quality expectations and the software development architecture, which are the basis for the architecture transformation process described in Section 6. Finally, we present certain conclusions in Section 7.

2 System Overview

The ABB robot controller was initially designed in the beginning of the 1990's. It was required that the controller should be capable of use in different types of ABB robots, and thus the architecture is a product line architecture. In essence, the controller has a layered, and within layers an object-oriented, architecture. The implementation consists of approximately 2500 KLOC of C language source code divided into 400-500 classes, organized in 15 subsystems, which makes it a complex embedded system. The system consists of three computers that are tightly connected: the main computer that basically generates the path to follow, the axis computer, which controls each axis of the manipulator, and finally the I/O computer, which interacts with external sensors and actuators.

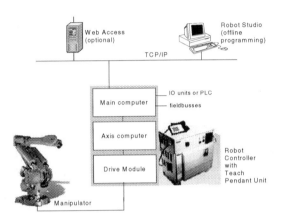

Fig. 1. System overview of an industrial robot system from ABB Robotics.

Only the main computer of the three computer nodes in the original system provides system-users with limited openness. This openness enables end-users to write their robot programming logic in the form of RAPID, an imperative language. A typical RAPID program contains commands to move the manipulator arm to different positions, making decisions based on input signals and setting output signals. This can be done through off-line programming tools on a PC, or on-line programming on a hand-held device designated a Teach Pendant Unit.

The system was originally designed to support easy porting to new HW-architectures and new operating systems. A level of openness beyond that possible with the RAPID language was not initially required. Furthermore, the system was not initially designed to support temporal analysis. Opening up the system for certain low-level extensions, e.g. adding new tasks, would require the introduction of such analyzability.

3 Defining the Open Platform for the Robot Controller Software System

In this section we define the platform openness from several different points of view. In order to prepare a successful architectural design, it is necessary to understand these different points of view, because all have an impact on architectural decisions.

As shown in Figure 2, we can consider the complete functionality of the system as a combination of functions or services provided by the system in different *system modes* of operation. Some of the modes are associated with normal performance of the system's task, while others represent degraded operation modes as responses to errors in the system. Defining the system modes is one of the steps in defining the *operational profiles* as described by Musa in [16]. According to Musa, system modes are a set of functions or operations that are grouped for convenience when analyzing execution behavior. Specifying degraded operation modes and modes available in different phases of the system's mission is important when system failure assumptions are considered in a system design [10]. The main system modes for the robot controller are the following (illustrated in Figure 2):

- *Initialization mode* – the mode in which the system operates during system startup. This mode is characterized by rapid dynamic changes of the system configuration between stopped mode and normal operation mode.
- *Safe-init mode* - the mode in which the system operates, if the system for some reason, is unable to start in the normal manner.
- *System update and configuration mode* - the mode in which new software may be added to or existing software replaced in the system.
- *Normal operation mode* – the mode in which the system's performs its primary functionality.
- *Fail-safe mode* – if an unrecoverable error is detected during normal operation, the system transitions into this mode. In this mode, the system is optimized for fault-tracing in the system by a maintenance engineer.

The functionality available in these modes, the number of system components and the way the components are connected to each other, are different in the different modes. On the top level, the system can only be in one of these modes at a time. This does not imply that some maintenance functions are not found in, e.g. normal operation mode, but rather that the majority of the functions present in each mode are still related to the primary purpose of that mode in the system.

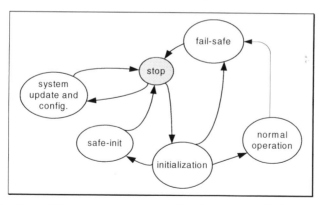

Fig. 2. Functions of the system are experienced by the user as multiple system modes.

The *functions*, also referred to as *services*, that we have described, are implemented either by the platform of the open system, or by components added to the platform. Further, added components should only be able to modify the behavior of a selected number of the platform services as illustrated in Figure 3.

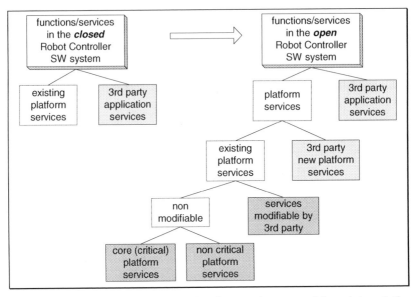

Fig. 3. In a system with an open platform, functions can be a part of the existing platform or extensions to the platform.

We use the designation platform *extensions* for system components that implement third party platform services or that implement modifications of the existing platform services. We will discuss extensions in two different contexts – the *software development architecture* and the *software operational architecture* of the system.

3.1 The Software Development Architecture

In this section, we will introduce the terminology used throughout the rest of the paper when we refer to the different components of the final system and illustrate the phases of the system development in which these components are added to the system.

The development artifacts, their relationships and dependencies can also be described as a system architecture as such. We refer to such an architecture as *software development architecture*. As discussed in [2] this architecture could be treated as an architecture on its own, not just as a different view of the single system architecture. In Figure 5, we show components in the software development architecture that can be developed independently:

- *Open Base Platform* – implements existing platform services, which can be modifiable or non-modifiable.
- *Extensions* – implement new platform services or modifications to the existing modifiable Open Base Platform services.
- *Extended Open Platform* – an instance of a platform, which is a composition of the Open Base Platform and all the installed extensions for that particular instance of the platform.
- *Application Programs and Configuration* – application logic written in the RAPID language and application configuration data.

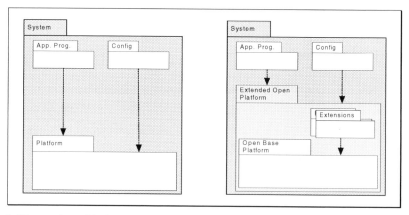

Fig. 4. The number of independently developed packages increases from the closed platform (left) to the open platform (right).

The left-hand part of Figure 4 shows the robot controller platform without the possibility of adding platform extensions. The right-hand part of the figure shows the open robot controller to which platform extensions can be added. *Packages* represent components that can be developed independently and within different organizational boundaries. A package may contain the implementation of several extension components. The arrows between the packages show their dependencies. When a system in the product line is implemented, the same Open Base Platform component is always used, while there are many possible choices of extension packages, applications and configurations.

3.2   Extensions and Software Operational Architecture

While, in the previous section, we showed how different components are related in the development architecture of the product-line system, in this section we describe how platform components fit into the system's operational architecture. Because the system has a layered architecture, we use a high-level layered view to describe it. We say that a system is more open if components can be added to lower layers in its architecture. To make the description more illustrative, we compare the robot controller to an open desktop platform.

3.2.1   Open Platforms in the Desktop Applications Domain

Examples of open platforms are Microsoft Windows© and Linux operating system platforms. Microsoft Windows© is more relevant to our case because we do not discuss open source openness, but rather openness in terms of the possibility of increasing the system capabilities. In the case of Windows© it is possible to extend the base platform on three different basic levels: device driver level, win32 programs and .Net applications. This is illustrated in Figure 5a.

The architecture of the system is such that each of the different extensibility mechanisms can only harm the system to a limited degree, device drivers causing the most harm and .Net application the least. Apart from basic or native ways to extend the platform, many of the applications define their own extensibility mechanisms, e.g.

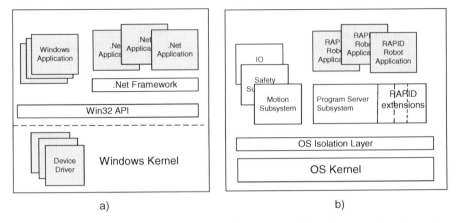

Fig. 5. Different ways to extend Windows© platform a) and ABB robot controller software b).

Internet Explorer and SQL Server. The differences between these applications are apparent in the process that accompanies the procedure of incorporating the extension functionality in the base system. Scripts are routinely downloaded and run on computers while browsing the Internet, whether requested by users or not. Application programs are mostly explicitly installed in the system but it is very unlikely that they will cause instability of the system as a whole. In the case of device drivers, a special organization designated Windows Hardware Quality Labs (WHQL), is responsible for certifying such drivers [14]. During the installation of device drivers, users of the platform are clearly notified if the driver has been verified by WHQL or not. The criticality of the device drivers is the driving force for adoption of the latest results from research communities into the device driver verification. An example of this is a recent adoption of the tool Static Driver Verifier, which is based on the model checking research [15]. This tool has a set of rules that can be automatically applied to device drivers, to check if they satisfy these rules.

3.2.2 Openness in the Robot Controller

The current way of adding functionality to the ABB robot controller, by adding RAPID programs, corresponds to adding .Net applications to Windows©. This is shown in Figure 5b. Two examples of low-level extensions to the robot controller platform that are currently restricted are extensions to the robot programming language RAPID and the addition of new subsystems/tasks. Let us consider an example.

Basic commands in the programming of a robot are motion commands which instruct the robot to move its arms to different positions. Some of the basic motion commands are implemented as RAPID extensions and perform their tasks by communicating with the motion subsystem. The basic part of the Program Server contains the execution engine for RAPID programs, and has features such as single stepping and executing the program backwards, i.e. running the robot backwards. The robot programming language consists of a predefined set of commands. It is desirable that new instructions can be added to permit easier programming, e.g. to permit the easier use of special tools by the robot. Such extensions may require adding new tasks or subsystems which would need an open access to the lower level services in the system.

Such extensions may have a significant impact on the system behavior, e.g. the temporal behavior. Traditionally, this has been restricted by the base platform development organization because of the prohibitive costs of verifying that they cause no harm to the system.

4 Describing the Design Approach

Understanding which types of extensions can be implemented and where they fit in the architecture is not sufficient when reasoning about, evaluating and motivating architectural decisions regarding the open robot controller platform. It is at least equally important to understand the constraints of the environment. Even though this part of the development process is usually considered as requirements engineering, the requirements engineering is closely related to architectural design and the line between the two cannot easily be drawn. As pointed out in [11], the idea that requirements should always state what a system should do rather than how it should do it, is an attractive idea but too simplistic in practice. The goals to be accomplished and the constraints on the solution must be modeled and described in such a way that it is easy to evaluate the design decision in relation to them.

A naive approach to transforming the robot controller platform into an open platform could be the following:

- turn internal interfaces into public interfaces.
- use the public interfaces to develop extensions with off-the-shelf development environments, compilers etc.
- define how extensions become a part of the platform.

In such an approach, the existing operational architecture is left unchanged. This approach is not acceptable if quality concerns are to be taken into account. In order to come to a satisfactory design solution, we need a design method that explicitly takes quality attributes into account. In the remainder of this section, we will describe several design approaches which focus on quality attributes and the approach we have used in this case study.

4.1 Different Approaches with Focus on Quality Attributes

In software quality research, different *quality models* exist, e.g. the ISO 9126 model and the model proposed by Dromey [5]. A quality model of a system can be described as a framework to capture the quality expectations of a system. Dromey emphasizes the importance of creating a quality model that is specific to a product [5]. This quality model is designated a *product quality model* and contains a *quality model*, a *software product model* and a link between them, as illustrated in Figure 6. The quality model should reflect the expectations that origin from the specific domain. A refinement of this model is necessary so that it can be linked with the product model. The software product model is the solution side of the model and describes the design or implementation. In the construction of the product quality model, a combination of the top-down and bottom-up approach is used. The quality model is constructed top-down starting from the most general quality attributes of the domain and then refining them to more specific quality attributes. The software product model is more likely to be constructed bottom-up because of, e.g., the use of COTS and legacy components. The quality of the individual components and the ways the components are combined in the product, have a dominant impact on the system quality.

The quality model consists of high-level quality attributes that are system non-tangible properties. Quality attributes can be classified to the following two groups:

- *Operational* quality attributes
- Examples of operational quality attributes are: usability, reliability, availability, safety, security, confidentiality, integrity, performance and maintainability.
- *Non-operational* quality attributes
- Examples of non-operational qualities are: maintainability, evolvability (reuse over time and across products in a product line), portability, verifiability, integrate-ability and deploy-ability.

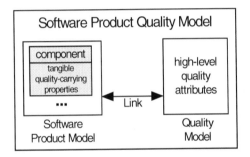

Fig. 6. Dromey's software product quality model.

Since high-level quality attributes are non-tangible and can only be measured through other tangible properties, Dromey suggests that they should be refined to more specific qualities and *characteristics* [6] , in order to create a finer grained quality model. Characteristics are tangible properties of a system that contribute to operational and-non operational qualities. Examples of characteristics are: machine independent, modular, static. Usability can, for instance, be further refined as learnability (easy to learn how to use), transparency (easy to remember how to use), customizability (can adjust to specific needs), operability (easy to access the functionality).

By analyzing the software product quality model, we have come to the conclusion that design tradeoffs between quality attributes are actually tradeoffs in choices of components and different ways of composing the components.

The software architecture community has been very active in trying to find a way to take quality attributes into account during architectural design. Good examples are two recent books on Software Architecture [3,4]. Even though the work described in these books relates to software systems, much of the reasoning can be applied more broadly to computer-based systems. In the architectural analysis, tradeoffs are made between all relevant quality attributes, not only between dependability attributes.

NFR (Non-Functional Requirements) is another approach to dealing with quality attributes which is used within the requirements engineering community. An example is NFR Framework described by Chang et al in [12]. NFR Framework uses a process-oriented approach and a qualitative approach to dealing with NFR, because quantitative measurement of an incomplete software system (its design) is considered to be even more difficult than measurement of the final product. NFR Framework defines soft-goals interdependency graphs for representing and analyzing NFR as well as dealing with tradeoffs.

A generic framework named *dependability-explicit development model* is described by Kaaniche, Laprie and Blanquart in [10]. This framework allows dependability-related activities to be structured and incorporated into the different phases of the *system creation process*. The activities are grouped in four processes: *fault prevention, fault tolerance, fault removal*, and *fault forecasting*. Because the dependability-explicit development model is a generic framework, customization is probably required for a given system. It is recognized that factors such as the complexity of the system, the priority of the dependability attributes and the confidence level to be achieved, cost limitations and standards, all influence the selection of optimal solutions.

4.2 The Approach Used in This Case Study

As explained in the previous sections, the Open Base Platform is the basic building block in the software product-line architecture of the robot controller. The software system and its components are designed and implemented in several stages, and within different organizational boundaries. This needs to be taken into account during the design of the Open Base Platform. In our opinion, the approaches presented in Section 4.1 are too general to be directly applicable to our case. For instance, the dependability-explicit development model takes only a subset of the relevant quality attributes (the dependability attributes) into account and gives no support to the development of flexible product-line architecture, which is important in the case of the robot controller. The approach in our case study contains elements of the architecture transformation method and the product-line design method described by Bosch [4], and also elements from the dependability-explicit development model [10]. The approach can be described in the following way:

- We describe the quality goals for the system in terms of constraints and quality attributes organized in two models or views: the operational constraints and quality attributes that capture the dependability objectives, and the non-operational constraints and quality attributes, i.e. qualities related to the development architecture. Quality attributes are organized in such a way that makes evaluation of different design decisions easier. We also describe some important constraints that determine allocation of dependability objectives among the system components. This is further described in Section 5.
- We describe and use an architectural transformation-based design method when designing the open platform architecture. In this method, we use the previously defined objectives to evaluate and guide our decisions. The method and its application to the robot controller system are described in Section 6.

5 Modeling Design Constraints for the Robot Controller Software – The First Step in Architecture Design

In this section we present a *quality view* of the robot controller software that includes two dimensions. The first dimension assigns the operational quality attributes of the industrial robot system to the robot controller software system's operational modes. The second dimension is a development architecture dimension that contains non-operational quality attributes. The purpose of these two dimensions is to permit the organization of quality attributes in a structured way that is suitable for qualitative reasoning in architectural design. Such organization makes the relations between quality attributes more clear, than e.g. having only a flat prioritized list of quality attributes. In a product-line-based approach, it is important to understand how the quality attributes of the platform, which constitute the base-component of the product line, are related to the quality of the products.

5.1 Operational Constraints

In many software system examples and studies, the analysis begins with software as the top system level. However, when software is embedded in a larger system, a systems approach is necessary when reasoning about quality attributes. In this section, we begin from the quality attributes implied by the industrial robotics domain and derive quality attributes down to the robot controller software system modes.

5.1.1 System Level Operational Quality Attributes
for Industrial Robotics Domain

The most important operational quality attributes for industrial robots are the following: dependability attributes, usability (e.g. ease of reconfiguration and operation), and performance (e.g. speed of manipulation, movement precision, and handling weight). For the dependability attributes we adopt the terminology presented in [1]. Dependability is described by the following attributes: *Reliability, Availability, Safety, Integrity, Confidentiality*, and *Maintainability*.

Security related attributes, i.e. confidentiality and integrity, are usually of less importance for industrial robots as robots tend to be physically isolated, or only connected to a control network together with other industrial devices. However, integrity of data which is not security-related is very important. For instance, it is not acceptable that, e.g. a task in the system should cause a hazard situation by damaging the logic of the safety subsystem. In some cases, integrity of the system is required in the sense that an unauthorized person may not change operational parameters for a robot. All other dependability attributes are highly relevant.

Even though the contact between humans and robots in an industrial environment is restricted (robots work in cells, which are physically isolated by a fence), safety can never be underestimated since an unsafe system can cause considerable physical damage to the expensive robot equipment and its environment. For example, larger types of robots are powerful machines currently capable of manipulating a weight of over 500 kg. Industrial robots are included in the category of safety-critical systems which can be implemented as "fail-safe", i.e. they have a fail-safe mode.

The industrial/business environment in which robots are used is such that it is crucial to have a very high degree of *availability* and *reliability*. Unreliability leads to non-availability, which means unscheduled production stops associated with what can be huge costs. Because of the complexity of, for example, a car production line, the non-availability of a single robot will result in the stopping of the entire production line. The failure of a single robot with a welding tool caught inside a car body could cause the loss of up to one-day's production from the production line.

Maintainability is important in the sense that it is related to availability. The shorter the unscheduled maintenance time, the higher the availability of the system. Regularly scheduled preventive maintenance cannot be avoided since the robot system contains mechanical parts.

When it comes to the dependability threats, i.e. fault, error and failures, both hardware and software faults must be considered. The robot controller software has both the roles of sending control sequences to the hardware and predicting preventive hardware maintenance.

There are many different fault-tolerance methods that can be applied to industrial robots. However, error recovery with temporary graceful degradation of performance is not acceptable. A robot either works or it does not work; an individual robot cannot perform its tasks by working more slowly - it being only one link in a production chain, or because of the nature, such as arc welding, of the process concerned.

5.1.2 Robot Controller Software System Operational Qualities

In Figure 1 a typical robotics system and its subsystems is shown. The system architecture is such that the domain dependability quality attributes discussed in Section 5.1.1 do not affect all of the subsystems in the same way. How domain requirements are propagated to subsystems may differ between different robotics systems depending on their design and implementation. When propagated from the system level, quality attributes required of the robot controller software subsystem can be described as following:

- *Safety* – The robot controller has software logic responsible for the collision detection safety feature.
- *Reliability* and *availability* – The robot controller is responsible for generating correct coordinates (values), and with predefined time intervals so that signals can be constantly sent to the manipulator while it is moving. If incorrect values are sent, the manipulator will move in the wrong direction and if no values are sent, the manipulator will not know in which direction to continue its movements and it will stop in the fail-safe mode.
- *Integrity* – Configuration data integrity during maintenance and integrity of data structures in normal operation is very important because of its large impact on reliability and availability.
- *Performance* – Examples of important performance values for a robot are speed of manipulation, and repetitive and absolute accuracy. In software these issues relate to computational efficiency and data transfer efficiency.
- *Maintainability* – In the case of failures, it must be easy to identify and recognize the faulty component in the system and replace it. The manipulator, which is an electro-mechanical device, must be maintained on a regular basis as it is subject to degradation faults. Because of this, any preventive, corrective or perfective updates to the robot controller software and hardware can be done at the same time without affecting the complete robot system availability.

For the purpose of a detailed design, these quality attribute descriptions must be defined more precisely but they are sufficient for the purposes of this paper.

5.1.3 Operational Qualities for the Robot Controller Software System Modes

Different robot controller software system modes, discussed in Section 3, are likely to have different or differently prioritized operational quality attributes. The goal of this section is not to go into the detailed design of each of the modes, but to model quality attributes expectations on the functionality in the modes. In Figure 7 we visualize how quality attribute requirements described in Section 5.1.2 are propagated to the individual system modes, resulting in the lists of dependability goals to be satisfied in the different modes.

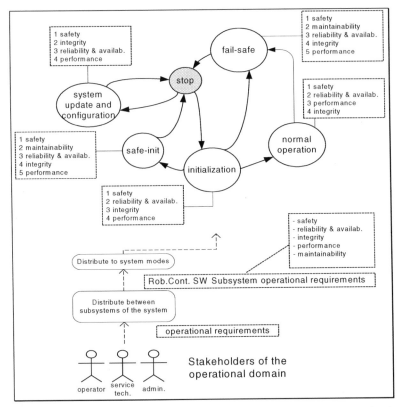

Fig. 7. Operational system modes with quality attributes assigned to them. As development stakeholders are not present here, the model is not dependent on their concerns.

As mentioned in Section 3, these modes have significantly different numbers of components and their interconnections. Because the normal mode of operation is the mode of the system's primary purpose, it is easy to neglect the other modes. From the software system quality perspective, it is absolutely crucial that the transitions between the modes are predictable and reliable. If the software system is corrupted on this level, it may not be able to start again. This implies that reliability and integrity are very important attributes at the top software system level.

5.1.4   New Operational Constraints for the Open Platform

For the open platform, new operational constraints also exist which are not necessarily of quality attribute type. An example is constraints on the allocation of dependability objectives that specify allowed effects of third party extensions to the core non-modifiable open platform functionality. Examples of such constraints are:

- The safety feature "collision detection" is a core non-modifiable feature allocated to the Open Base Platform components only, and can not be affected by platform extensions.
- The integrity of the top level software system mode transition sequence is allocated to Open Base Platform components only and it must not be affected by extensions in such a way that for example, the system is unable to start.

5.2   Software Development Architecture and Constraints
in the Development Domain

In this section we discuss the non-operational quality attributes that are important in the design and implementation of a system in the product line. In general, a system must be designed to fulfil both the operational requirements and the development requirements. Unlike dependability attributes, generally accepted definitions of which exist within the research community, there is a lack of generally accepted terminology and definitions for other quality attributes. For the quality attributes we refer to, we use intuitive names to refer to their meaning.

To identify the non-operational quality attributes, we first identify the *development stakeholders* and then bind their concerns to the packages in the development architecture that we introduced in the Section 3.1. It is generally recognized that quality concerns are dependent on the stakeholders and their views. The way that stakeholders are identified is still, to a large extent, an ad hoc procedure. A recent attempt by Preiss to systematize the stakeholder identification is described in [18]. Stakeholders are divided into *goal stakeholders* and *means stakeholders* and also according to the product lifecycle phases (*development stakeholders* and *operation stakeholder*). In this paper, we discuss only the *means* stakeholders, those who are responsible for designing and building the system. The concerns of the *system operation stakeholders* were described through the domain and system analysis of the robotic system in Section 5.1.

The important development stakeholders for industrial robotics and their concerns are presented in Figure 8. Using the terminology from Section 4, some of the concerns would be expressed as characteristics, e.g. standard compliance, and some as non-operational qualities, e.g. reuse. In Figure 8, we show only direct concerns of the stakeholders, but concerns of all other stakeholders are indirectly propagated to the Open Base Platform developer. The more effort invested in the design of the base platform level to address these concerns, the greater is the probability that the quality of all the components of the system will be improved. This is one of the very important goals of our design work.

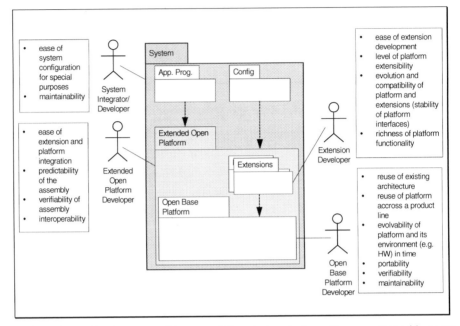

Fig. 8. Software development architecture of the robot controller software system with *means* stakeholders and their direct (first-level) concerns.

5.3 Other Important Requirements and Constraints

Operational and development qualities do not give us a complete model of the constraints on the software system design. There are other important constraints that can have a significant impact on the system design. The major tradeoffs in large and complex systems are usually associated with economics and business goals [3]. While we describe none of these constraints, they should definitely be defined and taken into account in the design phase. In the terms of means and goals stakeholders, mentioned in Section 5.2, these constraints are related to the goal stakeholders.

6   Robot Controller Software System Architecture Transformations

In this section we describe the design process for a more open software product line, which includes the architectural transformation process for the Open Base Platform. Referring to Figure 8, we are in the position of the developer of Open Base Platform. Our design goals are the following:

1. Direct goals from the Figure 8, such as reusing as much as possible of the existing assets, including the architecture.
2. Indirect development goals from the Figure 8, which are to help other development stakeholders to meet their goals. If extensions are difficult to develop and integrate

into the Open Base Platform, it decreases the likelihood that many new extensions will be developed.

3. To meet dependability objectives allocated to the Open Base Platform operational architecture components. These objectives were described in Section 5.1 through the domain analysis and the assignment of dependability goals to system operational modes.

4. To provide fault prevention means in the form of software tools, to other development stakeholders, in order to help meet the system dependability goals. This goal is closely related to item 2 in this list. If the complexity of the system integration and extension development is high, it increases the likelihood that the reliability of the system will be lower.

5. To meet other constraints, e.g. business goals discussed in Section 5.3.

These goals are independent of whether there is or not an existing robot controller software system. As we have an existing system from which to begin, we can describe our design goals in a slightly different way – we need to transform the system to address the changed and new requirements while still fulfilling the requirements that have not changed. From the discussions in the previous sections, we obtain the list of changes in the system and its environment, which can be attributed to the increased openness. This list is presented in Table 1.

Table 1. Changes in the robot controller software system and its environment, which can be attributed to the increased openness in the platform.

1	Some of the system *characteristics* have changed: • The amount of non-critical code in the system is very likely to increase. This increases the overall system complexity and the likelihood of faults being present in the system. • Adding extensions to the system increases resource utilization in the system which increases the risk of the system running out of critical resources during operation.
2	The system development environment has changed significantly, as shown in Figures 4 and 8. Concerns of the new stakeholders, i.e. developers of the Extended Open Platform and developers of extensions, need to be addressed by our design.
3	New operational constraints on allocation of dependability objectives between the system's components have emerged (described in Section 5.1.4).
4	Other new objectives exist, e.g. business objectives, which are not discussed in this paper.

To design a system, which is perceived as a high quality system from several different perspectives, all of these new goals must be addressed. Dependability of the system during operations can be categorized as a subset of these goals. System operational qualities as described in Section 5.1.3 are independent of the level of openness in the system. From the operational perspective, who has designed and implemented a component is irrelevant. However, this does not mean that there is no link between the development process/architecture and the operational architecture. The relationships between the different artifacts of the architectural design are visualized in Figure 9.

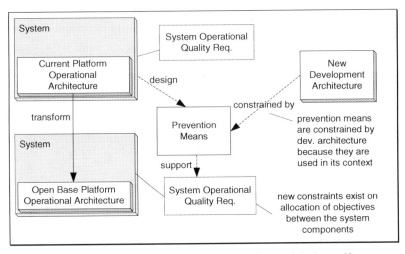

Fig. 9. Relationships between the software architectural design artifacts.

The current operational architecture of the platform is transformed into an Open Base Platform operational architecture. The platforms are the basis for systems that have the same operational quality attributes. However, for the more open system, new constraints exist on the allocation of dependability objectives between the system components. Fault prevention means, such as evaluation of the properties of the composition of the base platform and extensions, enforcements of restrictions on programming language features, are used to achieve the quality goals of the final system. The development architecture is changed and it dictates how and when fault prevention means can be applied.

6.1 Architectural Design

It is known that it is hard to define what software architecture is [2]. Furthermore, there are differences between what is considered an architecture in industry and in the research [8]. Fowler argues that all important system level design decisions that are hard to change are architectural decisions [7]. What is considered to be important is subjective and dependent on the opinion of the system expert.

One of the findings from our recent case study involving architects from seven large industrial companies was that an architects awareness of the process that is used to develop a product should be increased and process issues should be taken into account in architectural design [17]. Since the Base Open Platform is the basis for all products in the product line, it must provide a set of tools that can be used to support the process of completing the design and implementation of the system. An example of such a tool is a tool that checks that extensions to the platform are designed in such a way that they conform to the architectural principles of the base platform as described in Section 6.3. This is the design level support for operational quality goals of the system. We strongly believe that it is the software architects who should decide: which tools are suitable, what design properties of the system should they check and what are their limitations. In that sense, these tools become a part of the software architecture on the system level.

When designing a software architecture, Bosch [4] suggests preparing a functional design first and then performing architectural transformations to take quality attributes into account. Transformations that may be required could be as simple as adding a new functional component to the system, or may require changes such as the use of different architectural styles or patterns. This depends on the nature of a quality attribute. In our case, the functional design is already available because we began from an existing system. Furthermore, the existing system supports operational quality attributes as described in Section 5.1. The list of changes in the system environment was presented in Table 1. Design transformations must be performed to meet the new constraints within the context of the new development architecture.

The outline of the software architecture design method for the transformation of the system with the closed platform into a system with the open platform is shown in Figure 10. Initially, the open platform architecture is the same as the existing platform architecture. A number of architectural patterns in the existing platform architecture already provide a good basis for openness, such as: broker pattern, publish-subscribe and the layered-architecture. Then we estimate if the quality attributes and the constraints are satisfied or not. If not, we consider if prevention measures can be successfully applied to satisfy our concerns. If such is the case, we need to add the appropriate support, in the development environment, e.g. tools, language restrictions. If prevention measures are not sufficient, then we need to apply transformation of the platform operational architecture, e.g. to apply additional fault tolerance measures. Using prevention measures as much as possible helps to reuse the existing operational architecture, i.e. minimize its modifications, one of the goals mentioned in Figure 8. The resulting architecture is designated Open Base Platform operational architecture.

The platform transformations are performed now, but there is no complete system at this point. Many different systems can be designed using this platform as a basis. The platform design is completed when extensions are added to the platform, resulting in an Extended Open Platform. In the design of the Open Base Platform architecture, the effects of adding extensions to the platform are evaluated qualitatively, but the final configuration is not known. Evaluating the effects of adding extensions, e.g. new tasks, requires a tool support that can be used in a simple way outside the organization that designed the platform.

The following list summarizes the dependability means techniques that are applied in the platform architecture transformation phase, to address threats raised by the items in Table 1:

- Fault Tolerance techniques
  - o Because of the increased amount of non-critical code in the system (item 1), the system must be partitioned in several *fault-containment zones* representing multiple levels of criticality. The same technique addresses the concern introduced by item 4, on allocation of dependability objectives between the system components.
  - o Adding new components increases resource utilization and requires that *watch-dog* techniques be used to monitor the usage of critical system resources. Since the robot controller system may have fail-safe behavior, the watch-dog initiates roll-forward-recovery to the *failure* system mode.
- Fault Prevention techniques
  - o When new components are added to the Open Base Platform, the architecture of such a new system must be re-evaluated for important properties such as timeli-

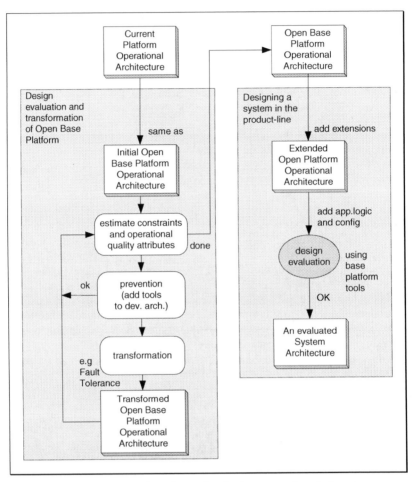

Fig. 10. Architectural transformation of the closed robot controller platform to an open platform. The open platform architecture is the basis for many different systems in the software product line.

ness. Qualitative reasoning about such properties is difficult. We have therefore introduced a software tool for a quantitative evaluation of the system design that checks for errors such as the violation of deadlines and queue underflow or overflow. Normally, the queue containing coordinate references must never be empty. If, however, it does become empty, the robot does not know what to do and will transit into a fail-safe state.

- Fault Removal techniques
  - o When components of a system are developed by different organizations, *fault diagnosis* that records the cause of errors in terms of both location and type is important. Fault diagnosis is the first step in fault handling [1]. However, in our case the goal is not to perform other steps in fault handling, e.g. isolation, reconfiguration, reinitialization, but to give precise information to an external agent.

Monitoring and debugging in the distributed real time system is challenging. In [20], Thane describes a method for software-based replay debugging of distributed real-time systems. A case study of the use of this method for the ABB robot controller is described in [21]. When this kind of diagnostic component is introduced in the Open Base Platform, it works in the same way for all components in the system.

6.2   Fault Tolerance Design Techniques to Support New Tasks

In addition to the architecture level transformations to support extensions to the Open Base Platform, lower level design transformations and techniques are needed to support different types of extensions. There is a difference between providing support for the addition of a new task to the system and adding a module that implements a new RAPID language command. The impact of changes to the system to support these different types of extensions is local and we therefore treat them as design level changes.

There are three important issues when transforming the architecture to support the addition of tasks, in addition to basic middleware broker support for installing tasks. These are:

- Which interfaces should be provided?
- How is the added task supervised during operation to detect erroneous behavior?
- Which type of exception handling should be used?

The basic system includes a set of interfaces for different required functionalities. The interfaces provided can be classified as critical or non-critical. The critical interfaces provide access to functionality that can impair the basic operational behavior of a robot, such as motion control. A failure in a task that is classified as critical will lead to an emergency stop. A task classified as non-critical is a task that only makes passive use of the information in the system and in the event of a failure, will not require the immediate stopping of the robot. An example of such a non-critical function is a web-server that presents certain statistics from the operations. Other fault handling measures can be taken instead, such as disabling the functionality provided by the extension. An added task that uses interfaces of both classes is classified as critical.

Supervising the behavior of an added task is supported in two ways, (i) assertions provided in each of the services and (ii) supervision of the assigned CPU bandwidth. The CPU-bandwidth is supervised by extending the basic operating system with functionality for monitoring execution time of each added task during each cycle of execution (from the time a task becomes ready until it will be waiting for the next cycle of execution). The basic idea is, thus, to prohibit the added task of delaying lower priority tasks longer than specified off-line. If the task uses too much CPU-bandwidth, different measures will be taken depending on the criticality of the task, as mentioned above.

In the case of a critical task, one can use an exception routine that is invoked before the severe impact occurs and allow that exception routine to finalize the computation with less accuracy. This concept is called imprecise computation or performance polymorphism as suggested in [13] and [19]. However, this approach is not acceptable in our case, since performance polymorphism can yield an application that delivers uneven quality. In the case of a non critical task we can adopt such an approach. In the first version of the design, a controlled shut down of the task is per-

proach. In the first version of the design, a controlled shut down of the task is performed and an error message provided to the operator.

6.3 Software Architecture Tools for Evaluation of Real-Time Properties

As shown in Figure 10, the evaluation of the Extended Open Platform Architecture is performed by other than the Open Base Platform developers. In [3], when the authors discuss product-line architectures, they point out that the documentation needs to explain valid and invalid variation bindings in a system based on the product-line architecture. We find this necessary, but not sufficient in our case; a tool support must also be provided. It is difficult to evaluate the impact of the combined extension on the temporal behaviour of the system, because of the system size and the number of interdependencies. A robot control system is a composition of Open Base Platform, extensions, configuration options (e.g. different field busses, the robot model, different software options such as spot- or arc- welding) and the user-programmed behaviour in the RAPID language. System compositions resulting from these components have different timing behaviour but in some cases, the magnitude of these differences might be insignificant. With extensions, the base system must not only be verified in different configurations, but also in combination with extensions that are to be used. These extensions can potentially have a large impact on the system timing and the developers of the extended base platform should not be required to know the details of the internal structure of the system in order to estimate the extension impact on the system. A way to address this issue is to describe system components using models and then analyze the system properties based on these models, as shown in Figure 11.

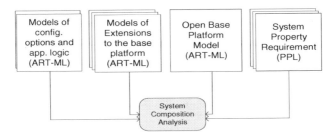

Fig. 11. The ART framework when used for real-time property validation in the design phase.

We propose a set of tools and methods for analyzing the impact on timing properties when changing the system. We call this framework ART [22]. It provides means for creating, analyzing and validating models of real-time systems. As illustrated in Figure 11, the general idea of this framework is to create a model of the system components using the modelling language ART-ML and, by using a suitable analysis method, to determine how the timing is affected by a change in the system. The analysis tool takes a system model containing the base system and extensions as input. It also needs a set of system-timing properties to analyze, formulated in the probabilistic query language PPL. In the current version of the framework, simulation based analysis is used. The tool evaluates the specified properties against the model.

7   Conclusions

Making changes to existing complex systems is never an easy task. These systems are created and fine-tuned using years of experience and maintenance, to satisfy the demanding functionality and quality requirements of the domains in which they are used. When changes are considered, it is vital to understand the impact of those changes, and then to find or develop adequate techniques to address the new or changed concerns and expectations.

In this paper, we use ABB robot controller, a complex real-time system, to analyze the impact on the system when the openness of the system is increased. As pointed out in [18], many development projects primarily take into account the operational domain stakeholders and their concerns. From the broader quality point of view when analyzing the impact of increasing system openness, we come to the conclusion that the impact on the system is primarily on the development side. Further, we recognize changes in some operational characteristics of the system that may affect system operational qualities and dependability. The amount of non-critical code in the system increases as well as resource usage. Because system reliability is a vital property of the system, and because the use of fault-tolerance means supporting fail-operational semantics is limited (because of cost or complexity), the importance of fault-prevention is emphasized, and tools supporting evaluation of the design decisions are proposed. The separation of system components into critical and non-critical components and their isolation in fault-containment regions is used to support fail-safe operational semantics.

We believe that most of the reasoning in this paper is applicable in general to the robotics domain, but also partly to other systems in the embedded domain, which require openness in the sense described in this paper.

References

1. Avizienis A., Laprie J.C., and Randell B.: Fundamental Concepts of Dependability, report 01-145, LAAS, 2001.
2. Baragry J. and Reed K.: Why we need a different view of software architecture, Working IEEE/IFIP Conference on Software Architecture, 2001.
3. Bass L., Clements P., and Kazman R.: Software Architecture in Practice, Addison-Wesley, 2003.
4. Bosch J.: Design & Use of Software Architectures, Addison-Wesley, 2000.
5. Dromey G.: Cornering the Chimera, IEEE Software, volume 13, issue 1, 1996.
6. Dromey G.: Software Product Quality: Theory, Model, and Practice, Software Quality Institute Griffith University Australia, http://www.sqi.gu.edu.au, 1998.
7. Fowler M.: Who needs an architect?, IEEE Software, 2003.
8. Graaf B., Lormans M., and Toetenel H.: Embedded Software Engineering: The State of the Practice, IEEE Software, 2003.
9. Issarny V.: Software Architectures of Dependable Systems: From Closed To Open Systems, ICSE 2002 Workshop on Architecting Dependable Systems, 2002.
10. Kaaniche M., Laprie J.C., and Blanquart J.P.: Dependability Engineering of Complex Computing Systems, 6th IEEE Conference on Engineering of Complex Computer Systems ICECCS, 2000.
11. Kotonya G. and Sommerville I.: Requirements Engineering - Processes and Techniques, John Wiley & Sons Ltd, 1997.

12. Lawrence C.(editor): Non-Functional Requirements in Software Engineering, Kluwer, 2000.
13. Liu J.W.S et al: Imprecise computations, Proceedings of the IEEE, volume 82, issue 1, 1994.
14. Microsoft Corporation, Windows Hardware and Driver Central homepage, http://www.microsoft.com/whdc/, 2003.
15. Microsoft Research, http://research.microsoft.com/slam/, SLAM Project 2003.
16. Musa J.D.: Operational profiles in software-reliability engineering, IEEE Software, volume 10, issue 2, 1993.
17. Mustapic G. et al: Influences between Software Architecture and its Environment in Industrial Systems - a Case Study, http://www.idt.mdh.se, Technical Report, Mälardalen University, Sweden, 2004
18. Preiss O. and Wegmann A.: Stakeholder discovery and classification based on systems science principles, Second Pacific-Asia Conference on Quality Software, 2001.
19. Takashio K. and Tokoro M.: An Object-Oriented Language for Distributed Real-Time Systems, OOPSLA'92, Vancouver, 1992.
20. Thane H.: Monitoring, Testing and Debugging of Distributed Real-Time Systems, Doctoral Thesis, Royal Institute of Technology, KTH, Mechatronics Laboratory, TRITA-MMK 2000:16, Sweden, 2000
21. Thane H. et al: Replay Debugging of Real-Time Systems using Time Machines, Parallel and Distributed Processing Symposium, Nice, France, 2003.
22. Wall A., Andersson J., and Norstrom C.: Probabilistic Simulation-based Analysis of Complex Real-Time Systems, 6th IEEE International Symposium on Object-oriented Real-time distributed Computing, Hakodate, Hokkaido, Japan, 2002.

Model Driven Architecture – An Industry Perspective

Chris Raistrick[1] and Tony Bloomfield[2]

[1] Kennedy Carter Ltd., Hatchlands, East Clandon, Surrey GU4 7RT, UK
chris@kc.com
[2] BAE Systems (Avionics) Ltd., Sensor Systems Division, Crewe Toll
Ferry Road, Edinburgh EH5 2XS, UK
tony.bloomfield@baesystems.com

Abstract. Model Driven Architecture (MDA) is an initiative of the Object Management Group (OMG) to promote an enhanced system development process based on the clear separation of application logic from the underlying platform technology and to generate software automatically from platform independent models, rather than relying on traditional largely manual code development processes. The avionics industry has identified several areas in which the MDA approach can potentially drive down the rapidly inflating cost of software development and maintenance of the very complex and safety critical systems both those in development and those currently in-service. This paper discusses some of the research work that is currently being undertaken within the avionics industry and specifically in collaboration with Kennedy Carter Ltd.(Software Consultants) to investigate the use of MDA to address the inefficiencies in the process of delivering and certifying avionics software. The conclusion is that the MDA approach represents how future avionics systems will be built.

1 Introduction

The rapid growth in the software content of military aircraft systems has dramatically increased the development and lifecycle maintenance costs of the avionics system as a proportion of the total platform. The identification and adoption of design methods that will potentially reduce or reverse this trend is therefore key to ensuring the affordability of the future avionics systems in the next twenty years.

The adoption of modern modelling, simulation and prototyping techniques in order to dramatically improve the engineering process and so cut the cost of specifying, designing and developing complex software systems is regarded as key to this.

These concepts are at the heart of Model Driven Architecture (MDA), which is an initiative of the Object Management Group (OMG) to promote an enhanced system development process based on the clear separation of platform independent and platform specific issues (see [1]). Executable Model Driven Architecture is a practical instantiation of the OMG's MDA developed by Kennedy Carter Ltd. based upon executable UML models and translation to the implementation, supporting 100% code generation.

The origins of translation-based development can be traced back to the well-established Shlaer-Mellor methodology (see [2] through [5]), illustrated in Figure 1.

R. de Lemos et al. (Eds.): Architecting Dependable Systems II, LNCS 3069, pp. 330–350, 2004.
© Springer-Verlag Berlin Heidelberg 2004

Executable UML (xUML) is a subset of the Unified Modelling Language incorporating a complete Action Language that allows system developers to build executable system models and then use these models to produce high quality code for their target systems. Executable MDA defines the process and xUML defines the language for expressing the models.

The iUML (intelligent UML) and iCCG (intelligent Configurable Code Generator) tools are proprietary to Kennedy Carter Ltd.

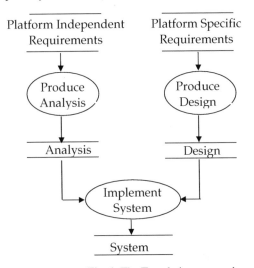

Fig. 1. The Translation approach.

The iUML tool suite has been designed to support every aspect of Executable MDA. It comprises three components, namely:

- iUML Modeller – which supports the creation and manipulation of executable object models using the Executable UML formalism.
- iUML Generator – which generates the code required to execute a model in the iUML Simulator.
- iUML Simulator (iSIM) – which executes, tests and debugs the executable object models created using object modeller.

The iCCG tool, as its name implies, is a tool for the specification of Code Generators. It provides the framework for extracting the information from an iUML model, and a translation engine, which generates the resulting code.

The following sections identify how the Executable MDA approach is being researched and applied to four cost saving strategies, namely:

- **Automation of the software development process.** The traditional approach to software development has been the "waterfall" method, whereby 3 models of the system under development are produced – the analysis model, the design model and the code. Manual processes based upon this lifecycle model lack objective completion criteria, and require multiple overlapping views of the system to be maintained, often resulting in obsolete analysis and design documentation. It has already been shown in mature avionics applications currently in service, that a system developed using a translation-based MDA approach results in better productivity and the elimination of a whole class of errors introduced during software design (refer to section 2.3 of this document for examples).

- **Managing legacy systems in a cost-effective fashion.** The software gestation period of many systems currently in service can be of the order of a decade or more. In the modern rapidly evolving software industry, this can mean that the methods and tools used to develop these systems can be obsolete even before the system comes into service. Migration strategies have to be identified to safeguard the massive investments (sometimes many man-centuries of effort) that have gone into these products. An MDA method and tool approach offers a solution to this problem.

- **Mapping software to modular computer systems.** Traditional avionics systems have consisted of federations of black boxes developed by various manufacturers using a variety of software standards and platform technologies. Large cost savings can be achieved if all the software in a modern avionics system is hosted in a single rack of standard processing modules. However this approach introduces a whole new set of challenges in mapping the software applications to the modules in such a way that absence of mutual interference is guaranteed, and to support reconfiguration of applications in case of hardware failure. The MDA approach of addressing the partitioning and mapping issues as a totally separate subject matter is regarded as fundamental to solving these challenges.

- **Support for modular or incremental certification.** Modern avionics systems have to be subject to a very expensive process of certification prior to entry into service. Current practice does not support incremental or modular certification, so any change to a part of an avionics system can mean that the whole must be totally recertified. MDA is a repeatable process, which relies on automation, and provides a strategy of strong modularisation using mappings which identify explicit dependencies about which structured reasoning, testing and risk assessment can be applied. MDA offers a strategy of modular safety case construction in support of the needs of this approach.

2   Automation of the Software Development Process

The classic analysis / design / code development process is faulty. It has a number of facets that act as a barrier to success:

- The manually maintained deliverables of the process embody significant overlap. Every fact in the analysis model appears again in the design model and every fact in the design model appears again in the code. With constantly changing requirements, this level of redundancy is untenable. There is barely time to specify the system once, let alone three times.

- Each component of the design is subjected to its own, personal, design phase. This results in a plethora of different design and coding strategies, which renders the components a source of enduring mystery and intrigue for the unfortunate maintainers.

We need a better process. The emerging industry standard process is Model Driven Architecture (MDA).

MDA facilitates abstraction and automation. Abstraction establishes highly reusable layers of capability, each providing guaranteed services to the layers above, and requiring services of the layers below. The following sections explain how automation eliminates the need to maintain derived artefacts, such as design and code.

Let us first examine the notions of layering, as illustrated in the context of an avionics system in Figure 2. A key notion in MDA is that of "platform independence". This is a slightly dangerous term, as it rather depends upon the definition of "platform". The domain model provides a number of types of platform independence:

- Aircraft platform independence
  - The *Hardware Interface* domain isolates the application from knowledge of the specific hardware (weapons and sensors) on the aircraft.
  - The *Communications* domain hides the specific protocols and technologies used for communication.
  - The *Pilot Interface* domain isolates the devices and formats used for communication with the pilot.
- Execution platform independence
  - The Software Architecture domain provides a "virtual UML machine" by offering services common to all UML models (store objects, send signals, execute actions), allowing the UML models to be mapped to any underlying software and hardware execution platform.

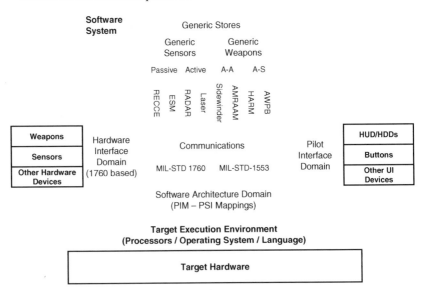

Fig. 2. Layers in an avionics system.

It should be noted, however, that the UML models making up the layered domains are not totally platform independent; they depend upon the UML virtual machine platform. The UML virtual platform, or virtual machine, provides an execution environment for any UML model, supporting standard UML notions such as creation and deletion of objects and links, generation of signal events, processing of state machines and execution of actions.

Automation plays a key role in eliminating the duplication of information prevalent in classic approaches. Rather than having the developers manually maintain several viewpoints (analysis / design / code / interface control documents), we automatically derive the design, code and required documents from the platform independent models. How? By building other platform independent models that embody the rules by which one artefact is derived from another. Hence a code generator is built as just another executable UML model, which takes as its primary input an executable UML model of the application or a service, and produces as its main output, target code.

The Platform Independent Model (PIM) to Platform Specific Model (PSM) mapping rules, embodied in such a model, *encapsulate the design decisions* that define how components of the platform specific implementation are to be generated from components of the platform independent model.

This allows the requirements to be *fully specified* in an abstract, implementation-independent, formalism, then *translated* onto a variety of execution platforms. The absence of platform specific detail from these models makes them much simpler than their platform specific equivalents, making them easier to check, which in turn leads to higher levels of dependability.

2.1 Summary of the Executable MDA Process

The MDA process offers a level of sophistication that puts avionics software engineering on a par with the engineering disciplines used to build the aircraft itself, in which the engineers:

1. Build *precise, predictive models*;
2. Subject the models to *rigorous testing prior to implementation*;
3. Establish a well-defined and *automated construction process*;
4. Construct the product from *large reusable components*.

The MDA process and primary deliverables are summarised in this context by Figure 3.

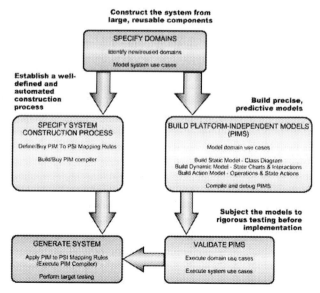

Fig. 3. The MDA process and work products.

2.2 Dependability

It is important to note that this process involves two kinds of component; the components (domains) that make up the application and the translation engines used to map the domains onto the selected target platform. Clearly, for development of a dependable system, the dependability of both types of component must be established. In this scheme, both types of component are expressed as UML models, and the verification process is identical; each component is subjected to a set of test cases to demonstrate compliance with requirements. Because we are using a fully defined formalism, we are able to subject the models to mathematical analysis and reasoning to establish their integrity, as explained later.

Since the Platform Independent Models (PIM) are built with an unambiguous and executable formalism, and the mappings from PIM to Platform Specific Models (PSM) and Platform Specific Implementation (PSI) can be fully specified, it is feasible to generate 100% of the code required to execute the system, with minimal opportunities for introducing errors that might compromise the dependability. Code generators can be bought off-the-shelf or can, with suitable tooling, be constructed or tailored for a particular project or organisation (see Figure 4).

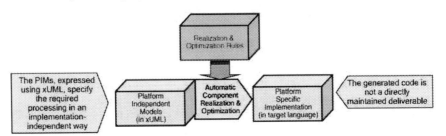

Fig. 4. Automatic code generation.

Note also that the use of code generation technology allows easy and consistent incorporation of relevant industry standards. For example, in a high integrity avionics application, we may wish to achieve:

1. Use of Spark Ada for safety critical systems
2. Conformance to the Generic Open Architecture (GOA) preferred standards for avionics domains (SAE AIR5316 – see http://www.sae.org)
3. Conformance to Generic Aircraft-Store Interface Framework (GASIF) (SAE AIR 5532 – see http://www.sae.org)

It is the code generator, in the form of a UML model, which embodies the policies by which these technologies and standards are deployed. This removes the need for all engineers to become experts in these areas, and further increases system dependability, by eliminating the opportunity for manual injection of unsystematic errors and inconsistencies during implementation.

2.3 Verification

Executable UML is strongly oriented towards development of highly dependable, high integrity systems, and there are a number of code generators that allow the PIM to be thoroughly tested and debugged in a simulation environment. Examples of such products include those produced by Project Technology Inc. (see [7]) and Kennedy Carter Ltd. (see [8]). This allows systems to be verified on one platform prior to being deployed on another. For example, this approach has been used for the development of very large federations of components, which are simulated and verified using the High Level Architecture (HLA) prior to being regenerated onto the target architecture (see [6]).

Below are examples of how executable UML has been successfully used to develop high dependability systems:

Lockheed Martin - F16 Modular Mission Computer at Fort Worth, Texas (see [9]): It has used the OMG's MDA to develop the F-16 Modular Mission Computer Application Software. Their goal was to achieve cross-platform compatibility and increased productivity and quality, all in the context of the environment of avionics software development.

The Lockheed Martin authored report concludes with a list of the benefits that were realized:

- The application models are expressed in a completely platform independent way and so can be reused across multiple hardware and software platforms;
- UML modellers are isolated from the software and hardware details and so can concentrate on a thorough exploration of the problem space;
- The hardware and software platforms can be upgraded without impacting the application models;
- Models can be tested at the earliest opportunity by executing them in the iUML Simulation environment;
- Rework is reduced with validated models;
- The mapping from PIM to PSM is specified in xUML with iCCG and is highly reusable;
- Code generation eliminates manual coding and eliminates the defects traditionally introduced in the coding phase;
- Defect injection (and the resulting rework) is reduced by automating the software phase in which most defects are injected "On a typical program, after Requirements Definition *approximately 2/3 of the defects are injected during implementation (coding)*";
- Maintenance of the application source code is eliminated, while maintenance of the xUML models is ensured;
- Nearly all implementation-specific design tasks (all but the design decisions represented by design tag values) are performed by the code generator, not the software developers.

Taken altogether these MDA benefits *have reduced application development time by 20%* on the F-16 MMC program in addition to helping them achieve complete cross-platform compatibility.

BAE Systems – Stingray Torpedo (see [10]): An objective of the project was to develop a tool to convert automatically the Software Design into Ada 95 code for use in a real time embedded system to support the Tactical Software Development on the Stingray Torpedo Life Extension Project. This was to be implemented by a small task centred team, using a selection of specialist software compiler technologies to ensure a high quality product while utilizing only a small number of Ada programmers and achieving a reduced development time.

With no previous experience of code generation, the team identified the development strategy, produced the design and utilized the appropriate technologies to realize the product. Novel use of compiler technologies, and 4 years of highly focused work took the concept to a fully developed product achieving 100% automated Ada 95 code generation. The code generator cost approximately 2 man-years of development time for the first prototype and, so far, has resulted in *a saving of 40 man-years* of software coding.

The customer (UK Ministry of Defence) is extremely confident in the quality of the product produced by this leading edge technology and the use of the code generator *allows much faster turn-round time between design changes* and in-water redeployment. Because of the modular approach taken with the design, maintenance is relatively straightforward and the product can be used in Object Oriented real-time embedded applications especially where *mission criticality* is an important consideration.

The three major benefits that have resulted from the innovative approach taken by the ground breaking design team are *improved software productivity, repeatable build process* and *improved software quality*; all of which contribute to and enhance the cost-effectiveness of the overall development lifecycle at BAE Systems. The sea trials of SRLE were the most successful of any product developed by the company.

3 Managing Legacy Systems in a Cost-Effective Fashion

The establishment of UML as the dominant formalism for representing system and software designs will inevitably result in tool vendors reducing their investment and support in other formalisms, and focussing their efforts on developing increasingly capable UML tools.

Most large systems embody components that were built many years ago, using tools that were, at the time, considered leading edge, but which are now often vendor unsupported and hosted on unsupportable platforms. It is not economically feasible, nor necessary, to re-engineer all such components. However, the issue of tool obsolescence may act as a driver towards adopting modern UML tools as a way of continuing to maintain and develop such legacy components.

In enhancing a software development process, many of the components we wish to build are components to be *deployed at development time*, which can become part of the tool chain used to build the deployed system. Therefore, there are advantages if the modelling and simulation tools are capable of producing components to support the MDA design flow as well as the components for the avionics system.

MDA exploits the emergence of a class of tools, which empower model translation such as that illustrated in Figure 4, and allow metamodel manipulation. These metamodels are simply "models of models", built for a particular purpose. For example, we might build a metamodel of the Structured Analysis (SA) formalism, which knows how to transform itself into the UML notation, expressed as a UML metamodel. Lack of space precludes inclusion of the complete metamodel, but the fragment in Figure 5

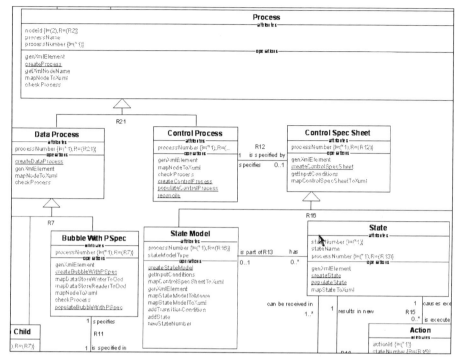

Fig. 5. Part of the structured analysis metamodel.

illustrates the level of abstraction of the SA metamodel. Similarly Figure 6 shows a fragment of the metamodel of the xUML formalism.

These metamodels include operations, which enable their automatic transformation into other models (e.g. SA to UML) or other formalisms (e.g. UML to code). To do this, we need the ability to build executable metamodels in the same environment as the component models for the target system.

The following section describes a generic process by which such a migration can be automated, allowing software maintenance to be continued using the original method but with new tools.

The example here is one of migrating models built using the Real-Time Structured Analysis method on the Teamwork tool, originally developed by Cadre. However, the approach can be used for any method and tool combination. Note that the modelling tool is used to model and generate the translation tools used during development, as well as to model and generate the application. The process for migration, resulting in the tool chain is illustrated in Figure 7.

The steps are as follows:

1. Build a metamodel of the old tool export format (in the case the textual notation used to store Teamwork models known as CDIF[1] – see Figure 8).

---

[1] CDIF (CASE data interchange format) is a proposed standard, which addresses model and method independent transfer between CASE tools.

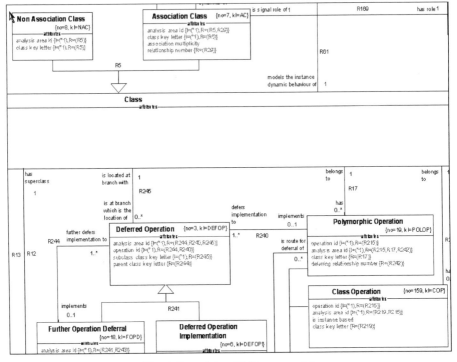

Fig. 6. Part of the xUML metamodel.

2. Build a metamodel of the old formalism (in this case Real Time Structured Analysis (RTSA) as shown in Figure 5).
3. Specify the mappings from the CDIF metamodel to the RTSA metamodel, as illustrated by the UML action language shown in Figure 9, which maps a CDIF process component to a RTSA process.
4. Build a mapping from the RTSA metamodel to the UML metamodel, shown in Figure 6.
5. Build a mapping from the UML metamodel to the new tool database (Figure 6). The overall process is summarised in Figure 7.

Once the basic migration has been automated, the tool chain can be further enhanced by the automation of parts of the development process, as illustrated in Figure 10. The following two enhancements are enabled by the use of an executable formalism (UML).

1. Model checking (and automatic fixing if desired);
2. Model transformation, for example, automatic generation of design and code from the RTSA model.

The result is a process, which is more strongly oriented towards dependability, by allowing earlier identification of defects, and reducing the scope for human error during the implementation phase.

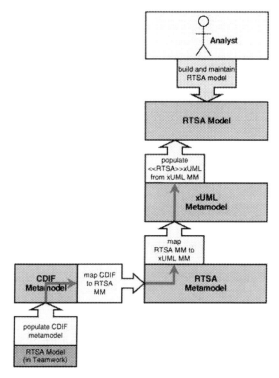

Fig. 7. SA to UML tool migration process.

4 Mapping Software to Modular Computer Systems

Traditional avionics architectures have consisted of a federation of black boxes, produced by various manufacturers. The adoption of modular avionics computer architecture compatible with the adoption of an open integrated modular software architecture is regarded as a major cost saving strategy. The goals of such an architecture are:

1. Technology Transparency - The underlying hardware should not have any impact on an application either during development or execution.
2. Scheduled Maintenance - The system should have inbuilt capability to operate in the presence of failures so that extended Maintenance Free Operating Periods (MFOPS) can be achieved.
3. Incremental Update - The system should be designed such that applications can be inserted/altered with minimum impact on other applications and on the supporting safety case.

The requirement is to develop and then to map a number of avionics applications to a rack of Processing Modules. The applications that are active at any time in the mission can be selected as function of the current operational mode (e.g. take-off, reconnaissance, attack etc.). In order to cater for failure conditions, it must be possible to re-map active applications to different non-failed modules (a certain amount of redundancy is catered for). These possible mappings are referred to as system configurations.

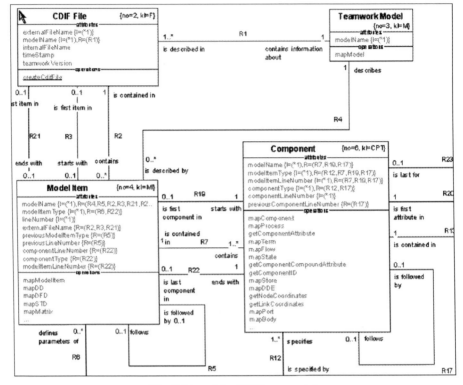

Fig. 8. Part of the CDIF metamodel.

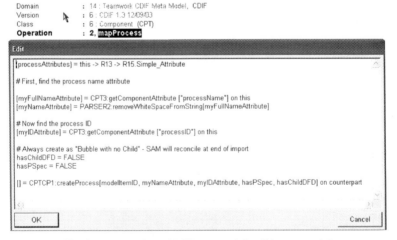

Fig. 9. Mapping from CDIF metamodel to SA metamodel.

The chosen process architecture is based upon the same principles as MDA, in that it comprises layers of abstraction, each providing services to the layer above, and requiring services of the layer below (see Figure 11).

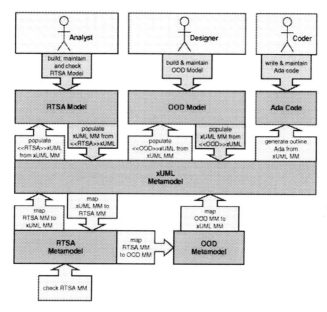

Fig. 10. Enhanced tool chain.

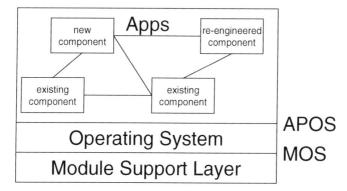

Fig. 11. IMS with existing, new and re-engineered applications.

In MDA, a layered set of platform-independent models are constructed, also known as *domains,* each of which encapsulates a single subject matter and provides services to its "clients" and requires services of its "servers". The application components running under IMS can be partitioned according to this principle. The benefit of domain partitioning is that it allows changes and upgrades to be made to one component while minimising the impact on other components.

An application can consist of one or more processes each being an independent execution environment. A process can in turn consist of one or more threads of execution, which communicate with any other thread in the system through logical connections, which are called virtual channels (VCs), see Figure 12.

One or more processes from any application, may be allocated to each Processing Module, provided they do not exceed their memory and bandwidth allocation, and

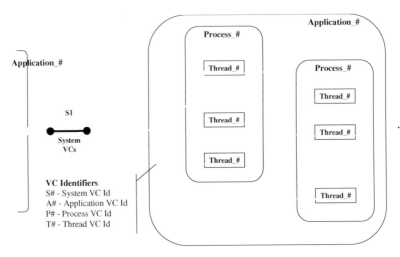

Fig. 12. Logical mapping of processes.

subject to security or safety constraints, which dictate which processes can share the same Module. Virtual channels that connect these processes are mapped to physical network connections.

This implies a sophisticated operating system that can manage the dynamic reconfiguration of the system at run-time in response to operational modes and fault conditions (as shown in Figure 11). Such an operating system requires instructions on how it is to behave for reconfiguration or error handling etc., and these are stored in a "runtime blueprint".

During development it is highly desirable to develop the applications independently of the hardware and then to devise a mechanism for specifying the complex mapping combinations to the target hardware. This concept fits hand-in-glove with the concepts of Model Driven Architecture and the concepts of Platform Independent Models (PIM's) and mappings from the PIM's to the Platform Specific Implementations (PSI's).

The strategy adopted is to develop the Applications as a set of Platform Independent Models. In research that has been carried out to date this has been performed using the Kennedy Carter iUML-modelling tool. The Platform Independent Models are expressed in Executable UML (xUML).

Decisions have to be made by the systems developers on how these Platform Independent Models are to be organised logically into processes, the concurrency model for these processes which defines the threads, and the communication paths between these threads which define the virtual channels. The mechanism for performing these operations is known as tagging. These tags do not in any way effect the structure of the PIM's, they are merely an overlay that is used as information required by the code generator.

Meanwhile the mappings from the PIM to PSI's (i.e. the processes to the processing modules) have been defined and these are captured in another Kennedy Carter tool known as the iCCG (configurable code generator tool). The iCCG tool contains a meta-model of the xUML formalism, which is populated by instances of the xUML

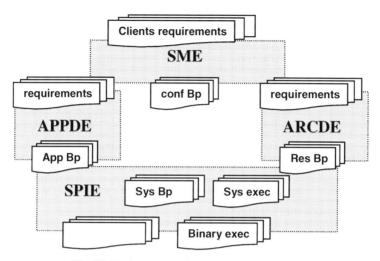

Fig. 13. Environments of the development process.

components contained in the application under development. This meta-model of xUML is actually expressed in xUML. The mapping rules are incorporated into this iCCG model as methods on the meta-model classes, which when invoked automatically output the code for the target system (expressed in a High Level Language such as Ada 83).

This results in a set of executables that can be loaded into the target system, but how to define the mappings? As already stated the mappings are defined at run-time using the "runtime blueprint".

The runtime blueprint includes information about the applications, the target hardware, all the possible configurations and the mapping solutions between these.

The solution that has been devised is to create three design-time blueprints that capture the necessary information about the application, the hardware resources and the configurations respectively. The mapping solutions are derived from these blueprints and captured in a fourth design-time blueprint known as the system blueprint. The run-time blueprint is a translation of information in the system blueprint, which is distributed around the various processing elements of the system.

The four development environments and how they fit with the generation of blueprints is shown in Figure 13.

The System Modelling Environment (SME) is where the overall system is modelled and results in the Configuration blueprint. The Application Development Environment (APPDE) is where the Application is developed. The Architecture Description Environment (ARCDE) is where the hardware architecture is defined. The System Prototyping and Integration Environment (SPIE) is where the system is prototyped and integrated.

Once again the technique of creating meta-models expressed in xUML has been utilised to define the contents and organisation of the four design-time blueprints. During the development process these are populated to define the actual instantiated blueprints. It must be emphasised that many processes and tools other than the UML modelling tools must be pressed into service to solve the complex mapping solutions;

these blueprints only represent a repository for the results. In the case of the application, the iCCG tool can be used to populate the application blueprint because all the logical organisation decisions (processes, threads and VC's) have been captured in the aforementioned tags.

It can be seen from research work carried out to date that this Model Driven Architecture approach offers a significant capability in support of this modular computer technology.

5 Support for Modular or Incremental Certification

Prior to deployment, the system developed will need to be approved for use in its specific domain. In the avionics application domain, systems need to be shown to meet the requirements of airworthiness authorities. This would be standards such as the RTCA / EUROCAE standard DO-178-B "Software Considerations in Airborne Systems and Equipment Certification" (see [11]) or the UK Ministry of Defence standards, such as Def Stan 00-55 "Requirements for Safety Related software in Defence Equipment" (see [12]). Other domains will have similar requirements, and the standards applied for a given domain vary between countries and territories.

Achieving certification is not trivial, especially as the standards relate both to product technologies and the development processes used to deliver them. Building an argument for certification is therefore a significant cost, one we would prefer to avoid recurring on every single change or variation of the system developed. For example, referring back to the avionics system illustrated in Figure 2, a change to the technologies used to implement the pilot interface should not require the entire avionics system to be re-certified. The term "incremental certification" is used to communicate the idea that only the parts of the system subject to a change are also subject to re-certification.

MDA supports incremental certification in a number of distinct ways:

- Separation of concerns – Each domain is separate from the other domains used to construct a system model. The domains may make up layers (as in the avionics example – see Figure 2) or may be at the same level of abstraction but represent different aspects such as one domain for sensors, another for weapons. The intention is that a change to one domain is limited to that domain so that certification effort can be restricted.
- Well-defined domains – Innovative technologies tend to be disruptive in that they require many of the underlying assumptions of the systems that utilise them to be re-considered. This can have a large impact on emergent system properties, where the full implications of a small change can be difficult to perceive. This is particularly the case for non-functional properties such as safety assessment where many of the key properties (such as, maintenance-free operation periods – MFOPs) are implicit within the system definition. The domains support the concept that innovations can be resolved more systematically within their own technological context, so that the implications for other domains are better understood in terms of service provision, impact and any supporting additional requirements in other domains to exploit innovations.
- Reuse – Once domains have been internally resolved, they can be subject to specific test strategies to test maturity and integrity. For example, DO-178B requires

that software with a safety-related role in the system be subjected to full Multi Criteria Decision Coverage (MC-DC) analysis, along with several other low-level indepth requirements. Using MDA, this testing can be carried out in a single domain and re-used for all instances of that domain across several systems. This makes more cost effective use of low level verification effort, leveraging the costs of deploying such techniques, and addressing the (significant) risk of inconsistencies in approaches to testing across different systems development projects.

- Mapping definition – Mappings between domains make explicit the dependencies between them. This supports structured reasoning about interactions and the context in which they occur. By making these dependencies explicit, different scenarios for system operation can be defined, and subject to testing or risk assessment.
- Assessing models, not code – Certification is in the context of systems, not just software. Arguments for certification are more compelling and robust if the assessment is based on system and architecture properties rather than the (more volatile) specifics of the software. Using MDA, the system model can be used to assert safety properties that are upheld in the software generated from it by code generation mappings. The system model can be validated directly against requirements and verified against test suites without descending into the detail of software implementation – which is likely to be less meaningful to certification and more volatile.
- Early resolution of safety/certification concerns – The definition of domains and the mappings between them provides a basic architecture for the system where key data flows, service calls and resource dependencies can be identified and assessed in the context of hazard identification. This kind of system model permits early identification of potential weaknesses that might threaten certification. For example, Def Stan 00-56 (see [13]) provides that system components at the highest safety integrity level (SIL 4) can be broken down into two components of a lower integrity level (SIL 3), so long as the two SIL 3 components can be shown to be independent. Early resolution of architecture using domains can identify where such a strategy might be appropriate between two safety critical domains.
- Use of "Commercial Off The Shelf" (COTS) – Use of COTS technology is a practical reality in most system development projects because commercial markets innovate faster than military or other niche markets. MDA helps to integrate these technologies into a mature development process without compromising system certification. So long as an interface can be defined between the COTS domain and the other system domains, that interface can be subjected to the same rigorous approach and arguments without the need to build arguments specific to individual COTS releases.

These benefits arise because the system development process is better resolved under MDA and less technology dependent. The challenge to achieving incremental certification using traditional systems development processes – such as the V lifecycle recommended in "Aerospace Recommended Practice" (ARP) (see [14])- is that the process is seen as monolithic, and any change requires certification to start again at the beginning. Such certification processes are too complex and interwoven to unpick and resolve change impact. The ARP is by no means unique in this regard; most "high integrity" processes have similar weaknesses, precisely because they attempt to associate dependability with control.

MDA provides an underlying infrastructure with more precise coupling between components. This structure can then be reflected in the safety argument constructed to support a certification argument. Dependability and precision come from improved understanding and interaction across domains, rather than attempts to control them all simultaneously. For example, an argument for correct translation from a UML model to an Ada program could take the form of three main claims:

1. The UML metamodel is correct in terms of the UML language reference manual (LRM).
2. The Ada metamodel is correct in terms of the Ada language reference manual.
3. The mapping between (1) and (2) above is defined and complete.

The argument would then proceed by decomposing the metamodel and the mappings into their component parts and reasoning that these support the three claims above (see Figure 14). The arguments about metamodels would consider all the entities represented in that metamodel, whereas each association in the mapping would need to be analysed to demonstrate:

- Relevance – There is a valid state of the source metamodel that triggers the mapping association. For example, UML classes are a relevant part of the system model and must be represented in the Ada code generated.
- Structural Integrity – The semantic meaning of the source metamodel is not altered by the mapping. This would be shown by reference to a mapping specification showing how UML components should be represented as Ada components. For example, representing a class as an Ada package.
- Symbolical Integrity – Showing that data connections are preserved by the mapping translation. For example, the Ada package name is the same as, or closely derived from, the UML class, preserving traceability between model and code.

An illustration of how such an argument can be structured and built up systematically is shown in Figure 14. It uses a methodology called "Goal Structuring Notation" (GSN) (see [15]) to document the argument.

By adopting this argument approach, or something similar, each metamodel and mapping specification is shown explicitly in the overall argument and implications of change can be resolved without reconstructing the entire argument structure.

The claims in Figure 14 have small diamonds to show that further decomposition will be required. These claims will need to be broken down into claims on specific components of the metamodel or mapping as appropriate until the claim has been decomposed to a point where it can be discharged by direct reference to evidence. For example, the claim about structural integrity of the mapping could be broken down into the specific operations used to define that mapping in the xUML metamodel. Each specific operation could then be proved to discharge the mapping specification using a mathematical approach such as weakest precondition calculus (see [15])

The approach could be taken further, documenting specific certification arguments useful to specific technologies, and evidence about specific software routines (such as MC-DC testing) retained in a library for re-use on other systems making use of the same software release.

Incremental certification is therefore delivered through a structured and systematic approach to arguing about safety that reflects the structure of the MDA process and the product architecture adopted prior to code generation. Many tangible benefits and

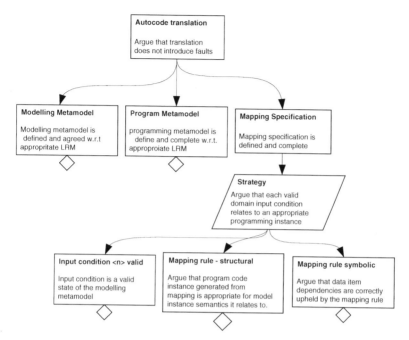

Fig. 14. Example safety argument fragment showing highest-level claims.

improvements in productivity of system assessment can be delivered by adopting this straightforward approach.

6 Conclusions and Future Work

MDA with executable UML offers an approach that embodies all the key ingredients of a process for developing dependable systems, by offering:

1. A uniform strategy for preserving investment in existing models built using unsupported tools, by automatically migrating them to profiled UML models for subsequent maintenance and development using state of the art UML tools.
2. A clean separation of application behaviour from the platform specific implementation using technologies such as Integrated Modular Avionics (IMA), allowing the full potential of IMA to be realised in a consistent and dependable way.
3. A semantically well defined formalism that can be used as the basis for modular certification of safety related systems.
4. The ability to generate not only the components of the target system, but components of the development tool chain, providing scope for model translation and offering "executable specifications" that can be tested early and mapped reliably onto the target, leading to greater levels of dependency.

MDA is a new approach for most organizations, and therefore carries additional training and learning curve costs and also currently the availability of production quality code generators is currently limited.

MDA requires developers to work at a more abstract level than code. Although experience shows that most do not have any difficulty making the adjustment, there will be some who find this change of emphasis difficult to achieve.

Building upon the initial success of MDA deployment so far, work is now proceeding on the enhancement of the Ada code mapping rules to cover the entire xUML formalism. Work is also underway to develop a generic "adapter/router" component to provide a standard way to interface re-engineered xUML components with pre-existing components, as illustrated in the Figure 15.

These techniques are now being applied to another avionics system in the same organization, in response to the customer's need for a faster and cheaper upgrade capability.

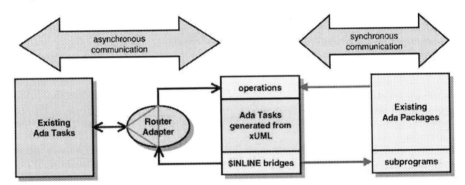

Fig. 15. Interfacing xUML components to legacy components.

Acknowledgements

The help and support of Steve Crook-Dawkins from the Department of Computer Science, University of York, in the preparation of this paper and his participation in some of the research work described here, is acknowledged.

References

1. Object Management Group - Model Driven Architecture - www.omg.org/mda
2. S. Shlaer, S. J. Mellor. *Object Oriented System Analysis: Modelling the World in Data.* Yourdon Press Computing Series. (March 1988).
3. S. Shlaer, S. J. Mellor. *Object Lifecycles: Modelling the World in States.* Yourdon Press Computing Series. (April 1991).
4. S. J. Mellor, M. Balcer. *Executable UML. A Foundation for UML.* Addison-Wesley Pub Co; 1st edition. (May 2002)
5. C. Raistrick et al. *Model Driven Architecture with Executable UML.* Cambridge University Press. (March 2004).
6. High Level Architecture https://www.dmso.mil/public/transition/hla.
7. Project Technology Inc. http://www.projtech.com/prods/index.html
8. Kenedy Carter Ltd. http://www.kc.com/products/iuml/index.html

9. Lockheed Martin - F16 Modular Mission Computer:
   http://www.omg.org/mda/mda_files/New_MDA.ppt
10. BAE Systems - Stingray Torpedo: http://www.kc.com/case_study/baesystems.html
11. RTCA Inc, "Software Considerations in Airborne Systems and Equipment Certification" DO-178B, RTCA SC-167, EUROCAE WG-12, Washington DC. (December 1992).
12. UK Ministry of Defence, "Def Stan 00-55: Requirements for Safety Related Software in Defence Equipment" Part 1 Requirements and Part 2 Guidance, UK MoD, Glasgow. (August 1997).
13. UK Ministry of Defence, "Def Stan 00-56: Safety Management Requirements for Defence Systems" Part 1 Requirements and Part 2 Guidance, UK MoD, Glasgow. (August 1997).
14. SAE, Systems Integration Task Group, "Guidelines and Methods for Conducting the Safety Assessment Process on Civil Airborne Systems and Equipment", ARP 4761, SAE S 18 Committee. (November 1994).
15. T.P. Kelly. *Arguing Safety – A Systematic Approach to Managing Safety Cases*. University of York. Department of Computer Science. DPhil Thesis YCST 99/05. (September 1998).

Author Index